INTERNATIONAL LAW
NORMS, ACTORS, PROCESS

ASPEN CASEBOOK SERIES

INTERNATIONAL LAW
NORMS, ACTORS, PROCESS

A Problem-Oriented Approach

Fourth Edition

Jeffrey L. Dunoff
Laura H. Carnell Professor of Law
Temple University Beasley School of Law

Steven R. Ratner
Bruno Simma Collegiate Professor of Law
University of Michigan Law School

David Wippman
Dean and William S. Pattee Professor of Law
University of Minnesota Law School

Printed in the United States of America.

3 4 5 6 7 8 9 0

ISBN 978-1-4548-4951-3

Library of Congress Cataloging-in-Publication Data

Dunoff, Jeffrey L., 1960- author.
   International law : norms, actors, process : a problem-oriented approach / Jeffrey L. Dunoff, Professor of Law, Temple University Beasley School of Law; Steven R. Ratner, Bruno Simma Collegiate Professor of Law, University of Michigan Law School; David Wippman, Dean and William S. Pattee Professor of Law, University of Minnesota Law School. – Fourth edition.
      pages cm
   Includes bibliographical references and index.
   ISBN 978-1-4548-4951-3 (alk. paper)
1. International law. I. Ratner, Steven R., author. II. Wippman, David, 1954- author. III. Title.
   KZ3410.D86 2015
   341–dc23
                          2015011078

Certified Chain of Custody
Promoting Sustainable Forestry

www.sfiprogram.org
SFI-01042

SFI label applies to the text stock

About Wolters Kluwer Law & Business

Wolters Kluwer Law & Business is a leading global provider of intelligent information and digital solutions for legal and business professionals in key specialty areas, and respected educational resources for professors and law students. Wolters Kluwer Law & Business connects legal and business professionals as well as those in the education market with timely, specialized authoritative content and information-enabled solutions to support success through productivity, accuracy and mobility.

Serving customers worldwide, Wolters Kluwer Law & Business products include those under the Aspen Publishers, CCH, Kluwer Law International, Loislaw, ftwilliam.com and MediRegs family of products.

CCH products have been a trusted resource since 1913, and are highly regarded resources for legal, securities, antitrust and trade regulation, government contracting, banking, pension, payroll, employment and labor, and healthcare reimbursement and compliance professionals.

Aspen Publishers products provide essential information to attorneys, business professionals and law students. Written by preeminent authorities, the product line offers analytical and practical information in a range of specialty practice areas from securities law and intellectual property to mergers and acquisitions and pension/benefits. Aspen's trusted legal education resources provide professors and students with high-quality, up-to-date and effective resources for successful instruction and study in all areas of the law.

Kluwer Law International products provide the global business community with reliable international legal information in English. Legal practitioners, corporate counsel and business executives around the world rely on Kluwer Law journals, looseleafs, books, and electronic products for comprehensive information in many areas of international legal practice.

Loislaw is a comprehensive online legal research product providing legal content to law firm practitioners of various specializations. Loislaw provides attorneys with the ability to quickly and efficiently find the necessary legal information they need, when and where they need it, by facilitating access to primary law as well as state-specific law, records, forms and treatises.

ftwilliam.com offers employee benefits professionals the highest quality plan documents (retirement, welfare and non-qualified) and government forms (5500/PBGC, 1099 and IRS) software at highly competitive prices.

MediRegs products provide integrated health care compliance content and software solutions for professionals in healthcare, higher education and life sciences, including professionals in accounting, law and consulting.

Wolters Kluwer Law & Business, a division of Wolters Kluwer, is headquartered in New York. Wolters Kluwer is a market-leading global information services company focused on professionals.

To

Theresa, Elizabeth, and Joel

Nancy, Benjamin, and Isabel

and

Brianna and Lauren

Summary of Contents

Contents

PART I
Introduction to International Law and Law Making   1

Contents

Part V
Interdependence and Integration: The Challenge of Collective Action Problems

Chapter 10
Responding to the First Global Commons Issue: The Law of the Sea

Chapter 11
Protecting the International Environment   **603**

Chapter 14
Conceptual Challenges to International Law: Legitimacy, Relevance, and Justice

Preface

Our book is designed to provide a general introduction to the range and reach—and the possibilities and limits—of contemporary international law. To do so, the book is built around a series of current problems that illustrate international law in action. These materials are intended to convey an understanding of the profound transformations that mark international law in the current era, and of recent theories and developments that challenge some of the discipline's most basic assumptions. Today's students and tomorrow's international lawyers will benefit from a casebook prepared with these fundamental shifts in the nature of the subject in mind.

The book is also designed to convey to students a keen sense of the process for the making, interpretation, and application of international legal norms, rather than focusing on law as a set of detailed rules or doctrines. It is our experience as teachers that the best way to get students interested in these processes and to show their relevance to modern society is to rely as much as possible on real situations where the law has made—or not made—a difference. Using real-world problems permits students to consider the formation and application of international law in the specific contexts in which such problems arise, and to appreciate the complexity and interrelated character of international legal issues as they appear to lawyers in practice. Moreover, we believe that only through an examination of international law's principal actors, methods of law making, and key subjects can a student fully understand what it means to have law in a context that lacks a single legislature, executive, or judiciary.

The problems are chosen, in part, for their importance or intrinsic interest and, in part, to highlight many of the profound transformations that characterize international law in the twenty-first century. Thus, throughout the text we focus on creative new forms of law making, including "soft" law, as well as treaty regimes; the increased importance of non-state actors, such as corporations, sub-state units, and non-governmental organizations; new compliance strategies; the growth of critical subject areas, notably international criminal law and international economic law; and the erosion of traditional divisions among these subjects. Given our focus on current international legal controversies, we omit a number of classic doctrinal areas that receive extended treatment in other texts but that do not raise critical process-related issues as dramatically as those we have chosen.

We recognize that no limited number of problems can present the entire spectrum of international law. Indeed, we have consciously avoided the temptation to create a treatise, or to present encyclopedic treatments of the limited range of issues covered. Instead, our overriding goal has been to create a book that serves as an effective teaching tool. To this end, each chapter begins with a short introduction to the particular field of international law at issue, and each problem begins with an overview and a set of key goals designed to orient the student to the materials that follow. Problems are followed by relevant primary and secondary source materials. These materials are both interdisciplinary and multi-perspectival and are intended to enrich the student's understanding of relevant issues. Notes and questions are kept to a minimum.

This book is organized into six parts, each consisting of two or more chapters for a total of fourteen chapters. Part I introduces students to international law and law making.

Chapter 1 uses two problems to illustrate both basic concepts and the changing nature of contemporary international law. Chapter 2 uses a series of problems to serve as vehicles for a discussion of treaties, customary international law, and soft law. Part II focuses on the principal participants (other than individuals) in the international legal system. Chapter 3 reviews the processes of state formation and dissolution, self-determination, recognition, governmental change, and related issues, as well as the legal status and powers of international organizations. In recognition of the prominence that non-state actors have assumed in contemporary international law, Chapter 4 includes three problems that explore the variety and roles that these entities play.

Part III explores the interactions between international and domestic law. Chapter 5 focuses on the impact of international law in domestic systems, while Chapter 6 explores the ways that states assert their authority abroad. Part IV focuses on the use of international law to protect human dignity. Chapter 7 covers human rights, including both civil and political rights, and economic, social, and cultural rights. We also include two chapters on rapidly evolving areas: Chapter 8 examines the legal regulation of the conduct of war, and Chapter 9 covers issues of individual accountability for human rights abuses. Part V focuses on issues generated by the interdependence of states and the need for collective action to protect international common resources and to facilitate international economic activity. Chapter 10 covers the law of the sea; Chapter 11 examines international environmental law; and Chapter 12 explores international economic law.

We take seriously the challenges of those who question the relevance, legitimacy, and justice of international law. Most casebooks bury these issues near the end of an introductory chapter, after which the issues disappear. As a conceptual matter, we think that starting a book with these issues often appears to be unduly defensive; as a practical matter, we think that discussing these issues before students have studied international law is unlikely to be productive. We also think the issues are too important to be treated in this way. Thus, we raise questions about the relevance and efficacy of international law throughout the text. We devote Part VI, the final part of the book, to an examination of the most important challenges to international law. Chapter 13 examines the use of force in international affairs. In Chapter 14, the book's final chapter, we focus more explicitly on the legitimacy, relevance, and justice of international law, through an examination of several contemporary issues, including the legal issues raised by the September 11, 2001 attacks on the United States and their aftermath.

The book is designed to stimulate interest in, and thinking about, international law. It is an invitation to share our commitment to exploration of the uses and limits of international law—where it succeeds, where it fails, and how it can be improved. We welcome your comments and suggestions.

Jeffrey L. Dunoff
Steven R. Ratner
David Wippman

April 2015

Acknowledgments

This volume is the product of countless interchanges with students, colleagues, and others who have contributed to the ideas in it. We begin by thanking all our students, whose reactions to this book as it progressed were our surest signal of where we needed to do more work.

At Temple Law School, we acknowledge with appreciation the outstanding work by Professor Dunoff's research assistants, including Kim Bartman, Brooke Birnbaum, Jon Cagan, Laurie Dow, Ben Franks, Sean Handler, Nhan Nguyen, Lori Odessa, Veronica Rice, Daniel Simons, Maggie Soboleski, Keith Verrier, and Allison Wells. We also thank John Necci, Ethel Fiderer, Steve Pavlo, and others at the Temple Law School Library, and Joel Houkom, Joshua Loftus, Freddie Sanford, and the secretarial staff at the Law School. Special thanks to Professor Dunoff's Temple colleagues for their support throughout this project. We wish to acknowledge Dean JoAnne Epps, former Dean Robert Reinstein and Temple University Beasley School of Law for generous financial assistance in support of this project.

At the University of Texas School of Law, we thank research assistants Molly Leder and Elizabeth Herre for their superlative work. Professor Ratner also thanks his former Columbia Law School student, Amin Kassam, for excellent research assistance. At the Tarlton Law Library, we appreciate the assistance of Jonathan Pratter in locating some of our more unusual sources. Professor Ratner's tremendous faculty assistants, Melonie Alspaugh and Katrin Flechsig, made the many details of the publication process for the first edition flow smoothly. His colleagues at Texas were a constant source of pedagogical ideas for the book, and he particularly appreciates the insights of Douglas Laycock. Dean William Powers provided generous financial assistance with all aspects of this project.

At the University of Michigan Law School, we thank Betsy Fisher, Scott Risner, Raphaelle Monty, and Stephen Rooke for their research assistance; Kimberly Latta and Karen Pritula for their superlative work on various production aspects of the book; and Deans Evan Caminker and Mark West for financial assistance in the form of the Wolfson and Cook Scholarship Funds.

At Cornell Law School, we would like to thank Ilana Buschkin, Jean Carmalt, Alayne Fleischmann, Maureen McKee, Benjamin Meier, and Victoria Orlowski for excellent research, cite-checking, and editing. Anne Cahanin and Pamela Finnigan provided outstanding and unflagging secretarial and administrative support. We also thank the Cornell Law School Library staff for their invaluable assistance in tracking down elusive documents. Professor Wippman acknowledges with great appreciation the faculty at Cornell Law School, particularly Professors John Barcelo and Muna Ndulo, for their advice, encouragement, and support. Dean Stewart Schwab and the Cornell Law School offered generous financial assistance in support of this project.

At the University of Minnesota Law School, we thank Rebecca Cassler and Elizabeth Super for their research assistance and Julie Johnson for her excellent administrative assistance. Dean Wippman also acknowledges with great appreciation advice from Professors Oren Gross and Fionnuala Ni Aolain on this edition.

We have benefitted greatly from the perceptive comments of our colleagues at other schools who taught from prior editions, as well as earlier drafts of this text, including

Karima Bennoune, Daniel Bodansky, David Caron, Kal Raustiala, and Peter Spiro. We are also grateful to Christopher Borgen, Alan Boyle, Gregory Fox, Philippe Gautier, Laurence Helfer, Duncan Hollis, Frederick Kirgis, John Knox, Sean Murphy, Michael Ratner, Anthea Roberts, Amy Sinden, and Ingrid Wuerth for various comments, suggestions, and assistance on aspects of the book. Bernard Oxman and J. Ashley Roach offered critically helpful commentary on all of Chapter 10. Aspen Publishers' anonymous reviewers offered many useful suggestions for which we are most grateful.

Many of the photographs that appear in the book were located and obtained through the hard work of our professional picture researcher, Corinne Szabo, whose unfailing assistance we gratefully appreciate.

We also thank our colleagues at Aspen Publishing, in particular Susan Boulanger, Melody Davies, John Devins, Troy Froebe, Carol McGeehan, Susan Junkin, Christie Rears, Annalisa Rodriguez, and Kathy Langone.

Finally, we thank our families, to whom this book is dedicated, for graciously tolerating the long hours required to complete this task—and for their creative efforts to devise enjoyable distractions from it.

The authors are grateful for permission to reprint material from the following sources:

Accord on Fire and Safety in Bangladesh; www.bangladeshaccord.org (2013). Reprinted by permission.

Amnesty International. "Rwanda: Gacaca: A Question of Justice," AI Index AFR 47/007/2002 (December 2002). Copyright © Amnesty International. Reprinted by permission.

Anand, R.P. "The Influence of History on the Literature of International Law," in The Structure and Process of International Law (R. St. J. Mac Donald and D. M. Johnston eds. 1983). Copyright © Martinus Nijhoff. Reprinted by permission.

Anderson, Kenneth. "What NGO Accountability Means—and Does Not Mean." Reproduced with permission from 103 Am. J. Int'l L. 170 (2009). Copyright © The American Society of International Law.

Anghie, Antony. "Finding the Peripheries: Sovereignty and Colonialism in Nineteenth-Century International Law," 40 Harv. Int'l L.J. 1 (1999). Copyright © 1999 by the President and Fellows of Harvard College and the Harvard International Law Journal.

An-Na'im, Abdullah Ahmed. "Human Rights in the Muslim World: Socio-Political Conditions and Scriptural Imperatives," 3 Harv. Hum. Rts. J. 13 (1990).

Baumol, William J., and Oates, Wallace E. Economics, Environmental Policy and the Quality of Life (1979). Reprinted by permission of William J. Baumol and Wallace E. Oates.

Benedick, Richard Elliot. Ozone Diplomacy: New Directions in Safeguarding the Planet. Copyright © 1991, 1998 by the President and Fellows of Harvard College. Reprinted by permission of the publisher.

Bodansky, Daniel. "The Legitimacy of International Governance: A Coming Challenge for International Environmental Law?" Reproduced with permission from 93 Am. J. Int'l L. 596 (1999). Copyright © The American Society of International Law.

Borgen, Christopher J. "The Language of Law and the Practice of Politics: Great Powers and the Rhetoric of Self-Determination in the Cases of Kosovo and South Ossetia," 10 Chi. J. Int'l L. 1 (2008). Reproduced with permission of the Chicago Journal of International Law.

Bronner, Ethan. "Population talks: the flip side; Unofficial groups get chance to tell world their views," The Boston Globe, Sept. 8, 1994. Republished with permission of The Boston Globe. Permission conveyed through Copyright Clearance Center, Inc.

Charnovitz, Steven. "The Illegitimacy of Preventing NGO Participation," 36 Brook. J. Int'l L. 891, 905-909 (2011). Reprinted by permission.

Chinkin, Christine. "Kosovo: A 'Good' or 'Bad' War?" Reproduced with permission from 93 Am. J. Int'l L. 841 (1999). Copyright © The American Society of International Law.

Couvreur, Philippe (Registrar, International Court of Justice, The Hague). Case Concerning the Gabcikovo-Nagymoros Project, Opinion of the Court, p. 26, Sketch Map No. 3. Permission granted by the Registrar of the Court.

Daskal, Jennifer, Ashley Deeks and Ryan Goodman. Strikes in Syria: The International Law Framework, Just Security, http://justsecurity.org/15479/strikes-syria-international-law-framework-daskal-deeks-goodman/. Reprinted by permission.

Donnelly, Jack. "Cultural Relativism and Universal Human Rights," 6 Hum. Rts. Q. 410 (1984). Copyright © The Johns Hopkins University Press. Reprinted with permission of The Johns Hopkins University Press.

Farer, Tom. "A Paradigm of Legitimate Intervention," in Enforcing Restraint: Collective Intervention in Internal Conflicts, edited by Lori Fisler Damrosch (1993). Council on Foreign Relations Press.

Franck, Thomas M., and Patel, Faiza. "The Gulf Crisis in International and Foreign Relations Law: UN Police Action in Lieu of War: 'The Old Order Changeth.'" Reproduced with permission from 85 Am. J. Int'l L. 63 (1991). Copyright © The American Society of International Law.

Gerretsen, Chas, "Messe de la Junta, General Augusto Pinochet, Santiago de Chile, September 19, 1973."© Chas Gerretsen/The Netherlands Photo Archive.

Greenpeace. July 10th, 1985: The Greenpeace Flagship Rainbow Warrior in Auckland Harbour after bombing by French secret service agents—crew member Fernando Pereira was killed in the blast. © Greenpeace.

Gya, Giji, and Global Policy Forum, Table in Chapter 14 reproduced with permission of Global Policy Forum.

Hardin, Garrett. "Tragedy of the Commons," 162 Science 1243 (1968). Excerpted with permission. Copyright © 1968 American Association for the Advancement of Science.

Hart, H. L. A. The Concept of Law. Copyright © Oxford University Press 1961. Reprinted by permission of Oxford University Press.

Held, David. "Cosmopolitanism: globalisation tamed?," 29 Review of International Studies 465 (2003). Reprinted by permission of Cambridge University Press.

Henkin, Louis. How Nations Behave (2d ed. 1979). Reprinted with permission of Columbia University Press.

Hersh, Seymour. "King's Ransom: How Vulnerable Are the Saudi Royals?" The New Yorker, Oct. 22, 2001, at 35.

Hudec, Robert E. "The New WTO Dispute Settlement Procedure: An Overview of the First Three Years," 8 Minnesota Journal of Global Trade 1 (1999). Reprinted with the permission of the publisher, University of Minnesota and Minnesota Journal of Global Trade.

Hurd, Ian. "The International Rule of Law: Law and the Limits of Politics," 28 Ethics and Int'l Affairs 39, 42-48 (2014). Copyright © 2014 Carnegie Council for Ethics in International Affairs. Reprinted with the permission of Cambridge University Press.

Hurrell, Andrew. "Global Inequality and International Institutions," 32 Metaphilosophy 34 (2004). Reprinted by permission of John Wiley & Sons.

International Humanitarian Law: Answers to Your Questions (ICRC, 1998). Reprinted by permission of the International Committee of the Red Cross.

International Legal Materials. Permission to reprint the following: Award on the Merits in Dispute Between Texaco Overseas Petroleum Company/California Asiatic Oil Company and the Government of Libyan Arab Republic, 17 I.L.M. 1 (1977); Guidelines on the Treatment of Foreign Direct Investment, 31 I.L.M. 1363 (1992); Conference on Yugoslavia: Arbitration Commission Opinion Nos. 1, 2, 3, 4, and 6, 31 I.L.M. 1494, 1497, 1499, 1501, 1507 (1992); Declaration on the Guidelines on the Recognition of New States in Eastern Europe and in the Soviet Union, 31 I.L.M. 1486 (1992); Agreement for the Implementation of the Provisions of the United Nations Convention on the Law of the Sea of 10 December 1982 Relating to the Conservation and Management of Straddling Fish Stocks and Highly Migratory Fish Stocks. 34 I.L.M. 1542 (1995); Public Committee Against Torture in Israel, Judgment Concerning the Legality of the General Security Service's Interrogation Methods, 38 I.L.M. 1471 (1999). Copyright © The American Society of International Law.

International Telecommunication Union, "Explanation of Membership Policies," *http://www.itu.int/members/sectmem/participation.html.*© International Telecommunication Union. Reprinted with permission.

Jacobson, Harold K. Networks of Interdependence: International Organizations and the Global Political System. Reprinted by permission of Merelyn Jacobson.

Kausikan, Bilihari. "Asia's Different Standard," 92 Foreign Policy 24 (1993). Copyright © 1993 by the Carnegie Endowment for International Peace. Reprinted by permission.

Kearney, Richard, and Dalton, Robert. "The Treaty on Treaties." Reproduced with permission from 64 Am. J. Int'l L. 495 (1970). Copyright © The American Society of International Law.

Kennedy, David. "When Renewal Repeats: Thinking Against the Box," 22 N.Y.U. J. Int'l. L. & Pol. 33 (2000). Reproduced with permission of the New York University Journal of International Law and Politics.

Kingsbury, Benedict. "Sovereignty and Inequality," 9 Eur. J. Int'l L. 599 (1998). Copyright © Oxford University Press. Reprinted by permission of Oxford University Press.

Koskenniemi, Martti. "The Politics of International Law," 1 Eur. J. Int'l L. 7 (1990). Copyright © Oxford University Press. Reprinted by permission of Oxford University Press.

Krasner, Stephen. Sovereignty: Organized Hypocrisy (1999). Copyright © 1999 by Princeton University Press. Reprinted by permission of Princeton University Press.

Krauthammer, Charles. "The Curse of Legalism: International Law? It's Purely Advisory," The New Republic, Nov. 6, 1989, at 44. Copyright © 1989 The New Republic, LLC. Reprinted by permission of The New Republic.

Levi, Werner. Contemporary International Law (2 ed. 1991). Reprinted by permission of the author.

Lietzau, William K. "The United States and the International Criminal Court: International Criminal Law After Rome: Concerns from a U.S. Military Perspective," 64 Law & Contemp. Prob. 119. Copyright © Duke University School of Law. Reprinted by permission.

Lutz, Ellen, and Sikkink, Kathryn. "International Human Rights Law in Practice: The Justice Cascade: The Evolution and Impact of Foreign Human Rights Trials in Latin America," 2 Chicago J. Int'l L. 1 (2001). Reproduced with permission of the Chicago Journal of International Law.

MacLaren, Malcolm, and Schwendimann, Felix. "An Exercise in the Development of International Law: The New ICRC Study on Customary International Humanitarian Law," 6 German L.J. (2005). Copyright © 2005 German Law Journal.

Malanczuk, Peter. Akehurst's Modern Introduction to International Law (7th ed. 1997). Reproduced with permission from Thomson Publishing Services.

Map of the Nile Basin in Chapter 11 was created for this text by Dana Costello.

Map of Syria adapted from Nissenbaum, Dion. "Months of Airstrikes Fail to Slow Islamic State in Syria" http://www.wsj.com/articles/u-s-led-airstrikes-fail-to-slow-islamic-state-in-syria-1421271618. Reprinted with permission of The Wall Street Journal, Copyright © 2015 Dow Jones & Company, Inc. All Rights Reserved Worldwide. License numbers 3582200615140 and 3582200720475.

Marie-Henckaerts, Jean, "Study on Customary International Humanitarian Law: A Contribution to the Understanding and Respect for the Rule of Law in Armed Conflict" 87 Int'l Rev. Red Cross 175 (2005). Reprinted with permission from the International Committee of the Red Cross.

Mathews, Jessica, "Power Shift," Foreign Affairs, Jan/Feb. 1997, at 50. Copyright © Council on Foreign Relations.

Milanovic, Marko, "Norm Conflict in International Law: Whither Human Rights?" 20 Duke J. Comp. & Int'l L. 69 (2009). Reprinted with permission from the Duke Journal of Comparative and International Law.

Mutua, Makau. "What is TWAIL?" Reproduced with permission from 94 ASIL Proc. 31, 34-35 (2000). Copyright © The American Society of International Law.

Nagel, Thomas. "The Problem of Global Justice," 33 Phil. & Pub. Aff. 113 (2005). Reprinted by permission of John Wiley and Sons.

Photo of the Japanese Factory Ship, the Nisshin Maru. Copyright © WENN Ltd / Alamy. Reprinted by permission.

Photo of Veiled Woman by Books, March 25, 2005, Agence France-Presse. Reproduced with permission from Getty Images.

Pogge, Thomas W. "Responsibilities for Poverty-Related Ill Health," 16 Ethics & International Affairs 71 (2002). Reprinted by permission of John Wiley and Sons.

Ratner, Steven R. "Belgium's War Crimes Statute: A Postmortem," Reproduced with permission from 97 Am. J. Int'l L. 888 (2003). Copyright © The American Society of International Law.

Ratner, Steven R. The Thin Justice of International Law: A Moral Reckoning of the Law of Nations 341-43 (2015). Reprinted by permission of Oxford University Press.

Reisman, W. Michael. "Law From the Policy Perspective," in International Law Essays, edited by Myres S. McDougal and W. Michael Reisman. Copyright © 1981 Foundation Press. Reprinted by permission, Foundation Press.

Reisman, W. Michael. "The Lessons of Qana," 22 Yale J. Int'l L. 381 (1997).

Reisman, W. Michael. "The Political Consequences of the General Assembly Advisory Opinion," in The International Court of Justice and Nuclear Weapons, edited by Laurence Boisson de Chazournes and Philippe Sands (1991). Reprinted with the permission of Cambridge University Press.

Shihata, Ibrahim. The Legal Treatment of Foreign Direct Investment. (Kluwer Academic Publishers, 1993). Reprinted with kind permission of Kluwer Law International and Mrs. Ibrahim Shihata.

Spiro, Peter J. "New Global Potentates: Nongovernmental Organizations and the 'Unregulated' Marketplace," 18 Cardozo L. Rev. 957 (1996). Copyright © 1996 Cardozo Law Review. Reprinted by permission of Cardozo Law Review.

Szasz, Paul. "Legal Authority for the Possible Use of Force Against Iraq." Reproduced with permission from 92 Am. Soc'y Int'l L. Proc. 136 (1998). Copyright © The American Society of International Law.

Taylor, Carmen, "A jet airliner is lined up on one of the World Trade Center towers in New York Tuesday, Sept. 11, 2001." Associated Press, KHBS KHOG. Reprinted with permission of AP/Wide World Photos.

Michael Walzer. Coda: Can the Good Guys Win? 24 Eur. J. Int'l L.433-434 (2013). Reprinted by permission of the European Journal of International Law.

Wedgwood, Ruth. "NATO's Campaign in Yugoslavia." Reproduced with permission from 93 Am. J. Int'l L. 828 (1999). Copyright © The American Society of International Law.

Wiener, Jonathan Baert. Global Environmental Regulation: Instrument Choice in Legal Context, 108 Yale L.J. 677 (1999). Reprinted by permission of The Yale Law Journal Company and William S. Hein Company from the Yale Law Journal, Vol. 108, page 677.

Wright, Shelley. "Women and the Global Economic Order: A Feminist Perspective," 10 Am. U. Int'l L. Rev. 861 (1995). Reprinted with the permission of the publisher, Washington College of Law of The American University and American University International Law Review.

Authors' Note

In order to provide a sense of the appearance of original international legal documents, we have attempted as much as possible to retain the formatting of documents as they appear in the original, authoritative source. In some cases, this results in different typefaces in the text. For convenience, additions to excerpted material are indicated by brackets. Deletions are indicated by ellipses, unless the deletions occur at the beginning of court or tribunal decisions or dissents. Citations and footnotes are generally omitted from excerpted materials without using an ellipsis. Footnotes that appear in excerpted materials retain the numbering of the originals; footnotes denoted by an asterisk are the authors'.

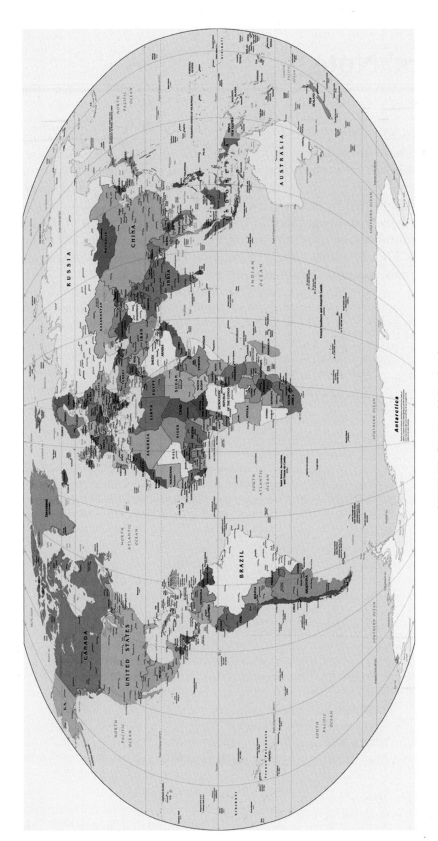

SOURCE: CIA World Factbook
Political Map of the World 2015

PART I

Introduction to International Law and Law Making

International law, in one form or another, dates back thousands of years, and reflects the felt need of most independent political communities for agreed norms and processes to regulate their interactions. Part I of this casebook is designed to introduce you to the issues, processes, actors, and norms that constitute modern international law, and to the ways in which international legal norms are generated, interpreted, and applied. The problems in Part I illustrate in microcosm the kinds of issues that confront international decision makers and the ways in which international legal norms and processes may be used to analyze and resolve such issues.

Chapter 1 provides an overview of the evolution and historical development of international law and institutions in the context of two quite different problems that together illustrate the richness and complexity of contemporary international law and its role in international decision making. The first problem, the clash between Chad and Libya over control of the Aouzou Strip during the 1980s, represents a classic international law dispute. The actors are states, the issue in dispute is control over territory, the governing legal instruments are treaties, and the forum for decision is an international court. Similar issues have arisen countless times over the last several hundred years, and the legal principles relied upon by the International Court of Justice in reaching its decision would be instantly recognizable to lawyers from a much earlier era. The Chad-Libya problem highlights the continuing importance of states and territory in the international legal and political order and raises questions concerning the effect of international law and institutions on interstate relations and state behavior.

The second problem in Chapter 1, the *Rainbow Warrior* affair, illustrates some of the dramatic changes that have reshaped international law in the post-World War II era, including the rising prominence of non-state actors and issue areas such as human rights and the environment. The problem centers on the French government's decision to destroy a vessel used by a non-governmental organization to protest the effects of French nuclear testing on the environment. The actors include states, non-governmental organizations, individuals, and a variety of international organizations. The issues involve a complex mix of international security, trade, and environmental concerns, and illustrate the sometimes complicated relationship between international and domestic legal systems. Like the Chad-Libya problem,

1

the *Rainbow Warrior* affair also raises difficult questions concerning the manner and extent to which international law influences the behavior of international actors, though in a very different context.

Chapter 1 concludes by sketching some of the conceptual challenges that characterize the field, noting both the increasing legalization of international relations and the gaps, inadequacies, and problems that remain. Finally, Chapter 1 outlines some of the many different conceptual approaches that could be applied to understand international law, from natural law to positivism to more recent interdisciplinary methodologies.

Chapter 2 provides the basic analytical framework for understanding the generation, interpretation, and application of international legal norms. The chapter relies on several concrete problems to illustrate how states come to agree on international legal norms, why states and other actors might prefer one form of international law to another in a given context, and the processes by which international legal norms change over time. Together, Chapters 1 and 2 provide an overview of the field of international law as well as some of the analytical and substantive tools needed for analyzing the subject-specific problems that appear in the chapters that follow.

1

Tracing the Evolution of International Law Through Two Problems

I. THE CHAD-LIBYA WAR OVER THE AOUZOU STRIP

In the middle of the Sahara desert lies a narrow area of barren land known as the Aouzou Strip. Sparsely inhabited by a few thousand people, the Strip sits on the border between Libya and Chad. The Strip has virtually no economic potential to either Chad or Libya, either on its surface or below; nor has either state seen the Strip as having any military or strategic value, given its isolation from population centers and its inhospitable climate. Yet since the independence of Libya from Italian colonial rule in 1951 and of Chad from French colonial rule in 1960, the two states have fiercely contested—including through recourse to armed force—the location of their common border and thus title to the Strip.

The essence of Chad's claim to the territory is that the border was fixed by a treaty—but not a treaty between Libya and Chad. Rather, Chad has asserted that the 1955 Treaty of Friendship and Good Neighbourliness between Libya and France included an acceptance by Libya of France's claims to the borders of its colonial possessions in Africa. These borders had been the subject of earlier agreements not between France and Libya, but between France and the previous colonial powers in the area—namely, Italy and Britain. Chad claimed that the 1955 Treaty that recognized the validity of these colonial agreements bound Libya. Libya asserted title not only to the Strip but to significant amounts of territory south of it, asserting the invalidity of the 1955 Treaty that France allegedly coerced Libya's king into signing; the lack of any recognition in that treaty of the Chad-Libya border; the allegiance to Libya of inhabitants of the region; and the prior title to the territory held by the Ottoman Empire and Italy, the predecessor colonial powers to Libya.

Libya asserted its claims in a variety of ways. In the early 1970s, it supported a rebellion by inhabitants of northern Chad against the central government; after the central

3

government lost control of the Strip, Libya set up a de facto military administration of the region. Diplomatic negotiations mediated by the Organization of African Unity (OAU) failed to reach a solution. In 1980, as Chad's civil war intensified, Libya invaded areas of Chad outside the Strip and ousted the official government in favor of its pro-Libyan rival. The invasion was strongly condemned by the OAU. In 1982, after the OAU threatened to cancel its summit scheduled to take place in Tripoli, Libya agreed to pull its troops out of much of the country.

In 1983, with Libya still occupying much of northern Chad (including the Strip), the Chad government appealed to the UN Security Council to demand Libya's withdrawal. The Soviet Union vetoed a UN resolution calling for the withdrawal. Chad succeeded in ousting the Libyan military from northern Chad—except for the Strip—in 1987. After two more years of OAU-sponsored negotiations, the two states agreed in August 1989 to settle the border dispute by political means within one year or, if they failed to do so, to submit it for determination to the International Court of Justice (ICJ), the judicial organ of the United Nations, in The Hague. In 1990, after the failure of negotiations, the two states asked the Court to determine their mutual border in accordance with principles of international law.

A. The Law of Nations in Its Traditional Incarnation

The dispute between Chad and Libya concerns international law, and not only political interactions, in two key senses. First, the parties themselves invoked legal arguments to assert their title to the disputed territory; and, second, they agreed, after much discussion and fighting, that they would allow a judicial body to resolve their dispute solely by recourse to legal rules. Throughout the pages that follow, the reader will see numerous problems in which the various actors—not always states—use legal arguments to make claims, justify their own actions, and acknowledge obligations. A decision by those parties to entrust the final resolution of their dispute to an international court is, however, relatively rare in the field of international law. Such regularized resort to tribunals for the settlement of international disputes represents an aspiration of many of the founders and modern practitioners of international law, but it is by no means the only way in which the law can prove decisive or influential to an outcome. We offer this case merely to demonstrate the role of law in the resolution of disputes without suggesting that the mechanism of a court decision is the only possible, or even the most common, arena for decision making.

The Aouzou Strip problem also provides an example of an international legal disagreement in its most traditional sense: the principal actors are states; the resource under dispute is territory; the legal instruments on which the two sides rely are quite formal—namely, treaties; the doctrinal arguments of the parties about the formal requisites of title to territory reflect concepts dating back to the conquest of much of the world by European states 500 years ago. This sort of dispute could easily have arisen 100 or 200 years ago (with colonial powers replacing the states of today as parties).

To gain a sense of how international law developed to address these interstate disputes, one must have some grasp of its history. Legal historians differ significantly, however, in arriving at an appropriate starting point for such history. From their earliest days, organized political communities have entered into agreements to regulate interactions they might have. For instance, in the thirteenth century B.C., the Egyptian pharaoh Rameses II entered into a Treaty of Peace, Alliance, and Extradition with a neighboring king; Asian kingdoms routinely engaged in similar practices. Ancient entities settled some disputes through accords, though recourse to war was a common enterprise. Most historians of international law nonetheless focus on Europe as the birthplace of international law as we know it today; as indicated in the following excerpt, they regard the law's key formative years as the time of the decline of the Holy Roman Empire and the birth of new states in Europe.

Werner Levi, *Contemporary International Law*
6-13 (2d ed. 1991)

Mainly as a result of new economic forces, the Holy Roman Empire broke down, which brought about the collapse of the at least nominally centralized order of Europe and foreshadowed the need for a different legal system. . . .

As new centers of independent power arose, laws regulating their coexistence and relations were needed, although until the age of absolutism had passed, these laws had to refer to the person of the rulers more than to political entities. Gradually, the relationships of subordination and superordination under the universalist reign of one emperor and pope were replaced by a system of coordination among sovereign rulers. The feudalistic entities with their relatively uncertain borders gave way to states based upon sharply defined territory. . . . The preeminent role of territory in international law began. . . .

Once the multitude of specific limited jurisdictions . . . was replaced by the principle of territoriality with one sovereign ruler as the basis of the state, a number of legal consequences followed. One was the absolute power and exclusive jurisdiction of one ruler in his or her territory. The second was the prohibition of interference by other monarchs in a state's internal affairs. The third was the rise of immunity. The fourth was the gradual elaboration of equality among states in diplomatic practice and of the principles regulating this practice. . . .

Many of the principles and norms developed during this time, especially those fortifying sovereignty, are still accepted today, with states replacing rulers as subjects of the law. But initially, the law was not applicable to peoples and territories outside Western society (except the United States when it became independent). . . . Rules legitimizing imperialism and its means . . . endured well into the twentieth century, until most colonies became independent.

EARLY WRITERS ON INTERNATIONAL LAW

During these first centuries in the development of international law, legal and political writers . . . collected existing norms and suggested new ones. And they provided the theoretical and philosophical foundations, justifications, and guidelines for the international legal system, always keeping in mind the interests of their countries.

. . . The Spaniard Francisco Vitoria (1480-1546) argued that Spain was obliged to treat the conquered Indians in the Americas humanely, and he even granted these Indians a limited right to conduct "just wars" against their cruel conquerors. But he defended Spain's right in principle to create overseas dependencies and to exploit them. Another Spaniard, Francisco Suárez (1548-1617), dealt with the by then obvious interactions of states and how to regulate them. Like all writers of the era he was particularly concerned with the nature of just war and rules for its conduct. The Italian Alberico Gentili (1552-1608) — in contrast to his Spanish colleagues, who were both professors of theology — emphasized the secular nature of international law. He therefore deduced the rules of the law not from some metaphysical source but from the practice of states and the writings of historians. He was thus the first representative of the "positivists," who argue that law is created by humans for definite conditions and purposes rather than by some supreme being for all eternity. . . .

Outstanding [among early treatises] was Hugo de Groot's (Grotius, 1583-1645) *De iure belli ac pacis* (On the Law of War and Peace), which brought him the sobriquet "father of international law." He became equally influential in writing on the laws of treaties, extra-territoriality, and the sea while focusing on the law of war and on the theoretical foundation of international law. Grotius believed that there was a law of nature (not necessarily divine) that could be implemented, not counteracted, by people using right reason. The combination of these two sources was, to Grotius, the foundation of international law. By this argument he avoided commitment to a particular religion and deliberately so, for he felt that to be effective, international law had to be acceptable to all, conceivably even "infidels." . . . Three doctrines [that are still relevant today] are the applicability of laws of war to all parties regardless of the justness of the war, freedom of the seas (argued in his book *Mare liberum* and a particularly important concept for a Dutchman to undo the claims of England and other states to dominion over the seas), and extraterritoriality of ambassadors. . . .

In spite of Grotius's influence, writers continued to argue in their treatment of international law either the naturalist or the positivist view, although they did so with varying degrees. The Germans Samuel Pufendorf (1632-1694) and Christian Wolff (1676-1756) and the Swiss Emmerich de Vattel (1714-1767) could generally be classified as naturalists. The Englishman Richard Zouche (1590-1660) represented the positivist school. But few of these writers were extremists, and most took account of state practice. . . .

THE NINETEENTH CENTURY

. . . When the French Revolution and others ended the age of absolutism, the state became identified with its people rather than with the person of its monarch. This change required adjustments in the law. A state's territory or people could no longer be treated as appendixes of the ruler. The state itself became the subject of international law. The state's form or government personnel no longer affected the state's rights or obligations. The separation of the ruler's person from the objective legal existence of the state fulfilled the political need of including non-Christian states (Turkey, Japan, China) into the international community of states.

In increasing measure, treaties, especially multilateral treaties, implemented and eventually surpassed in volume custom as a source of international norms. The growing importance and numbers of treaties also meant a simplification of their conclusion, the routinization of what used to be prestige matters, and, most important to the new and Communist states today, a greater effectiveness of the rule that states cannot be bound against their will or that they should participate in the making of rules binding them.

The material covered by treaties was greatly augmented, reflecting both the growing volume of interaction among states and the multiplication of state interests. Agreements were reached on rules of state conduct. Communications, trade and commerce, financial matters, scientific and health subjects, and humanitarian concerns surpassed politics in volume, not importance, as topics of international conferences, thereby inaugurating a trend that continues in the contemporary era. Treaties establishing international organizations, mainly in the "noncontroversial" field of communications, made their appearance.

Grotius's natural law approach can be seen in the following passages from his treatise on war and peace.

Hugo Grotius, *De Jure Belli ac Pacis Libri Tres, book 1*
9, 12-13, 15 (Francis Kelsey trans. 1925) (1625)

1. . . . That body of law . . . which is concerned with the mutual relations among states or rulers of states, whether derived from nature, or established by divine ordinances, or having its origin in custom and tacit agreement, few have touched upon. Up to the present time no one has treated it in a comprehensive and systematic manner; yet the welfare of mankind demands that this task be accomplished. . . .

3. Such a work is all the more necessary because in our day, as in former times, there is no lack of men who view this branch of law with contempt as having no reality outside of an empty name. On the lips of men quite generally is the saying of Euphemus, which Thucydides quotes, that in the case of a king or imperial city nothing is unjust which is expedient. . . .

Furthermore, the controversies which arise between peoples or kings generally have Mars as their arbiter. That war is irreconcilable with all law is a view held not alone by the ignorant populace. . . . Nothing is more common than the assertion of antagonism between law and arms. . . .

8. [M]aintenance of the social order . . . which is consonant with human intelligence, is the source of law properly so called. To this sphere of law belong the abstaining from that which is another's, the restoration to another of anything of his which we may have, together with any gain which we may have received from it, the obligation to fulfil promises, the making good of a loss incurred through our fault, and the inflicting of penalties upon men according to their deserts.

9. From this signification of the word law there has flowed another and more extended meaning. . . . [I]t is meet for the nature of man, within the limitations of human intelligence, to follow the direction of a well-tempered judgement, being neither led astray by fear or the allurement of immediate pleasure, nor carried away by rash impulse. Whatever is clearly at variance with such judgement is understood to be contrary also to the law of nature, that is, to the nature of man. . . .

17. [J]ust as the laws of each state have in view the advantage of that state, so by mutual consent it has become possible that certain laws should originate as between all states, or a great many states; and it is apparent that the laws thus originating had in view the advantage, not of particular states, but of the great society of states. And this is what is called the law of nations. . . .

The geographical ambit of international law and its approach to the diversity of actors in the international system during its formative centuries remains a subject of great importance. Levi's more Eurocentric vision is echoed in the first edition of the leading English-language treatise on international law.

Lassa Oppenheim, *International Law, vol. 1, Peace*
30-31, 34, 218-219, 266-267 (1905)

§26. . . . There is no doubt that the Law of Nations is a product of Christian civilisation. It originally arose between the States of Christendom only, and for hundreds of years was confined to these States. Between Christian and Mohammedan nations a condition of perpetual enmity prevailed in former centuries. And no constant intercourse existed in former times between Christian and Buddhistic States. But from about the beginning of the nineteenth century matters gradually changed. A condition of perpetual enmity between whole groups of nations exists no longer either in theory or in practice. And although there is still a broad and deep gulf between Christian civilisation and others, many interests, which knit Christian States together, knit likewise some non-Christian and Christian States.

§27. Thus the membership of the Family of Nations has of late necessarily been increased and the range of dominion of the Law of Nations has extended beyond its original limits. . . . [T]here are three conditions for the admission of new members into the circle of the Family of Nations. A State to be admitted must, first, be a civilised State which is in constant intercourse with members of the Family of Nations. Such State must, secondly, expressly or tacitly consent to be bound for its future international conduct by the rules of International Law. And, thirdly, those States which have hitherto formed the Family of Nations must expressly or tacitly consent to the reception of the new member. . . .

§29. The Law of Nations as a law between States based on the common consent of the members of the Family of Nations naturally does not contain any rules concerning the intercourse with and treatment of such States as are outside that circle. That this intercourse and treatment ought to be regulated by the principles of Christian morality is obvious. But actually a practice frequently prevails which is not only contrary to Christian morality, but arbitrary and barbarous. Be that as it may, it is discretion, and not International Law, according to which the members of the Family of Nations deal with such States as still remain outside that family. . . .

§169. The territory of a State may consist of one piece of the surface of the globe only, such as that of Switzerland, [or it] may also be dismembered and consist of several pieces, such as that of Great Britain. All States with colonies have a "dismembered territory." . . . Colonies rank as territory of the motherland, although they may enjoy complete self-government and therefore be called Colonial States. . . .

————————————

Consider the following two perspectives on the history of international law and the state of that law by the nineteenth century.

R.P. Anand, *The Influence of History on the Literature of International Law*

The Structure and Process of International Law 342-343 (R.St.J. MacDonald & D.M. Johnston eds., 1983)

There is little doubt that in some form or another, rules of inter-state conduct or what we now call international law can be traced to some of the most ancient civilizations, like China, India, Egypt and Assyria. Apart from just and humane rules of war and peace, one can find numerous rules and regulations on the law of treaties, right of asylum, treatment of aliens and foreign nationals, the immunities and privileges of ambassadors, modes of acquiring territory, and even glimpses of the law of the sea and maritime belt. . . . As Majid Khadduri points out: "In each civilization the population tended to develop within itself a community of political entities—a family of nations—whose interrelationships were regulated by a set of customary rules and practices, rather than being a single nation governed by a single authority and a single system of law. Several families of nations existed or coexisted in areas such as the ancient Near East, Greece and Rome, China, Islam and Western Christiandom, where at least one distinct civilization had developed in each of them. Within each civilization a body of principles and rules developed for regulating the conduct of states with one another in peace and war."

Although many of these systems of inter-state rules and practices were confined to one or two civilizations, and disappeared with the disappearance of those civilizations, it would be wrong to dismiss them as not international law or as of no consequence and merely "religious precepts" or moral obligations. . . . [N]ecessities in intercourse between nations in different civilizations probably provoked similar responses and similar rules and institutions, such as the immunity of foreign envoys and the establishment of durable treaty relationships. . . .

[L]ong before the emergence of Europe as the center of the world stage, relations between Europe and Asia were conducted on the basis of well-recognized rules of inter-state conduct which were supposed to be universally applicable to all states. [W]hen European adventurers arrived in Asia in the fifteenth century "they found themselves in the middle of a network of states and inter-state relations based on traditions which were more ancient than their own and in no way inferior to notions of European civilization." . . . European sovereign or semi-sovereign agencies which appeared on the Asian scene were automatically drawn into the Asian legal system and influenced by its rules. The confrontation of the Asian and European states "took place on a footing of equality and the ensuing commercial and political transactions, far from being in a legal vacuum, were governed by the law of nations as adjusted to local inter-state custom." The East Indies constituted the meeting ground of the Dutch, English, French and other European East India companies, on the one hand, and Asian sovereigns on the other. The more these contacts became intensified, the more they affected each other's practices with a common framework of diplomatic exchanges and treaty making.

Antony Anghie, *Finding the Peripheries: Sovereignty and Colonialism in Nineteenth-Century International Law*

40 Harv. Intl. L.J. 1, 22, 25, 29, 30, 49, 69, 79, 80 (1999)

. . . [A] central feature of positivism was the distinction it made between civilized and uncivilized states. The naturalist notion that a single, universally applicable law governed a naturally constituted society of nations was completely repudiated by jurists of the mid-nineteenth century. Instead, nineteenth-century writers such as Wheaton claimed that international law was the exclusive province of civilized societies. . . .

. . . [T]he distinction between the civilized and uncivilized was a fundamental tenet of positivist epistemology and thus profoundly shaped the concepts constituting the positivist framework. The racialization of positivist law followed inevitably from these premises—as demonstrated, for example, by the argument that law was the creation of unique, civilized, and social institutions and that only states possessing such institutions could be members of "international society." . . .

The concept of society enabled positivists to develop a number of strategies for explaining further why the non-European world was excluded from international law. One such strategy consisted of asserting that no law existed in certain non-European, barbaric regions. . . . A second strategy used to distinguish the civilized from the uncivilized consisted of asserting the fact that while certain societies may have had their own systems of law these were of such an alien character that no proper legal relations could develop between European and non-European states. . . .

The problem of the legal personality of non-European peoples could be most simply resolved by the actual act of colonization, which effectively extinguished this personality. Once colonization took place, the colonizing power assumed sovereignty over the non-European territory, and any European state carrying on business with that territory would deal with the colonial power. In this way, legal relations would once again take place between two European powers. . . .

Sovereignty manifested itself quite differently in the non-European world than in the European world. First, since the non-European world was not "sovereign," virtually no legal restrictions were imposed on the actions of European states with respect to non-European peoples. European states could engage in massive violence, invariably justified as necessary to pacify the natives and followed by the project of reshaping those societies in accordance with their particular vision of the world. [Second,] lacking sovereignty, non-European states exercised no rights recognizable by international law over their own territory. Any legal restrictions on the actions of European states towards non-European states resulted from contentions among European states regarding the same territory, not from the rights of the non-European states. This is evident in the partition of Africa, which was determined in accordance with the needs of the major European states. . . .

. . . [T]he nineteenth century offers us an example of a much broader theme: the importance of the existence of the "other" for the progress and development of the discipline itself. Seen from this perspective, the nineteenth century is both distinctive and conventional. Its method, focus, and techniques are in many ways unique. But in another respect, the nineteenth century is simply one example of the nexus between international law and the civilizing mission. The same mission was implemented by the vocabulary of naturalism in sixteenth-century international law. . . . [T]he only thing unique about the nineteenth century is that it explicitly adopted the civilizing mission and reflected these goals in its very vocabulary. The more alarming and likely possibility is that the civilizing mission is inherent in one form or another in the principal concepts and categories that govern our existence: ideas of modernity, progress, development, emancipation, and rights. . . .

International law by the nineteenth century had developed an entire doctrine to justify acquisition of territory by colonial powers. That law recognized, for instance, that European states could acquire so-called empty land or *terra nullius*, or land not already under the control of another state—based on its purported discovery by Europeans, notwithstanding its prior discovery, so to speak, by indigenous peoples who may have been living on the territory for thousands of years. It also justified the colonial presence by placing great weight on treaties of cession whereby indigenous peoples signed over control of their land to colonial powers, despite the coerced nature of many of these agreements. Colonial powers could divide their possessions as they saw fit, a process that reached its apogee in the Congress of Berlin in 1884-1885, when the European imperial powers drew up legal spheres of influence for most of Africa, and continued with numerous bilateral agreements setting individual frontiers, such as those cited by Chad and Libya in the Aouzou Strip controversy.

In the case of territorial disputes between colonial powers not resolved by treaty, arbitral tribunals recognized by the end of the century that effective control over the territory was the key to title. However, the views of the local populations played little if any role.

B. Resolution of the Chad-Libya Conflict

On February 3, 1994, three and a half years after Chad and Libya submitted the case, the ICJ ruled 16-1 (the sole dissenter was the judge that Libya was allowed to appoint under the Court's rules) that the Aouzou Strip in its entirety, as well as all lands south of it claimed by Libya, belonged to Chad. The Court first examined the text and context of the 1955 Treaty and concluded that, contrary to Libya's assertions, it "was aimed at settling all the frontier questions, and not just some of them." It then closely examined the various colonial agreements incorporated into the 1955 Treaty; these included agreements between Britain and France from 1898, 1899, and 1919, and between France and Italy from 1900 and 1902. The Court relied extensively on, and even reprinted, a French colonial map from 1899 (see next page) that showed the border agreed to by France and Britain that year, although the Court ultimately concluded that France and Britain adopted a slightly different line (more favorable to Chad) in their 1919 agreement. The line from the 1919 France-Britain agreement, combined with the line resulting from the France-Italy agreements, determined the border, as Chad had claimed. The Court continued:

Case Concerning the Territorial Dispute (Libya/Chad)

1994 I.C.J. 6 (Feb. 3)

66. Having concluded that a frontier resulted from the 1955 Treaty, and having established where that frontier lay, the Court is in a position to consider the subsequent attitudes of the Parties to the question of frontiers. No subsequent agreement, either between France and Libya, or between Chad and Libya, has called in question the frontier in this region deriving from the 1955 Treaty. On the contrary, if one considers treaties subsequent to the entry into force of the 1955 Treaty, there is support for the proposition that after 1955, the existence of a determined frontier was accepted and acted upon by the Parties. The Treaty between Libya and Chad of 2 March 1966 . . . deals with frontier questions. Articles 1 and 2 mention "the frontier" between the two countries, with no suggestion of there being any uncertainty about it. . . . If a serious dispute had indeed existed regarding frontiers, eleven years after the conclusion of the 1955 Treaty, one would expect it to have been reflected in the 1966 Treaty. . . .

68. The Court now turns to the attitudes of the Parties, subsequent to the 1955 Treaty, on occasions when matters pertinent to the frontiers came up before international fora. Libya achieved its independence nearly nine years before Chad; during that period, France submitted reports on this territory to the United Nations General Assembly. The report for 1955 . . . shows the area of Chad's territory as 1,284,000 square kilometres, which expressly includes [the Aouzou Strip]. . . . Moreover United Nations publications from 1960 onward continued to state the area of Chad as 1,284,000 square kilometres. . . . Libya did not challenge the territorial dimensions of Chad as set out by France.

69. As for Chad, it has consistently adopted the position that it does have a boundary with Libya, and that the territory of Chad includes the "Aouzou strip" . . . . [The Court describes various complaints by Chad to the UN and OAU about Libya's occupation of the Strip.]

72. [Although the 1955 Treaty allows either party to terminate it after 20 years,] the Treaty must, in the view of the Court, be taken to have determined a permanent frontier. . . . The establishment of this boundary is a fact which, from the outset, has had a legal life of its own, independently of the fate of the 1955 Treaty. Once agreed, the boundary

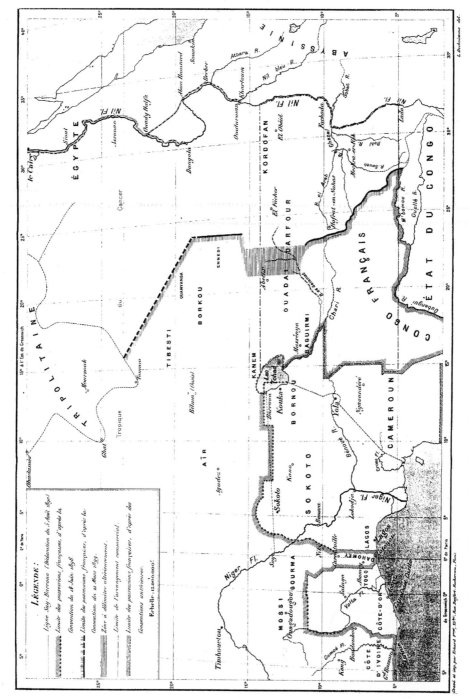

French Ministry of Foreign Affairs Map. 1899, reproduced in *Case Concerning the Territorial Dispute (Libya/Chad)*, 1994 I.C.J. 6, 40

12

stands, for any other approach would vitiate the fundamental principle of the stability of boundaries, the importance of which has been repeatedly emphasized by the Court. . . .

73. A boundary established by treaty thus achieves a permanence which the treaty itself does not necessarily enjoy. The treaty can cease to be in force without in any way affecting the continuance of the boundary. In this instance the Parties have not exercised their option to terminate the Treaty, but whether or not the option be exercised, the boundary remains. . . .

75. . . . The Court's conclusion that the Treaty contains an agreed boundary renders it unnecessary to consider the history of the "Borderlands" claimed by Libya on the basis of title inherited from the indigenous people, the Senoussi Order, the Ottoman Empire and Italy. . . .

76. Likewise, the effectiveness of occupation of the relevant areas in the past, and the question whether it was constant, peaceful and acknowledged, are not matters for determination in this case. . . . The concept of *terra nullius* and the nature of . . . Ottoman or French administration are likewise not germane to the issue. . . . The 1955 Treaty completely determined the boundary between Libya and Chad.

Within weeks of the ICJ's decision, Libya and Chad agreed to abide by it; in April 1994, they reached an agreement on the practicalities of the Libyan withdrawal, removal of mines, and demarcation of the border. They called for the United Nations to send a team of monitors to observe the withdrawal. In May, the UN Security Council established the United Nations Aouzou Strip Observer Group for this purpose. The team consisted of 15 military and civilian observers and cost the United Nations just over $67,000. On May 30, in accordance with the withdrawal schedule previously agreed upon, Libya completed its withdrawal, and the United Nations certified the result. Both governments consider the matter of the Strip's territorial sovereignty closed.

Notes and Questions

1. Why do you suppose that Libya and Chad considered the Aouzou Strip of such importance as to justify the use of armed force? Who would benefit from title over the Strip?

2. Why do you think the Court does not consider the historical circumstances surrounding the colonial agreements to which it refers? What are the differences among the ways that Oppenheim, Anand, and Anghie view the relationships between the European powers and local populations in Africa?

3. If there had been no treaties between the colonial powers on the location of the border, what factors should the Court have considered in arriving at its outcome? Would these factors be different from those a similar court would have examined a hundred years ago?

4. Why do you think the losing party—Libya—complied so readily with the ICJ's decision?

5. Do the facts and outcome represent a victory for the rule of law in international relations or simply a political loss for Libya?

C. International Law's Development in the Twentieth Century

The twentieth century brought about sea changes in the entire field of international law. As a historical matter, most originate in the gradual global transformation that began with World War I, as the populations of European states—and of some of their colonies—decimated themselves in combat over control of small pieces of land. As a result of that war, at least three constitutive changes in the international legal order began. First, European states began to accept that unlimited recourse to war to resolve disputes was counterproductive to their national interests and that recourse to war should be regulated legally. (The states of Europe and Latin America had already agreed, at meetings in The Hague in 1899 and 1907, that the *methods* by which wars were conducted should also be limited, leading to the development of the modern law of war.) By 1928, European and American governments had agreed upon the Treaty Providing for the Renunciation of War as an Instrument of National Policy, the so-called Kellogg-Briand Pact.

Second, in the territorial shakeup that ended World War I, European and U.S. leaders concluded that some ethnic groups in Europe that lacked their own state should determine their own political future. As a result, the victorious World War I Allies carved new states out of the defeated Central Powers based in significant part on the principle of national self-determination, part of American President Woodrow Wilson's Fourteen Points (announced in January 1918 as the U.S. goals in the war). In addition, European leaders agreed on a network of treaties and arrangements aimed at protecting ethnic minority groups within both new and newly enlarged states. This concern with self-determination and minority rights remained, however, quite circumscribed, for European states did not recognize their application to their colonies nor to minorities within the Allied states.

Third, after World War I, the independent states agreed upon a fundamental institutional arrangement to address questions of war and peace and develop legal norms in other areas, such as labor, health, and communications. This organization, the League of Nations, was created by the Versailles Treaty ending World War I. The League transcended prior forms of international cooperation by representing a true international organization, with decisionmaking bodies and a large, permanent Secretariat. Along with its specialized bodies, such as the International Telecommunication Union and the International Labour Office, the League studied and promoted international cooperation on numerous issues of transnational interest. The result was a shift in the way much international law was made, as the League took the lead in preparing multilateral treaties, encouraged states to reach bilateral agreements, and drafted many influential nontreaty instruments. In addition, the world's first standing global court—the Permanent Court of International Justice—began to decide a handful of cases, leading some to believe that the future for the settlement of disputes through international adjudication was bright indeed.

The prospects for legal arrangements to regulate international affairs were soon overshadowed by the sequential aggression of the fascist states—Japan, Italy, and Germany—in China, Ethiopia, and central Europe. The League's members showed no political will to enforce by economic sanctions or military force the legal commitments states had undertaken in the areas of recourse to force or protection of minorities, and America's absence from the League due to the U.S. Senate's rejection of the Versailles Treaty only worsened matters. Much of the apparent progress of international law proved illusory during the 1930s. The cataclysm that followed—50 million dead, Germany's campaign to exterminate European Jews and others, the obliteration of cities by both sides, the use of nuclear weapons, and the continued subjugation of colonial peoples—left little room for optimism about the possibility for the role, let alone the rule, of law in international relations.

Yet World War II proved the catalyst for the acceleration of the major trends that began before it started, as well as for the participation of new actors in the international legal process. Thus, states oversaw the change in substantive law with respect to the two core issues that had proved significant before the war—the use of force and human rights. (The role of new actors is discussed after the next problem in this chapter.) With respect to the first issue, governments agreed in the UN Charter to ban the use of force against states except in two situations—when a state was responding in self-defense and when the United Nations itself authorized force against a state. Wars hardly ceased as a result of the UN Charter, but states did begin to refrain from the sort of aggression against neighboring states, followed by annexation, that had characterized earlier years. The limits of the Charter's ban, however, quickly became clear as powerful states, principally the United States and the USSR, resorted to more subtle tactics to extend their spheres of influence, such as fomenting civil wars and carrying out covert actions.

World War II and events after it also brought renewed attention to the issue of self-determination and human rights. Because the war exacted such a large human and financial toll on the European powers, their grip on colonial possessions significantly weakened. By the late 1940s, two of the largest—British India and the Dutch East Indies—had achieved independence (in the former case through civil disobedience; in the latter through armed conflict) as India, Pakistan, and Indonesia. Most of the rest of Africa and Asia followed suit within a dozen years, usually without significant violence. The independence of these new states vastly changed the legal landscape, as they came to have a significant role in the development of international norms. Their perspectives, molded by centuries of colonial domination, exerted a major influence on the process of law making and its outcomes.

With respect to human rights, the tragedy of World War II led governments to devote significant resources to the creation of a corpus of law aimed at protecting individuals from their own governments. In December 1948, the UN General Assembly proclaimed the Universal Declaration of Human Rights, which sets out a list of civil and political rights as well as various economic, social, and cultural rights. While the Universal Declaration was not intended to be legally binding, many states consider it an authoritative interpretation of the Charter, setting forth in considerable detail the "human rights and fundamental freedoms" that UN members agreed in the Charter to promote and observe. States prepared and signed onto treaties covering genocide, civil and political rights, economic rights, racial discrimination, women's rights, apartheid, torture, and children's rights. Some states took this process, and human rights generally, more seriously than others; indeed, for most of the period after World War II, most governments merely paid lip service to the concept of human rights as a way of influencing or currying favor with others. Nevertheless, the growth of the human rights movement fundamentally challenged the notion that states were free to do what they wanted within their own borders.

In another important development related to human rights, the trials of German and Japanese political and military leaders after World War II helped solidify the notion of individual duties under international law. Many defendants argued that, because they were following superiors' orders, they were immune under international law. Instead, at Nuremberg, Tokyo, and in other postwar trials, thousands of individuals were tried and convicted, and hundreds were executed, dramatically demonstrating, as the Nuremberg Tribunal stated, that "crimes against international law are committed by men, not by abstract entities, and only by punishing individuals who commit such crimes can the provisions of international law be enforced." A number of the human rights treaties, including the 1948 Genocide Convention, make individuals, rather than just states, responsible for violations. In the 1990s, the UN Security Council established ad hoc tribunals with jurisdiction to try individuals for genocide, crimes against humanity, and war crimes. In 1998, states concluded the treaty to establish the International Criminal Court (ICC). The ICC Statute gives the Court jurisdiction over those same three offenses as well as aggression; in 2014, the Court completed its first trial.

New attitudes about the use of force and human rights were, in fact, only part of the change in government attitudes after the war, for the participants in defining that order were themselves increasing in number and taking on new roles. As we appraise these other developments in international law of the last 70 years, consider the following modern dispute of a type that has become more and more common in international relations.

II. THE *RAINBOW WARRIOR* AFFAIR

In 1978, the international non-governmental organization (NGO) Greenpeace purchased a converted research trawler, which it named the *Rainbow Warrior*. Over the next several years, Greenpeace used the *Rainbow Warrior* to publicize its protests against commercial whaling practices, the dumping of nuclear waste in the oceans, and offshore oil and gas operations. In July 1985, Greenpeace sent the *Rainbow Warrior* to the South Pacific to support New Zealand's decision to close its ports to ships carrying nuclear weapons. The vessel was then scheduled to proceed to France's nearby Mururoa Atoll to protest upcoming French underground nuclear testing in the atoll. On July 10, 1985, while the *Rainbow Warrior* was docked in Auckland Harbor, New Zealand, members of the French Directorate General of External Security (DGSE) placed a bomb aboard the vessel; the ensuing explosion resulted in the sinking and total destruction of the ship and the death of Fernando Pereira, a Dutch crew member.

Although most members of the French team quickly fled New Zealand, two agents — Major Alain Mafart and Captain Dominique Prieur — were arrested and charged with murder and arson under New Zealand law. While France initially denied any role in the bombing, in September 1985, France's Prime Minister admitted DGSE's involvement in the attack. At the same time, the French Defense Minister resigned, and the head of the DGSE was fired. In November, Mafart and Prieur pleaded guilty to charges of manslaughter and wilful damage to a ship by means of explosives and were each sentenced to ten years' imprisonment. The French Defense Minister informed the agents that the government would work for their release. At the same time, New Zealand informed France that it would seek compensation for damages caused by France's illegal actions. New Zealand also insisted that France compensate Greenpeace and Pereira's family.

Thereafter, France placed considerable pressure on New Zealand to release the two agents. France argued that the agents had been obeying superior orders and that, because France was prepared to assume responsibility, the agents should not be individually liable. New Zealand replied that neither New Zealand law nor international law excuse criminal acts on the grounds that they were committed pursuant to official orders. New Zealand was also reluctant to release the agents to France because French law did not authorize the serving out of a New Zealand sentence in France, and because the agents' acts were

July 10, 1985: The Greenpeace Flagship *Rainbow Warrior* in Auckland Harbor after
bombing by French secret service agents.
SOURCE: Greenpeace NZ © Greenpeace

not illegal under French law, which provides that when a "homicide, wounding or striking
[was] ordered by law or lawfully ordered authority, no felony or misdemeanor has been
committed."

In early 1986, France began to restrict certain New Zealand exports to France and
French territories. France also began to link resolution of the *Rainbow Warrior* dispute to
the question of future access to the European Community of New Zealand exports, including butter, which is vital to the New Zealand economy. In response, New Zealand filed a
formal complaint with the Organization for Economic Co-operation and Development
(OECD), an international organization promoting dialogue and open markets among
wealthy states, and initiated nonbinding consultation procedures under the General
Agreement on Tariffs and Trade (GATT), a multilateral treaty governing international
trade. In the meantime, bilateral negotiations continued.

Notes and Questions

1. On the merits, how do you think the various disputes between France and New
Zealand should have been resolved? How would you have predicted, in 1986, that they
would be resolved?

2. As a matter of process, how do you think the disputes between France and New
Zealand should be resolved? How would you have predicted they would be resolved?

On June 19, 1986, France and New Zealand agreed to submit all issues between them arising out of this episode to UN Secretary-General Javier Perez de Cuellar (of Peru) for a binding ruling. Once this agreement was reached, New Zealand withdrew its GATT and OECD complaints. Both sides submitted written statements to Perez de Cuellar, who, on July 6, issued the following decision:

Ruling Pertaining to the Differences between France and New Zealand Arising from the *Rainbow Warrior* Affair

19 UN Rep. Intl. Arb. Awards 199 (1986)

The issues that I need to consider are limited in number . . . . My ruling is as follows:

1. APOLOGY

New Zealand seeks an apology. France is prepared to give one. My ruling is that the Prime Minister of France should convey to the Prime Minister of New Zealand a formal and unqualified apology for the attack, contrary to international law, on the "*Rainbow Warrior*" by French service agents which took place on 10 July 1985.

2. COMPENSATION

New Zealand seeks compensation for the wrong done to it and France is ready to pay some compensation. The two sides, however, are some distance apart on quantum. New Zealand has said that the figure should not be less than US Dollars 9 million, France that it should not be more than US Dollars 4 million. My ruling is that the French Government should pay the sum of US Dollars 7 million to the Government of New Zealand as compensation for all the damage it has suffered.

3. THE TWO FRENCH SERVICE AGENTS

It is on this issue that the two Governments plainly had the greatest difficulty in their attempts to negotiate a solution to the whole issue on a bilateral basis before they took the decision to refer the matter to me.

The French Government seeks the immediate return of the two officers. It underlines that their imprisonment in New Zealand is not justified, taking into account in particular the fact that they acted under military orders and that France is ready to give an apology and to pay compensation to New Zealand for the damage suffered.

The New Zealand position is that the sinking of the "*Rainbow Warrior*" involved not only a breach of international law, but also the commission of a serious crime in New Zealand for which the two officers received a lengthy sentence from a New Zealand court. The New Zealand side states that their release to freedom would undermine the integrity of the New Zealand judicial system. In the course of bilateral negotiations with France, New Zealand was ready to explore possibilities for the prisoners serving their sentences outside New Zealand.

But it has been, and remains, essential to the New Zealand position that there should be no release to freedom, that any transfer should be to custody, and that there should be a means of verifying that.

The French response to that is that there is no basis either in international law or in French law on which the two could serve out any portion of their New Zealand sentence in France,* and that they could not be subjected to new criminal proceedings after a transfer into French hands.

On this point, if I am to fulfil my mandate adequately, I must find a solution in respect of the two officers which both respects and reconciles these conflicting positions.

My ruling is as follows:

(a) The Government of New Zealand should transfer Major Alain Mafart and Captain Dominique Prieur to the French military authorities. Immediately thereafter, Major Mafart and Captain Prieur should be transferred to a French military facility on an isolated island outside of Europe for a period of three years.

(b) They should be prohibited from leaving the island for any reason, except with the mutual consent of the two Governments. They should be isolated during their assignment on the island from persons other than military or associated personnel and immediate family and friends. . . . These conditions should be strictly complied with and appropriate action should be taken under the rules governing military discipline to enforce them.

(c) The French Government should every three months convey to the New Zealand Government and to the Secretary-General of the United Nations . . . full reports on the situation of Major Mafart and Captain Prieur in terms of the two preceding paragraphs in order to allow the New Zealand Government to be sure that they are being implemented.

(d) If the New Zealand Government so requests, a visit to the French military facility in question may be made, by mutual agreement by the two Governments, by an agreed third party.

(e) I have sought information on French military facilities outside Europe. On the basis of that information, I believe that the transfer of Major Mafart and Captain Prieur to the French military facility on the isolated island of Hao in French Polynesia would best facilitate the enforcement of the conditions which I have laid down in paragraphs (a) to (d) above. My ruling is that that should be their destination immediately after their transfer.

4. TRADE ISSUES

The New Zealand Government has taken the position that trade issues have been imported into the affair as a result of French action, either taken or in prospect. The French Government denies that, but it has indicated that it is willing to give some undertakings relating to trade, as sought by the New Zealand Government. I therefore rule that France should:

(a) Not oppose continuing imports of New Zealand butter into the United Kingdom in 1987 and 1988 at levels proposed by the Commission of the European Communities . . . ;

and

(b) Not take measures that might impair the implementation of the agreement between New Zealand and the European Economic Community on Trade in Mutton, Lamb and Goatmeat which entered into force on 20 October 1980. . . .

5. ARBITRATION

The New Zealand Government has argued that a mechanism should exist to ensure that any differences that may arise about the implementation of the agreements concluded

---

*In fact, many states have entered into treaties that permit the return of foreign convicts to their home state to serve out their sentence. —Eds.

as a result of my ruling can be referred for binding decision to an arbitral tribunal. The Government of France is not averse to that. My ruling is that an agreement to that effect should be concluded and provide that any dispute concerning the interpretation or application of the other agreements, which it has not been possible to resolve through the diplomatic channel, shall, at the request of either of the two Governments, be submitted to an arbitral tribunal. . . . The decisions of the tribunal . . . shall be binding on the two Governments.

6. The two Governments should conclude and bring into force as soon as possible binding agreements incorporating all of the above rulings. These agreements should provide that the undertaking relating to an apology, the payment of compensation and the transfer of Major Mafart and Captain Prieur should be implemented at the latest on 25 July 1986.

Three days later, France and New Zealand concluded agreements incorporating the substance of the Secretary-General's ruling. One agreement provided that Mafart and Prieur were to be "transferred to a French military facility on the island of Hao for a period of not less than three years. They will be prohibited from leaving the island for any reason, except with the mutual consent of the two governments." Major Mafart and Captain Prieur were transferred to French custody on the island of Hao on July 23, 1986. In addition, France reached a settlement with the family of Fernando Pereira that included a formal apology and payment of compensation totaling 2.3 million francs. France admitted that it was legally liable to Greenpeace, but these parties were unable to agree on appropriate compensation. After Greenpeace threatened to sue France in a New Zealand court, the parties agreed to submit the matter to binding international arbitration. After full briefing and argument, an ad hoc international arbitral tribunal consisting of a former New Zealand judge and two distinguished law professors awarded Greenpeace $5 million for the loss of the *Rainbow Warrior* and an additional $1.2 million "for aggravated damages," plus expenses, interest, and legal fees. Greenpeace representatives hailed the decision and stated that the precedent "will hold state security and intelligence agencies to account in the future."

On its face, the processes and outcome of the *Rainbow Warrior* affair seem to demonstrate international law's relevance, flexibility, and efficacy in the resolution of international disputes. Two states used independent third-party dispute resolution that upheld the norm against the use of force, one of the core principles of international law. In addition, a powerful state paid compensation to the family of a foreign national whose human rights had been violated and accepted legal responsibility for the damage its actions caused an international NGO.

But the *Rainbow Warrior* affair can also be understood as a much more nuanced and ambiguous tale about the relevance and effectiveness of international law. In fact, France and New Zealand had previously agreed to most of the Secretary-General's rulings during secret negotiations in Switzerland. However, given the high political visibility of this dispute, neither state was willing to take the domestic political risks associated with a compromise reached through bilateral negotiations. Both governments believed that a compromise agreement would be politically insulated if it had the imprimatur of an independent and neutral third party. The Secretary-General's prestige and authority made it easier for each government to persuade domestic constituencies to accept those elements of the compromise that were contrary to their interests.

Moreover, neither of the French agents spent three years on Hao Island. On December 11, 1987, the French government was advised that Mafart's medical condition required "an emergency return to a hospital in mainland France." The following day, France sought New Zealand's permission to evacuate Mafart and, at the same time, stressed that the only available means of transport was by military aircraft leaving Hao the next morning. New Zealand sought to have one of its doctors examine Mafart; France refused but offered to have a doctor designated by New Zealand examine Mafart as soon as he arrived in France. On December 14, without New Zealand's consent, Mafart was flown to Paris and given medical treatment. The same day, New Zealand delivered a note to France stating that it "regards this action as a serious breach of both the letter and the spirit of the obligations undertaken pursuant to the [Secretary-General's ruling]." The New Zealand doctor who examined Mafart in Paris later that day reported that, although he needed medical treatment unavailable on Hao, "it is . . . highly arguable whether an emergency evacuation as opposed to a planned urgent evacuation was necessary." Mafart never returned to Hao. France insisted that, for medical reasons, he was to remain in France.

On May 3, 1988, France advised New Zealand that Prieur was pregnant and in need of special medical attention unavailable on Hao. This time, France agreed that a New Zealand doctor could travel to Hao to examine Prieur. But on the following day, before the New Zealand doctor could arrive in Hao, France advised New Zealand that Prieur's father was dying of cancer in Paris and that she was needed at his bedside. On May 5, three days before French presidential elections, France informed New Zealand that "[t]he French Government considers it impossible, for obvious humanitarian reasons, to keep Mrs. Prieur on Hao while her father is dying in Paris. [She] will therefore immediately depart for Paris." Prieur arrived in Paris on May 6 without New Zealand's consent. Four days later, New Zealand sent a note to the French Foreign Ministry to "protest these actions in the strongest possible terms." Calling the actions "a further serious violation of the legal obligations under the Agreement," it offered to allow medical treatment for both agents in Tahiti (the capital of French Polynesia) or to send the dispute to arbitration under the terms of the Secretary-General's decision.

Prieur's father died on May 16. France argued that Prieur could not be sent back to Hao as long as her pregnancy continued; after her child was born, France asserted that she could not be sent back to Hao with a baby. After negotiations over the return of the agents proved inconclusive, New Zealand requested the establishment of an arbitral tribunal as provided in paragraph 5 of the Secretary-General's ruling. The panel, chaired by a former president and judge of the ICJ, ruled in favor of New Zealand. In the case of Major Mafart, the tribunal unanimously declared that France had breached its obligations to New Zealand by failing to order his return to Hao, although a majority held that his initial removal was not wrongful. In the case of Captain Prieur, the tribunal unanimously held that France committed a breach by not endeavoring in good faith to obtain New Zealand's consent to her removal from Hao, by subsequently removing her from Hao, and by failing to return her to Hao. A majority held, however, that as the three-year period that Mafart and Prieur were to serve on Hao had now passed, France's obligations were at an end, and accordingly the tribunal declined to order the agents' return. The tribunal unanimously declared "that the condemnation of the French Republic for its breaches of its treaty obligations to New Zealand, made public by the decision of the Tribunal, constitutes in the circumstances appropriate satisfaction for the legal and moral damage caused to New Zealand." Finally, although New Zealand had expressly rejected the award of monetary damages, the tribunal "recommended" that the two governments create a fund to promote close and friendly relations between the citizens of the two states and that the French government make an initial contribution of $2 million to the fund. Almost immediately thereafter, France contributed $2 million to a fund to promote friendly bilateral relations.

The *Rainbow Warrior* affair can also be understood to be part of a larger struggle by many states and NGOs against French nuclear testing in the South Pacific. While France's first nuclear tests were in the French Sahara in 1960, France shifted its testing site to the Mururoa Atoll after Algeria achieved independence. This decision and subsequent nuclear tests prompted a series of legal and political disputes between France and the region's states. Concern over French nuclear testing was also a major factor in the adoption of the South Pacific Nuclear Free Zone (SPNFZ) Treaty in 1985. The treaty establishes a nuclear free zone; states party to the treaty undertake not to possess or permit in their territory the testing of nuclear devices. This treaty was open only to members of the South Pacific Forum (SPF), a regional organization consisting of 15 South Pacific states. Thus, France was not a party to the treaty, and French testing continued until 1992, when France and other nuclear powers announced a moratorium on nuclear testing.

In June 1995, France announced that it would break this moratorium and conduct a final series of eight nuclear tests in the South Pacific. After France resumed testing in October 1995, the SPF suspended official links with France, and the European Parliament condemned the testing; the UN General Assembly urged the immediate cessation of the tests, and Greenpeace and other NGOs strongly protested the tests. France announced that it would conduct only six tests and that it would then shut down its testing site in the South Pacific. Finally, on March 25, 1996, France signed three SPNFZ Treaty protocols that were open to nuclear powers, including a protocol that prohibits nuclear testing in the South Pacific. New Zealand proclaimed that "France's signature [brought] an end to French nuclear testing in the South Pacific for all time." The SPF Chairman stated that these signings "mark the end of a tense and uncertain period when the region was a testing ground, and in certain respects a battleground, for nuclear testing by the nuclear powers."

Notes and Questions

1. Why did France agree to submit its disputes with New Zealand and Greenpeace to binding, third-party dispute resolution? What was the basis of the Secretary-General's ruling? Was the ruling something other than a form of political theater? What was the basis of the rulings by the various arbitral tribunals? Why did France agree to compensate Pereira's family and Greenpeace?

2. Who won here? Does the *Rainbow Warrior* affair represent a victory for the rule of law in international relations? Can you identify specific points in this incident where international law made a difference?

A. New Actors, New Issues, New Processes

The *Rainbow Warrior* affair illustrates some of the ways that the traditional understanding of international law reflected in the Chad-Libya dispute—as a body of rules binding upon states in their relations—has been supplemented by a new international legal process characterized by new actors, issues, and modalities of prescription and enforcement. Notably, this new international law has not replaced traditional international law; indeed, the "contemporary" *Rainbow Warrior* affair preceded the ICJ decision in the "traditional" dispute between Chad and Libya by nearly a decade. Rather, as we shall see throughout this book, international law is a complex and constantly evolving field; in some areas, traditional norms continue to operate relatively untouched by new norms and processes; in other areas there are deep tensions between the old and the new norms; and in yet other areas new legal principles have emerged and occupy the field. A few of the most notable features of contemporary international law are outlined below.

1. International Institutions

The institutionalization of international law that began in significant part with the League of Nations accelerated in the postwar era. The three bodies that considered disputes arising out of the *Rainbow Warrior* affair — the United Nations, the GATT, and the OECD — represent three of the most important types of international bodies that states create. The United Nations, formed when 51 states signed the UN Charter in 1945, is the paradigmatic example of a multilateral body formed to address a diverse set of issues. Like other international organizations, the United Nations acts through a number of organs. The UN Security Council has primary responsibility for maintaining international peace and security and was intended to oversee a charter-based collective security system. But Cold War rivalries quickly undermined this system, and the United Nations enjoyed only mixed success in efforts to maintain international peace and security. While the Security Council acted more assertively in the aftermath of the Cold War, it soon found itself confronting new types of challenges, including global pandemics, such as AIDS; environmental problems, such as climate change; and non-conventional security threats, such as terrorist networks.

While the UN is often judged on its ability to maintain international peace and security, the organization was also charged with promoting the peaceful settlement of international disputes. The UN Secretariat, headed by the Secretary-General, has helped to resolve a variety of international disputes, including *Rainbow Warrior,* through neutral fact finding, mediation, and other settlement-inducing activities. The ICJ, the UN's principal judicial organ, provides another possible forum for dispute resolution, as was seen in the Chad-Libya dispute. Ironically, the Court was not available in the *Rainbow Warrior* affair because France withdrew its consent to the Court's jurisdiction in response to a 1974 suit by New Zealand and Australia challenging French nuclear testing in the South Pacific. The General Assembly, composed of representatives of all member states, is the UN's main deliberative organ. Its resolutions, while not binding on states, have had a formative influence in the development of international law in many areas.

As governments and other international actors have come to regard more and more issues as requiring some form of international cooperation, they have created specialized organizations. Thus, the trade disputes arising out of the *Rainbow Warrior* affair were submitted to the GATT, which eventually evolved into the World Trade Organization (WTO), whose rules now govern over $23 trillion per year in international trade. It, along with the International Monetary Fund and the International Bank for Reconstruction and Development (World Bank), were the primary international bodies created in the postwar era to address international economic issues. Other international organizations address aviation (International Civil Aviation Organization), intellectual property (World Intellectual Property Organization), and health (World Health Organization). The decisions to create these bodies followed from technological developments that made interstate borders more permeable and the actions of one state more likely to influence others, a process labeled today as "globalization" but that has been occurring, in various forms, for centuries.

States have also created numerous regional organizations, such as the Organization of American States, to coordinate policies, including through legal instruments, at a subglobal level. Of these regional bodies, the European Economic Community — now *subglobal org. to coordinate polices*

the European Union (EU)—has emerged as the most powerful and fully developed. European Union members delegate authority for certain matters to independent EU institutions that represent the interests of the Union, its member countries, and its citizens. These institutions have generated a dense system of EU law that is separate from, and superior to, the domestic law of EU members. Other regional organizations that have assumed particular importance to interstate interactions include the Organization of American States, the North Atlantic Treaty Organization, the Organization of African Unity, the Organization for Security and Cooperation in Europe, and the Association of Southeast Asian Nations.

2. Non-State Actors

Actors other than states and organizations of states have come to play a critical role in the creation and enforcement of international law. Non-state actors have been integrally involved in international relations for many hundreds of years—whether as organized religions such as the Catholic Church or the large trading companies of the colonial area—and non-governmental organizations have had an influence in international law making at least since the time of the antislavery movement in the nineteenth century. Yet the twentieth century saw these entities play a much more prominent role in international legal arenas.

NGOs—private, voluntary citizens' groups—today help frame agendas, mobilize constituencies, attend intergovernmental conferences to lobby governments, and even provide key staff delegations to such conferences. In one particularly dramatic example of NGO influence on lawmaking processes, a coalition of 1,200 NGOs from more than 60 states initiated, and then convinced governments to negotiate, the 1997 Convention on the Prohibition of the Use, Stockpiling, Production, and Transfer of Anti-Personnel Mines and on their Destruction (the Landmines Convention). In addition to their enhanced roles in law making, NGOs also play a critical role in enforcing and promoting compliance with international legal norms. NGOs frequently investigate and publicize state violations of international law in order to shame states and build domestic constituencies for compliance. Although the ICJ and the WTO's Dispute Settlement Body only entertain state-to-state disputes, in many recently created dispute resolution fora, particularly in the human rights area, NGOs can institute cases or intervene as parties. For example, under amendments to the treaty creating the European Court of Human Rights, victims and NGOs can bring proceedings directly before the court. Similarly, NGOs can initiate proceedings before the World Bank Inspection Panel, which reviews complaints that the World Bank failed to comply with its own operational policies and procedures in the design, appraisal, or implementation of projects financed by the Bank.

The role of the individual in international law has also undergone significant development. As noted above, during the postwar era states have recognized an increasing number of international legal rights and obligations that individuals possess. Indeed, individual rights (of Pereira, the *Rainbow Warrior*'s Dutch crew member) and duties (of Mafart and Prieur) were both arguably in play in the *Rainbow Warrior* affair. Individuals also play enhanced roles in the implementation and enforcement of international law, in part through their increased access to international dispute resolution bodies—including, particularly, human rights bodies.

Finally, beyond NGOs and individuals, a number of other non-state actors, including indigenous peoples, ethnic minorities, subnational units in federal states, and business enterprises, now contribute to the creation and implementation of international law. At the same time, violent non-state actors, frequently labeled terrorists, have forced upon others their own notions of international order. The enhanced activities of all these groups, along with the development of individual rights and duties discussed above, has transformed the traditional "law of nations"—with states as the exclusive law makers and participants—into a dynamic discipline that touches on virtually all human relationships and transactions.

3. Non-Traditional Law Making and Enforcement

The rise of new actors has led to diverse and imaginative ways of both making and enforcing international law. The treaty remains the clearest expression of the expectations of states. But international organizations have served as the arenas for new forms of law making, including a form of administrative law making by executive bodies on which only some of the organization's members sit. When governments have been unwilling to agree on treaties, they have nonetheless prepared important instruments that are meant to, and in fact do, influence governmental behavior. These instruments, sometimes referred to as "soft law," cover areas ranging from foreign investment to telecommunications to human rights.

States, international organizations, NGOs, and others have also agreed on new methods for securing compliance with the law. Thematically, these ideas date back to the creation of the United Nations itself, as its members gave the Security Council the authority to order all states to carry out its directives on peace and security matters. Over the years, the Council has, in fact, ordered economic sanctions against a variety of states and non-state entities for committing acts that constitute threats to or breaches of international peace and security. In the trade arena, states gave the WTO the authority both to adjudicate disputes between member states and to allow a party that prevails in the dispute settlement process to raise tariffs as a means of sanctioning the loser. Even criminal law, with the prospect of sanctions against individuals, has been enforced at the international level. The United Nations created special criminal courts for the former Yugoslavia and Rwanda; an International Criminal Court, located at The Hague, hears cases involving genocide, crimes against humanity, and war crimes; and states have asserted unusual forms of jurisdiction to try foreign criminals for acts committed abroad. International organizations have also used new methods for monitoring state performance and inducing compliance with international legal norms, including reporting mechanisms that may embarrass a state into complying, and capacity building, technical assistance, and, less frequently, diplomatic, economic, and military sanctions.

Much of the impetus for these developments arose out of the end of the Cold War. During the years of intense Soviet-American ideological and military confrontation, opportunities for global cooperation on all areas of international concern were limited. Both superpowers and their allies used international fora as much to score points against the other side as to advance international cooperation. Each side viewed proposals for legal cooperation, however legitimate, with suspicion. During these years, international organizations were often polarized along East-West lines, included members of only one bloc (for instance, NATO had only U.S. allies), or excluded members of another (for example, the Association of Southeast Asian Nations and the Organization of American States excluded Communist states). As a result, their ability to address major areas of international concern was limited to areas where ideology played a relatively small role, such as health or telecommunications, or where East-West interests happened to coincide (such as with the creation of certain UN peacekeeping operations to stabilize regional conflicts).

The end of the Cold War drastically changed the situation, as an enormous obstacle to the development and implementation of international law disappeared. The opening up of the Soviet bloc also allowed the populations of those states to exert a greater influence on foreign policy, and NGOs began to become influential as well. These developments were no panacea for the rule of law, however. The termination of superpower support that had kept many world leaders in power led some to respond by playing parts of their populations against each other, with catastrophic consequences for human rights in Rwanda, Congo, the former Yugoslavia, and elsewhere. In addition, the weakness or complicity of some central governments resulted in havens for terrorist networks.

The early years of the twenty-first century have been a period of unsettling political and economic change. Emerging powers—such as China, Brazil, and India—have brought new visions of global order into political and legal debates. The increased power and resources of these and other new actors have, at times, spurred reform in international bodies and processes. At other times, the increasing multipolarity of international relations has slowed the pace of or stymied formalized international cooperation. For example, multilateral efforts to address global climate change have met with very limited success; the current round of global trade talks, launched in 2001, has long been stalemated and seems unlikely to make substantial progress anytime soon; and the international response to the 2008 global financial crisis was not centered in formal institutions, but rather in the relatively informal and ad hoc Group of 20. These and related developments have caused some international actors to seek the creation of alternative institutions, and others to ask whether new forms of global cooperation and law making are needed to address contemporary problems.

B. Conceptual Challenges

In the aggregate, the dramatic changes outlined above raise a number of practical, doctrinal, and conceptual challenges to those who seek to understand, practice, or improve international law. These challenges arise in part from the uneasy juxtaposition of the traditional understanding of international law and more recent processes; in part from increased global interdependence and the heightened need for international cooperation to solve transnational problems; and in part from changing conceptions of the power of the state. Below, we briefly introduce three conceptual challenges that speak to the place and meaning of international law today and that are relevant to all of the subsequent chapters of this book.

1. Legalization and Its Limits

Traditionally, scholars understood international law to address a narrow range of issues; today international law addresses almost every type of human activity. The *Rainbow Warrior* affair implicates just a few of the numerous fields that have either been created or expanded since 1945, including international environmental law, international trade law, international law on decolonization, and the international law of terrorism. Other recently developed areas, including human rights law, international criminal law, and international humanitarian law, receive extended treatment elsewhere in this text. The sheer increase in the kinds of issues and numbers of international agreements and bodies, standing alone, capture only part of the story. As we shall see throughout this text, many recent agreements and rules tend to be significantly more detailed and reach much more deeply into what was previously considered to be the domestic jurisdiction of states. Thus, both the *breadth* and *depth* of international law have increased, as the law regulates more areas than ever before and does so through processes and mechanisms that challenge a state's interest in keeping others out of its affairs—in a word, its sovereignty.

The result of these developments is, in essence, the increased legalization of international relations. Nevertheless, the move to law on the international plane is hardly uniform. While legalization has increased in some areas, such as international trade, in others, such as international monetary issues, legalization seems to ebb and flow. One goal of this book is to understand better this variation in the uses and effects of international law in different issue areas. In addition, through the problems examined in subsequent chapters, we explore the implicit claim that legalization encourages greater cooperation, the more effective and efficient resolution of international disputes, and a more equitable resolution of claims between parties of unequal bargaining power.

2. The Fragmentation of International Law and Regime Interaction

International law is created in highly decentralized processes, and at present, most international norms are made in specialized international legal regimes, such as trade, human rights, or environment. Each of these regimes has its own treaties, other norms, and institutions, all designed to advance certain values and outcomes. However, the goals advanced by any one regime are not always consistent with those of other specialized regimes. In recent years, this structural feature of international law, which some scholars have labelled "fragmentation," has given rise to significant difficulties in law creation, application, interpretation, and enforcement.

What should happen, for example, when norms from two or more international legal regimes are potentially applicable to a situation? Consider the transfer of hazardous waste from a firm in one state to a firm in another. This transaction implicates international environmental law, international trade law, the law of maritime transit, the law of the sea, and potentially other areas of international law. The simultaneous application of multiple bodies of law raises the possibility of regime collision and conflict. How should states and private parties act when norms from different international regimes are not consistent?

Relatedly, what should happen when the same or a related fact pattern comes before multiple courts or institutions? Chapter 3 discusses the 2008 armed conflict between Russia and Georgia; this conflict gave rise to disputes before both the ICJ and the European Court of Human Rights. Chapter 13 explores the ICJ opinion addressing armed conflict in the Democratic Republic of the Congo; communications arising out of the same conflict were filed before the African Commission on Human and People's Rights. How, if at all, should international tribunals treat decisions rendered by international bodies housed in other legal regimes?

Finally, what should happen when a court or other body embedded in one legal regime is asked to interpret or apply a norm originating in a different regime? Do human rights bodies, for example, have the legal or technical competence to apply international humanitarian law? Should a WTO dispute panel invoke non-WTO law, such as international environmental or labor law, when considering disputes?

At a deeper level, the proliferation of subject areas, rules, and institutions; the lack of coordination or a formal structure of relations among them; and real and potential conflicts all raise the question of whether international law as it now exists is sufficiently coherent to constitute a "system." Does international law define comprehensively the rights and duties of states, or are there important areas of international life beyond or outside international law's domain? Are the various doctrines of international law oriented toward a common set of goals or objectives? Are there general themes that unite various bilateral, regional, and global rules? Or is an international legal "system" either unrealistic or undesirable given nonhierarchical and decentralized processes of law making, interpretation, and application?

3. The Persistent Puzzle of Compliance

Episodes as diverse as the *Rainbow Warrior* affair and Russia's annexation of Crimea highlight another series of questions central to discussions of international law: when do states comply with their international legal obligations, and what strategies promote compliance? We consider compliance issues in some detail in Chapter 14, after the reader has had a chance to gauge how and whether international law actually works. For now, we simply identify several of the compliance theories that international relations scholars and international lawyers have developed.

For many years, the field of international relations was dominated by the so-called realists. Realists focus on the distribution of power and resources in the international arena as well as on its anarchic nature. They argue that nations comply with international law only when it is in their interests to do so; when interests conflict with norms, interests will prevail. Compliance thus depends on the most powerful states deciding to comply and ensuring that weaker states comply. Iraq violated international law when it invaded Kuwait; it only "complied" with international law and withdrew from Kuwait in response to enforcement actions by a coalition of stronger states.

So-called institutionalists agree that nations obey international law when it is in their interests to do so; however, they stress that states have both conflicting and mutual interests. Hence international regimes, comprised of institutions and norms on a particular subject (although not always what lawyers would consider law) serve as mechanisms for restraining states and for achieving common aims. Regimes and their norms promote compliance by reducing transaction costs, providing information and dispute resolution procedures, and providing a trigger and a focus for negative responses to noncompliance.

Finally, a so-called constructivist school argues that in an anarchic international order, states have no preexisting interests or identity; rather, their interests and identities are created—and changed—by and through their interactions with states and other actors. Under this view, participation in international institutions helps states achieve shared understandings. These understandings, in turn, alter a state's perception of its own interests.

International lawyers have developed their own explanations for compliance. A "Kantian" strand of thought asserts that compliance is a function of international law's legitimacy vis-à-vis its targets. Some scholars see such legitimacy as deriving from those targets' sense that an international rule or institution has been created by and operates under fair procedures. Others suggest that the key to compliance is found at the domestic level. They argue that so-called liberal states, with representative governments, independent judiciaries, and guarantees of political and civil rights, rely more heavily on legal rules in their international relations, and on international adjudication in resolving international disputes—at least in their relations with other liberal states. This would explain why, for example, compliance with the European human rights system (largely by liberal democracies) is stronger than it is with the developing African human rights system, which addresses a collection of democratic and authoritarian states.

Yet another set of legal scholars have identified a "managerial" model, where states induce compliance not through coercion but rather through cooperative, interactive processes of justification, discourse, and persuasion. Through these processes, legal norms are invoked, interpreted, and elaborated in ways that generate pressure for compliance. Managerialists share much in common with institutionalists, but, like scholars focusing on international legitimacy, they place a heavier reliance on the norms themselves rather than on institutions. A related "transnational legal process" school has added a domestic law element to the horizontal, interstate focus of the managerialists. They believe that state compliance occurs when international legal norms "come home"—that is, when they are debated, interpreted, and ultimately internalized by domestic legal actors.

Of course, compliance questions are hardly new to international law. One of the most compelling explanations was formulated more than a half century ago by French scholar Georges Scelle. Scelle observed that governmental officials play a dual function (*dédoublement fonctionnel*) in that they both make claims on behalf of their state and respond to the claims of other states against their state. Because any outrageous or illegal claims or acts governmental officials make or take will erode a legal norm and create precedents that another state might in the future use against their state, governments will restrain their behavior to conform to international law. Thus, for example, state *A* will respect the limits of the territorial sea of state *B* even if state *B* were too weak militarily to prevent state *A* from violating that norm, so that state *C* will likewise respect these limits vis-à-vis state *A*. This dynamic differs somewhat from reciprocity, another method of self-enforcement long understood by international lawyers, in that Scelle was concerned broadly with the precedential effect of illegal acts and not merely with whether the particular recipient of an illegal claim might be able to take action against the claimant.

As you study the materials that follow, consider how states might increase compliance, whether there is an optimal rate of compliance, and which—if any—of the above explanations ring true, or if different theories are relevant in different issue areas. Consider also whether compliance is even the correct issue on which to focus. High compliance rates may not prove that an international rule is effective, in the sense that it causes or even affects state behavior. For example, high compliance rates may reflect that international agreements simply codify the lowest common denominator among the parties. Thus, it is necessary to identify not only the reasons for compliance and the processes that induce compliance, but the types of rules, institutions, and processes that enable international law to produce effective change.

C. *Ways of Understanding International Law*

The exceedingly brief historical overview presented above outlines a process of great change over the centuries both in terms of the areas ripe for regulation by international law and in the process by which international law is made and implemented—the participants, the arenas, the outcomes. At the same time, the study of international law—the intellectual task of conceptualizing, describing, and evaluating international law—has also changed fundamentally. The excerpts above describe what was perhaps the most fundamental shift, from the natural-law approach that dominated the early years of European international law to the positive-law approach that gained ascendancy in the nineteenth century. Positivism—put simply, the theory that international law is no more nor less than the rules to which states have consented—remains the lingua franca of most international lawyers, especially in continental Europe.

But legal scholars have developed alternative methodologies for understanding or "doing" international law. In the 1940s and 1950s, Myres McDougal and Harold Lasswell of Yale Law School created a school of policy-oriented jurisprudence based on tenets of American legal realism. They saw international law not as a set of rules but as a process of authoritative decision making by which various actors (not just states) clarify and implement their common interests in accordance with their expectations of appropriate processes and of effectiveness in controlling behavior. They placed particular emphasis on the distinction between rules and operations, or between law as written down and law as actually observed. This so-called New Haven School remains influential in both the

United States and abroad. In the 1960s, Abram Chayes, Thomas Ehrlich, and Andreas Lowenfeld helped develop an approach, since known as international legal process, which focuses on law as a constraint on international decision makers and events in international affairs. They developed a variety of case studies to show how government officials did or did not take international law into account in various crises.

The 1960s and 1970s also saw the increased influence of scholars with a decidedly post-colonial perspective on international law. Hailing primarily from former colonial countries, these scholars questioned the legitimacy of much of international law as emanating from the profound injustices of the colonial system and sought to develop ways for the law to rectify North-South inequities. Some, like Georges Abi-Saab and C.A. Amerasinghe, were particularly concerned with issues of sovereignty over natural resources and exploitation of the South by Northern investors, but this new generation addressed numerous other issues too. These scholars, and their current protégés, would find allies in the 1970s and 1980s in American and European scholars seeking to apply the methodology of critical legal studies to international law. This self-described "New Stream" has focused on the contradictions, hypocrisies, and failings not only of the rules themselves but of the ways actors invoke and talk about international law. Like the deconstructionist movement of literary theory and philosophy to which they owe great homage, the New Stream advocates place great emphasis on the use and misuse of language and culture in international legal discourse. In the 1980s, a related critical methodology emerged from scholars seeking to apply tools of feminist jurisprudence to international law. Many scholars are now examining how international norms reflect the domination of men in the international system. Although they are particularly concerned about issues of women's rights, they seek to uncover deep structural challenges to international law as insufficiently attentive to the interests and roles of women.

The 1990s and early 2000s saw many scholars apply distinctively interdisciplinary methodologies to international law. Scholars initiated a movement to incorporate into international law the insights of international relations theory. This scholarship has encouraged inquiry into questions such as compliance with norms, the stability and effectiveness of international institutions, and causal mechanisms explaining how particular rules and institutions influence international actors. In a similar vein, other scholars began to explore whether economic analysis could usefully be applied to international law problems, while still others applied game theoretic insights and public choice theory to international legal issues.

Within the past decade, various scholars have developed new conceptual frameworks for understanding and critiquing international law. A group of "global administrative law" scholars argue that much modern global governance takes the form of regulation and administration created not in high-profile diplomatic conferences or treaty negotiations but in less visible settings that constitute a "global administrative space." Scholars urge that these processes be reformed along lines that advance transparency, consultation, participation, and reasoned decision making. Other scholars argue for the application of constitutional principles to improve the effectiveness and fairness of the international legal order. Arguments among "international constitutionalists" over the conceptual coherence and normative desirability of constitutional orders outside the state were echoed in contentious public debates over the European Union's proposed constitutional treaty. Finally, "global legal pluralism" constitutes a third emerging conceptual approach to international law. Drawing on earlier anthropological traditions that examined the interactions between official and non-state law in colonial settings, global legal pluralists highlight the multiplicity of legal norms that can apply to an event or person, and suggest a highly decentralized approach to the management of legal diversity. Each of these approaches seeks to describe and analyze international law's current challenges, including particularly those associated with regime interaction.

The proliferation of methodologies and normative approaches means, of course, that each could form the basis for its own casebook. Positivism dominates most casebooks, but the founders of the policy-oriented jurisprudence and international legal process schools developed their own, admittedly idiosyncratic, teaching materials as well. This book adopts a more eclectic approach, not seeing these methods as inconsistent but rather as providing different lenses through which to examine the problems—and the opportunities—that those who practice international law confront.

2

Making Law
in a Decentralized System

The status of international law as "law" is often contested. In part, skepticism concerning international law stems from the way in which it is made, interpreted, and enforced. The international system lacks a central legislature to enact legislation; there is no executive to apply or enforce the law that is made; and there is no centralized judiciary to interpret the law and adjudicate disputes. Nonetheless, international lawyers, diplomats, government policy makers, representatives of international organizations, non-governmental actors, and others routinely invoke international law to justify, insist upon, or limit particular courses of action; individuals frequently rely on international law to assert claims in national and international fora; and international and domestic tribunals regularly apply international law to decide disputes. In short, as international lawyers frequently point out, international law is made, applied, interpreted, and (sometimes) enforced through a variety of processes that will be explored throughout this volume.

This chapter introduces the primary ways in which international law is made. Article 38 of the Statute of the International Court of Justice, which forms part of the United Nations Charter, provides the traditional starting point. It describes the law that the International Court of Justice (ICJ), the UN's principal judicial organ, should apply to resolve disputes:

Statute of the International Court of Justice, Article 38

1. The Court, whose function is to decide in accordance with international law such disputes as are submitted to it, shall apply:

a. international conventions, whether general or particular, establishing rules expressly recognized by the contesting states;

b. international custom, as evidence of a general practice accepted as law;

c. the general principles of law recognized by civilized nations;

d. . . . judicial decisions and the teachings of the most highly qualified publicists of the various nations, as subsidiary means for the determination of rules of law.

Article 38, though helpful, is only a starting point in two important respects. First, it suggests that courts and other decision makers simply find existing international law in one of several predefined "sources" and then apply it as appropriate to a given dispute. This reflects an unduly static and impoverished description of international law, which can also be understood in many other ways. Some scholars, for example, see international law as a process of decision making, a form of communication, or a mask for political power, among other things. These and various other approaches to international law are considered more fully in other chapters of this book.

Second, although treaties and custom, which are listed first in Article 38, remain the principal means by which international law is made, they are increasingly supplemented by alternative forms of law, which stem from the lawmaking and standard-setting activities of international organizations, regional bodies, multinational enterprises, and non-governmental organizations. The role of these actors in law making will become increasingly apparent as you study subsequent chapters. In particular, the lawmaking function of international organizations is considered in Chapters 3, 11, and 12.

The order of the sources of law listed in Article 38 does not reflect a formal hierarchy, but it is nonetheless suggestive. Article 38 is a directive to the judges on the ICJ. For a court faced with a legal dispute, treaties may be a preferred form of law for several reasons. First, despite issues of interpretation, their content is relatively easy to determine. Second, treaties in most cases reflect the formal consent of the states that ratified them to be bound by their terms. Third, treaties may be a more familiar source of law to national policy makers and their constituents than other sources of international law, and decisions based on a treaty may therefore find greater acceptance by those to whom the decisions are addressed.

Nonetheless, treaties may also have disadvantages in relation to other forms of law. In some situations, for example a state's assertion of jurisdiction over acts or persons abroad, custom may prove to have broader applicability than a treaty. Customary international law evolves from state practice. It does not require the formal negotiation and express consent associated with treaties. A rule of customary international law binds all states that have not objected to the rule while it is in the process of formation. Despite the proliferation of treaties in recent years, custom continues to govern many issues that are not regulated by treaty; on other issues, custom and treaties may to a large extent coincide.

In some situations, the informality of so-called soft law may prove preferable to utilization of a treaty or custom. "Soft law" may be loosely defined as declared norms of conduct understood as legally nonbinding by those accepting the norms. Soft law instruments assume innumerable forms, ranging from declarations of international organizations, to industry codes of conduct, to experts' reports. Soft law instruments, though not enforceable by legal sanction, are often framed in legal language and in many respects may possess an authority comparable to that of treaties or custom. Soft law is not mentioned in Article 38 of the ICJ's Statute, which derives from a similar provision in the 1929 Statute of the Permanent Court of International Justice. But soft law instruments have proliferated in recent years and must be considered a vital part of the international lawmaking process.

In other instances, issues may arise that cannot be resolved by application of either treaty or custom. There are gaps in the coverage of these forms of international law, which courts and other decision makers sometimes attempt to fill by reliance on general principles common to most national legal systems. Thus, decision makers sometimes borrow from national legal systems principles such as *res judicata* or estoppel to resolve international disputes.

This chapter examines treaties, custom, soft law, and general principles in turn, although, as the following materials make clear, different sources of international law are often interrelated and simultaneously applicable to a given situation. Judicial decisions and the teachings of publicists, mentioned in Article 38 as "subsidiary means for the determination of rules of law," are not considered separately, but their role should become evident as you examine them in connection with the other forms of law described above.

I. CREATING AND USING TREATIES: THE WHALING REGIME

Japanese whaling ship, 2014
SOURCE: WENN Ltd./Alamy

In recent years, bilateral and multilateral treaties have multiplied at an almost exponential pace. The United Nations Treaty Series, which includes all treaties deposited with the UN Secretary-General, now fills more than 2,700 volumes, with 60 or more new volumes published every year. The series contains over 200,000 treaties and related instruments, covering almost every conceivable subject. Most treaties are bilateral, but many involve dozens of states. Increasingly, treaties are being used to codify existing international law and to develop new law. Treaties also serve as the constitutive instruments of international organizations, such as the United Nations and the International Civil Aviation Organization, which often engage in their own lawmaking activities. The complexity and diversity of contemporary treaties, their multiple forms, and the different approaches to their conclusion and implementation will become increasingly evident as you consider the role of treaties in connection with different problems presented throughout this volume.

Like contracts in municipal legal systems, treaties create rights and obligations for the parties to them. In many cases, treaties specify particular quid pro quo arrangements relating to narrow or specific interests of the parties, such as a treaty allocating fishing rights in a particular area or one defining the terms by which individuals accused of crimes may be extradited from one country to another. In other cases, treaties may take on some of the characteristics of general legislation by establishing broad rules to govern state conduct in areas such as human rights, trade, or the environment. The vicissitudes of modern efforts to regulate whaling illustrate some of the legal issues that may arise in connection with treaties and their interrelation with other legal and political issues. Many of those related issues—including the operation and lawmaking role of international organizations, the relationship between international and national law, and the scope and effectiveness of efforts to regulate the global commons—will be explored in greater detail in later chapters.

The goals for this problem include:

- to understand the processes and accompanying basic rules of treaty formation, interpretation, modification, breach, and termination;
- to understand the ways in which treaties resemble and differ from both contracts and legislation; and
- to understand some of the strengths and weaknesses of treaties as a means to establish norms and regulate conduct.

A. The Problem

For hundreds of years, whales have been hunted commercially for their meat, blubber, and oil. By the nineteenth century, whaling was an important industry in Japan, Scandinavia, Russia, and to some extent the United States. But in the early twentieth century, new technologies, including steam engines, exploding harpoon guns, and factory ships that permitted captured whales to be processed at sea, threatened to reduce stocks below commercially viable levels and drive some species close to extinction. Whaling states responded by adopting multilateral treaties in 1931 and 1937 to limit the killing of certain categories of whales. When these early efforts at regulation proved unsuccessful, the United States convened an international conference on whaling. The resulting International Convention for the Regulation of Whaling (ICRW) established the International Whaling Commission (IWC), made up of one representative from each state party. The Convention included a Schedule providing "regulations with respect to the conservation and utilization of whale resources." The Schedule is an integral part of the Convention, but the Commission may amend the Schedule's provisions, including catch limits, by a three-quarters majority of the members voting on a given issue. The role of the Commission, as described on its Web site,

> is to keep under review and revise as necessary the measures laid down in the Schedule. . . .
> These measures, among other things, provide for the complete protection of certain
> species; designate specified areas as whale sanctuaries; set limits on the numbers and size
> of whales which may be taken; prescribe open and closed seasons and areas for whaling;
> and prohibit the capture of suckling calves and female whales accompanied by calves.

In 1950, the IWC established a Scientific Committee, composed of scientists nominated by member states. The Committee reviews research on whaling and assists the IWC in making "scientific findings" to assist in decisions on amendments to the Schedule.

In its first several decades, the IWC used quotas in an attempt to limit the taking of whales. However, whaling states dominated the IWC, paid relatively little attention to the advice of the Scientific Committee, and set quotas so high that whale stocks were dangerously depleted. That began to change in the early 1970s, as growing environmental awareness generated a global anti-whaling movement. Anti-whaling nations began to ratify the Convention and join the IWC. Even some pro-whaling states, particularly the United States, began to advocate for conservation-minded policies. New scientific studies demonstrating the intelligence of whales and growing awareness that some species could be hunted to extinction bolstered the anti-whaling forces.

By the late 1970s, the anti-whaling states at the IWC were in ascendance. In 1982, by a 25-7 vote, with five abstentions, the IWC imposed a general moratorium on commercial whaling, to take effect in the 1985-1986 whaling season. In 1994, the IWC established the 50-million-square-mile Southern Ocean Sanctuary, by a vote of 23-1, with Japan providing the sole negative vote.

The moratorium was expected to be a temporary measure that would allow whale stocks to recover and permit further research to determine sustainable levels of whale hunting. The moratorium included two compromise clauses. One permitted aboriginal subsistence whaling to protect the interests of aboriginal groups for which whaling is of cultural importance. The other permitted states to issue licenses to their nationals to capture and kill whales for the purpose of scientific research.

Whaling states responded to the moratorium in different ways. Norway, Russia, and Denmark (representing Greenland and the Faroe Islands) each took advantage of a provision in Article V of the treaty that allows a state that objects to an IWC amendment to opt out of it. Iceland withdrew from the treaty in 1992 and re-acceded ten years later with a reservation to the moratorium. Japan objected to the moratorium when it was established, but withdrew the objection under pressure from the United States and other countries. Japan then began a new whaling program under the Convention's exception for scientific research.

Although the moratorium was originally intended as a temporary measure, stark divisions within the IWC have blocked efforts to amend or eliminate it. Pro- and anti-whaling nations accuse each other of vote buying and efforts to pack the Commission with supporters. Greenpeace and other anti-whaling groups, and some governments, accuse Japan in particular of using foreign aid to induce countries to join the IWC and support Japan's positions. Pro-whaling states note that anti-whaling countries also use foreign aid to their advantage and complain that countries admitted to the European Union are encouraged to join the IWC and oppose whaling. Whatever the reason, pro-whaling states (including a number of landlocked countries) have joined the IWC in greater numbers than anti-whaling states in recent years. As a result, the IWC, with 89 members, is almost equally balanced between pro- and anti-whaling members.

The IWC can claim some conservation success. In the 1930s, as many as 40,000 whales a year were hunted and killed. With the 1986 moratorium on commercial whaling, that number has been reduced to a few thousand a year. The whaling that continues remains highly controversial. But with a three-quarters majority required for amendments to the Schedule, the IWC can make little progress on most issues.

One particularly contentious issue has been Japan's continued whaling under the Treaty's scientific research exception. Critics accuse Japan of continuing to conduct commercial whaling under the guise of research. Japan argues that research is necessary to determine the health and extent of existing whale stocks and to set sustainable catch levels.

B. Why Do States Enter into Treaties?

The parties to the ICRW have spent substantial time and energy over many years negotiating the original treaty and subsequent amendments, and arguing over the treaty's purpose, interpretation, and enforcement. Why? For lawyers, the answer might at first seem obvious. Treaties are by definition legally binding. States must enter into treaties, then, to obtain binding commitments from other states; such legally binding commitments may assist the parties in pursuing their interests for the same reasons that legally binding contracts assist private parties in pursuing their interests. But what does it mean to say that treaties are legally binding? And why should states prefer treaties to other forms of commitment, such as informal agreements among governments?

International lawyers recognize, of course, that the international legal system does not have enforcement mechanisms comparable to those of effective national legal systems. There is a significant and increasing number of international courts and arbitral bodies but none have overarching general compulsory jurisdiction. There are various bodies with executive powers, such as the UN Security Council, but no international police force. As a result, states usually cannot count on outside actors to interpret agreements, decide on their validity, or enforce them in case of dispute. Yet international lawyers note, as Professor Louis Henkin famously observed, that "almost all nations observe . . . almost all of their [international] obligations almost all of the time." Louis Henkin, How Nations Behave 47 (1979). Some of the reasons why states often comply with their international legal obligations were identified in Chapter 1 and will be explored in subsequent chapters. But even if states often fulfill their treaty obligations, that still leaves open the question of why they enter into those obligations in the first place.

Political scientists who adhere to realist theories of international relations largely discount treaties—and international law generally. In their view, the international system is anarchic, in the sense that no central authority exists over states with power to compel compliance with international rules. As a result, treaties and international law generally exert little influence over state behavior. Instead, states pursue their interests, with outcomes of state interactions determined by the relative power of the states involved. States will enter into a treaty when convenient, interpret a treaty as they wish, and break a treaty when changing interests render it inconvenient.

Many political scientists, especially those of the so-called institutionalist school, accept some of the premises of the realists but reach quite different conclusions. In general, institutionalists accept the realist claim that the international system is anarchic, but they argue that states nonetheless have powerful incentives for entering into treaties beyond the simple pursuit of interests through power. The institutionalists, drawing on economics and game theory, suggest that states often enter into treaties to achieve mutually beneficial outcomes, forsaking short-term efforts to maximize power in favor of pursuing long-term goals. As Professors Kenneth Abbott and Duncan Snidal put it, "rationalists . . . view international agreements as 'contracts' created to resolve problems of coordination, collaboration, or domestic politics. . . ." Kenneth Abbott & Duncan Snidal, *Hard and Soft Law in International Governance*, 54 Intl. Org. 421, 424 (2000).

From this standpoint, one advantage of treaties is that they may enable states to make their commitments credible. Professor Charles Lipson offers the following account.

Charles Lipson, *Why Are Some International Agreements Informal?*

45 Intl. Org. 495, 508-512 (1991)

The decision to encode a bargain in treaty form is primarily a decision to highlight the importance of the agreement and, even more, to underscore the durability and significance of the underlying promises. . . . In the absence of international institutions that permit effective self-binding or offer external guarantees for promises, treaties use conventional forms to signify a seriousness of commitment. . . .

The effect of treaties, then, is to raise the political costs of noncompliance. . . . The more formal and public the agreement, the higher the reputational costs of noncompliance. . . . States deliberately choose to impose these costs on themselves in order to benefit from the counterpromises (or actions) of others. Given the inherent constraints of international institutions, these formal pledges are as close as states can come to precommitment—to a contractual exchange of promises. . . .

In a world of imperfect information, . . . reputation has value. . . . The threat of such loss [of reputational capital] promotes compliance, although it cannot guarantee it. Whether it succeeds depends on (1) the immediate gains from breaking an agreement, (2) the lost stream of future benefits and the rate of discount applied to that stream, and (3) the expected costs to reputation from specific violations.

. . .

The price of noncompliance takes several forms. First, there is loss of reputation as a reliable partner. . . . Second, the violation or perceived violation of a treaty may give rise to specific, costly retaliation, ranging from simple withdrawal of cooperation in one area to broader forms of noncooperation and specific sanctions. . . . Finally, treaty violations may recast national reputation in a still broader and more dramatic way, depicting a nation that is not only untrustworthy but is also a deceitful enemy, one that makes promises in order to deceive.

Professor Lipson's account identifies some of the ways in which treaties assist states in making credible commitments. As Kenneth Abbott and Duncan Snidal point out, treaties may also enhance the credibility of states by "constraining self-serving auto-interpretation" of commitments, "mobiliz[ing] legally oriented interest and advocacy groups, such as the organized bar," "expand[ing] the role of legal bureaucracies within foreign offices and other government agencies," and modifying domestic actors' "plans and actions in reliance on such commitments, increasing the audience costs of violations." In addition, treaties may "reduce[] the transaction costs of subsequent interactions among states" as they seek to apply and elaborate agreed rules and enforce commitments. Abbott & Snidal, *supra*, at 427-428, 430.

Further, Abbott and Snidal note that treaties may also serve the interests of private actors, who may organize within and across states to pursue shared objectives and values through interstate agreements. Alternatively, treaties may serve the interests of government officials, who may support particular agreements "as a way of making credible commitments to influential private actors in return for electoral support." *Id.* at 453.

International lawyers and political scientists have developed a variety of other theories to explain why states enter into international agreements and why they prefer some types of agreements to others. The latter question is considered later in this chapter. In other chapters we consider alternative theories concerning the motivations of states and other actors for reaching international agreements in different issue areas, and their incentives for compliance with those agreements.

Notes and Questions

1. The original 15 parties to the ICRW were all pro-whaling states, interested in preserving the whaling industry. What alternatives to a treaty might these states have considered to promote their shared interests in commercial whaling? Would public statements by each government concerning their intentions regarding limits on whaling have served just as well as a formal treaty?

2. Do you agree with Professor Lipson that treaties raise the political costs of noncompliance? What other advantages might treaties have over less formal interstate agreements?

C. Treaties as Frameworks for Further Regulation

The ICRW consists of 11 articles, spanning just a few pages. But as noted in the Preamble, the Convention aspires "to establish a system of international regulation for the whale fisheries. . . ." The Convention does this by creating a Commission and empowering it to amend the Schedule with a three-quarters majority vote on everything from fixing "protected and unprotected species" to deciding on open and closed waters, seasons, catch limits, "time, methods, and intensity of whaling," and the equipment that may be used. In this respect, the ICRW resembles a relatively recent phenomenon in international law — the framework convention.

Framework conventions are typically relatively brief and general agreements that the parties anticipate will be fleshed out by subsequent and more detailed agreements or protocols. They are most commonly used in the field of international environmental law, on issues where the parties anticipate that evolving technologies and new scientific information will facilitate future substantive commitments. But framework conventions may be used in any field, and their form and specific characteristics vary widely. Framework conventions often establish bodies like the IWC, which can make decisions and establish regulations potentially binding on all parties by votes that do not require unanimity. This structure facilitates consideration of changing circumstances and permits faster responses to new information and shifting state interests than would be possible if states were forced to negotiate a succession of new treaties.

Regulatory bodies like the IWC, created by treaty but with their own rule-making capacity, have proliferated in recent years in an increasingly wide range of fields, including international environmental issues, immigration, terrorism, money laundering, and international investment. In many respects, these bodies operate on the international level much as administrative agencies function in a national legal system. They conduct studies and policy reviews and issue recommendations and sometimes binding decisions and regulations, often in ways that directly affect national policies and decision making.

International law scholars have begun to refer to the work of bodies like the IWC as a form of global administrative law. They note the increasing interpenetration of national and international forms of regulation, the shift of some lawmaking functions from the national to the international plane, and the problems of legitimacy, transparency, and accountability that may arise when international institutions engage in transnational regulation. We will return to some of these issues in Part V, which examines complex international efforts to manage transboundary and global problems involving the law of the sea, trade, and the environment.

D. Applying Treaty Law to the Whaling Convention

Over time, states and other actors have agreed upon norms to govern treaty formation, interpretation, modification, breach, and termination. Each of these issues is considered below in connection with one or another aspect of the whaling regime.

1. Background on Treaty Law

Most of the international law norms applicable to treaties have been codified in the Vienna Convention on the Law of Treaties, which was adopted by states at an international conference in 1969. As of 2014, 114 states are parties to the Convention. The Vienna Convention reflects two decades of study and deliberation by members of the

International Law Commission, a body of independent experts operating under UN auspices. Many of the Vienna Convention's provisions restate or codify customary international law already in place prior to the treaty's adoption. Other Convention provisions reflect a deliberate effort to modify existing law or to create new law, a process referred to as progressive development.

The Vienna Convention's rules are now so widely accepted that even some provisions that might have constituted "progressive development" when the treaty was drafted have acquired the status of custom. The United States is not a party to the treaty, but the Executive Branch has described the Convention as "the authoritative guide to current treaty law and practice."

The Vienna Convention provides the following definition of a treaty:

Vienna Convention on the Law of Treaties

1155 U.N.T.S. 331 (1969)

Article 2
Use of Terms

1. For purposes of the present Convention: (a) "treaty" means an international agreement concluded between States in written form and governed by international law, whether embodied in a single instrument or in two or more related instruments and whatever its particular designation. . . .

Article 3
International Agreements Not
Within the Scope of the Present Convention

The fact that the present Convention does not apply to international agreements concluded between States and other subjects of international law or between such other subjects of international law, or to international agreements not in written form, shall not affect: (a) the legal force of such agreements. . . .

As suggested in Article 2 of the Convention, treaties take many forms and can be denominated by many different terms, including "agreement," "protocol," "concordat," "pact," "accord," and "charter." Treaties may be written or oral (although the Vienna Convention applies only to written treaties), bilateral or multilateral, for a fixed term or indefinite. The limitations on the scope of the Convention contained in Article 3 reflect the desire of the Convention's drafters to facilitate agreement on the rules applicable to the most common kinds of international agreements. The commentary to the International Law Commission's final draft of the Convention makes clear that the Vienna Convention rules may be relevant to international agreements involving parties other than states (e.g., insurgent groups, international organizations) and to oral agreements.

Multilateral treaties govern a rapidly growing range of issues, so to some extent, the treaty-making process is an analogue to the legislative process in national legal systems. However, the treaty-making process is highly decentralized, and the actors involved vary enormously, depending upon the treaty. A treaty may be initiated by international organizations, individual states, or non-governmental organizations, acting individually or collectively. Sometimes a treaty may be preceded by a declaration or other form of soft law; sometimes treaties emerge from lengthy periods of study by international agencies such as the International Law Commission, with multiple expert reports and proposals and innumerable drafts of particular provisions; sometimes initial drafts of treaties are presented to interested states by an individual government, an international organization, or an NGO. Negotiations by states may take many years, sometimes culminating in an intensive burst of negotiations at an international conference; in other instances, negotiations may take a matter of months or weeks. Typically, only governments are formally parties to the negotiation of multilateral treaties, but NGOs increasingly play a major role in many treaty negotiations, and their representatives are sometimes added to the delegations representing individual states. At some point, the organization or state leading the negotiations will submit a text to the participating states for adoption, by consensus or by a process of voting on particular provisions or the text as a whole. Multilateral treaties often provide for signature subject to ratification or approval. States that sign a treaty accept the text as adopted and indicate their intent to be bound by the treaty, subject to completion of national law requirements for treaty ratification. Under Article 18 of the Vienna Convention, states that have signed but not yet ratified a treaty must not take any action to defeat the treaty's object and purpose. Treaties are usually open for signature until a specified date, though states can often become parties after the date for signature passes by a process of accession. Some treaties, especially human rights treaties, may remain open for signature indefinitely. Multilateral treaties often condition entry into force on signature or ratification by a specified minimum number of states.

Notes and Questions

1. States often enter into formal agreements that by their terms expressly disavow the creation of any legal obligations. The Final Act of the Conference on Security and Cooperation in Europe, signed in Helsinki in 1975, set out the terms of an agreement between the Eastern and Western blocs on a wide range of security and human rights issues. The Final Act was understood and intended to be politically but not legally binding. Agreements of this sort are considered more fully below.

States also frequently enter into informal and usually unwritten "gentlemen's agreements" to govern matters such as the nationality of the individual who heads a particular international agency or the regions to be represented in subsidiary bodies of international organizations. In 1999, for example, U.S. objections to the European Union candidate for executive director of the International Monetary Fund were viewed by some states as a violation of such an agreement. What is the legal status of these "gentlemen's agreements"? Do they qualify as treaties under the Vienna Convention definition? Does the intention of the parties determine whether such agreements are legally binding? If so, how do you ascertain the intention of the parties?

During negotiations on the Vienna Convention, several states urged that the intent to create rights and obligations under international law be included in the Convention's definition of "treaty." The commentary to the final draft explained that "the Commission concluded that . . . the element of intention is embraced in the phrase 'governed by international law,' and it decided not to make any mention of the element of intention in the definition."

2. Can unilateral statements create binding international legal obligations equivalent to a treaty? In 1919, the Norwegian Minister of Foreign Affairs, speaking for his government, declared that Norway would not interfere with Danish plans concerning Greenland, an assurance sought by Denmark. The declaration was made in the course of negotiations over Greenland's status, which included a statement by Denmark that it would not press any claim to Spitzbergen, an archipelago claimed by Norway. In *The*

Legal Status of Eastern Greenland (Nor. v. Den.), P.C.I.J. Rep. Series A/B, No. 53 (1933), the Permanent Court of International Justice (the predecessor to the ICJ), referring to the Norwegian foreign minister's statement, concluded that "a reply of this nature given by the Minister of Foreign Affairs on behalf of his government in response to a request by the diplomatic representative of a foreign Power, in regard to a question falling within his province, is binding upon the country to which the Minister belongs." In subsequent cases, the ICJ made clear that the effect of a unilateral statement depends upon the intention of the state in question. Speaking of a unilateral declaration by the government of France that it would halt nuclear tests in the South Pacific, the ICJ stated:

> When it is the intention of the State making the declaration that it should become bound according to its terms, that intention confers on the declaration the character of a legal undertaking. . . . In these circumstances, nothing in the nature of a *quid pro quo*, nor any subsequent acceptance of the declaration, nor even any reply or reaction from other States, is required for the declaration to take effect. . . .

Nuclear Tests (Austl. v. France), 1974 I.C.J. 253, 267. The Court did not decide whether unilateral engagements should be treated as the equivalent of treaty obligations but noted that all international legal obligations, from whatever source, should be governed by the principle of good faith. The ICJ returned to the issue of unilateral statements in *Armed Activities on the Territory of the Congo* (Dem. Rep. Congo v. Rwanda). In that case, the DRC sought to rely on a statement by the Rwandan Justice Minister, who told the UN Human Rights Commission that "reservations [to human rights treaties] not yet withdrawn will shortly be withdrawn." The DRC argued that the statement constituted a unilateral commitment to withdraw Rwanda's reservation to Article IX of the Genocide Convention. The Court noted that "with increasing frequency in modern international relations other persons [than the President or Foreign Minister] representing a State in specific fields may be authorized by that State to bind it by their statements in respect of matters falling within their purview," but added that "a statement of this kind can create legal obligations only if it is made in clear and specific terms." The Court found that the statement at issue was not sufficiently specific because it did not identify the treaties to which it applied or the time frame for withdrawal.

Under what circumstances, if any, are unilateral statements enforceable under domestic law? Should unilateral declarations by governments be treated as the equivalent of treaty obligations? Should such declarations be deemed legally binding on some other ground, such as estoppel?

2. Making Treaties: Who May Participate in Treaty Regimes?

One of the peculiarities of the debates over whaling is that two of the handful of entities that continue to whale—Greenland and the Faroe Islands—are not directly represented in the IWC. Although both possess substantial autonomy and participate directly in some international bodies, both are territories of Denmark, which represents them in the IWC. Greenland was granted "home rule" in 2008, and now exercises full authority over most domestic matters, from policing and immigration to financial regulation and business activity. Similarly, the Faroe Islands have been a self-governing territory within Denmark since 1948. In both cases, Denmark retains control over national defense, monetary policy, and foreign affairs.

International organizations vary widely in their treatment of territories and groups within states. Some international organizations allow them full membership. Others may afford substate actors more limited roles, such as observer status, or the opportunity to participate in debate on specific issues. The results are sometimes confusing. For example, when Denmark joined the European Economic Community, the Faroe Islands did not join with it and thus were excluded from EU membership when Denmark joined the EU. But the Faroe Islands are considered part of Denmark's territorial scope for purposes of Denmark's membership in the WTO. Thus, in a WTO dispute with the EU, the Faroe Islands represents itself, acting as "the Kingdom of Denmark, in respect of the Faroe Islands."

Under Article III of the ICRW, each Contracting Government is entitled to only one member and one vote in the IWC. As a result, Greenland and the Faroe Islands must both be represented by Denmark. Greenland and the Faroe Islands both permit whale hunting (although the latter focuses on small cetaceans largely outside the purview of the IWC); Denmark does not allow whaling. At IWC meetings, the Danish representative must carefully distinguish among the three entities when speaking on positions that might be supported by one but not by the others. Denmark, in turn, is part of the European Union, which has urged its members to take common positions on foreign policy issues, including in the IWC. Almost all EU members oppose whaling, putting Denmark out of step when it speaks up for greater catch levels for Greenland.

The Vienna Convention speaks only of the capacity of states to enter treaties:

Article 6
Capacity of States to Conclude Treaties

Every State possesses capacity to conclude treaties.

The early drafts of Article 6 provided that some entities other than states also possessed the capacity to enter into treaties, and specifically identified international organizations and member states of federal unions, depending on the provisions of the federal constitution at issue. During the debate on Article 6, the United States argued that

> To limit the scope of the term "other subjects of international law" to international organizations, the Holy See and cases such as an insurgent community would . . . be too restrictive; for colonies and similar entities given some measure of authority in foreign relations, especially when approaching statehood, should not have to be in a state of insurgency to be capable of concluding a valid international agreement. . . . [S]o far as such a colony or entity is entrusted with a measure of authority by the parent State in the conduct of its foreign relations, it necessarily becomes a subject of international law [and] it would be paradoxical if at the present time areas approaching independence could not be encouraged by being entrusted with authority to conclude agreements in their own name.

Article 6 was eventually reduced to its present form in keeping with the decision of the International Law Commission to confine the Vienna Convention to treaties between states. Nonetheless, political subdivisions of states, insurgent communities, and various other non-state actors are sometimes treated as possessing the capacity to enter international agreements for particular purposes.

Notes and Questions

1. Should autonomous territories such as Greenland and the Faroe Islands have the authority to join treaties such as the ICRW directly? What complications might ensue if political units other than states are treated as possessing treaty-making capacity?

2. If Greenland should object to a position taken in the IWC by Denmark, does or should Greenland have any recourse under international law?

3. Invalidating Treaties: Coercion and Consent

In 2009, in the aftermath of the global financial crisis, Iceland entered into accession talks with the European Union. Iceland's economy is closely tied to Europe, with over half of Iceland's exports sold in the EU. As part of the accession talks, Iceland was under strong pressure to abandon whaling, in keeping with EU policy. But in 2014, before the issue could come to a head, Iceland withdrew from the talks, following the election of an anti-accession government.

Treaty negotiations (like contract negotiations) involve sometimes contentious bargaining between parties with different interests. But at what point, if any, does hard bargaining turn into impermissible coercion?

Not unlike the law of contracts in most national legal systems, the Vienna Convention on the Law of Treaties contains a number of provisions pursuant to which a treaty may be held invalid. Many of those provisions, including provisions relating to error, fraud, and the corruption of a representative of a state, relate to the validity of a state's consent to the treaty at issue. One of the most hotly contested issues during the drafting of the VCLT involved coercion. The Convention provides:

Article 52
Coercion of a State by the Threat or Use of Force

A treaty is void if its conclusion has been procured by the threat or use of force in violation of the principles of international law embodied in the Charter of the United Nations.

In the course of the negotiations, many socialist and developing states favored inclusion of an article that would invalidate "unequal treaties." Treaties might be deemed unequal either because one party is in a position to dictate terms to the other party by applying economic or political pressure or because the terms of the treaty greatly favor one party at the expense of the other. As a practical matter, these two forms of inequality go together, because, almost by definition, states that are in an equal bargaining position will not reach one-sided agreements.

Those who supported a provision on the invalidity of unequal treaties relied in part on the principle of the sovereign equality of states, one of the core principles of international law embodied in Article 2(1) of the UN Charter. Of course, the equality of states is juridical only. As a practical matter, states vary enormously in size, resources, population, military capacity, and economic strength. These disparities necessarily place some states in stronger bargaining positions than others in the negotiation of particular treaties. As a general matter, such inequalities do not preclude the conclusion of a valid treaty any more than similar inequalities in the bargaining positions of private parties preclude the formation of valid private contracts.

On the other hand, there are doctrines in the municipal law of many states that invalidate contracts procured through pressure, even when such pressure falls short of coercion, or that invalidate contracts that are unduly onerous to one of the parties. States that challenged the validity of "unequal treaties" focused on colonial-era treaties, especially those granting metropolitan states extensive trade, mineral, or other rights in their former colonies as an implicit condition of independence, and on neocolonial treaties viewed by some as perpetuating colonialism through economic domination.

By contrast, most Western states viewed the notion of unequal treaties as vague, easily manipulated, and likely to jeopardize the stability of treaty relations. The issue came to a head in connection with the drafting of Article 52. States sympathetic to the notion of unequal treaties urged a broad definition of "coercion," one that would encompass political and economic pressure and permit the invalidation of imposed or "unequal" treaties.

Two U.S. government participants in the Vienna Convention negotiations describe the debate and its outcome:

> Afghanistan, Algeria, Bolivia, Congo (Brazzaville), Ecuador, Ghana, Guinea, India, Iran, Kenya, Kuwait, Mali, Pakistan, Sierra Leone, Syria, United Arab Republic, United Republic of Tanzania, Yugoslavia and Zambia proposed that the International Law Commission text . . . be amended by defining force to include any "economic or political pressure."

> The nineteen-state amendment was vociferously supported and vehemently attacked in the committee debate. . . .

> The proponents of the amendment made it quite clear in the committee of the whole that their amendment was directed toward "economic needs." . . . The Algerian representative advanced the thesis:

>> [T]he era of the colonial treaty was past or disappearing, but there was no overlooking the fact that some countries had resorted to new and more insidious methods, suited to the present state of international relations, in an attempt to maintain and perpetuate bonds of subjection. Economic pressure, which was a characteristic of neo-colonialism, was becoming increasingly common in relations between certain countries and the newly independent States.

>> Political independence could not be an end in itself; it was even illusory if it was not backed by genuine economic independence. That was why some countries had chosen the political, economic and social system they regarded as best calculated to overcome under-development as quickly as possible. That choice provoked intense opposition from certain interests which saw their privileges threatened and then sought through economic pressure to abolish or at least restrict the right of peoples to self-determination. Such neo-colonialist practices . . . should therefore be denounced with the utmost rigour.

> Statements of this character reinforced the already deep misgivings as to the effect of the amendment held by the states concerned with the stability of treaties. . . .

> The course of the debate had made it clear that if the amendment were put to the vote it would carry by quite a substantial majority. On the other hand, in private discussions it had been made quite clear to the proponents that adoption could wreck the conference because states concerned with the stability of treaties found the proposal intolerable.

> To reduce tension, discussion of the article was adjourned and private negotiations resorted to. A compromise solution was reached after some days of cooling off. The amendment was withdrawn. In its place, a draft declaration condemning threat or use of pressure in any form by a state to coerce any other state to conclude a treaty was unanimously adopted by the committee. Although at one point during the plenary it appeared that the compromise might be unraveling, it was adhered to by both sides. The declaration finally approved by the conference in 1969 is annexed to the Final Act.

Richard Kearney & Robert Dalton, *The Treaty on Treaties*, 64 Am. J. Intl. L. 495, 533-535 (1970).

Notes and Questions

1. Should economic and military coercion be seen as different in kind or simply as different points along a continuum?

2. In March 1999, NATO forces started bombing targets in the Federal Republic of Yugoslavia (FRY) to force it to end human rights abuses in Kosovo and to accept a political settlement on the future status of Kosovo. (Further background on NATO's action and discussion of related legal issues appear in Chapters 8 and 13.) After an extensive air campaign lasting several months, the FRY signed an agreement accepting NATO's terms for ending the conflict. Could the FRY later declare that agreement void under Article 52?

4. Invalidity and *Jus Cogens*

Treaties may also be rendered void if they violate peremptory (*jus cogens*) norms of international law. *Jus cogens* norms are norms deemed to be so fundamental to the existence of a just international legal order that states cannot derogate from them, even by agreement. By contrast, other norms of general international law may be modified by agreement, at least with respect to the relations of the parties to the agreement.

No state has yet argued that continued whaling violates *jus cogens* norms. But that day may not be far off. A number of scholars have identified various principles of international environmental law calling for avoidance of undue harm to the environment as candidates for future *jus cogens* status.

The relevant articles of the Vienna Convention provide:

Article 53
Treaties Conflicting with a Peremptory Norm of General International Law
(jus cogens)

A treaty is void if, at the time of its conclusion, it conflicts with a peremptory norm of general international law. For the purposes of the present Convention, a peremptory norm of general international law is a norm accepted and recognized by the international community of States as a whole as a norm from which no derogation is permitted and which can be modified only by a subsequent norm of general international law having the same character.

Article 64
Emergence of a New Peremptory Norm of General International Law
(jus cogens)

If a new peremptory norm of general international law emerges, any existing treaty which is in conflict with that norm becomes void and terminates.

Since it is possible for states to derogate by agreement from ordinary rules of general international law, Articles 53 and 64 of the Vienna Convention suggest the existence of a hierarchy of norms in international law. As a result, the inclusion of provisions on *jus cogens* in the Vienna Convention generated considerable debate. Some states, including the United States, expressed concern about the possible disruption to treaty relations such provisions might cause; others disagreed on whether to include a list of peremptory norms in Article 53 and on which norms such a list might encompass. Luxembourg raised a more fundamental objection, one in keeping with the view of many positivist lawyers:

> [Luxembourg] interprets the Commission's object as being to introduce as a cause of nullity criteria of morality and "public policy" such as are used in internal law to determine the compatibility of private contracts with fundamental concepts of the social

order; and it questions whether such concepts are suitable for transfer to international relations which are characterized by the lack of any authority, political or judicial, capable of imposing on all States standards of international justice and morality.

The commentary on the International Law Commission's final draft of Article 53 defended the inclusion of provisions on *jus cogens* in the Convention:

(1) The view that in the last analysis there is no rule of international law from which States cannot at their own free will contract out has become increasingly difficult to sustain. . . . [T]he law of the Charter concerning the prohibition of the use of force in itself constitutes a conspicuous example of a rule in international law having the character of *jus cogens*. . . . [O]nly one [government has] questioned the existence of rules of *jus cogens* in the international law of today. Accordingly, the Commission concluded that in codifying the law of treaties it must start from the basis that today there are certain rules from which States are not competent to derogate at all by a treaty arrangement, and which may be changed only by another rule of the same character.

(2) The formulation of the article is not free from difficulty, since there is no simple criterion by which to identify a general rule of international law as having the character of *jus cogens*. Moreover, the majority of the general rules of international law do not have that character, and States may contract out of them by treaty. It would therefore be going much too far to state that a treaty is void if its provisions conflict with a rule of general international law. Nor would it be correct to say that a provision in a treaty possesses the character of *jus cogens* merely because the parties have stipulated that no derogation from that provision is to be permitted, so that another treaty which conflicted with that provision would be void. Such a stipulation may be inserted in any treaty with respect to any subject-matter for any reasons which may seem good to the parties. . . .

(3) The emergence of rules having the character of *jus cogens* is comparatively recent, while international law is in process of rapid development. The Commission considered the right course to be to provide in general terms that a treaty is void if it conflicts with a rule of *jus cogens* and to leave the full content of this rule to be worked out in State practice and in the jurisprudence of international tribunals. Some members of the Commission felt that there might be advantage in specifying, by way of illustration, some of the most obvious and best settled rules of *jus cogens* in order to indicate by these examples the general nature and scope of the rule contained in the article. Examples suggested included (a) a treaty contemplating an unlawful use of force contrary to the principles of the Charter, (b) a treaty contemplating the performance of any other act criminal under international law, and (c) a treaty contemplating or conniving at the commission of acts, such as trade in slaves, piracy or genocide, in the suppression of which every State is called upon to co-operate. . . . [T]reaties violating human rights, the equality of States or the principle of self-determination were mentioned as other possible examples.

Notes and Questions

1. Should international law recognize peremptory norms? What norms should qualify? As a practical matter, how can a peremptory norm, once established, be modified? Is there an analogue to peremptory norms in national legal systems?

2. In 1998, the Economic Community of West African States (ECOWAS), a regional group of 15 states founded in 1975, adopted a Protocol Relating to the Mechanism for Conflict Prevention, Management, Resolution, Peacekeeping and Security. The Protocol established a nine-member Mediation and Security Council, empowered to decide by a two-thirds vote on ECOWAS responses to conflicts in member states. Among other things,

the Mediation and Security Council shall "authorise all forms of intervention and decide particularly on the deployment of political and military missions" pursuant to triggering conditions that include "serious and massive violation of human rights and the rule of law"; "an overthrow or attempted overthrow of a democratically elected government"; and "[a]ny other situation as may be decided by the Mediation and Security Council." Similarly, Article 4(h) of the African Union Constitutive Act of 2000 identifies as one of the Union's operative principles "the right of the Union to intervene in a Member State pursuant to a decision of the Assembly in respect of grave circumstances, namely: war crimes, genocide and crimes against humanity." The subsequent Protocol Relating to the Establishment of the Peace and Security Council of the African Union contains provisions establishing an AU Peace and Security Council that may among other things "authorize the mounting and deployment of peace support missions." The UN Charter prohibits any use of force in international relations that is not authorized by the Security Council or taken in self-defense. This prohibition, which is also part of customary international law, is generally deemed the paradigm example of a *jus cogens* norm. Should the ECOWAS and AU protocols therefore be treated as void for purporting to authorize military intervention in member states without Security Council authorization?

5. Interpreting Treaties

In May 2010, after diplomatic efforts to end Japan's special permit whaling program stalled, Australia sued Japan in the ICJ, claiming that Japan's special permit whaling program violated the 1982 moratorium. The parties' arguments, and the Court's decision, turned principally on differing interpretations of the object and purpose of the ICRW, as set forth in its Preamble, and of the meaning of Article VIII of the Convention.

The Preamble to the ICRW states:

CONSIDERING that the history of whaling has seen over-fishing of one area after another and of one species of whale after another to such a degree that it is essential to protect all species of whales from further over-fishing;

RECOGNIZING that the whale stocks are susceptible of natural increases if whaling is properly regulated, and that increases in the size of whale stocks will permit increases in the numbers of whales which may be captured without endangering these natural resources; . . .

DESIRING to establish a system of international regulation for the whale fisheries to ensure proper and effective conservation and development of whale stocks . . . ; and

HAVING decided to conclude a convention to provide for the proper conservation of whale stocks and thus make possible the orderly development of the whaling industry. . . .

Article VIII provides:

1. Notwithstanding anything contained in this Convention, any Contracting Government may grant to any of its nationals a special permit authorizing that national to kill, take, and treat whales for purposes of scientific research subject to such restrictions as to number and subject to such other conditions as the Contracting Government thinks fit, and the killing, taking, and treating of whales in accordance with the provisions of this Article shall be exempt from the operation of this Convention. Each Contracting Government shall report at once to the Commission all such authorizations which it has granted. . . .

In making their arguments, both Australia and Japan relied heavily on the Vienna Convention's rules of treaty interpretation. The key provisions of the Vienna Convention are considered below.

Article 31
General Rule of Interpretation

1. A treaty shall be interpreted in good faith in accordance with the ordinary meaning to be given to the terms of the treaty in their context and in the light of its object and purpose.

2. The context for the purpose of the interpretation of a treaty shall comprise, in addition to the text, including its preamble and annexes:

(a) any agreement relating to the treaty which was made between all the parties in connection with the conclusion of the treaty; (b) any instrument which was made by one or more parties in connection with the conclusion of the treaty and accepted by the other parties as an instrument related to the treaty.

3. There shall be taken into account, together with the context:

(a) any subsequent agreement between the parties regarding the interpretation of the treaty or the application of its provisions; (b) any subsequent practice in the application of the treaty which establishes the agreement of the parties regarding its interpretation; (c) any relevant rules of international law applicable in the relations between the parties.

4. A special meaning shall be given to a term if it is established that the parties so intended.

Article 32
Supplementary Means of Interpretation

Recourse may be had to supplementary means of interpretation, including the preparatory work of the treaty and the circumstances of its conclusion, in order to confirm the meaning resulting from the application of article 31, or to determine the meaning when the interpretation according to article 31:

(a) leaves the meaning ambiguous or obscure; or (b) leads to a result which is manifestly absurd or unreasonable.

———————————

The Vienna Convention's articles on treaty interpretation were adopted by unanimous vote and largely reflect preexisting customary international law. Nonetheless, there was extensive discussion at the drafting conference on the formulation of both Articles 31 and 32 and whether to include them at all. The principal issue to be resolved was whether and to what extent the intentions of the parties and the object and purpose of an agreement should supplement consideration of the text of the treaty in the process of interpretation. The final commentary to Articles 31 and 32 notes:

(2) Jurists also differ to some extent in their basic approach to the interpretation of treaties according to the relative weight which they give to:

(a) The text of the treaty as the authentic expression of the intentions of the parties;

(b) The intentions of the parties as a subjective element distinct from the text; and

(c) The declared or apparent objects and purposes of the treaty.

Some place the main emphasis on the intentions of the parties and in consequence admit a liberal recourse to the *travaux préparatoires* [the preparatory work of the treaty] and to other evidence of the intentions of the contracting States as means of interpretation. Some give great weight to the object and purpose of the treaty and are in consequence more ready, especially in the case of general multilateral treaties, to admit teleological interpretations of the text which go beyond, or even diverge from, the original intentions of the parties as expressed in the text. The majority, however, emphasizes the primacy of the text as the basis for the interpretation of a treaty, while at the same time giving a certain place to extrinsic evidence of the intentions of the parties and to the objects and purposes of the treaty as means of interpretation.

––––––––––––

Australia and Japan agreed that Japan's whaling program would violate the 1982 moratorium unless Japan's whaling fell within the terms of Article VIII. But they disagreed on the proper interpretation of Article VIII, its role within the Convention, and whether Japan's program was in fact undertaken for purposes of scientific research. They also disagreed on whether the numerous resolutions and recommendations of the IWC, some adopted unanimously and some by large or narrow margins, constituted subsequent practice within the meaning of VCLT Article 31. New Zealand intervened in the case, generally supporting Australia.

In its Memorial, Australia argued that the ordinary meaning of Article VIII, supported by the drafting history and the subsequent practice of the IWC:

> leads to the following conclusions:
> (1) Article VIII special permits are to be treated as exceptional.
> (2) The application of Article VIII is to be determined on an objective basis—it is not self-judging. That is, a Contracting Government is not entitled to determine unilaterally that it is free to issue special permits according to its own asserted view that the killing, taking or treating of whales under those permits is "for purposes of scientific research".
> (3) A program of whaling "for purposes of scientific research" under Article VIII must possess certain essential characteristics drawn from generally accepted scientific practice . . . .
> (4) Activities carried out for "purposes" of scientific research must be carried out for those purposes and not for any other purpose.
> (5) Article VIII must be implemented in good faith.

Memorial of Australia, *Whaling in the Antarctic (Austl. v. Japan),* 9 May 2011 at 141.

In its Counter-Memorial, Japan responded that Article VIII:

> does not stipulate that special permit whaling is permitted as an exception under the ICRW to the more general provisions on whaling: on the contrary, it stipulates that special permit whaling is "exempt from the operation of this Convention". Special permit whaling under Article VIII is entirely outside the scope of the ICRW.

Counter-Memorial of Japan, *Whaling in the Antarctic (Austl. v. Japan),* 9 March 2012 at 324.

Japan argued further that Article VIII was unambiguous in permitting "each Contracting Government to authorize its nationals to engage in special permit whaling" and therefore that "recourse to the supplementary means of interpretation set out in VCLT Article 32" was unnecessary. Nonetheless, "for the sake of completeness," Japan reviewed the ICRW's legislative history:

> 7.29 There are four specific points arising in the *travaux préparatoires* to which attention should be drawn.

7.30 First, the importance of whaling as an activity, an industry, and a source of natural resources was repeatedly affirmed.

7.31 On the day of the opening session of the Conference, delegates . . . referred to the whaling industries as "extremely important industries in which an enormous amount of money is sunk and . . . producing [sic] very vital commodities, oil among other things" and said that "we must look after the whaling industries" and that "[w]haling is of paramount importance to mankind".

7.33 Second, the importance of scientific research and the continuous collection of biological data was repeatedly affirmed . One speaker said that "[t]here is perhaps no area of biology in which we know so little as we do in the case of life in the seas and oceans of the world"; another "indicated that the [IWC] would have need for all of the biological information it could obtain from all possible sources, in order that it might take such information into consideration at the time amendments to the various provisions of the Schedule were taken up". . . .

7.37 Third, it was clearly understood that the IWC would not itself conduct that scientific research and data collection . That was a matter that was deliberately left to the Contracting Governments . . . .

7.41 Fourth, while the possibility was suggested of requiring a Contracting Government that was proposing to authorize special permit whaling to consult with the IWC before doing so, that suggestion was rejected . . . .

Excerpts of the ICJ's decision and several of the separate and dissenting opinions follow.

Whaling in the Anatarctic
(Austl. v. Japan: New Zealand Intervening)
2014 I.C.J. (March 31)

[After rejecting Japan's objections to its jurisdiction and reviewing the background to the ICRW, the Court focuses on the meaning of Article VIII, viewing it neither as the broad exemption from the rest of the Convention's provisions claimed by Japan nor as the limited exception to other aspects of the Convention urged by Australia and New Zealand:]

55. The Court notes that Article VIII is an integral part of the Convention. It therefore has to be interpreted in light of the object and purpose of the Convention and taking into account other provisions of the Convention, including the Schedule. However, since Article VIII, paragraph 1, specifies that "the killing, taking, and treating of whales in accordance with the provisions of this Article shall be exempt from the operation of this Convention", whaling conducted under a special permit which meets the conditions of Article VIII is not subject to the obligations under the Schedule concerning the moratorium on the catching of whales for commercial purposes, the prohibition of commercial whaling in the Southern Ocean Sanctuary and the moratorium relating to factory ships.

56. The preamble of the ICRW indicates that the Convention pursues the purpose of ensuring the conservation of all species of whales while allowing for their sustainable exploitation. [After noting that some parts of the Preamble support conservation as a goal, while other parts support the exploitation of whales as a goal, the Court continues:] The objectives of the ICRW are further indicated in the final paragraph of the preamble, which states that the Contracting Parties "decided to conclude a convention to provide for the proper conservation of whale stocks and thus make possible the orderly development of the whaling industry". Amendments to the Schedule and recommendations by

the IWC may put an emphasis on one or the other objective pursued by the Convention, but cannot alter its object and purpose.

57. In order to buttress their arguments concerning the interpretation of Article VIII, paragraph 1, Australia and Japan have respectively emphasized conservation and sustainable exploitation as the object and purpose of the Convention in the light of which the provision should be interpreted. According to Australia, Article VIII, paragraph 1, should be interpreted restrictively because it allows the taking of whales, thus providing an exception to the general rules of the Convention which give effect to its object and purpose of conservation. . . . This approach is contested by Japan, which argues in particular that the power to authorize the taking of whales for purposes of scientific research should be viewed in the context of the freedom to engage in whaling enjoyed by States under customary international law.

58. Taking into account the preamble and other relevant provisions of the Convention referred to above, the Court observes that neither a restrictive nor an expansive interpretation of Article VIII is justified. The Court notes that programmes for purposes of scientific research should foster scientific knowledge; they may pursue an aim other than either conservation or sustainable exploitation of whale stocks. This is also reflected in the Guidelines issued by the IWC for the review of scientific permit proposals by the Scientific Committee. . . .

[The Court concludes that it should apply an objective standard of review to assess whether Japan's program was genuinely "for the purposes of scientific research" (rather than using the "arbitrary or capricious" or bad faith test proposed by Japan). Australia argued that scientific research required a testable hypothesis, "appropriate methods," i.e., non-lethal means where feasible, peer review, and avoidance of harm to whale stocks. In response to Australia's argument about methods, the Court states:]

78. . . . Australia asserts that Article VIII, paragraph 1, authorizes the granting of special permits to kill, take and treat whales only when non-lethal methods are not available. . . . Australia refers to [IWC] Resolution 1986-2 (which recommends that when considering a proposed special permit, a State party should take into account whether "the objectives of the research are not practically and scientifically feasible through non-lethal research techniques") . . . .

83. Article VIII expressly contemplates the use of lethal methods, and the Court is of the view that Australia and New Zealand overstate the legal significance of the recommendatory resolutions and Guidelines on which they rely. First, many IWC resolutions were adopted without the support of all States parties to the Convention and, in particular, without the concurrence of Japan. Thus, such instruments cannot be regarded as subsequent agreement to an interpretation of Article VIII, nor as subsequent practice establishing an agreement of the parties regarding the interpretation of the treaty . . . .

Secondly, as a matter of substance, the relevant resolutions and Guidelines that have been approved by consensus call upon States parties to take into account whether research objectives can practically and scientifically be achieved by using non-lethal research methods, but they do not establish a requirement that lethal methods be used only when other methods are not available.

The Court however observes that the States parties to the ICRW have a duty to co-operate with the IWC and the Scientific Committee and thus should give due regard to recommendations calling for an assessment of the feasibility of non-lethal alternatives.

[The Court rejects some of the other components of Australia's proposed four-part test, and focuses on the question "whether the elements of a programme's design and implementation are reasonable in relation to its stated scientific objectives." After an extensive analysis, including detailed comparison of Japan's original research program (JARPA I) with the program under dispute (JARPA II), the Court finds that Japan's whaling program was not for scientific purposes. The Court identifies several reasons for this conclusion, including 1) Japan's failure to consider the feasibility of non-lethal methods, and 2) the expanded scale of JARPA II compared to JARPA I, in a manner suggesting sample sizes under the former "were not driven by strictly scientific considerations." The Court then holds:]

227. Taken as a whole, the Court considers that JARPA II involves activities that can broadly be characterized as scientific research, but that the evidence does not establish that the programme's design and implementation are reasonable in relation to achieving its stated objectives. The Court concludes that the special permits granted by Japan for the killing, taking and treating of whales in connection with JARPA II are not "for purposes of scientific research" pursuant to Article VIII, paragraph 1, of the Convention.

245. The Court observes that JARPA II is an ongoing programme. Under these circumstances, measures that go beyond declaratory relief are warranted. The Court therefore will order that Japan shall revoke any extant authorization, permit or licence to kill, take or treat whales in relation to JARPA II, and refrain from granting any further permits under Article VIII, paragraph 1, of the Convention, in pursuance of that programme.

247. For these reasons,
THE COURT,

(2) By twelve votes to four,

Finds that the special permits granted by Japan in connection with JARPA II do not fall within the provisions of Article VIII, paragraph 1, of the International Convention for the Regulation of Whaling;

(7) By twelve votes to four,

Decides that Japan shall revoke any extant authorization, permit or licence granted in relation to JARPA II, and refrain from granting any further permits in pursuance of that programme.

[Judges Owada (Japan), Abraham (France), Bennouna (Morroco), and Yusuf (Somalia) cast the dissenting votes.]

Dissenting Opinion of Judge Owada

2014 I.C.J. (March 31)

4. . . . It is argued on the one hand that there has been an evolution in the economic-social vista of the world surrounding whales and whaling over the years since 1946, and that this is to be reflected in the interpretation and the application of the Convention. It is argued, on the other hand, that the juridico-institutional basis of the Convention has not changed since it was drafted, based as it was on the well-established principles of international law relating to the conservation and management of fishing resources, including whales, and that this basic character of the Convention should essentially be maintained. This to my mind is the fundamental divide that separates the legal positions of the Applicant, Australia, and New Zealand as an intervener under Article 63 of the Statute, and that of the Respondent, Japan.

[After a brief review of the treaty's background, Preamble, and legislative history, Judge Owada concludes that "the object and purpose of the Convention is to pursue the goal of achieving the twin purposes of the sustainability of the maximum sustainable yield ('MSY') of the stocks in question and the viability of the whaling industry." He continues:]

12. . . . The Judgment [does not try] to analyse the raison d'être of the Convention as reflected in its Preamble, except for the laconic statement that "[t]he functions conferred on the Commission have made the Convention *an evolving instrument*" (emphasis added). It does not specify what this implies. Any international agreement can be evolving inasmuch as it is susceptible to modification by the agreement of the parties. The fact that the Commission is given the power to adopt amendments to the Schedule as an integral part of the Convention, which can become binding upon those States parties which do not raise an objection, and that the Commission has amended the Schedule many times in this sense would not support the thesis that the Convention is an "evolving instrument" as such. The Convention is not malleable as such in the legal sense, according to the changes in the surrounding socio-economic environments.

16. . . . The argument advanced with regard to this situation by the Applicant, and developed further by the Intervener, that the Convention has gone through an evolution during these 60 years in accordance with the change in the environment surrounding whales and whaling, and especially in the growth in the community interest of the world that whales be preserved as precious animals, would seem to be an argument that would be tantamount to an attempt to change the rules of the game as provided for in the Convention and accepted by the Contracting Parties in 1946.

[Judge Owada goes on to state that the Convention created a "self-contained regulatory regime for the regulation of whales and whaling," and that killing whales for scientific research under Article VIII is not an exception to the regime, but rather a way to carry out "an important function within this regulatory regime by collecting scientific materials and data required for the promotion of the objectives and purposes of the Convention. . . ." He concludes:]

46. [T]the activities carried out pursuant to JARPA II can be characterized as "reasonable" activities for purposes of scientific research. It may well be that JARPA II is far from a perfect programme, but the evidence presented to the Court has clearly shown that it provides some useful scientific information . . . .

Separate Opinion of Judge *Ad Hoc* Charlesworth

2014 I.C.J. (March 31)

5. . . . Although the Court acknowledges at a general level that resolutions adopted by consensus or by a unanimous vote "may be relevant for the interpretation of the Convention or its Schedule", with respect to lethal research methods it states that any such resolutions "do not establish a requirement that lethal methods be used only when other methods are not available". In my view, however, the applicable resolutions establish a principle that lethal methods should be of last resort in scientific research programmes under Article VIII. [After citing resolutions in support of this position, Judge Charlesworth continues:]

6. The precautionary approach to environmental regulation also reinforces this analysis of the conditions in which lethal research methods may be undertaken. The approach was formulated in Principle 15 of the Rio Declaration on Environment and Development in 1992 as "[w]here there are threats of serious or irreversible damage, lack of full scientific certainty shall not be used as a reason for postponing cost-effective measures to prevent environmental degradation". The precautionary approach entails the avoidance of activities that may threaten the environment even in the face of scientific uncertainty

about the direct or indirect effects of such activities. It gives priority to the prevention of harm to the environment in its broadest sense, including biological diversity, resource conservation and management and human health. The essence of the precautionary approach has informed the development of international environmental law and is recognized implicitly or explicitly in instruments dealing with a wide range of subject-matter, from the regulation of the oceans and international watercourses to the conservation and management of fish stocks, the conservation of endangered species and biosafety.

10. [After citing several ICJ decisions endorsing reliance on the precautionary approach in treaty interpretation, Judge Charlesworth concludes:] Both Parties to this dispute endorsed the precautionary approach at a theoretical level, although they disagreed about its application to the facts. In my view, the precautionary approach requires that non-lethal methods of research be used wherever possible. In relation to Article VIII, which contemplates the killing of the subject of research by the research activity, an implication of the precautionary approach is that lethal methods must be shown to be indispensable to the purposes of scientific research on whales.

Notes and Questions

1. What is the object and purpose of the ICRW? Short of a formal amendment to a treaty, can the object and purpose of a treaty change with changes in membership, community values, or socioeconomic conditions? With changes in related areas of international law?

2. Is the ordinary meaning of the terms of Article VIII clear? As Judge Keith notes in a concurring opinion, Article VIII "does not say that a Contracting Government may grant a special permit for 'what it considers to be' scientific research." On the other hand, it does state that a "Contracting Government may grant to any of its nationals a special permit . . . subject to such restrictions as to number and subject to such other conditions *as the Contracting Government thinks fit* . . ." (emphasis added). How much discretion does Article VIII grant a state issuing a special permit?

3. Why does the VCLT permit treaty interpreters to take into account the subsequent practice of state parties? Do you agree with the Court's treatment of IWC resolutions as a form of subsequent practice? Should only resolutions adopted unanimously count as subsequent practice?

4. Under Article 31 of the ICJ Statute, "a State party to a case before the International Court of Justice which does not have a judge of its nationality on the Bench may choose a person to sit as judge ad hoc in that specific case. . . ." Australia appointed Judge Charlesworth. Do you agree with her that the precautionary principle should influence the interpretation of Article VIII? Is it a relevant rule of international law within the meaning of VCLT Article 31(3)? Should it matter whether Japan supports application of the precautionary principle, either in general or in this case?

5. Should the rules of interpretation be the same for all treaties? Or are environmental treaties, for example, more likely to evolve in ways that call for greater flexibility in interpretation?

6. Treaty Withdrawal, Breach, and Termination

In the months leading up to the ICJ's decision in *Whaling in the Antarctic*, Japan suggested it might withdraw from the treaty in the event of an adverse ruling. When the decision was announced, however, Japan canceled its 2014-2015 Antarctic whale hunt; this was the first time the hunt was cancelled in the last 24 years. Japan stated it would abide by the ICJ's ruling, even though it "regrets and is deeply disappointed by the decision." At the same time, Japanese officials indicated they would develop a new whaling research program in light of the ICJ decision, and would likely begin the new program in the 2015-2016 whaling season. Japan also continued to hunt whales in the northern Pacific, under a program not covered by the ICJ decision.

Most treaties specify their duration or the conditions under which a state may withdraw or the treaty may be terminated. Article 54 of the Vienna Convention provides that withdrawal or termination may take place "(a) in conformity with the provisions of the treaty; or (b) at any time by consent of all the parties after consultation with the other contracting States." The ICRW states that "[a]ny Contracting Government may withdraw from this Convention on 30th June, of any year by giving notice on or before 1st January of the same year to the depository Government. . . ." As of January 2014, eight states have withdrawn from the Convention; another eight have withdrawn but ratified a second time; and three states (Netherlands, Sweden, and Norway) have withdrawn twice and are again parties after having ratified a third time.

But many treaties do not contain any specific provisions regarding their duration or termination. With respect to such treaties, the Vienna Convention provides:

Article 56
Denunciation of or Withdrawal from a Treaty Containing No Provision Regarding Termination, Denunciation or Withdrawal

1. A treaty which contains no provision regarding its termination and which does not provide for denunciation or withdrawal is not subject to denunciation or withdrawal unless:

> (a) it is established that the parties intended to admit the possibility of denunciation or withdrawal; or (b) a right of denunciation or withdrawal may be implied by the nature of the treaty.

2. A party shall give not less than twelve months' notice of its intention to denounce or withdraw from a treaty under paragraph 1.

In the contract law of most states, a material breach by one party, that is, a breach that goes to the heart of the agreement, will usually entitle the other party or parties either to suspend the operation of the contract or to terminate it and seek damages. International law (as reflected in the Vienna Convention on the Law of Treaties) contains similar provisions regarding the breach of a treaty.

Article 60
Termination or Suspension of the Operation of a Treaty as a Consequence of Its Breach

1. A material breach of a bilateral treaty by one of the parties entitles the other to invoke the breach as a ground for terminating the treaty or suspending its operation in whole or in part.

2. A material breach of a multilateral treaty by one of the parties entitles:

> (a) the other parties by unanimous agreement to suspend the operation of the treaty in whole or in part or to terminate it either: (i) in the relations between themselves and the defaulting State, or (ii) as between all the parties;

(b) a party specially affected by the breach to invoke it as a ground for suspending the operation of the treaty in whole or in part in the relations between itself and the defaulting State;

(c) any party other than the defaulting State to invoke the breach as a ground for suspending the operation of the treaty in whole or in part with respect to itself if the treaty is of such a character that a material breach of its provisions by one party radically changes the position of every party with respect to the further performance of its obligations under the treaty.

3. A material breach of a treaty, for the purposes of this article, consists in:

(a) a repudiation of the treaty not sanctioned by the present Convention; or (b) the violation of a provision essential to the accomplishment of the object or purpose of the treaty.

4. The foregoing paragraphs are without prejudice to any provision in the treaty applicable in the event of a breach.

5. Paragraphs 1 to 3 do not apply to provisions relating to the protection of the human person contained in treaties of a humanitarian character, in particular to provisions prohibiting any form of reprisals against persons protected by such treaties.

In many cases, as with Japan's breach of the ICRW, termination or suspension in response to a breach will be of little or no value to other parties to the treaty. In theory, other parties may seek reparations for a breach, as they might for any other violation of an international obligation. In the *Whaling in the Antarctic* case, however, Australia did not request reparations, perhaps because it did not suffer any direct monetary harm as a result of Japanese special permit whaling.

With some limitations, customary international law also permits states injured by another state's breach of a treaty (or of any international obligation owed to the injured state) to impose countermeasures. Countermeasures entail a state's refusal to perform obligations owed to another state in order to induce the latter state to remedy a breach of its legal duty owed to the former state. For example, if one state denies landing rights to aircraft from another state in breach of an aviation agreement between the two states, the injured state may deny landing rights in reciprocal fashion, in order to induce the first state to comply with the parties' agreement. The International Law Commission, in its 2001 Articles on Responsibility of States for Internationally Wrongful Acts, proposed the following restatement of the Law governing countermeasures:

Article 49
Object and limits of countermeasures

1. An injured State may only take countermeasures against a State which is responsible for an internationally wrongful act in order to induce that State to comply with its obligations under part two [outlining a state's responsibility to cease any internationally wrongful acts and to make full reparation for such acts].

2. Countermeasures are limited to the non-performance for the time being of international obligations of the State taking the measures towards the responsible State.

3. Countermeasures shall, as far as possible, be taken in such a way as to permit the resumption of performance of the obligations in question.

The Articles state further that countermeasures must be "commensurate with the injury suffered" (Article 51) and should "be terminated as soon as the responsible State has complied with its obligations" (Article 53). In some cases, as in the case of Japan's breach of the ICRW, countermeasures cannot be perfectly reciprocal; Australia could not resume whaling without breaching obligations to other treaty parties and hurting its own interests. Accordingly, countermeasures may involve suspension of the performance of some other obligation owed under the same or a different treaty, or under other norms of international law.

States may also have options other than treaty termination, reparations, or countermeasures to respond to a breach (or, for that matter, to pressure a state to accept and comply with particular treaty provisions in the first place). The United States, for example, has periodically relied on economic sanctions or the threat of economic sanctions to pressure Japan and other countries to stop whaling. In particular, the United States has threatened or imposed restrictions on imports and reductions in fishing rights in U.S. waters. Moreover, efforts to stop whaling are not confined to governments. Numerous NGOs vigorously lobby states and international organizations to adopt anti-whaling positions. Some NGOs, most notably a group called the Sea Shepherd Conservation Society, use "direct action" tactics. Since its founding in 1977, Sea Shepherd vessels have monitored, shadowed, harassed, and sometimes rammed and sunk whaling ships, prompting arrests, lawsuits, and accusations of ecological terrorism.

Notes and Questions

1. Why might a state withdraw from a treaty only to ratify it a second (or third) time?

2. How should one determine whether a right of denunciation is implicit in the nature of a treaty? An early draft of Article 56 listed treaties "effecting a final settlement of an international dispute" as among the kinds of treaties that should ordinarily be viewed as continuing indefinitely. As a general matter, what other kinds of treaties should presumptively be viewed as continuing indefinitely? As permitting a right of denunciation by their nature?

3. If Japan resumes special permit whaling in ways other states deem violate the ICRW, what means beyond suspension or termination of the treaty would likely be most effective in securing compliance?

The ICRW and related international efforts to restrict whaling have had considerable success. Only a handful of countries still engage in whaling, whale stocks have at least partly recovered, and the greatest threats to whales now come from pollution, shipping traffic, and climate change, not commercial whaling.

But the IWC, closely divided between pro- and anti-whaling states, remains largely paralyzed. In 2007, the IWC began a process, called the "Future of the IWC," intended to reach a consensus proposal for the future regulation of whaling. In 2010, an IWC working group released for public discussion a "proposed consensus decision" that for the next 10 years would have brought all whaling under the authority of the IWC, set catch limits well below those currently set by whaling countries, and barred new whaling operations by non-IWC members. According to the working group, its proposal would reduce by 14,000 the number of whales killed during the 10-year period and permit the IWC to work on other important conservation issues, including the effects of pollution and climate change. But when the proposal was made public, anti-whaling critics attacked it as a "whaler's convention" on the theory that by legitimizing some whale hunting, even if at a lower level than would otherwise occur, the proposal was backing away from the zero-kill goal of the 1982 moratorium. Critics from pro-whaling countries attacked the proposal as expanding international regulation at the expense of local practices. As a result, the working group's chair was forced to resign and the proposal was scrapped.

In thinking about the utility of the ICRW whaling regime, in particular, and treaties as a form of international regulation, in general, consider the following assessment:

Ian Hurd, *Almost Saving Whales: The Ambiguity of Success at the International Whaling Commission*

26 Ethics & Int'l Aff. 103, 110-111 (2012)

The IWC case also highlights the subtle means by which international law shapes state behavior. A legal skeptic might use the case to illustrate how self-interested states are capable of evading legal obligations, and this might be considered evidence of the weakness or irrelevance of international law. But such a view is too simplistic, since it requires ignoring the ways in which states are making use of the rules to justify and legalize their behavior. The pro-whaling states reveal themselves to be intensely interested in how the rules are written and in finding means to fit their behavior within them. The effect of the law is evident in all the ways that states have adapted their language and their policies as a consequence: some have given up whaling altogether; others have reconstituted their hunts as scientific; and still others have made the effort to redefine their legal obligations by opting out of the moratorium. It is clear that these changes are not all in the direction anticipated by the designers of the ban, but nonetheless they show the complex ways that international law interacts with state behavior.

More directly, the whaling regime has increased the social and political costs of whaling. Many whaling states have been offered strong incentives from the United States to abandon the practice. And many non-whaling small states, in turn, have been offered inducements to vote with pro-whaling governments in the IWC. Thus, whale hunting is an increasingly expensive proposition, both politically and financially. . . .

A gap between compliance and law is usually called noncompliance or rule breaking. But in international law the matter is not so clear. Governments are active agents in making, interpreting, and limiting international law, and they are therefore equipped with various tools to structure their legal obligations around their desired policies. It is not self-evident what counts as "rule following" in international law or what counts as "rule breaking."

E. Reservations to Treaties

Until fairly recently, the acceptance of all treaty terms by all parties to a treaty was essential to the conclusion of the agreement. This uniform acceptance of all of the provisions of a treaty is the norm for most treaties. In some cases, however, one or more states wishes to become a party to a multilateral treaty but refuses to accept one or more of the treaty's provisions. In such cases, states may seek to enter a reservation to the treaty to limit or exclude the application of one or more of the treaty's terms to the reserving state, provided that the treaty does not expressly prohibit the reservation at issue.

When the IWC adopted its moratorium on commercial whaling in 1982, Iceland (under pressure from the United States) did not object. Instead, like Japan, it began a special permit whaling program under Article VIII of the ICRW. Following sharp criticism of the scientific merits of its research program, Iceland in 1992 withdrew from the ICRW. In 1994, the IWC adopted a Revised Management Procedure (RMP) as a "scientifically robust method for calculating safe catch limits." However, the Commission agreed not to lift the moratorium until a Revised Management Scheme (RMS), covering matters such as inspection and observation, was in place to ensure that new catch limits were respected. But the IWC has not been able to agree on an RMS.

In 2001, Iceland sought to rejoin the ICRW, with a reservation to the moratorium established by paragraph 10(e) of the ICRW Schedule. Iceland's reservation added:

> Notwithstanding the aforementioned reservation, the Government of Iceland will not authorise whaling for commercial purposes by Icelandic vessels while progress is being made in negotiations within the IWC on the RMS. This does not apply, however, in case of the so-called moratorium on whaling for commercial purposes . . . not being lifted within a reasonable time after the completion of the RMS. Under no circumstances will whaling for commercial purposes be authorised without a sound scientific basis and an effective management and enforcement scheme.

Not surprisingly, Iceland's reservation prompted sharp debate. As summarized below, the law in this area is complex and still evolving.

The International Court of Justice first had occasion to consider the permissibility of reservations to a multilateral convention following promulgation of the Genocide Convention in 1948. By the end of 1950, eight states had indicated their intent to ratify the Convention with reservations concerning various articles, especially Article 9, which provided for reference of disputes to the ICJ. In an advisory opinion issued in 1951, the Court, in a 7-5 decision, articulated reasons for moving away from the old rule, at least with regard to human rights treaties.

Reservations to the Convention on the Prevention and Punishment of the Crime of Genocide

1951 I.C.J. 15 (May 28)

It is well established that in its treaty relations a State cannot be bound without its consent, and that consequently no reservation can be effective against any State without its agreement thereto. It is also a generally recognized principle that a multilateral convention is the result of an agreement freely concluded upon its clauses and that consequently none of the contracting parties is entitled to frustrate or impair, by means of unilateral decisions or particular agreements, the purpose and *raison d'être* of the convention. To this principle was linked the notion of the integrity of the convention as adopted, a notion which in its traditional concept involved the proposition that no reservation was valid unless it was accepted by all the contracting parties without exception, as would have been the case if it had been stated during the negotiations.

This concept, which is directly inspired by the notion of contract, is of undisputed value as a principle. However, as regards the Genocide Convention, it is proper to refer to a variety of circumstances which would lead to a more flexible application of this principle. . . .

The Genocide Convention was . . . intended by the General Assembly and by the contracting parties to be definitely universal in scope. It was in fact approved on December 9th, 1948, by a resolution which was unanimously adopted by fifty-six States.

The objects of such a convention must also be considered. The Convention was manifestly adopted for a purely humanitarian and civilizing purpose. . . . In such a convention the contracting States do not have any interests of their own; they merely have, one and all, a common interest, namely, the accomplishment of those high purposes which are the *raison d'être* of the convention. Consequently, in a convention of this type one cannot speak of individual advantages or disadvantages to States, or of the maintenance of a perfect contractual balance between rights and duties. . . . The foregoing considerations, when applied to the question of reservations, and more particularly to the effects of objections to reservations, lead to the following conclusions.

The object and purpose of the Genocide Convention imply that it was the intention of the General Assembly and of the States which adopted it that as many States as possible should participate. The complete exclusion from the Convention of one or more States would not only restrict the scope of its application, but would detract from the authority of the moral and humanitarian principles which are its basis. It is inconceivable that the contracting parties readily contemplated that an objection to a minor reservation should produce such a result. But even less could the contracting parties have intended to sacrifice the very object of the Convention in favour of a vain desire to secure as many participants as possible. The object and purpose of the Convention thus limit both the freedom of making reservations and that of objecting to them. It follows that it is the compatibility of a reservation with the object and purpose of the Convention that must furnish the criterion for the attitude of a State in making the reservation on accession as well as for the appraisal by a State in objecting to the reservation. Such is the rule of conduct which must guide every State in the appraisal which it must make, individually and from its own standpoint, of the admissibility of any reservation. . . .

The drafters of the Vienna Convention adopted much of the ICJ's approach to treaty reservations, in language that applies to all treaties, not just to human rights treaties:

Article 20
Acceptance of and Objection to Reservations

1. A reservation expressly authorized by a treaty does not require any subsequent acceptance by the other contracting States unless the treaty so provides.

2. When it appears from the limited number of the negotiating States and the object and purpose of a treaty that the application of the treaty in its entirety between all the parties is an essential condition of the consent of each one to be bound by the treaty, a reservation requires acceptance by all the parties.

3. When a treaty is a constituent instrument of an international organization and unless it otherwise provides, a reservation requires the acceptance of the competent organ of that organization.

4. In cases not falling under the preceding paragraphs and unless the treaty otherwise provides:

(a) acceptance by another contracting State of a reservation constitutes the reserving State a party to the treaty in relation to that other State if or when the treaty is in force for those States; (b) an objection by another contracting State to a reservation does not preclude the entry into force of the treaty as between the objecting and reserving States unless a contrary intention is definitely expressed by the objecting State; (c) an act expressing a State's consent to be bound by the treaty and containing a reservation is effective as soon as at least one other contracting State has accepted the reservation. . . .

Article 21
Legal Effects of Reservations and of Objections to Reservations

1. A reservation established with regard to another party . . .

(a) modifies for the reserving State in its relations with that other party the provisions of the treaty to which the reservation relates to the extent of the reservation; and (b) modifies those provisions to the same extent for that other party in its relations with the reserving State.

2. The reservation does not modify the provisions of the treaty for the other parties to the treaty *inter se*.

3. When a State objecting to a reservation has not opposed the entry into force of the treaty between itself and the reserving State, the provisions to which the reservation relates do not apply as between the two States to the extent of the reservation.

In 2006, the International Court of Justice had occasion to revisit its 1951 judgment on the permissibility of reservations to the Genocide Convention. In *Armed Activities on the Territory of the Congo* (Dem. Rep. Congo v. Rwanda), 2006 I.C.J. 126, the Court had to determine whether Rwanda's reservation to Article IX of the Genocide Convention precluded the exercise of the Court's jurisdiction over the Democratic Republic of Congo's complaint. The Court held that Rwanda's reservation related to the Court's jurisdiction, not to Rwanda's substantive obligations regarding genocide. Accordingly, the Court decided it could not:

> 67. . . . conclude that the reservation of Rwanda in question, which is meant to exclude a particular method of settling a dispute relating to the interpretation, application or fulfilment of the Convention, is to be regarded as being incompatible with the object and purpose of the Convention.

In a joint separate opinion, Judges Higgins, Kooijmans, Elaraby, Owada, and Simma agreed with the outcome but expressed concern over "some issues underlying" the Court's opinion:

> 9. The Court in 1951 was clearly not unaware of the hazards inherent in its answers, in the sense that they would entail a veritable web of diverse reciprocal commitments within the framework of a multilateral convention. . . .
>
> 10. In the event, the problems which the Court could already envisage in 1951 have turned out to be vastly greater than it could have foreseen. The Genocide Convention stood virtually alone in the sphere of human rights in 1951. Since then it has been added to by a multitude of multilateral conventions, to which States have not hesitated to enter a plethora of reservations—often of a nature that gives serious concern as to compatibility with the object and purpose of the treaty concerned. And the vast majority of States, who the Court in 1951 envisaged would scrutinize and object to such reservations, have failed to engage in this task.
>
> [The opinion notes that since 1951 regional courts and treaty bodies such as the Human Rights Committee have sometimes pronounced on the validity of specific reservations. The opinion continues:]
>
> 16. . . . The practice of such bodies is not to be viewed as "making an exception" to the law as determined in 1951 by the International Court; we take the view that it is rather a development to cover what the Court was never asked at that time, and to address new issues that have arisen subsequently.
>
> 21. We believe it is now clear that it had not been intended to suggest that the fact that a reservation relates to jurisdiction rather than substance necessarily results in its compatibility with the object and purpose of a convention. Much will depend upon the particular convention concerned and the particular reservation. . . .
>
> 26. Judicial settlement of claims relating to genocide is highly desirable. At the same time, it cannot be said that the entire scheme of the Genocide Convention would necessarily collapse if some States make reservations to Article IX. Were it so, adherence to the jurisdiction of the Court could have been made compulsory. . . .

may also authorize other UN organs or specialized agencies to request advisory opinions on "legal questions arising within the scope of their activities." Advisory opinions are not legally binding but nonetheless have substantial persuasive value. The Court's 1951 opinion in the Genocide Convention case contributed directly to the adoption of the Vienna Convention articles on reservations quoted above.

2. Was Iceland's reservation to the ICRW compatible with the object and purpose of the treaty? What was the effect of the decision by some states to object to Iceland's reservation but nonetheless accept Iceland as a party to the treaty? Was the outcome different for the states that accepted Iceland's reservation?

3. Does Article 20(3) of the VCLT give the IWC the authority to decide on the acceptability of Iceland's reservation? What values does Article 20(3) promote? If a state makes a reservation that a body created pursuant to the treaty determines to be incompatible with the object and purpose of the treaty, is the reserving state still a party to the treaty? See the discussion of reservations to human rights treaties in Chapter 7.

F. Treaties and Sovereignty

Historically, states have been free to make unilateral decisions concerning the exploitation of resources in their own territory and in common areas outside the jurisdiction of other states, including the high seas. Treaties like the ICRW limit the freedom of states to make such decisions. Such constraints are often seen as infringements on national sovereignty. Not surprisingly, opponents of international restrictions on whaling sometimes invoke sovereignty as a reason Japan should withdraw from the ICRW, something Japan periodically threatens to do.

Sovereignty is a concept regularly invoked in international discourse, but its meaning is notoriously difficult to pin down. In many instances, sovereignty is used as shorthand for a particular legal principle or a subset of the attributes associated with statehood. Sovereignty is often invoked in opposition to a state's participation in various treaty regimes, usually by domestic groups who object to what they perceive as a loss of national decisionmaking authority over the areas subject to regulation by the treaty.

Inevitably, every treaty limits a state's freedom to act to some degree, just as a private contract constrains the behavior of the parties to it. In *S.S. Wimbledon* (U.K., France, Italy, Japan, Germ.), 1923 P.C.I.J. (Ser. A), No.1, the Permanent Court of International Justice discussed Germany's reliance on sovereignty as a reason to escape limitations placed on Germany by the Treaty of Versailles. Under the treaty, Germany accepted a permanent right of passage through the Kiel Canal for vessels of all nationalities. Following the outbreak of war between Russia and Poland, however, Germany sought to protect its neutral status by denying transit to a ship carrying arms for one of the belligerents. When charged with a breach of the treaty, Germany argued that a state's ability to declare itself neutral was "an essential part of her sovereignty," and that by signing the Versailles Treaty, Germany "neither could nor intended to renounce by anticipation" what it described as the "inalienable right of states to liberty of action." The Permanent Court held that "the right of entering into international engagements is an attribute of State sovereignty," and that therefore the limitations a state accepts under a treaty cannot later be renounced as impermissible infringements on that state's sovereignty. *Id.* at 25.

The meaning of the term "sovereignty" has varied widely since medieval times. A common understanding of the term in modern public international law is that it entails "the whole body of rights and attributes which a State possesses in its territory, to the exclusion of all other States, and also in its relations with other States." *Corfu Channel Case* (U.K. v. Alb.), 1949 I.C.J. 39, 43 (opinion of Judge Alvarez). Similarly, Professor Helmut Steinberger defines "sovereignty" as "the basic international legal status of a State that is not subject, within its territorial jurisdiction, to the governmental, executive, legislative, or judicial jurisdiction of a foreign State or to foreign law other than public international law." Helmut Steinberger, *Sovereignty*, in Encyclopedia of Public International Law 500, 512 (1992). But as Professor Louis Henkin points out in the following excerpt, the term "sovereignty" often obscures more than it reveals:

Louis Henkin, *International Law: Politics and Values*

8-10 (1995)

Sovereignty, strictly, is the locus of ultimate legitimate authority in a political society, once the Prince or "the Crown," later parliament or the people. It is an internal concept and does not have, need not have, any implication for relations between one state and another.

Sovereignty, a conception deriving from the relations between a prince and his/her subjects, is not a necessary or appropriate external attribute for the abstraction we call a state. Nor is it the appropriate term or concept to define the relation between that abstraction and its counterpart abstractions, other states. For international relations, surely for international law, it is a term largely unnecessary and better avoided.

One can more meaningfully describe the state system—without invoking or implying "sovereignty"—as a social contract among entities which come together to establish a system of law and institutions for their governance, ceding some of their original autonomy, retaining the rest. What they retain is not "sovereignty" but the remainder of what they ceded to the needs of governance.

. . . As applied to a state, elements long identified with "sovereignty" are inevitably only metaphors, fictions, fictions upon fictions; some of them, however, do constitute essential characteristics and indicia of statehood today. These include principally: independence, equality, autonomy, "personhood," territorial authority, integrity and inviolability, impermeability and "privacy."

Notes and Questions

1. Does Japan's participation in the ICRW limit Japan's sovereignty? What benefits, if any, does Japan receive from membership in the ICRW?

2. If Professor Henkin is correct that the term "sovereignty" is ambiguous and "better avoided," why do states so often invoke it? Are states likely to invoke the term for different purposes for different audiences?

States typically enter treaties to advance particular interests, knowing that the price for doing so is the acceptance of some constraints on their own decision making. At the same time, states realize that changes in context, state interests, or treaty membership might create a situation in which the burdens of treaty participation outweigh the benefits. These risks are magnified when a treaty creates an institution like the IWC and empowers it to make binding decisions by less than a unanimous vote.

States have a number of devices available to them to mitigate such risks, and the ICRW employs many of these devices. The treaty includes two significant exceptions to IWC limits on whaling, for scientific research and aboriginal subsistence whaling. In addition, states are free to object to IWC Schedule amendments and thereby render them inapplicable to the objectors. States may also accede to the Convention with reservations to particular provisions, as Iceland and other states have done. Under Article IX of the ICRW, states can withdraw from the Convention after a specified period of advance notice. But these devices also limit the reach of the Convention and therefore its effectiveness. Striking the right balance between establishing a treaty regime that can adapt flexibly to new circumstances, such as changes in scientific knowledge, new technologies, market shifts, changes in community values, and changes in treaty membership, on the one hand, and protecting the interests of the original parties, on the other, is notoriously difficult, particularly when treaties are open-ended in duration.

II. CUSTOM AND SOFT LAW: REGULATING FOREIGN DIRECT INVESTMENT

In its list of the sources of international law, Article 38 of the Statute of the International Court of Justice includes "international custom, as evidence of a general practice accepted as law." Although listed after treaties, custom was, at least until World War II, widely viewed as equal to or more important than treaties in the development of international law. In recent years, treaties have overtaken custom for many purposes, and they are often preferred as a form of law making because of their relative specificity. Nonetheless, many areas of international relations are not covered by treaties, and even in areas that are regulated by treaty, many states are not parties to the relevant instruments. Accordingly, custom continues to play a vital role in international law.

Increasingly, states are also using non-traditional forms of law making to supplement treaties and custom as means for the regulation of international activities and relations. This trend is most evident in the promulgation in recent years of a wide variety of quasi-legal instruments, from industry codes of conduct to guidelines issued by international organizations, to achieve multiple and varied purposes, which have collectively fallen under the general rubric of soft law.

The goals for this problem include:

- to understand the processes and basic rules that govern the formation and modification of customary international law and the role different actors play in establishing custom;
- to understand the differences between custom and soft law and the role each plays in enabling international actors to pursue their interests; and
- to understand the factors that might lead different actors to prefer one type of international law over another.

A. *The Problem*

Foreign direct investment—the transfer of capital by an investor from one country to another, accompanied by a claim to the income produced by the assets acquired or generated with that capital—takes many forms. It may involve the establishment of a foreign company or subsidiary or the purchase of shares in a foreign corporation. As discussed more fully in Chapter 12, global foreign direct investment (FDI) has increased substantially over the last 15 years. As shown in the chart below, global FDI peaked in 2007, falling sharply with the 2008 global financial crisis. FDI levels have increased since then, though they are still well below the 2007 peak.

Figure 1. Global FDI flows, 2004-2013*

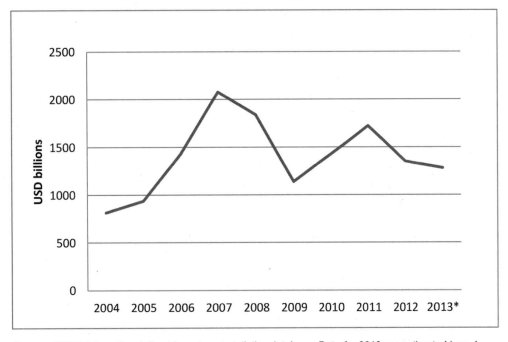

Source: OECD International direct investment statistics database. Data for 2013 are estimated based upon a linear projection of the first three quarters of 2013.

In many countries, foreign direct investment provides an important source of capital. In 2013, five countries received almost 50 percent of global FDI: China, the United States, Brazil, Canada, and Russia. But foreign direct investment has also proven highly controversial; some governments have tried to restrict it, and some non-governmental organizations (NGOs) have argued that in countries with inadequate financial controls and problems of official corruption, it may do more harm than good. Many countries, including developed countries, restrict foreign investment for political and economic reasons. Often investment in particular sectors of the economy deemed essential to national security, such as telecommunications and defense-related industries, is restricted or even precluded altogether. In some developing countries, foreign investors may not purchase more than 50 percent of the stock of some domestic enterprises.

Disputes between foreign investors and their host states arise with some frequency, but the legal principles applicable to these disputes, and the political environment within which these disputes have been settled, have varied dramatically. During the colonial era, international law supported the political dominance generally enjoyed by the developed world vis-à-vis the developing world. The colonial powers enjoyed complete freedom to exploit the economic resources of their colonies as they saw fit, and this pattern of economic exploitation came to characterize the relations between developed and developing countries generally. Commercial enterprises based in developed countries could generally count on the political support of their home states in securing access to the wealth of the developing world on inordinately favorable terms. The developing states received little if any economic benefit from Western investment and had little or no legal basis for pursuing claims against Western companies. By virtue of "concession" agreements with host states, Western companies gained control over much of the oil wealth of the Middle East, the mineral wealth of Africa, and the agricultural and other resources of Latin America.

Following World War II, however, the relationships between developed and developing countries changed dramatically. The Western states accepted that relations with developing countries had to be based on the principle of sovereign equality. As decolonization progressed, developing states joined international organizations, including the United Nations, in numbers large enough to pass numerous resolutions demanding greater economic equality with developed states. This process peaked in the 1970s, when the UN General Assembly passed a series of resolutions intended to establish a "New International Economic Order." These resolutions included the Charter of Economic Rights and Duties of States, excerpted below.

As part of this process of demanding economic and political equality with the developed world, developing states began to engage in large-scale expropriations of certain assets belonging to foreign investors. The best-known set of expropriations occurred in the Middle East, where host states nationalized the holdings of many Western oil companies. These nationalizations triggered vigorous debate on the applicable law. Developed states insisted on compensation for the full economic value of their investments; developing states denied that full compensation was required under international law and insisted that such issues should be governed by domestic law.

This debate harkened back to an earlier dispute between the United States and Mexico. Between 1915 and the late 1930s, Mexico expropriated numerous properties owned by U.S. nationals, including agricultural lands and petroleum concessions. In the lengthy diplomatic exchange that followed, Mexico denied that it was under any international legal obligation to pay compensation. It insisted instead that Mexican law (which did require some compensation) applied. United States Secretary of State Cordell Hull, in what came to be known as the Hull doctrine, insisted that Mexico was obligated to pay prompt, adequate, and effective compensation.

The Mexican Minister of Foreign Affairs to the American Ambassador, August 3, 1938:

My government maintains . . . that there is in international law no rule universally accepted in theory nor carried out in practice, which makes obligatory the payment of immediate compensation nor even of deferred compensation, for expropriations of a general and impersonal character like those which Mexico has carried out for the purpose of redistribution of the land. . . .

Secretary of State Hull to the Mexican Ambassador, August 22, 1938:

The government of the United States merely adverts to a self-evident fact when it notes that the applicable precedents and recognized authorities on international law support its declaration that, under every rule of law and equity, no government is entitled to expropriate private property, for whatever purpose, without provision for prompt, adequate, and effective payment therefor. In addition, clauses appearing in the constitutions of almost all nations today, and in particular in the constitutions of the American republics, embody the principle of just compensation. These, in themselves, are declaratory of the like principle in the law of nations.

The universal acceptance of this rule of the law of nations, which, in truth, is merely a statement of common justice and fair-dealing, does not in the view of this Government admit of any divergence of opinion. . . .

The Mexican Minister of Foreign Affairs to the American Ambassador:

This attitude of Mexico is not, as Your Excellency's Government affirms, either unusual or subversive. Numerous nations, in reorganizing their economy, have been under the necessity of modifying their legislation in such manner that the expropriation of individual interests nevertheless does not call for immediate compensation and, in many cases, not even subsequent compensation; because such acts were inspired by legitimate causes and the aspirations of social justice, they have not been considered unusual or contrary to international law.

Green Hackworth, 3 Digest of International Law 660-665 (1942).

The United States-Mexico dispute replayed itself many times in later years, as radical changes in the political administration of developing states often translated into abrupt policy changes regarding the role of foreign investors in the local economy. In a number of countries, revolutions were followed by the wholesale nationalization of particular industries, especially those related to mineral extraction. In many of these cases, enterprises owned in whole or in substantial part by foreign nationals were the primary targets of nationalization.

The UN General Assembly debated the legal principles relating to nationalization of foreign investment on many occasions. In 1962, the General Assembly adopted the following resolution, supported by both developed and developing countries.

Permanent Sovereignty over Natural Resources

G.A. Res. 1803 (1962)

4. Nationalization, expropriation or requisitioning shall be based on grounds or reasons of public utility, security or the national interest which are recognized as overriding purely individual or private interests, both domestic and foreign. In such cases the owner shall be paid appropriate compensation in accordance with the rules in force in the State taking such measures in the exercise of its sovereignty and in accordance with international law. In any case where the question of compensation gives rise to a controversy, the national jurisdiction of the State taking such measures shall be exhausted. However, upon agreement by sovereign States and other parties concerned, settlement of the dispute should be made through arbitration or international adjudication. . . .

In the early 1970s, as the movement to establish the New International Economic Order was in full swing, the General Assembly adopted a different approach to nationalizations, as reflected in the following resolutions:

Permanent Sovereignty over Natural Resources

G.A. Res. 3171 (1973)

The General Assembly . . .
1. *Strongly reaffirms* the inalienable rights of States to permanent sovereignty over all their natural resources. . . .

3. *Affirms* that the application of the principle of nationalization carried out by States, as an expression of their sovereignty in order to safeguard their natural resources, implies that each State is entitled to determine the amount of possible compensation and the mode of payment, and that any disputes which might arise should be settled in accordance with the national legislation of each State carrying out such measures. . . .

Charter of Economic Rights and Duties of States (CERDS)

G.A. Res. 3281 (1974)

1. Every State has and shall freely exercise full permanent sovereignty, including possession, use and disposal, over all its wealth, natural resources and economic activities.

2. Each State has the right . . .

c) To nationalize, expropriate or transfer ownership of foreign property, in which case appropriate compensation should be paid by the State adopting such measures, taking into account its relevant laws and regulations and all circumstances that the State considers pertinent. In any case where the question of compensation gives rise to a controversy, it shall be settled under the domestic law of the nationalizing State and by its tribunals, unless it is freely and mutually agreed by all States concerned that other peaceful means be sought on the basis of the sovereign equality of States and in accordance with the principle of free choice of means.

In the years that followed, the international legal principles applicable to nationalizations continued to generate vigorous dispute. Developing countries usually acknowledged that some compensation was owed for expropriated foreign investments, but they differed sharply with Western, capital-exporting countries on the means for valuing the investments at issue and the form compensation should take. Both sets of countries invoked international law and pointed to resolutions of the General Assembly and various indicators of state practice in support of their positions.

These disputes have often been resolved through negotiated settlements. In some cases, those settlements take the form of agreements between the host state and the expropriated investors. In such cases, the value of the settlement depends on the relative bargaining power of the parties. In other cases, the host state and the home state of the investors agree on a lump sum to be paid over to the home state and later distributed by the home state to individual investors in accordance with particular criteria and claims-resolution procedures. In most lump-sum settlement arrangements, claimants receive only a modest amount in relation to the actual economic value of their loss. Developed countries accept such arrangements as the best available outcome, given the limited capacity of developing states to pay foreign investors' claims and the desire of developed countries to maintain or restore acceptable diplomatic relations with expropriating states. At the same time, to protect the interests of their investors, developed states have increasingly entered into Friendship, Commerce, and Navigation treaties, and later, bilateral investment treaties (BITs) with developing states. These treaties include guarantees of fair and equitable treatment for foreign investors, as determined by international law. Among other things, the treaties require the payment of the full economic value of expropriated investments.

Despite these various means of resolving host state-investor disputes, a number of important cases have been referred to international arbitration. Two of those cases are excerpted in Section C below.

B. Background on the Formation of Customary International Law

Custom has served as a form of law since ancient times. Common practices among the Greek city-states gave rise to rules governing war, trade, and other relations. Similarly, Roman law recognized custom as a source. In theory, usage or repeated state acts become custom over time, as divergent practices of various states converge and achieve a level of uniformity, consistency, and regularity that in turn generates a sense of legal obligation, often referred to as *opinio juris*. The drafters of the Restatement (Third) of the Foreign Relations Law of the United States therefore describe custom as law that "results from a general and consistent practice of states followed by them from a sense of legal obligation."

Many scholars describe custom as based on implicit state consent. Rules form because states engage in or acquiesce in particular practices and eventually recognize them as obligatory. In keeping with positivist notions that states can only be bound by their consent, international law permits states to opt out of an emerging customary international law rule by objecting to the rule as it develops. As a practical matter, however, states rarely exercise this right of persistent objection. Moreover, a rule once formed is binding on states that did not object, even if they did not have the opportunity to object. Thus, new states, including those that emerged from decolonization, are bound by all general customary international law in effect at the time they achieve statehood.

1. State Practice

State practice takes numerous forms. These forms include diplomatic contacts and correspondence, public statements of government officials, legislative and executive acts, military manuals and actions by military commanders, treaties and executive agreements, decisions of international and national courts and tribunals, and decisions, declarations, and resolutions of international organizations, among many others. State practice also includes inaction, at least in circumstances in which a state's failure to object to actions by another state may imply acquiescence in those actions. The significance of any particular evidence of state practice may vary enormously depending on the circumstances. In the case of resolutions of international organizations, for example, much will depend on whether the resolution purports to declare existing law or simply recommends a particular course of action. It will also depend on the number of states voting for and against, as well as the extent to which the states involved are directly affected by the subject matter of the resolution. Decisions of international tribunals are not state practice per se but may contribute to the formation of customary international law by their persuasive value and influence on subsequent state practice. The extent to which state practice must be general and consistent varies with the circumstances. As Jean-Marie Henckaerts, co-author of a massive International Committee of the Red Cross study on customary international law, explains:

. . . To establish a rule of customary international law, State practice has to be virtually uniform, extensive and representative.

Let us look more closely at what this means. First, for State practice to create a rule of customary international law, it must be virtually uniform. Different States must not have engaged in substantially different conduct. The jurisprudence of the International Court of Justice shows that contrary practice which, at first sight, appears to undermine the uniformity of the practice concerned, does not prevent the formation of a rule of customary international law as long as this contrary practice is condemned by other States or denied by the government itself. Through such condemnation or denial, the rule in question is actually confirmed. . . .

Second, for a rule of general customary international law to come into existence, the State practice concerned must be both extensive and representative. It does not, however, need to be universal; a "general" practice suffices. No precise number or percentage of States is required. One reason it is impossible to put an exact figure on the extent of participation required is that the criterion is in a sense qualitative rather than quantitative. That is to say, it is not simply a question of how many States participate in the practice, but also which States. In the words of the International Court of Justice in the North Sea Continental Shelf cases, the practice must "include that of States whose interests are specially affected."

This consideration has two implications: (1) if all "specially affected States" are represented, it is not essential for a majority of States to have actively participated, but they must have at least acquiesced in the practice of "specially affected States"; and (2) if "specially affected States" do not accept the practice, it cannot mature into a rule of customary international law, even though unanimity is not required as explained. Who is "specially affected" under international humanitarian law may vary according to circumstances. Concerning the legality of the use of blinding laser weapons, for example, "specially affected States" include those identified as having been in the process of developing such weapons, even though other States could potentially suffer from their use. . . .

Jean-Marie Henckaerts, *Study on customary international humanitarian law: A contribution to the understanding and respect for the rule of law in armed conflict*, 87 Intl. Rev. Red Cross 175, 179 (2005).

The time required for state practice to mature into custom also varies with the circumstances. In 2000, the International Law Association's Committee on the Formation of Customary (General) International Law issued a Statement of Principles Applicable to the Formation of General Customary International Law. (The International Law Association (ILA) is a distinguished organization of international lawyers and academics founded in 1873.) The statement noted:

(a) In the North Sea Continental Shelf cases the ICJ observed that "Although the passage of only a short period of time is not necessarily, or of itself, a bar to the formation of a new rule of customary international law on the basis of what was originally a purely conventional rule, an indispensable requirement would be that within the period in question, short though it might be, State practice, including that of States whose interests are specially affected, should have been both extensive and virtually uniform in the sense of the provision invoked. . . ."

(b) The quotation from the ICJ just cited makes it clear that . . . there is no specific time requirement: it is all a question of accumulating a practice of sufficient density, in terms of uniformity, extent and representativeness. Some customary rules have sprung up quite quickly: for instance, sovereignty over air space, and the régime of the continental shelf, because a substantial and representative quantity of State practice grew up rather rapidly in response to a new situation.

(c) However, in the nature of things some time will normally need to elapse before a practice matures into a rule. The development of the continental shelf is an example of how the process often works. In 1945, President Truman proclaimed the "jurisdiction and control" of the USA over the adjacent continental shelf. Other States with important interests in their own continental shelf, such as the United Kingdom, followed suit. Some others, though their own interests were affected, failed to object. What started out as, first, a unilateral claim and undertaking, next a bilateral set of obligations, and then a body of particular customary law restricted to a confined (though not regionally defined) group of States, gradually ramified into a rule of general law. The process took several years to be completed. Even in the present era of easy and instantaneous communications, if a State or group of States adopts a practice, others will need to consider how (if at all) they wish to respond. These responses may give rise to further responses, and so on. All of this will usually involve some delay.

The *North Sea Continental Shelf* cases and the evolution of the continental shelf legal regime are discussed in more detail in Chapter 10.

2. *Opinio Juris*

Not all state practice results in customary law. Indeed, there are many instances of repeated state practice that reflect simply convenience or courtesy — for example, the forms of address used for ambassadors or other government officials — but not law. Consistent state practice becomes law when states follow the practice out of a sense of legal obligation encapsulated in the phrase *opinio juris sive necessitatis*. Unfortunately for international lawyers, however, states often act without express reference to rules of international law. Accordingly, the subjective element implicit in customary international law, the belief that a practice is in fact binding, must often be inferred from the nature and circumstances of the practice itself. In many cases, judges and international law scholars may help identify and establish such inferences through careful review of the relevant practice and their work is therefore listed in Article 38 of the Statute of the International Court of Justice as a subsidiary means for determining the law.

Whether proof of *opinio juris* is essential to the recognition of a new rule of customary international law is controversial. The International Law Association's Committee on Formation of Customary (General) International Law concluded in 2000 that "it is not necessary to the formation of such a rule that such a belief exists, either generally or on the part of any particular State":

(c) It may well be true (though trivial) to observe that States will usually or always hold an *opinio juris* about an established rule of law. . . . [T]herefore . . . where it can be shown that an *opinio juris* exists about a practice, that will be sufficient [to prove the existence of a rule of customary international law]. But this tells us nothing about the necessity of this subjective state for the formation of a new rule of customary law. . . . And in fact, it is hard to see how a State, if properly advised, could entertain the belief that its conduct is permitted (or required) by existing law when that conduct is, by definition, a departure from it. States actively engaged in the creation of a new customary rule may well wish or accept that the practice in question will give rise to a legal rule, but it is logically impossible for them to have an *opinio juris* in the literal and traditional

law is simply a violation of that law, a contribution to the formation of new law, or both, is equally difficult. In other cases, state practice may be so inconsistent or incomplete that decision makers must look to other sources of law for guidance. As you read the following cases, consider what kinds of practice count toward the creation of custom, the extent to which practice must be widespread and consistent, the time period over which the practice at issue extends, the point at which emerging custom can be properly described as binding law, the relationship between custom and treaties, and the means by which customary law once established may be changed.

In 1900, the U.S. Supreme Court had to determine the validity of the condemnation of two Spanish fishing vessels as prizes of war. The Court's decision illustrates some of the issues involved in identifying and applying a rule of customary international law.

The Paquete Habana

175 U.S. 677 (1900)

MR. JUSTICE GRAY delivered the opinion of the court.

There are two appeals from decrees of the District Court of the Southern District of Florida, condemning two fishing vessels and their cargoes as prize of war.

Each vessel was a fishing smack, running in and out of Havana, and regularly engaged in fishing on the coast of Cuba; [each] sailed under the Spanish flag. . . . Until stopped by the blockading squadron, [the *Paquete Habana*] had no knowledge of the existence of the war, or of any blockade. She had no arms or ammunition on board, and made no attempt to run the blockade after she knew of its existence, nor any resistance at the time of the capture. . . .

Both the fishing vessels were brought by their captors into Key West. . . . [A] final decree of condemnation and sale was entered, "the court not being satisfied that as a matter of law, without any ordinance, treaty or proclamation, fishing vessels of this class are exempt from seizure."

Each vessel was thereupon sold by auction; the Paquete Habana for the sum of $490; and the Lola for the sum of $800. . . .

We are then brought to the consideration of the question whether . . . the fishing smacks were subject to capture by the armed vessels of the United States during the recent war with Spain.

By an ancient usage among civilized nations, beginning centuries ago, and gradually ripening into a rule of international law, coast fishing vessels, pursuing their vocation of catching and bringing in fresh fish, have been recognized as exempt, with their cargoes and crews, from capture as prize of war.

This doctrine, however, has been earnestly contested at the bar; and no complete collection of the instances illustrating it is to be found, so far as we are aware, in a single published work, although many are referred to and discussed by the writers on international law. . . . It is therefore worth the while to trace the history of the rule, from the earliest accessible sources, through the increasing recognition of it, with occasional setbacks, to what we may now justly consider as its final establishment in our own country and generally throughout the civilized world.

The earliest acts of any government on the subject, mentioned in the books, either emanated from, or were approved by, a King of England. [The Court then reviews orders issued by King Henry IV in 1403 and 1406, pursuant to a treaty with France, directing that fishermen from France, Flanders, and Brittany be permitted to carry out their trade without hindrance, provided they should not "do or attempt, or presume to do or attempt, anything that could prejudice the King, or his kingdom of England, or his subjects." The Court next describes a 1521 treaty between the Emperor Charles V and Francis I of France, pursuant to which subjects of either sovereign could "safely and freely, everywhere in the sea, take herrings and every other kind of fish, the existing war by land and sea notwithstanding," for a limited period. The Court then notes French and Dutch edicts issued in 1536 to permit herring fishing during wartime, and describes the early authority of French admirals to grant "fishing truces" in time of war, a custom that continued until late in the seventeenth century, when France abandoned it in the face of a refusal by other states to extend reciprocal treatment to French fishermen. The Court then turns to a review of eighteenth century practice.]

The doctrine which exempts coast fishermen with their vessels and cargoes from capture as prize of war has been familiar to the United States from the time of the War of Independence.

On June 5, 1779, Louis XVI, our ally in that war, addressed a letter to his admiral, informing him that the wish he had always had of alleviating, as far as he could, the hardships of war, had directed his attention to that class of his subjects which devoted itself to the trade of fishing, and had no other means of livelihood; that he had thought that the example which he should give to his enemies, and which could have no other source than the sentiments of humanity which inspired him, would determine them to allow to fishermen the same facilities which he should consent to grant; and that he had therefore given orders to the commanders of all his ships not to disturb English fishermen, nor to arrest their vessels laden with fresh fish, even if not caught by those vessels; provided they had no offensive arms, and were not proved to have made any signals creating a suspicion of intelligence with the enemy; and the admiral was directed to communicate the King's intentions to all officers under his control. By a royal order in council of November 6, 1780, the former orders were confirmed; and the capture and ransom, by a French cruiser, of The John and Sarah, an English vessel, coming from Holland, laden with fresh fish, were pronounced to be illegal.

[The Court then reviews British practice and treaties between the United States and Prussia exempting fishermen from molestation during war, and concludes that: "Since the United States became a nation, the only serious interruptions, so far as we are informed, of the general recognition of the exemption of coast fishing vessels from hostile capture, arose out of the mutual suspicions and recriminations of England and France during the wars of the French Revolution." The Court describes at some length the disputes between England and France over the treatment of fishermen, and the occasions on which each captured fishermen of the other, and then comments upon Lord Stowell's judgment upholding a British seizure of a Dutch fishing vessel in 1798.]

[Lord Stowell's] opinion begins by admitting the known custom in former wars not to capture such vessels—adding, however, "but this was a rule of comity only, and not of legal decision." . . . But the period of a hundred years which has since elapsed is amply sufficient to have enabled what originally may have rested in custom or comity, courtesy or concession, to grow, by the general assent of civilized nations, into a settled rule of international law. As well said by Sir James Mackintosh: "In the present century a slow and silent, but very substantial mitigation has taken place in the practice of war; and in proportion as that mitigated practice has received the sanction of time, it is raised from the rank of mere usage, and becomes part of the law of nations." Discourse on the Law of Nations, 38; 1 Miscellaneous Works, 360.

The French prize tribunals, both before and after Lord Stowell's decision, took a wholly different view of the general question. [The Court cites decisions finding the capture of English and Portuguese fishing vessels to be in violation of international law.]

The English government . . . more than once unqualifiedly prohibited the molestation of fishing vessels employed in catching and bringing to market fresh fish. [The Court cites English orders in council of 1806 and 1810 relating to Prussia and France, respectively.] In the war with Mexico in 1846, the United States recognized the exemption of coast fishing boats from capture. . . . [After further discussion of British, French, Mexican, and U.S. practice, the Court continues:] Since the English orders in council of 1806 and 1810 . . . in favor of fishing vessels employed in catching and bringing to market fresh fish, no instance has been found in which the exemption from capture of private coast fishing vessels, honestly pursuing their peaceful industry, has been denied by England, or by any other nation. . . .

International law is part of our law, and must be ascertained and administered by the courts of justice of appropriate jurisdiction, as often as questions of right depending upon it are duly presented for their determination. For this purpose, where there is no treaty, and no controlling executive or legislative act or judicial decision, resort must be had to the customs and usages of civilized nations; and, as evidence of these, to the works of jurists and commentators, who by years of labor, research and experience, have made themselves peculiarly well acquainted with the subjects of which they treat. Such works are resorted to by judicial tribunals, not for the speculations of their authors concerning what the law ought to be, but for trustworthy evidence of what the law really is. *Hilton v. Guyot*, 159 U.S. 113, 163, 164, 214, 215 [1895]. . . .

[The Court then reviews in detail the works of commentators from England, France, Argentina, Germany, Netherlands, Portugal, Spain, Austria, Italy, and other states and concludes:] This review of the precedents and authorities on the subject appears to us abundantly to demonstrate that at the present day, by the general consent of the civilized nations of the world, and independently of any express treaty or other public act, it is an established rule of international law, founded on considerations of humanity to a poor and industrious order of men, and of the mutual convenience of belligerent States, that coast fishing vessels, with their implements and supplies, cargoes and crews, unarmed, and honestly pursuing their peaceful calling of catching and bringing in fresh fish, are exempt from capture as prize of war. . . .

This rule of international law is one which prize courts, administering the law of nations, are bound to take judicial notice of, and to give effect to, in the absence of any treaty or other public act of their own government in relation to the matter. . . .

[In rejecting the argument that "a distinct exemption in a treaty or other public act of the Government" was necessary to exempt coastal fishing vessels from seizure, the Court notes:] To this subject, in more than one aspect, are singularly applicable the words uttered by Mr. Justice Strong, speaking for this court: "Undoubtedly, no single nation can change the law of the sea. That law is of universal obligation, and no statute of one or two nations can create obligations for the world. Like all the laws of nations, it rests upon the common consent of civilized communities. It is of force, not because it was prescribed by any superior power, but because it has been generally accepted as a rule of conduct. Whatever may have been its origin, whether in the usages of navigation, or in the ordinances of maritime States, or in both, it has become the law of the sea only by the concurrent sanction of those nations who may be said to constitute the commercial world. Many of the usages which prevail, and which have the force of law, doubtless originated in the positive prescriptions of some single State, which were at first of limited effect, but which, when generally accepted, became of universal obligation." "This is not giving to the statutes of any nation extra-territorial effect. It is not treating them as general maritime laws; but it is recognition of the historical fact that by common consent of mankind these rules have been acquiesced in as of general obligation. Of that fact, we think, we may take judicial notice. Foreign municipal laws must indeed be proved as facts, but it is not so with the law of nations." *The Scotia*, 14 Wall. 170, 187, 188 [1871].

The position taken by the United States during the recent war with Spain was quite in accord with the rule of international law, now generally recognized by civilized nations, in regard to coast fishing vessels.

. . . On April 22, the President issued a proclamation, declaring that the United States had instituted and would maintain [its] blockade, "in pursuance of the laws of the United States, and the law of nations applicable to such cases." . . .

On April 28, 1898 (after the capture of the two fishing vessels now in question), Admiral Sampson telegraphed to the Secretary of the Navy as follows: "I find that a large number of fishing schooners are attempting to get into Havana from their fishing grounds near the Florida reefs and coasts. They are generally manned by excellent seamen, belonging to the maritime inscription of Spain, who have already served in the Spanish navy, and who are liable to further service. As these trained men are naval reserves, have a semi-military character, and would be most valuable to the Spaniards as artillerymen, either afloat or ashore, I recommend that they should be detained as prisoners of war, and that I should be authorized to deliver them to the commanding officer of the army at Key West." To that communication the Secretary of the Navy, on April 30, 1898, guardedly answered: "Spanish fishing vessels attempting to violate blockade are subject, with crew, to capture, and any such vessel or crew considered likely to aid enemy may be detained." Bureau of Navigation Report of 1898, appx. 178. The Admiral's despatch assumed that he was not authorized, without express order, to arrest coast fishermen peaceably pursuing their calling; and the necessary implication and evident intent of the response of the Navy Department were that Spanish coast fishing vessels and their crews should not be interfered with, so long as they neither attempted to violate the blockade, nor were considered likely to aid the enemy. . . .

Upon the facts proved in either case, it is the duty of this court, sitting as the highest prize court of the United States, and administering the law of nations, to declare and adjudge that the capture was unlawful, and without probable cause; and it is therefore, in each case,

Ordered, that the decree of the District Court be reversed, and the proceeds of the sale of the vessel, together with the proceeds of any sale of her cargo, be restored to the claimant, with damages and costs.

Notes and Questions

1. The Court describes the formation of a customary international law rule against confiscation of fishing vessels as the "ripening" of an "ancient usage among civilized nations." What does the Court mean by "ripening," and how can such a process give rise to a rule of international law? How much time must elapse before a usage can be deemed to have "ripened" into a rule of customary international law, and how can one ascertain when that has happened?

2. What indicators of state practice support the Court's conclusion? The Court notes that France temporarily discontinued its practice of exempting fishing vessels from seizure in the late seventeenth century in response to the refusal of other states to exempt French fishermen. What is the effect of this interruption in the "ripening" of the rule at issue? How uniform must state practice be to support the formation of a rule of custom? Does it matter if a few countries fail to follow a practice generally followed by most other states?

3. Which countries' practice does the Court examine in attempting to determine the existence and content of a rule governing the treatment of fishing vessels during wartime? Is it reasonable to assume that most other countries acquiesced in the practice of a handful of dominant maritime powers? Does a state's silence on an issue indicate acquiescence? Note that a rule of customary international law binds all states that do not object to the rule as it is forming. By contrast, states that do not affirmatively ratify a treaty are not bound by it, even if it is a general multilateral treaty.

4. Is customary international law based on state consent? If not, why is it binding? Would states generally better satisfy their lawmaking objectives by negotiating multilateral treaties instead of waiting for customary rules to develop and crystallize into law?

5. Do you agree with the ILA Committee on Formation of Customary (General) International law that *opinio juris* should not be deemed a necessary element in the formation of a new rule of customary international law, or with the ILC's claim that it is necessary? Is there any discussion of *opinio juris* in the *Paquete Habana*? Can *opinio juris* be inferred from statements of writers on international law who opine that a particular rule has attained the status of custom? Determining the existence of *opinio juris* with regard to a particular state practice can be extremely difficult. For an opinion of the ICJ discussing this issue, see *The North Sea Continental Shelf* case, discussed in Chapter 10.

6. As a general matter, why might states refrain from the seizure of coastal fishing vessels in the absence of an applicable legal rule? Two commentators, after reviewing state practice on this issue, conclude that state behavior in this regard can best be explained as a "coincidence of interest":

> The most parsimonious explanation for the evidence is that states seized fishing vessels when they had a military reason to do so, whether the reason was to reward sailors under the rules of prize, to clear away obstructions or spies, or to terrorize the population—and they did not seize fishing vessels when they had a military reason not to do so, for example, to avoid the trouble or to maintain naval discipline. One might conjecture that a few cases, perhaps some of the interactions between France and England, are attributable to the solution of bilateral repeated prisoner's dilemmas. Most cases, however, are best attributable to simple lack of anything to cooperate about. If one insists on looking for a general pattern, one might conclude that most of the time states did not seize fishing vessels after the Napoleonic Wars because most of the time they were not at war, and when they were at war, their navies had better uses. One may dignify this pattern of behavior with the CIL [customary international law] label, if one wants, as long as one understands that it hardly reflects international cooperation or anything that is noteworthy or desirable, and it is certainly not the result of states acting out of a sense of legal or moral obligation.

Jack Goldsmith & Eric Posner, *A Theory of Customary International Law*, Chicago Working Paper in Law and Economics 69-70 (1999).

7. What happens when states broadly subscribe to a norm in their public declarations but frequently violate the norm in practice? In a 1984 suit in which Nicaragua accused

the United States of illegally assisting rebel forces seeking to overthrow the Nicaraguan government, the ICJ considered that question in its discussion of customary international law governing the use of force. The Court opined:

> It is not to be expected that in the practice of States the application of the rules in question should have been perfect, in the sense that States should have refrained, with complete consistency, from the use of force or from intervention in each other's internal affairs. The Court does not consider that, for a rule to be established as customary, the corresponding practice must be in absolutely rigorous conformity with the rule. In order to deduce the existence of customary rules, the Court deems it sufficient that the conduct of States should, in general, be consistent with such rules, and that instances of State conduct inconsistent with a given rule should generally have been treated as breaches of that rule, not as indications of the recognition of a new rule. If a State acts in a way prima facie incompatible with a recognized rule, but defends its conduct by appealing to exceptions or justifications contained within the rule itself, . . . the significance of that attitude is to confirm rather than to weaken the rule.

Case Concerning Military and Paramilitary Activities In and Against Nicaragua (Nicar. v. U.S.), 1986 I.C.J. 14.

C. *Discerning and Applying Custom: Foreign Direct Investment (FDI) and Expropriation*

In the two cases that follow, international arbitrators apply customary international law to determine the standard of compensation to be paid for the expropriation of foreign enterprises. In attempting to identify the relevant customary norms, the arbitrators consider, among other things, the UN General Assembly resolutions excerpted in Section A above. The first case involved Libya's nationalization of various Western oil properties. When Libya became an independent state in 1951, its economic prospects were bleak. But the discovery of large oil deposits in 1959 soon transformed Libya from a poverty-stricken country to a wealthy one. To achieve this transformation, Libya granted deeds of concession to Western oil companies to encourage them to undertake the costly and risky efforts necessary to find and develop Libya's oil deposits. The concessions conferred broad rights on the oil companies, enabling them to earn substantial profits on their investments. In the early 1970s, Libya began to insist on substantial equity participation in the Western oil company concessions, anywhere from 51 to 100 percent. In 1973 and 1974, Libya nationalized the interests and properties in Libya of nine international oil companies, including Texaco Overseas Petroleum Company (TOPCO), a Texaco subsidiary, and California Asiatic Oil Company (CAOC), a Standard Oil subsidiary. The timing was dictated in part by Libya's desire to retaliate for U.S. support for Israel and U.S. efforts to coordinate opposition to the 1973 Arab oil embargo.

In response to the nationalization, TOPCO and CAOC invoked the arbitration clauses in their deeds of concession. They sent notices to the Libyan government requesting arbitration and appointed their arbitrator. When Libya responded by denying that there was any arbitrable dispute, TOPCO and CAOC requested Manfred Lachs, the President of the ICJ, to appoint a sole arbitrator, as provided for in the deeds of concession. Lachs appointed René-Jean Dupuy, Professor of Law at the University of Nice. In the following excerpt, Dupuy considers the effect of General Assembly resolutions on the customary international law relating to expropriation.

**Award on the Merits in Dispute Between Texaco Overseas
Petroleum Company/California Asiatic Oil Company
and the Government of the Libyan Arab Republic**

17 I.L.M. 1 (1978)

... Substantial differences ... exist between Resolution 1803 (XVII) and the subsequent Resolutions as regards the role of international law in the exercise of permanent sovereignty over natural resources. . . . [T]his Tribunal is obligated to consider the legal validity of the above-mentioned Resolutions and the possible existence of a custom resulting therefrom.

83. . . . This Tribunal will recall first that, under Article 10 of the U.N. Charter, the General Assembly only issues "recommendations", which have long appeared to be texts having no binding force and carrying no obligations for the Member States. . . .

Refusal to recognize any legal validity of United Nations Resolutions must, however, be qualified according to the various texts enacted by the United Nations. These are very different and have varying legal value, but it is impossible to deny that the United Nations' activities have had a significant influence on the content of contemporary international law. In appraising the legal validity of the above-mentioned Resolutions, this Tribunal will take account of the criteria usually taken into consideration, i.e., the examination of voting conditions and the analysis of the provisions concerned.

84. (1) With respect to the first point, Resolution 1803 (XVII) of 14 December 1962 was passed by the General Assembly by 87 votes to 2, with 12 abstentions. It is particularly important to note that the majority voted for this text, including many States of the Third World, but also several Western developed countries with market economies, including the most important one, the United States. The principles stated in this Resolution were therefore assented to by a great many States representing not only all geographical areas but also all economic systems.

From this point of view, this Tribunal notes that the affirmative vote of several developed countries with a market economy was made possible in particular by the inclusion in the Resolution of two references to international law, and one passage relating to the importance of international cooperation for economic development.

85. On the contrary, it appears to this Tribunal that the conditions under which Resolutions 3171 (XXVII) . . . and 3281 (XXIX) (Charter of the Economic Rights and Duties of States) [were adopted] were notably different:

—Resolution 3171 (XXVII) was adopted by a recorded vote of 108 votes to 1, with 16 abstentions, but this Tribunal notes that a separate vote was requested with respect to the paragraph in the operative part mentioned in the Libyan Government's Memorandum whereby the General Assembly stated that the application of the principle according to which nationalizations effected by States as the expression of their sovereignty implied that it is within the right of each State to determine the amount of possible compensation and the means of their payment, and that any dispute which might arise should be settled in conformity with the national law of each State instituting measures of this kind. As a consequence of a roll-call, this paragraph was adopted by 86 votes to 11 (Federal Republic of Germany, Belgium, Spain, United States, France, Israel, Italy, Japan, The Netherlands, Portugal, United Kingdom), with 28 abstentions (South Africa, Australia, Austria, Barbados, Canada, Ivory Coast, Denmark, Finland, Ghana, Greece, Haiti, India, Indonesia, Ireland, Luxembourg, Malawi, Malaysia, Nepal, Nicaragua, Norway, New Zealand, Philippines, Rwanda, Singapore, Sri Lanka, Sweden, Thailand, Turkey).

This specific paragraph concerning nationalizations, disregarding the role of international law, not only was not consented to by the most important Western countries, but caused a number of the developing countries to abstain. . . .

—The conditions under which Resolution 3281 (XXIX), proclaiming the Charter of Economic Rights and Duties of States, was adopted also show unambiguously that there was no general consensus of the States with respect to the most important provisions and in particular those concerning nationalization. Having been the subject matter of a roll-call vote, the Charter was adopted by 118 votes to 6, with 10 abstentions. The analysis of votes on specific sections of the Charter is most significant insofar as the present case is concerned. From this point of view, paragraph 2 (c) of Article 2 of the Charter, which limits consideration of the characteristics of compensation to the State and does not refer to international law, was voted by 104 to 16, with 6 abstentions, all of the industrialized countries with market economies having abstained or having voted against it. . . .

86. . . . [T]he absence of any binding force of the resolutions of the General Assembly of the United Nations implies that such resolutions must be accepted by the members of the United Nations in order to be legally binding. In this respect, the Tribunal notes that only Resolution 1803 (XVII) of 14 December 1962 was supported by a majority of Member States representing all of the various groups. By contrast, the other Resolutions mentioned above . . . were supported by a majority of States but not by any of the developed countries with market economies which carry on the largest part of international trade.

87. . . . [I]t appears essential to this Tribunal to distinguish between those provisions stating the existence of a right on which the generality of the States has expressed agreement and those provisions introducing new principles which were rejected by certain representative groups of States and having nothing more than a *de lege ferenda* [the law as it should be] value only in the eyes of the States which have adopted them; as far as the others are concerned, the rejection of these same principles implies that they consider them as being *contra legem.* With respect to the former, which proclaim rules recognized by the community of nations, they do not create a custom but confirm one by formulating it and specifying its scope, thereby making it possible to determine whether or not one is confronted with a legal rule. . . .

On the basis of the circumstances of adoption mentioned above and by expressing an *opinio juris communis*, Resolution 1803 (XVII) seems to this Tribunal to reflect the state of customary law existing in this field. . . .

88. While Resolution 1803 (XVII) appears to a large extent as the expression of a real general will, this is not at all the case with respect to the other Resolutions mentioned above. . . . In particular, as regards the Charter of Economic Rights and Duties of States, several factors contribute to denying legal value to those provisions of the document which are of interest in the instant case.

—In the first place, Article 2 of this Charter must be analyzed as a political rather than as a legal declaration concerned with the ideological strategy of development and, as such, supported only by non-industrialized States.

—In the second place, this Tribunal notes that in the draft submitted by the Group of 77 [a grouping of developing states formed in 1964 to promote the collective economic interests of its now 133 members] . . . the General Assembly was invited to adopt the Charter "as a first measure of codification and progressive development" within the field of the international law of development. However, because of the opposition of several States, this description was deleted from the text submitted to the vote of the Assembly. . . .

89. Such an attitude is further reinforced by an examination of the general practice of relations between States with respect to investments. This practice is in conformity, not with the provisions of Article 2 (c) of the above-mentioned Charter conferring exclusive jurisdiction on domestic legislation and courts, but with the exception stated at the end of this paragraph. Thus a great many investment agreements entered into between industrial States or their nationals, on the one hand, and developing countries, on the other, state, in an objective way, the standards of compensation and further provide, in case of dispute regarding the level of such compensation, the possibility of resorting to an international tribunal. . . .

Some eight months after Dupuy rendered his award on the merits, finding Libya obligated to carry out the terms of the deeds of concession, TOPCO, CAOC, and Libya reached a settlement. In return for Libyan oil valued at $152 million, delivered over the course of the next 15 months, TOPCO and CAOC terminated the arbitration proceedings.

The second case arose in the aftermath of the Iranian revolution, when the Islamic Republic of Iran expropriated numerous foreign enterprises. Among other things, the Iranian government expropriated the interest held by SEDCO, the subsidiary of a U.S. corporation, in the SEDIRAN drilling company. Under the subsequently negotiated Algiers Accords, the United States and Iran agreed to resolve this and other commercial disputes through arbitration before a special arbitral tribunal created by the Accords—the Iran-U.S. Claims Tribunal. In the decision excerpted below, the Tribunal considers "the standard of compensation to be applied in determining any compensable damages resulting from" the expropriation of SEDCO's interest in SEDIRAN.

Interlocutory Award in Case Concerning SEDCO, Inc. v. National Iranian Oil Company and the Islamic Republic of Iran

Iran-United States Claims Tribunal, 10 Iran-U.S. Cl. Rep. 180 (1986)

II. CONTENTIONS OF THE PARTIES

. . . SEDCO claims to be entitled to full ("prompt, adequate and effective") compensation by virtue of customary international law. SEDCO contends that in the case of an ongoing business enterprise like SEDIRAN the full market value means going concern value including not only net assets but also good will and anticipated future earnings. . . .

The standard of "full" (or "prompt, adequate and effective") compensation in fact has never been the standpoint of international law, Respondents assert. Customary international law, according to Respondents, requires "appropriate" compensation to be measured in the light of all the circumstances of the case, and assessed with "unjust enrichment" as the guiding principle. Should any enrichment on the part of Respondents entitling Claimant to compensation be found, such compensation should be calculated according to the net book value of the company, a valuation basis allegedly widely used in compensation settlements in the oil industry.

III. Conclusions of the Tribunal

"[T]he overwhelming practice and the prevailing legal opinion" before World War II supported the view that customary international law required compensation equivalent to the full value of the property taken. . . . It is only since those days that this traditional legal standpoint has been challenged by a number of States and commentators.

Assessment of the present state of customary law on this subject on the basis of the conduct of States in actual practice is difficult, *inter alia*, because of the questionable evidentiary value for customary international law of much of the practice available. This is particularly true in regard to "lump sum" agreements between States (a practice often claimed to support the position of less than full compensation), as well as to compensation settlements negotiated between States and foreign companies. Both types of agreements can be so greatly inspired by non-judicial considerations—e.g., resumption of diplomatic or trading relations—that it is extremely difficult to draw from them conclusions as to *opinio juris*, i.e., the determination that the content of such settlements was thought by the States involved to be required by international law. . . . The bilateral investment treaty practice of States, which much more often than not reflects the traditional international law standard of compensation for expropriation, more nearly constitutes an accurate measure of the High Contracting Parties' views as to customary international law, but also carries with it some of the same evidentiary limitations as lump sum agreements. Both kinds of agreements involve in some degree bargaining in a context to which "*opinio juris* seems a stranger."

Those arguing that there has been an erosion of the traditional international law standard of full compensation often cite also resolutions and declarations of the United Nations General Assembly. Respondents in this case, for example, refer in particular to the Declaration on the Establishment of a New International Economic Order and the Charter of Economic Rights and Duties of States ("Charter") as well as the earlier Resolution 1803, of 14 December 1962, on Permanent Sovereignty over Natural Resources.

United Nations General Assembly Resolutions are not directly binding upon States and generally are not evidence of customary law. Nevertheless, it is generally accepted that such resolutions in certain specified circumstances may be regarded as evidence of customary international law or can contribute—among other factors—to the creation of such law.

There is considerable unanimity in international arbitral practice and scholarly opinion that of the resolutions cited above, it is Resolution 1803, and not either of the two later resolutions, which at least reflects, if it does not evidence, current international law. . . .

. . . [Resolution 1803] has been argued, on the one hand, to express the traditional standard of compensation with different words and, on the other hand, to signify an erosion of this standard.

Those learned writers who have argued, however, that the adoption of Resolution 1803, against the background of general recognition of the permanent sovereignty of States over natural resources, evidenced or brought about a change in customary international law so that less than full compensation should be the applicable standard, have focused mainly on the possible impact of the Resolution on the issue of compensation in the context of a formal systematic large-scale nationalization, e.g., of an entire industry or a natural resource, a circumstance not argued by either of the Parties to have been present in the instant case.

details which could be used by host states in determining whether to resort to expropriation and what compensation to pay in such cases. By making these details known in
advance as acceptable international standards, it was hoped that disputes over this matter
could be avoided or, that if disputes arose, they would be more amenable to amicable
settlement. . . .

As mentioned above, the principal controversy focused on the standard to be used
in assessing the amount of compensation due. The use of the compromise term "appropriate" does not necessarily conflict with the better-known formula of "prompt, adequate
and effective." The latter term is preferred by governments of developed countries and
many western international law writings, and is also used in many bilateral investment
treaties. The approach adopted in the draft guideline set the general standard of compensation as "appropriate," but immediately defined this term in the following section
of the guideline, by stating that compensation which was adequate, effective and paid
without undue delay would be deemed generally to be appropriate. This approach tried
to accommodate the seemingly conflicting views on this matter and accepted the Hull
formula as a general standard, thereby encouraging its use without requiring it in all
circumstances.

[After completing its initial draft guidelines, the Working Group circulated them to
numerous governments and a variety of business groups for comment. The United States
and some of the business groups were sharply critical of a number of the draft guidelines
and, in particular, draft guideline IV, relating to expropriation. Shihata describes the U.S.
reaction:]

[The U.S.] argued that the standard of compensation should be the Hull formula,
in other words, that the compensation should be "prompt, adequate and effective," without any qualification. [T]he U.S. wanted the deletion of all the qualifications in the draft
allowing for exceptional deviations from the Hull doctrine, such as where the host country faced foreign exchange stringencies or in the case of large scale, non-discriminatory
nationalizations taken in the context of broad social reforms or in other exceptional cases
of war and the like (draft guideline IV, sections 8 and 10). . . .

Following the informal meeting of the [Bank's] Executive Directors, the U.S.
Executive Director arranged for a meeting between the members of the Working Group
and a high level U.S. delegation to discuss the substance of the U.S. comments. In this
meeting it became clear that the U.S. was objecting to the idea of preparing any guidelines that would provide standards less favorable to investors than those provided for in
the most recent bilateral investment treaties concluded by the U.S. At that time, the U.S.
was heavily involved in negotiating such bilateral treaties with the Russian Federation
and a number of other former Soviet Republics and was also involved with Canada and
Mexico in the completion of the North American Free Trade Agreement (NAFTA). In
the judgement of the Working Group, a set of guidelines addressing the world community and submitted for issuance by a world forum could not be identical to the bilateral
investment treaties concluded by a few countries which, to a large extent, follow the lines
of a standard text prepared by one party. In fact, the number of U.S. bilateral investment
treaties was small compared to the number of treaties concluded by other major industrial countries which should also be taken into account, along with other sources. . . .

More generally, the U.S. delegation indicated that the proposed guidelines represented, in their view, the lowest common denominator. . . . The Working Group responded
to this comment by stating that the guidelines, far from representing the lowest common
denominator, were in fact based on a combination of existing principles and commendable practices identified with a view to their usefulness and acceptability. In many respects,
the draft guidelines constituted a progressive development of customary international

law and presented a set of liberal recommendations on the subject compared to the practice of many countries, including developed countries. They could not, however, ignore general trends in state practice without risking becoming an academic exercise with little practical value from a legal viewpoint.

Other developed countries had a variety of criticisms but were generally more positive than the United States. Developing countries provided relatively little input.

The Working Group revised the guidelines and the revised version, excerpted below, was unanimously endorsed by the Bank's Development Committee and published in 1992.

Guidelines on the Treatment of Foreign Direct Investment

31 I.L.M. 1379 (1992)

The Development Committee

Recognizing

that a greater flow of foreign direct investment brings substantial benefits to bear on the world economy and on the economies of developing countries in particular, . . .

that these guidelines are not ultimate standards but an important step in the evolution of generally acceptable international standards which complement, but do not substitute for, bilateral investment treaties,

therefore *calls the attention* of member countries to the following Guidelines as useful parameters in the admission and treatment of private foreign investment in their territories, without prejudice to the binding rules of international law at this stage of its development. . . .

IV. Expropriation and Unilateral Alterations or Termination of Contracts

1. A State may not expropriate or otherwise take in whole or in part a foreign private investment in its territory, or take measures which have similar effects, except where this is done in accordance with applicable legal procedures, in pursuance in good faith of a public purpose, without discrimination on the basis of nationality and against the payment of appropriate compensation.

2. Compensation for a specific investment taken by the State will, according to the details provided below, be deemed "appropriate" if it is adequate, effective and prompt.

3. Compensation will be deemed "adequate" if it is based on the fair market value of the taken asset as such value is determined immediately before the time at which the taking occurred or the decision to take the asset became publicly known.

4. Determination of the "fair market value" will be acceptable if conducted according to a method agreed by the State and the foreign investor (hereinafter referred to as the parties) or by a tribunal or another body designated by the parties.

5. In the absence of a determination agreed by, or based on the agreement of, the parties, the fair market value will be acceptable if determined by the State according to reasonable criteria related to the market value of the investment, i.e., in an amount that a willing buyer would normally pay to a willing seller after taking into account the nature of the investment, the circumstances in which it would operate in the future and its specific characteristics. . . .

7. Compensation will be deemed "effective" if it is paid in the currency brought in by the investor where it remains convertible, in another currency designated as freely usable by the International Monetary Fund or in any other currency accepted by the investor.

8. Compensation will be deemed to be "prompt" in normal circumstances if it is paid without delay. In cases where the State faces exceptional circumstances, as reflected in an arrangement for the use of the resources of the International Monetary Fund or under similar objective circumstances of established foreign exchange stringencies, compensation . . . may be paid in installments within a period which will be as short as possible and which will not in any case exceed five years from the time of the taking, provided that reasonable, market-related interest applies to the deferred payments in the same currency. . . .

10. In case of comprehensive non-discriminatory nationalizations effected in the process of large scale social reforms under exceptional circumstances of revolution, war and similar exigencies, the compensation may be determined through negotiations between the host State and the investors' home State and failing this, through international arbitration. . . .

The World Bank Guidelines have had a mixed reception. On the one hand, the Guidelines have contributed to an evolving consensus in favor of strengthened protections for investors. They have influenced national legislation and bilateral treaties relating to the treatment of foreign direct investment and have been cited in arbitration decisions.

On the other hand, the Guidelines have been partly superseded by the same forces that helped create the conditions making the Guidelines possible. The nationalizations and expropriations that fueled debate over the customary international law obligations governing foreign direct investment peaked in the 1970s, and declined sharply in the 1980s and 1990s, though now they have begun to pick up again. With the collapse of socialism as a possible economic alternative to capitalism, developing countries throughout the world increasingly found themselves in competition with each other to attract foreign direct investment. Accepting treaty conditions favorable to investors is one way to compete. Accordingly, despite U.S. fears that the Guidelines might impede the negotiation of bilateral investment treaties, such treaties have proliferated. Most developing countries, and virtually all developed states, continue to enter into new BITs. Where such treaties are in force, they take precedence over the Guidelines.

The impact of BITs on customary international law regarding expropriation is debated. Professor Sonarajah offers a skeptical view:

> Consistent acceptance of a norm in bilateral treaties could convert that norm into a principle of international law. But, it is unlikely that such a view can be taken of bilateral investment treaty provisions on compensation. It has already been pointed out that the divergence in standards used and the fact that many of them provide for valuation of compensation to be made by national authorities make the possibility of such treaties creating a norm as to the standard of compensation remote.

M. Sornarajah, *The International Law of Foreign Investment* 40-41 (2d ed. 2004). In recent years, however, a number of arbitral tribunals have concluded that consistent state practice through the use of BITs and other investment agreements has reshaped customary international law. As one tribunal put it:

> The requirement of compensation to be "just" and representative of the "genuine value of the investment affected" evokes the famous Hull Formula, which provided for

the payment of prompt, adequate and effective compensation for the taking of foreign owned property. That formula was controversial. . . . But in the end, the international community put aside this controversy, surmounting it by the conclusion of more than 2,200 bilateral (and a few multilateral) investment treaties. Today these treaties are truly universal in their reach and essential provisions. They concordantly provide for payment of "just compensation," representing the "genuine" or "fair market" value of the property taken. . . .

The possibility of payment of compensation determined by the law of the host State or by the circumstances of the host State has disappeared from contemporary international law as it is expressed in investment treaties in such extraordinary numbers, and with such concordant provisions, as to have reshaped the body of customary international law itself.

CME Czech Republic B.V. v. Czech Republic, Final Award, March 14, 2003, paras. 497-498.

Many states, including the United States, have sought the promulgation of a comprehensive, multilateral treaty governing foreign direct investment. Supporters wanted a uniform set of rules to govern foreign investment comparable to the rules on trade associated with the World Trade Organization. In particular, supporters hoped for liberal rules on admission of investments, treatment for all foreign investors equivalent to that given to nationals or most favored nations, whichever was more favorable, strong legal protections in cases of expropriations, including the prompt, adequate, and effective standard for compensation, and effective dispute settlement procedures.

The OECD began to draft such an agreement, the proposed Multilateral Agreement on Investment (MAI), in 1995, building on existing BITs, the World Bank Guidelines, NAFTA, and various other multilateral agreements with investment provisions. Initially, it appeared that the MAI was headed for rapid completion and broad acceptance. But the MAI soon ran into major obstacles. The United States insisted on investor protections comparable to those in the typical U.S. BIT; other states feared that developing countries would not accept investor protections stronger than those contained in most European BITs, which are generally less favorable to investors than U.S. BITs. Participants in the negotiations disagreed on the nature and extent of possible exceptions to the general principles of the treaty, including exceptions for public order, culture, and regional economic integration organizations. Perhaps most important, MAI supporters encountered unexpectedly strong opposition from environmental and labor groups, who feared the new treaty would impair national efforts at strengthening environmental and labor standards. As a result, the effort to create the MAI ground to a halt. Similar efforts to create a comprehensive set of investment rules in the WTO and elsewhere have met with only limited success.

Although FDI declined substantially during the global financial crisis that began in fall 2008, FDI has been growing in recent years and remains a major driver of the international economy. Moreover, despite the proliferation of BITs and related agreements specifying prompt, adequate, and effective as the standard for compensation for expropriated assets, disputes over expropriation continue. In some cases, these disputes are resolved through negotiation or international arbitration. In Ecuador, for example, a U.S. oil company won a $1.76 billion award in 2013, following Ecuador's termination of the company's participation contract. From 2007 to 2010, Venezuela nationalized a range of companies and assets, in industries such as oil, cement, and food processing. In May 2009, Venezuela's National Assembly passed legislation empowering the president to extend the government's control over the oil industry. The legislation states that foreign service firms should be paid book value for their assets, less deductions for labor and environmental costs, that payment may take the form of bonds rather than cash, and that disputes should be resolved exclusively in Venezuelan courts. Venezuela's actions have generated multiple suits against it before the International Centre for Settlement of Investment Disputes and other fora. For more on expropriation, see Chapter 12.

Notes and Questions

1. What role should the World Bank Guidelines play in a dispute over the compensation to be paid to a foreign investor for the expropriation of the investor's property, assuming no BIT or other treaty is directly on point?

2. How should one judge the effectiveness of soft law instruments such as the World Bank Guidelines? What are the advantages and disadvantages of such instruments in comparison to treaties or custom?

3. How would a decision maker know whether the World Bank Guidelines are becoming or have become hard law in the sense of conferring legally binding rights on investors? If the guidelines are becoming hard law, might one expect the Guidelines to be invoked in international arbitrations? In other fora?

4. Recall the discussion at the beginning of this section on the ways in which different legal instruments may be hard or soft on various criteria. How hard or soft are the World Bank Guidelines? Note that the Guidelines are not legally binding, but they do help to clarify the meaning of "appropriate compensation," a previously vague concept in customary international law. What are the implications of failure to comply with soft law instruments such as the Guidelines?

F. Note on Incorporating Principles from Domestic Law

Article 38 of the Statute of the International Court of Justice identifies "general principles of law recognized by civilized nations" as a source of law separate from (and therefore implicitly independent of) treaties and custom. As a source of law, general principles are the subject of considerable debate, with respect to both their content and their jurisprudential underpinnings. Some positivist scholars maintain that general principles can be treated as binding only when states manifest their consent through widespread recognition of such principles as international law. Other scholars suggest general principles can be derived in part from natural law, without reference to state consent. Most scholars, however, regard general principles as those principles so basic to developed legal orders that they arise in most national legal systems and can therefore be ascertained through an objective, comparative assessment of municipal law in the relevant states.

In the South West Africa cases, which challenged apartheid as it was administered under the League of Nations mandate system, the applicants relied on general principles (in addition to treaties and custom) for recognition of non-discrimination as a legal norm. In his dissenting opinion, Judge Tanaka considered the nature and evolution of general principles as a source of international law.

Dissenting Opinion of Judge Tanaka

1966 I.C.J. Rep. 6 (July 18)

The question is whether the legal norm of non-discrimination or non-separation denying the practice of apartheid can be recognized as a principle enunciated in [Article 38, 1(c) of the ICJ Statute]. . . .

To decide this question we must clarify the meaning of "general principles of law". To restrict the meaning to private law principles or principles of procedural law seems from the viewpoint of literal interpretation untenable. So far as the "general principles of law" are not qualified, the "law" must be understood to embrace all branches of law, including municipal law, public law, constitutional and administrative law, private law, commercial law, substantive and procedural law, etc.

Nevertheless, analogies drawn from these laws should not be made mechanically, that is to say, to borrow the expression of Lord McNair, "by means of importing private law institutions 'lock, stock and barrel' ready-made and fully equipped with a set of rules".

What international law can with advantage borrow from these sources must be from the viewpoint of underlying or guiding "principles". These principles, therefore, must not be limited to statutory provisions and institutions of national laws: they must be extended to the fundamental concepts of each branch of law as well as to law in general so far as these can be considered as "recognized by civilized nations."

Accordingly, the general principles of law in the sense of Article 38, paragraph 1 (c), are not limited to certain basic principles of law such as the limitation of State sovereignty, third-party judgment, limitation of the right of self-defence, *pacta sunt servanda*, respect for acquired rights, liability for unlawful harm to one's neighbour, the principle of good faith, etc. . . .

It is beyond all doubt that the presence of laws against racial discrimination and segregation in the municipal systems of virtually every State can be established by comparative law studies. . . .

Originally, general principles are considered to be certain private law principles found by the comparative law method and applicable by way of analogy to matters of an international character . . . as we see in the case of the application of some rules of contract law to the interpretation of treaties. In the case of the international protection of human rights, on the contrary, what is involved is not the application by analogy of a principle or a norm of private law to a matter of international character, but the recognition of the juridical validity of a similar legal fact without any distinction as between the municipal and the international legal sphere.

In short, human rights . . . are not the product of a particular juridical system in the hierarchy of the legal order. . . . The uniformity of national laws on the protection of human rights is not derived, as in the cases of the law of contracts and commercial and maritime transactions, from considerations of expediency by the legislative organs or from the creative power of the custom of a community, but it already exists in spite of its more-or-less vague form. This is of nature *jus naturale* in roman law.

[After concluding that the protection of human rights falls within the general principles of international law, Tanaka continues:]

[I]n Article 38, paragraph 1 (c), some natural law elements are inherent. It extends the concept of the source of international law beyond the limit of legal positivism according to which, the States being bound only by their own will, international law is nothing but the law of the consent and auto-limitation of the State. But this viewpoint, we believe, was clearly overruled by Article 38, paragraph 1 (c), by the fact that this provision does not require the consent of States as a condition of the recognition of the general principles. . . .

The principle of equality before the law . . . is stipulated in the list of human rights recognized by the municipal system of virtually every State no matter whether the form of government be republican or monarchical and in spite of any differences in the degree of precision of the relevant provisions. This principle has become an integral part of the constitutions of most of the civilized countries in the world. . . .

From what we have seen above, the alleged norm of non-discrimination and non-separation, being based on the United Nations Charter, particularly Articles 55 (c), 56, and on numerous resolutions and declarations of the General Assembly and other organs of the United Nations, and owing to its nature as a general principle, can be regarded as a source of international law according to the provisions of Article 38, paragraph 1 (a) - (c).

In practice, courts and other tribunals rely on general principles largely as an adjunct to treaties and custom, to be invoked as necessary to supplement or extend those other forms of law or to fill gaps created when treaty and custom fail to supply all of the relevant rules for decision of a particular dispute. Principles invoked are usually general rules of procedure, evidence, or liability. For example, the Permanent Court of International Justice announced in the *Chorzow Factory* case that "it is a general conception of law that every violation of an engagement involves an obligation to make reparation." *Chorzow Factory* (Ger. v. Pol.), 1928 P.C.I.J. (Ser. A., No. 17) at 29. Other tribunals have relied on general principles for such basic precepts of law as *res judicata*, estoppel, that "a party cannot take advantage of his own wrong," that no one shall judge his or her own case, that the passage of time may bar a claim through prescription or laches, and that circumstantial evidence may be probative. Similarly, general principles have been accepted as sources for rules viewed as intrinsic to the logical function of a legal system, such as the rule that a law later in time takes precedence over an earlier law if both are from the same source. In recent years, general principles have been invoked with particular frequency in the context of international criminal law proceedings, as recently created international criminal tribunals draw on the hundreds of years of experience of national courts in dealing with criminal law matters.

PART II

Participants in the International Legal Process

Treaties, custom, soft law, and other outcomes of the international lawmaking process result from the interaction of diverse participants, each making claims about the lawfulness of its own conduct or that of another actor. Identifying these participants more explicitly and understanding the roles they play in the international legal process is essential and is the goal of the following two chapters. Chapter 3 addresses states and organizations of states, entities that orthodox international law regards as the principal, if not sole, relevant actors. Chapter 4 examines entities other than states that contemporary international law treats as key participants, namely non-governmental organizations (NGOs), corporations, and substate entities, in particular states of the United States.

Both particip*ants* and particip*ation* come in a variety of forms. The actors themselves may be territorially organized, as are states, subfederal entities (such as U.S. states), or autonomous units within states (such as Hong Kong). Indeed, the notion that states possess unique authority and control over territory has served as the foundation for their predominant—though far from exclusive—role in international law. International organizations start as an agent of the states that create them (usually via treaty), but can come to take on an identity separate from their members, as their organs or officials implement the organization's goals. Still, other key participants lack such a nexus to territory. NGOs are principally entities based on shared agendas, comprised of like-minded individuals within one or more states. Business entities are organized for an economic goal. And all these actors are, in a sense, the result of decisions by individuals to combine their talents in different spheres and for various purposes.

Why pursue international law's treatment of these participants as a discrete subject of inquiry rather than merely the substantive norms they eventually agree upon? First, the norms resulting from law making very much reflect who is involved in that law making. It is thus critical to understand what access to lawmaking arenas the international legal process provides. Second, international legal norms themselves address the question of participation. That is, international law has rules as to which entities are entitled to take part in different stages of the legal process. Third, to comprehend the meaning of international norms (or any norms for that matter) requires examining who exactly has rights and duties. International law has

101

recognized many rights and duties for states, but fewer for non-state actors. Finally, the implementation of norms depends very much upon different roles played by various actors. Thus, international organizations and NGOs will have significant roles in securing compliance with international law.

THE STATE AND BEYOND

The very term "law of nations" captured the idea that international law was for much of its history a law by and about states. As Stephen Krasner explains, a community that has achieved statehood (as opposed to the other ways in which actors might participate) has a special place in international law and relations. It possesses a bundle of attributes he calls (in a term that might make international lawyers cringe a bit) "international legal sovereignty":

Stephen D. Krasner, *Sovereignty: Organized Hypocrisy*
14-20 (1999)

. . . [I]nternational legal sovereignty has been concerned with establishing the status of a political entity in the international system. Is a state recognized by other states? Is it accepted as a juridical equal? Are its representatives entitled to diplomatic immunity? Can it be a member of international organizations? Can its representatives enter into agreements with other entities? . . .

Almost all rulers have sought international legal sovereignty, the recognition of other states, because it provides them with both material and normative resources. Sovereignty can be conceived of as "a ticket of general admission to the international arena." All recognized states have juridical equality. International law is based on the consent of states. Recognized states can enter into treaties with each other, and these treaties will generally be operative even if the government changes. Dependent or subordinate territories do not generally have the right to conclude international agreements (although, as with everything else in the international system, there are exceptions), giving the central or recognized authority a monopoly over formal arrangements with other states. . . .

By facilitating accords, international legal sovereignty offers the possibility for rulers to secure external resources that can enhance their ability to stay in power and to promote the security, economic, and ideational interests of their constituents. The rulers of internationally recognized states can sit at the table. Entering into certain kinds of contracts, such as alliances, can enhance security by reducing uncertainty about the commitment of other actors. Membership in international financial institutions opens the possibility, although not the assurance, of securing foreign capital. Even if rulers have entered into accords that have far-reaching effects on their domestic autonomy, such as the European Union, they have nothing to lose by retaining their international legal sovereignty, including their formal right to withdraw from any international agreements. . . .

. . . The attractiveness of international legal sovereignty can also be understood from a more sociological or cognitive perspective. Recognition as a state is a widely, almost universally understood construct in the contemporary world. . . . Recognition gives the ruler the opportunity to play on the international stage; even if it is only a bit part, parading at the United Nations or shaking hands with the president of the United States or the chancellor of Germany, can enhance the standing of a ruler among his or her own followers. . . .

In light of this special role for states, Chapter 3 seeks to elaborate how international law has regulated the creation, transformation, and institutionalized cooperation of states.

Notwithstanding the many advantages of statehood on the global plane, individuals and groups seeking a place in making and applying international law have never assumed that only the state should possess rights (substantive or participatory) or duties. As discussed in Chapter 1, other organized entities have long played a role in international affairs. Although states have resisted recognizing these other entities as bona fide international actors and have preferred to see them as creatures of a particular state, these entities have continued to pursue their own interests independently. They have appraised the behavior of other actors and responded to attempts by those actors to judge their actions. This participation began long ago but accelerated in the second half of the twentieth century. Jessica Mathews has written:

Jessica Mathews, *Power Shift*

For. Aff. 50, 50-51 (Jan./Feb. 1997)

The end of the Cold War has brought no mere adjustment among states but a novel redistribution of power among states, markets, and civil society. National governments are not simply losing autonomy in a globalizing economy. They are sharing powers . . . with businesses, with international organizations, and with a multitude of citizens groups, known as nongovernmental organizations (NGOs). . . .

The absolutes of the Westphalian system—territorially fixed states where everything of value lies within some states' borders; a single, secular authority governing each territory and representing it outside its borders; and no authority above states—are all dissolving. Increasingly, resources and threats that matter, including money, information, pollution, and popular culture, circulate and shape lives and economies with little regard for political boundaries. . . . Even the most powerful states find the marketplace and international public opinion compelling them more often to follow a particular course. . . .

The most powerful engine of change in the relative decline of states and the rise of nonstate actors is the computer and telecommunications revolution. . . . Widely accessible and affordable technology has broken governments' monopoly on the collection and management of large amounts of information and deprived governments of the deference they enjoyed because of it. In every sphere of activity, instantaneous access to information and the ability to put it to use multiplies the number of players who matter and reduces the number who command great authority. . . .

In a similar vein, the political scientist Susan Strange has found corporations and market forces so powerful and impervious to government control as to speak of the "retreat of the state," and Peter Spiro has questioned whether non-governmental organizations constitute a new form of "global potentates."

Formal doctrine has nonetheless been slow to accept this reality, but the trend toward increased participation by these non-state actors seems irreversible. Chapter 4 thus examines how these actors have managed to achieve an independent voice on the international stage. In particular, it focuses upon the tensions between the strategies these actors undertake and the paradigm that grants certain roles only to states. The result is, if not a full-fledged "retreat" of the state, an undeniable challenge to its hitherto dominant role in international law.

3

The Traditional Actors: States and International Organizations

The organization of human communities into states remains a principal fact of political life in the international arena. States have been the dominant unit in international relations since at least the Peace of Westphalia in 1648, and much legal regulation of international relations still centers on the resolution of claims by states. Orthodox international law doctrine regarded states as the primary, or even sole, actors in international law—the only entities that scholars considered to enjoy full "international legal personality," meaning that they could create and be the subject of international legal obligations. This view has meshed with the dominant view of international relations theory as well as diplomacy—realism—that regards states as the critical actors in international relations.

In this chapter, we seek to gain an understanding of the state as a participant in the legal process. The chapter begins by analyzing how states are formed and whether international norms have emerged to regulate or constrain that process. We then turn to the process by which states change, whether through disintegration, secession, or other means. Third, we turn to the institutions within states that have legal authority and control—namely, governments—and consider the extent to which international law concerns itself with such internal matters. Finally, this chapter considers the formation of international institutions composed of states and how such organizations can become independent players in the interstate system. As we examine these norms of participation, the basic assumption that states are the primary actors in international law and international relations itself becomes the subject of scrutiny.

I. THE FORMATION AND BREAKUP OF STATES: CRIMEA'S SEPARATION FROM UKRAINE

Although the world may seem like a system of old and stable states, much of the contemporary state system is very recent. Much of Africa, Asia, and even Eastern Europe is composed of relatively new, and in some cases unstable, states. The recent vintage and potential evanescence of the contemporary makeup of states means that legal issues constantly arise regarding the formation of states. The extent to which law actually controls or affects decision makers involved in the process of state formation—whether those within a putative state or those outside it deciding how to react to it—remains a central concern in the international legal process.

The goals for this Problem include:

- to understand the international legal rules and principles that address which entities constitute a state;
- to understand the various processes by which states are formed and the role of law in these processes;
- to understand which groups have the right to form their own state, and the legal effects of recognition by other states; and
- to understand the role of different international actors in resolving contested claims over statehood.

For at least the last 60 years, states have emerged on the global stage through the following processes:

1. Decolonization: This refers to the process by which states became independent from self-identified colonial empires, principally those of the United Kingdom and France, but also those of Spain and Portugal (principally in Latin America), Belgium, the Netherlands, Germany, the Ottoman Empire, and, to some extent, the United States. Independence might have resulted from the peaceful transfer of power (as with much of the British Empire) or wars of independence (as with French Indochina). Decolonization is virtually complete today. The United Nations has taken an active role in promoting and supervising decolonization.

2. Secession: With secession, one territory breaks off from a nonimperial state to form a new state, either peacefully or as a result of armed conflict. Since World War II, successful secession has been rare, but not nonexistent. Bangladesh (East Pakistan) seceded from Pakistan after a short war in 1971; Eritrea seceded from Ethiopia in 1993 after a conflict lasting more than 30 years; South Sudan seceded from Sudan in 2011 following a long struggle. The departure of the three Baltic states—Estonia, Latvia, and Lithuania—from the Soviet Union in 1990 may also be seen as a secession, although all three were independent states from the end of World War I until their annexation by the USSR in 1940, and the Soviet Union was in the process of dissolution at the time of their separation.

3. Dissolution: Dissolution is the process by which a state dissolves into two or more states, with the former state ceasing to exist. The most significant dissolutions in recent years have been those of Yugoslavia, the USSR, and Czechoslovakia, although other states (for instance, Somalia) may also be in the midst of such processes as well.

4. Merger: This is the creation of one state by the union of two states. The merger of North and South Yemen in 1990 and the merger of the Federal Republic of Germany and the German Democratic Republic in 1990 are prime examples. The two states may create an entirely new entity (Yemen), or one state may be absorbed into the second (Germany).

5. Peace Treaties: Historically, states have also emerged from peace settlements after major wars, such as with the creation of new states in Eastern Europe after World War I.

A. The Problem

Crimea is a peninsula jutting into the Black Sea, connected by a thin strip of land to Ukraine and separated by a narrow strait from Russia. Fifty-eight percent of Crimea's population identify themselves as ethnic Russian and speak Russian, 24 percent self-identify

Ukraine and its Neighbors
SOURCE: CIA World Factbook

as Ukrainian, and 12 percent belong the Tatar people, a Turkic-speaking Muslim minority. From 1920 to 1954, despite its location near Ukraine, Crimea was part of the Russian republic within the USSR. In 1954, Soviet premier Nikita Khrushchev transferred Crimea from the Russian republic to the Ukrainian republic—at that time a purely symbolic move as Crimea, along with the rest of Ukraine, remained within the USSR. During the years of the Soviet Union, Crimea was also the home of the USSR's Black Sea Fleet.

In 1991, as the USSR was dissolving into fifteen different states, Ukraine voted for independence; within Crimea only 54 percent favored independence because many of Crimea's Russians wished to remain linked with Russia. Following Ukraine's independence in 1991, Crimea became an "Autonomous Republic" within Ukraine, with significant authority to regulate local issues independently of the central government. A 1997 Ukraine-Russia treaty allowed Russia to maintain the former USSR fleet in Crimea, although any Russian troop increases or major troop movements required Ukrainian approval.

Ukraine as a whole features differing concentrations of ethnic groups, with high concentrations of ethnic Russians in the east (bordering Russia). Even so, ethnic Ukrainians comprise the majority of the population in all Ukrainian provinces except Crimea, and many ethnic Russians identify first as Ukrainian citizens. Since Ukrainian independence, there has been little evidence of discrimination against Russian speakers in Crimea or elsewhere in the country. UN human rights reviews of Ukraine in 2011, 2012, and 2013 mentioned allegations of ethnic discrimination against other ethnic groups, but not ethnic Russians.

Since the end of the USSR, Ukraine has sought closer ties with Western and Central Europe, with a long-term goal of membership in the European Union (EU). Many ethnic Russians in Ukraine and Crimea continue to value close ties to Russia. The Russian government, consistent with a centuries-old approach to its neighbors, fears that close ties between Ukraine and Europe will harm Russian interests.

In November 2013, after Ukraine's president, seemingly under pressure from Moscow, announced that he was abandoning a trade agreement with the EU in favor of ties with Russia, pro-EU protests began. In February 2014, the protestors took control of the capital, the president fled to Russia, and Ukraine's parliament replaced him with an interim, pro-Western government. In response, pro-Russia protests began in Crimea, with encouragement—and perhaps outright instigation—by Russia, calling for reunification of Crimea with Russia. Russia unilaterally increased its troop levels in Crimea, took control of several Ukrainian military bases, and amassed thousands of troops on the Russia-Ukraine border. Pro-Russia gunmen seized government buildings in Crimea and soon after in eastern Ukrainian cities; Russia disclaimed these forces as its own.

In March 2014, Crimea's parliament voted unanimously to declare independence and seek to join Russia if the population supported such a move in a referendum. Days later Crimea held a vote. The official results showed that over 95 percent of voters supported union with Russia. Russia then promptly signed a treaty with Crimea's leaders and amended its Constitution, thereby absorbing Crimea into Russia. Not since the end of World War II had one permanent member of the Security Council effectively absorbed part of its neighbor's territory. Russia's actions were denounced by the UN General Assembly, the EU, and the United States, although Russia vetoed any action in the UN Security Council. In the months that followed, other cities in eastern Ukraine, including the large city of Donetsk, declared their separation from Ukraine and desire to join Russia. Ukraine's government engaged in serious clashes with pro-Russia militias in these areas, leading to significant casualties on both sides. In response, the United States and European Union stepped up a series of economic sanctions on Russia, leading to Russian counter-sanctions.

B. What Is a State? Requisites of Statehood

Crimea's vote to form an independent state, and then to join the Russian federation, raised a key legal question—what are the international law criteria for a new state? The very actors that prescribe law have attempted to make law regarding the grounds for participation in that law making—for who may join the club or lose membership in it.

In the past, international law offered a deceptively simple, black-letter answer to these questions. As stated in the 1933 Convention on the Rights and Duties of States (the Montevideo Convention), concluded among 16 states in the Western hemisphere:

> The state as a person of international law should possess the following qualifications:
> a) a permanent population; b) a defined territory; c) government; d) capacity to enter into relations with the other states.

But in practice, global elites have interpreted the so-called Montevideo criteria quite flexibly. As for "permanent population," some entities recognized as states have very small populations, such as the Pacific Island state of Nauru (9,500), or the city-state of San Marino (33,000). The requirement of "a defined territory" has not prevented the international community from regarding as states entities with disputed or even unknown boundaries, such as Israel, with its half-century dispute with its Arab neighbors; the two Koreas, with their claims to each other's territory; or the states of the Arabian peninsula, whose desert borders were often unknown. New states have emerged even without a full capacity to enter into foreign relations with other states. The national defense of Liechtenstein and Monaco, both regarded for many years as states (and both members of numerous international organizations), is the responsibility of Switzerland and France, respectively. Micronesia, Palau, the Cook Islands, and Niue are termed "freely associated states": the defense of Micronesia and Palau is controlled by the United States under agreements of free association that accompanied their independence; the foreign and defense relations of the Cook Islands and Niue are controlled by New Zealand. The first two are members of the United Nations; the last two are not.

Equally important, what has been the reaction of the international community when a state loses one of the traits listed in the Montevideo Convention? This issue has arisen most visibly with respect to the third criterion, when a government has fled or been disbanded due to military occupation or when internal strife has eliminated any effective power of the central government. During World War II, states did not regard the occupation of most countries in Western Europe as eliminating their legal status as states; rather, such states were regarded as occupied nations. Similarly, Kuwait did not lose its legal status despite Iraq's occupation from August 1990 to April 1991. During much of the Cold War, the states of Eastern Europe effectively lost their ability to conduct foreign and defense relations independent of the USSR and yet continued to be regarded as states. Today, certain states remain under the firm control of neighbors, such as Bhutan vis-à-vis India. As for collapsed governments, no state has claimed that the collapse of central government control in Somalia and Afghanistan during much of the last three decades has deprived them of statehood.

Notes and Questions

1. What underlying purposes do the Montevideo criteria of statehood advance? Is it possible to imagine an entity that fulfills the purposes of statehood but lacks some of these attributes?

2. What would be the consequence of the view that entities that cease to fulfill all of the Montevideo criteria are no longer states with respect to the integrity of land, sea, and air boundaries; treaty relations; the holders of the entity's passports; and the assets of the entity in foreign lands?

3. During the days when Ukrainian forces had no control over Crimea and before its absorption by Russia, was it an independent state?

C. Separation Anxiety: Self-Determination and Its Limits

Statehood is not a static condition. As noted above, states are born (and disappear) through a variety of processes, both peaceful and violent. Does international law have norms regarding the legitimacy of separation from states? On the one hand, the traditional criteria suggest that statehood is about effective power: a state exists and enjoys all the benefits of statehood as long as the government enjoys effective control over the territory. States have generally recognized the right of a state to defend itself against internal threats to its unity, including through armed force. International law thus has a strong presumption in favor of the continuity of states. On the other hand, groups within a state might have legitimate reasons to separate from the state, including repression by the central government. Does international law make an ex ante choice between the existing state and those attempting to secede from it, or does it simply ratify the outcome of a civil war, whether victory for the government or for those seceding?

The starting point for the rules on separation is the "principle of equal rights and self-determination of peoples" in Article 1 of the UN Charter. But which group or groups—in the Crimea situation, for example—qualify as a "people" entitled to self-determination? The people of Ukraine as a whole, the people of Crimea, Russian speakers in Crimea (as well as elsewhere in Ukraine), or some other group? To help answer these questions, self-determination must be considered in its historical context.

1. The Pre-UN Charter Era

The primarily Eurocentric form of international law that emerged in the seventeenth century did not generally regard communities other than states as participants in the process of making international law. Instead, the law of nations became the handmaiden of the policies of many states to expand their spheres of influence through colonialism. Lands not under the control of any state were termed *terra nullius* (empty land), subject to legal acquisition by states. The peoples living in those lands were treated, for most purposes, no differently from the flora and fauna. Imperial powers differentiated between their core territory inhabited by their citizens—the metropolitan area—and colonial territories, whose inhabitants were not full members of the state.

International law developed an entire doctrine on colonies. For example, a territory became a so-called protectorate if its leaders had concluded some form of agreement with the metropole giving the latter certain authority over it, although these agreements were often coerced. Regardless of the locutions used, at the core of international law's approach to colonialism was the legal responsibility of the metropole over the territory and the corresponding right of the metropole to govern the colony as it saw fit. States could swap, combine, or divide up colonies as a matter of power politics. This practice reached its apogee in the Berlin West Africa Conference of 1884 and 1885, where 13 European states divided up much of the continent through an international agreement.

The Treaty of Versailles ending World War I constituted a significant shift in international law's treatment of colonial lands and peoples. The losing powers—Germany, Austria-Hungary, and the Ottoman Empire—were stripped of their colonies. Their overseas colonies were placed under a new legal regime, the Mandates system of the League of Nations, on the theory, as stated in the League's Covenant, that "for peoples not yet able to stand by themselves under the strenuous conditions of the modern world . . . the tutelage of such peoples should be entrusted to advanced nations who by reason of their resources, their experience or their geographical position can best undertake this responsibility." Covenant of the League of Nations, art. XXII. The victorious powers did not, however, place any of their own colonies under the Mandates system.

Peoples within Europe were treated differently. President Wilson had spoken during the war of the need for national groups to exercise self-government as much as feasible. In a 1918, speech to Congress, he stated: "Self-determination is not a mere phrase; it is an imperative principle of action which statesmen will henceforth ignore at their peril." The Allies adopted this position at their peace conferences in their treatment of the Central Powers. As a result, the Austro-Hungarian and Ottoman empires were dissolved and Russia and Germany lost territory, leading to the creation of new states: Czechoslovakia, Yugoslavia, Finland, Estonia, Latvia, Lithuania, and Poland. Borders were drawn to concentrate national groups within states to the extent politics and geography allowed for it. The new states had their own minorities, though the League recognized some minority rights for groups who found themselves outside the state where their ethnic kin were the majority (e.g., Hungarians in Romania or Germans in Poland).

Because of these new minorities, the League soon faced a number of self-determination claims. Among the claimants were the people of the Aaland Islands, an archipelago of about 300 small islands between southern Finland and southern Sweden. In the early nineteenth century, as a result of various wars between Sweden and Russia, Sweden, which had administered Finland and the adjacent islands, ceded all those lands to Russia. In 1917, after the outbreak of the Russian Revolution, Finland declared independence from Russia. The Aalanders, nearly all Swedish in familial origin and Swedish speakers, sought unification with their kin in Sweden. They insisted on a plebiscite for their status, which Finland refused to authorize. The League created an International Committee of Jurists to determine whether the League could address the issue or whether it was solely within the domestic jurisdiction of Finland (which, under the Covenant of the League, would deny it the ability to act). The Committee's report included the following passages:

Report of the International Committee of Jurists Entrusted by the Council of the League of Nations with the Task of Giving an Advisory Opinion upon the Legal Aspects of the Aaland Islands Question

League of Nations Official Journal, Special Supp. No. 3, at 5-10 (1920)

OCTOBER, 1920.

League of Nations — Official Journal.

THE PRINCIPLE OF SELF-DETERMINATION AND THE RIGHTS OF PEOPLES.

Although the principle of self-determination of peoples plays an important part in modern political thought, especially since the Great War, it must be pointed out that there is no mention of it in the Covenant of the League of Nations. The recognition of this principle in a certain number of international treaties cannot be considered as sufficient to put it upon the same footing as a positive rule of the Law of Nations.

On the contrary, in the absence of express provisions in international treaties, the right of disposing of national territory is essentially an attribute of the sovereignty of every State. Positive International Law does not recognise the right of national groups, as such, to separate themselves from the State of which they form part by the simple expression of a wish. . . . Generally speaking, the grant or refusal of the right to a portion of its population of determining its own political fate by plebiscite or by some other method, is, exclusively, an attribute of the sovereignty of every State which is definitively constituted. . . . Any other solution would amount to an infringement of sovereign rights of a State and would involve the risk of creating difficulties and a lack of stability which would not only be contrary to the very idea embodied in the term "State," but would also endanger the interests of the international community. . . .

The Commission, in affirming these principles, does not give an opinion concerning the question as to whether a manifest and continued abuse of sovereign power, to the detriment of a section of the population of a State, would, if such circumstances arose, give to an international dispute, arising therefrom, such a character that its object should be considered as one which is not confined to the domestic jurisdiction of the State concerned, but comes within the sphere of action of the League of Nations. . . .

DE FACTO AND DE JURE CONSIDERATIONS. THEIR INTERNATIONAL CHARACTER.

3. It must, however, be observed that all that has been said concerning the attributes of the sovereignty of a State, generally speaking, only applies to a nation which is definitively constituted as a sovereign State and an independent member of the international community and so long as it continues to possess these characteristics. From the point of view of both domestic and international law, the formation, transformation and dismemberment of States as a result of revolutions and wars create situations of fact which, to a large extent, cannot be met by the application of the normal rules of positive law. . . . [I]f the essential basis of these rules, that is to say, territorial sovereignty, is lacking, either because the State is not yet fully formed or because it is undergoing transformation or dissolution, the situation is obscure and uncertain from a legal point of view, and will not become clear until the period of development is completed and a definite new situation, which is normal in respect to territorial sovereignty, has been established.

This transition from a *de facto* situation to a normal situation *de jure* cannot be considered as one confined entirely within the domestic jurisdiction of a State. It tends to lead to readjustments between the members of the international community and to alterations in their territorial and legal status; consequently, this transition interests the community of States very deeply both from political and legal standpoints.

SELF-DETERMINATION AS APPLIED TO *DE FACTO* SITUATIONS. ITS FORMS.

Under such circumstances, the principle of self-determination of peoples may be called into play. New aspirations of certain sections of a nation, which are sometimes based on old traditions or on a common language and civilisation, may come to the surface and produce effects which must be taken into account in the interests of the internal and external peace of nations. . . .

HISTORICAL DEVELOPMENT OF FINLAND.

In the light of the foregoing, the question has to be decided as to whether, from the standpoint of territorial sovereignty, the situation of the Aaland Islands in the independent State of Finland is of a definite and normal character, or whether it is a transitory or not fully developed situation. . . .

THE PURPORT OF THE FINNISH DECLARATION OF INDEPENDENCE.

The Aaland Islands were undoubtedly part of Finland during the period of Russian rule. Must they, for this reason alone, be considered as definitely incorporated *de jure* in the State of Finland which was formed as a result of the events described above?

The Commission finds it impossible to admit this. The extent and nature of the political changes, which take place as facts and outside the domain of law, are necessarily limited by the results actually produced. . . . If one part of a State actually separates itself from that State, the separation is necessarily limited in its effect to the population of the territory which has taken part in the act of separation. . . . It may even be said that if a separation occurs from a political organism which is more or less autonomous, and which is itself *de facto* in process of political transformation, this organism cannot at the very moment when it transforms itself outside the domain of positive law invoke the principles of this law in order to force upon a national group a political status which the latter refuses to accept. . . .

For these reasons, Finland cannot claim that the future of the Aaland Islands should be the same as hers simply because of the one fact that the Islands formerly formed part of the Finnish political organisation in the Russian Empire.

Based on these views, the Committee decided that the question of the islands' status was not solely within the domestic jurisdiction of Finland and that the League's Council was competent to make a recommendation. The League then appointed a Commission of Rapporteurs (representatives of member states) to recommend a solution to the problem. Its report from 1921 included the following:

The Aaland Islands Question: Report Submitted to the Council of the League of Nations by the Commission of Rapporteurs

League of Nations Doc. B7/21/68/106 (1921)

First of all, we must eliminate an analogy which cannot be pleaded justly.

The Aalanders and the Swedes are wrong in citing the example of Finland, which, in determining her own fate, has succeeded, thanks to the results of the great war, in freeing herself from her dependence on Russia. . . . Finland has been an autonomous State since long before the war, i.e. from 1809. . . . [N]o one will dispute the natural right of the Finns, born of inherent justice, to proclaim their independence; but this right which Finland possessed does not provide any evidence in support of the demand of the Aalanders. The Aaland Archipelago is only a small part of the Finnish territory, and the Aaland population a small fraction of the Finnish nation. Now, it is evident that one cannot treat a small minority, a small fraction of a people, in the same manner and on the same footing as a nation taken as a whole.

. . . [Moreover,] Finland has been oppressed and persecuted, her tenderest feelings have been wounded by the disloyal and brutal conduct of Russia. The Aalanders have neither been persecuted nor oppressed by Finland. . . . It is true that, as a result of quite exceptional conditions, the Aaland population is threatened in its language and its culture. But this is not the result of a policy of oppression; on the contrary, we feel certain that it is possible to appeal to the good will of the Finnish Government to preserve and protect the language and the culture which are so precious to the Aalanders. . . .

. . . Is it possible to admit as an absolute rule that a minority of the population of a State, which is definitely constituted and perfectly capable of fulfilling its duties as such, has the right of separating itself from her in order to be incorporated in another State or to declare its independence? The answer can only be in the negative. To concede to minorities . . . the right of withdrawing from the community to which they belong, because it is their wish or their good pleasure, would be to destroy order and stability within States and to inaugurate anarchy in international life. . . .

The separation of a minority from the State of which it forms a part and its incorporation in another State can only be considered as an altogether exceptional solution, a last resort when the State lacks either the will or the power to enact and apply just and effective guarantees.

In the case of the Aalanders, the important question is the protection of their language—the Swedish language. . . . We appreciate the ardent desire, the resolute wish of the Aaland population, proud in its democratic simplicity and eager for independence, to preserve intact the Swedish language and culture—their heritage from their ancestors. The conviction that their language is threatened and can only be saved by union with Sweden has profoundly moved this gallant little race, which inhabits, from an international point of view, one of the most interesting regions of Europe. . . .

We recognise that the Aaland population, by reason of its insular position and its strong tradition, forms a group apart in Finland, not only distinct from the Finnish population, but also in certain respects distinct from the Swedish-speaking population. . . . We admit also that the fear fostered by the Aalanders of being little by little submerged by the Finnish invasion has good grounds. . . . If it were true that incorporation with Sweden was the only means of preserving its Swedish language for Aaland, we should not have hesitated to consider this solution. But such is not the case. There is no need for a separation. The Finnish State is ready to grant the inhabitants satisfactory guarantees and faithfully observe the engagement which it will enter into with them: of this we have no doubt. . . .

[The Commission then recommends strengthening the existing Finnish statute that gave autonomy to the islands regarding schools and language.]

However, in the event that Finland . . . refused to grant the Aaland population the guarantees which we have just detailed, there would be another possible solution, and it is exactly the one which we wish to eliminate. The interest of the Aalanders, the interests of a durable peace in the Baltic, would then force us to advise the separation of the islands from Finland, based on the wishes of the inhabitants which would be freely expressed by means of a plebiscite. . . .

_____

In the end, the League of Nations recommended that the islands remain part of Finland, but be subject to a special regime providing for their demilitarization and a special autonomy regime that included, for instance, the teaching of Swedish in schools. The parties accepted the recommendation, and this regime, which has been amended several times, survives to the present day.

2. Self-Determination After the UN Charter

In the years leading up to World War II, the notion of self-determination received a significant blow, as Adolf Hitler invoked it as an excuse for unifying German-speaking peoples in Europe into one Reich. Moreover, after the war, when the victorious Allies came together to prepare the UN Charter, those states with colonies still clung to them. As a result, the Charter offered only the briefest provisions about self-determination and essentially saw the principle as limited to states as they currently existed, rather than as applying to colonies or minorities within states.

United Nations Charter
_(1945)_

Article 1

[The purposes of the United Nations are:] 2. To develop friendly relations among nations based on respect for the principle of equal rights and self-determination of peoples, and to take other appropriate measures to strengthen universal peace. . . .

Article 73

Members of the United Nations which have or assume responsibilities for the administration of territories whose peoples have not yet attained a full measure of self-government recognize the principle that the interests of the inhabitants of these territories are paramount, and accept as a sacred trust the obligation to promote to the utmost . . . the well-being of the inhabitants of these territories, and, to this end:

    a. to ensure, with due respect for the culture of the peoples concerned, their political, economic, social, and educational advancement, their just treatment, and their protection against abuses;

    b. to develop self-government, to take due account of the political aspirations of the peoples, and to assist them in the progressive development of their free political institutions, according to the particular circumstances of each territory and its peoples and their varying stages of advancement. . . .

_____

In addition to these provisions, the drafters included in the Charter an International Trusteeship System under which the World War II Allies would administer former German, Italian, and Japanese colonies. Under the new system, the Administering states were obligated "to promote the political, economic, social and educational advancement of the inhabitants of the trust territories, and their progressive development towards self-government or independence as may be appropriate." UN Charter, art. 76. Most trust territories became independent in the 1950s and 1960s.

Despite the absence of a call for decolonization in the Charter, the colonial system soon lost legitimacy among most members of the new United Nations. Colonial territories achieved independence relatively peacefully, as in India and much of Africa, or through armed conflict, as in Indochina and Indonesia. This process began shortly after the war and was largely complete by the mid-1970s. By 1960, the newly independent states had become a dominant voice in the UN General Assembly. With support from the Soviet Union and its allies, they passed the following resolution. No states opposed the resolution, although nine (nearly all states with colonies) abstained.

Declaration on the Granting of Independence to Colonial Countries and Peoples
G.A. Res. 1514 (1960)

The General Assembly . . .

Declares that:

1. The subjection of peoples to alien subjugation, domination and exploitation constitutes a denial of fundamental human rights, is contrary to the Charter of the United Nations and is an impediment to the promotion of world peace and cooperation.

2. All peoples have the right to self-determination; by virtue of that right they freely determine their political status and freely pursue their economic, social and cultural development.

3. Inadequacy of political, economic, social or educational preparedness should never serve as a pretext for delaying independence.

4. All armed action or repressive measures of all kinds directed against dependent peoples shall cease in order to enable them to exercise peacefully and freely their right to complete independence, and the integrity of their national territory shall be respected.

5. Immediate steps shall be taken, in Trust and Non-Self-Governing Territories or all other territories which have not yet attained independence, to transfer all powers to the peoples of those territories, without any conditions or reservations, in accordance with their freely expressed will and desire, without any distinction as to race, creed or colour, in order to enable them to enjoy complete independence and freedom.

6. Any attempt aimed at the partial or total disruption of the national unity and the territorial integrity of a country is incompatible with the purposes and principles of the Charter of the United Nations. . . .

In the 1970s, in anticipation of the twenty-fifth anniversary of the United Nations, the members of the General Assembly prepared a lengthy resolution to restate or proclaim basic principles of international law concerning various aspects of the Charter. The long-titled resolution, adopted by consensus and commonly known as the Friendly Relations Declaration, included the following section that describes the contours of self-determination of states, the rights of different peoples, and the duties of states to promote self-determination:

Declaration on Principles of International Law Concerning Friendly Relations and Co-operation Among States in Accordance with the Charter of the United Nations

G.A. Res. 2625 (1970)

The principle of equal rights and self-determination of peoples . . .

The establishment of a sovereign and independent State, the free association or integration with an independent State or the emergence into any other political status freely determined by a people constitute modes of implementing the right of self-determination by that people.

Every State has the duty to refrain from any forcible action which deprives peoples referred to above in the elaboration of the present principle of their right to self-determination and freedom and independence. In their actions against and resistance to such forcible action in pursuit of the exercise of their right to self-determination, such peoples are entitled to seek and to receive support in accordance with the purposes and principles of the Charter of the United Nations.

The territory of a colony or other non-self-governing territory has, under the Charter of the United Nations, a status separate and distinct from the territory of the State administering it; and such separate and distinct status under the Charter shall exist until the people of the colony or non-self-governing territory have exercised their right of self-determination in accordance with the Charter, and particularly its purposes and principles.

Nothing in the foregoing paragraphs shall be construed as authorizing or encouraging any action which would dismember or impair, totally or in part, the territorial integrity or political unity of sovereign and independent States conducting themselves in compliance with the principle of equal rights and self-determination of peoples as described above and thus possessed of a government representing the whole people belonging to the territory without distinction as to race, creed or colour.

———————

Together, the 1960 and the 1970 Declarations, through somewhat convoluted language, elaborate on which peoples are granted which rights under the principles of self-determination. Thus:

- colonial peoples have right to full independence, and indeed the first paragraph of the 1970 Declaration makes clear that these peoples have other options as well.
- peoples within existing states do not have such a right, as the 1960 Declaration condemns disruptions of the "national unity" of a country, but the last paragraph of the 1970 Friendly Relations Declaration suggests that the unity of a state may be conditioned on its maintaining a certain kind of government.

Notes and Questions

1. What sort of options might colonial entities seek short of independence and why?

2. As you read the last paragraph of the Friendly Relations Declaration, consider whether it sets up conditions under which a state might not be entitled to its territorial integrity in the sense of an immunity from secession. How does this compare to the position of the League in the Aaland Islands case? What opening does that paragraph leave open for secession, and why would it offer it so obliquely?

3. As a normative matter, should any right to secede turn on the wishes of the seceding group or the whole state? Does the Friendly Relations Declaration create a huge new set of claimants for secession?

D. The Yugoslavia Precedents on Secession

In the years between the Friendly Relations Declaration and Crimea's attempted secession, international law on self-determination was tested and clarified during a number of important incidents. One of the most significant concerned the breakup of Yugoslavia beginning in 1990.

1. The Initial Dissolution

Yugoslavia, created after World War I from pre-war Serbia and land carved out of the Austro-Hungarian Empire, contained many ethnic groups organized into six republics:

The Former Yugoslavia

Serbia, Montenegro, Macedonia, Croatia, Bosnia-Herzegovina, and Slovenia. Most of the republics had a majority ethnic group along with significant minorities. Bosnia-Herzegovina did not contain a majority of any ethnic group but rather a plurality of Muslims and large populations of Serbs and Croats. Yugoslavia remained unified due to the strong authoritarian rule of its longtime dictator, Tito, but began to fray after his death in 1980.

In June 1991, Slovenia and Croatia declared independence, the former's independence eliciting only brief resistance from Belgrade but the latter's igniting significant armed conflict. Macedonia and Bosnia declared independence shortly thereafter. However, Serbs living in both Bosnia and Croatia opposed separation from their ethnic kin in Serbia. In January 1992, Serbs in Bosnia, acting through a self-proclaimed Assembly of the Serbian People of Bosnia-Herzegovina, declared the independence of the "Serbian Republic of Bosnia-Herzegovina."

With hostilities breaking out in Croatia and Bosnia, the European Community (EC)—the 12-member regional organization in Western Europe*—set up a Conference on Yugoslavia as a negotiation forum. The Conference created an arbitration commission, composed of the heads of five European constitutional courts, to address legal questions. The arbitration commission faced the issue of self-determination in response to a series of questions posed to it by the president of the Conference on Yugoslavia. First, the Conference president asked whether the events in Yugoslavia were best viewed as the secession of entities from Yugoslavia, as Serbia insisted, or the dissolution of the state itself, as the other republics claimed. In late 1991, the Commission published its opinion.

CONFERENCE ON YUGOSLAVIA ARBITRATION COMMISSION OPINION NO. 1

31 I.L.M. 1494 (1992)

1 - The Committee considers . . . . :

   b) that the State is commonly defined as a community which consists of a territory and a population subject to an organized political authority; that such a State is characterized by sovereignty;

   c) that, for the purpose of applying these criteria, the form of internal political organization and the constitutional provisions are mere facts, although it is necessary to take them into consideration in order to determine the Government's sway over the population and the territory;

   d) that in the case of a federal-type State, which embraces communities that possess a degree of autonomy and, moreover, participate in the exercise of political power within the framework of institutions common to the Federation, the existence of the State implies that the federal organs represent the components of the Federation and wield effective power. . . .

---

* Through the Treaty on European Union, the EC became part of a broader European Union after 1993. It currently has 28 members.

2 - The Arbitration Committee notes that:

a) - . . . the Republics have expressed their desire for independence [by referenda in Slovenia, Croatia, and Macedonia in 1990 and 1991, and by a resolution in Bosnia];

b) - The composition and workings of the essential organs of the Federation [of Yugoslavia], be they the Federal Presidency, the Federal Council, . . . the Constitutional Court or the Federal Army, no longer meet the criteria of participation and representativeness inherent in a federal State;

c) - The recourse to force has led to armed conflict between the different elements of the Federation which has caused the death of thousands of people and wrought considerable destruction within a few months. The authorities of the Federation and the Republics have shown themselves to be powerless to enforce respect for the succeeding ceasefire agreements . . . .

3 - Consequently, the Arbitration Committee is of the opinion:

- that the Socialist Federal Republic of Yugoslavia is in the process of dissolution;

- that it is incumbent upon the Republics to settle such problems of State succession as may arise from this process . . . ;

- that it is up to those Republics that so wish, to work together to form a new association endowed with the democratic institutions of their choice.

Soon after, the Commission was asked whether "the Serbian population in Croatia and Bosnia-Herzegovina, as one of the constituent peoples of Yugoslavia, ha[s] the right to self-determination." On January 11, 1992, the Commission responded.

CONFERENCE ON YUGOSLAVIA ARBITRATION COMMISSION OPINION NO. 2

31 I.L.M. 1497 (1992)

1. The Commission considers that international law as it currently stands does not spell out all the implications of the right to self-determination.

However, it is well established that, whatever the circumstances, the right to self-determination must not involve changes to existing frontiers at the time of independence (*uti possidetis juris*) except where the States concerned agree otherwise.

2. Where there are one or more groups within a State constituting one or more ethnic, religious or language communities, they have

the right to recognition of their identity under international law. [T]he now-peremptory-norms of international law require States to ensure respect for the rights of minorities. This requirement applies to all the Republics *vis-à-vis* the minorities on their territory.

The Serbian population in Bosnia-Hercegovina and Croatia must therefore be afforded every right accorded to minorities under international conventions as well as national and international guarantees consistent with the principles of international law. . . .

3. Article 1 of the two 1966 International Covenants on human rights establishes that the principle of the right to self-determination serves to safeguard human rights. By virtue of that right every individual may choose to belong to whatever ethnic, religious or language community he or she wishes.

In the Commission's view one possible consequence of this principle might be for the members of the Serbian population in Bosnia-Hercegovina and Croatia to be recognized under agreements between the Republics as having the nationality of their choice, with all the rights and obligations which that entails with respect to the States concerned.

4. The Arbitration Commission is therefore of the opinion:

  (i)   that the Serbian population in Bosnia-Hercegovina and Croatia is entitled to all the rights accorded to minorities and ethnic groups under international law . . . and
  (ii) that the Republics must afford the members of those minorities and ethnic groups all the human rights and fundamental freedoms recognized in international law, including, where appropriate, the right to choose their nationality.

For nearly four years after the Commission's opinion, Serbs and Croats in Bosnia fought the Muslim-led government for independence. In Bosnia, the conflict exacted its largest toll—at least 100,000 dead, including the war's worst single atrocity, the July 1995 massacre of 5,000 to 8,000 Bosnian Muslim men and boys at Srebrenica. The civil war ended with a Western-imposed peace treaty that left Bosnia formally united. But as a practical matter, Bosnia remained divided between the Muslim-Croat federation and the Serb-controlled Republika Srpska. Each had separate government structures, schools, and economies.

2. Kosovo's Secession from Serbia

Yugoslavia's dissolution was not, however, complete. Kosovo, a province of Serbia whose majority was ethnically Albanian, sought independence from what was left of Yugoslavia, namely Serbia and Montenegro. After Serbia rejected a plan for Kosovo's autonomy and its army killed several dozen civilians in Kosovo, the North Atlantic Treaty Organization (NATO), led by the United States, attacked Serbia to force it to withdraw from Kosovo. (See Chapter 13, Problem IV for more details on this episode of humanitarian intervention.) Serbia was forced to accept a UN administration for Kosovo, although it remained formally part of Serbia.

In late 2007, a UN negotiator proposed a plan for Kosovo's independence. It included a variety of obligations for Kosovo, including respect for human rights, protections for minorities, multi-ethnic national institutions, and decentralization of power. The Kosovar leadership supported the plan, but Serbia opposed it. The Security Council could not reach consensus on the plan due to strong resistance to it by Russia.

On February 17, 2008, Kosovo's parliament approved declared the territory's independence from Serbia:

The Assembly of Kosovo . . .

Observing that Kosovo is a special case arising from Yugoslavia's non-consensual breakup and is not a precedent for any other situation . . .

Recalling the years of internationally-sponsored negotiations between Belgrade and Pristina over the question of our future political status,

Regretting that no mutually-acceptable status outcome was possible . . .

Approves

KOSOVA DECLARATION OF INDEPENDENCE

1. We, the democratically-elected leaders of our people, hereby declare Kosovo to be an independent and sovereign state. This declaration reflects the will of our people. . . .

2. We declare Kosovo to be a democratic, secular and multi-ethnic republic, guided by the principles of non-discrimination and equal protection under the law. We shall protect and promote the rights of all communities in Kosovo and create the conditions necessary for their effective participation in political and decision-making processes.

3. We accept fully the obligations for Kosovo contained in the [UN independence] Plan, and welcome the framework it proposes to guide Kosovo in the years ahead. We shall implement in full those obligations . . . particularly those that protect and promote the rights of communities and their members.

8. With independence comes the duty of responsible membership in the international community. We accept fully this duty and shall abide by the principles of the United Nations Charter. . . .

Recognition of Kosovo as an independent state followed quickly but was hardly unanimous. Serb and Russian opposition to Kosovo's independence led to a lobbying campaign in the UN General Assembly to seek an advisory opinion from the ICJ about the legal status of Kosovo. In 2008, the General Assembly asked the ICJ for an advisory opinion on the following: "Is the unilateral declaration of independence by the Provisional Institutions of Self-Government of Kosovo in accordance with international law?"

On July 22, 2010, the ICJ found, by a vote of 10-4, that the declaration did not violate international law. The Court ruled that the declaration violated neither customary international law nor the UN Security Council resolution that set up the UN administration after the 1999 war. The Court emphasized the narrow scope of the request, noting that it did not concern the legality of Kosovo's purported secession or the status of Kosovo, but only the issuance of the declaration:

79. During the eighteenth, nineteenth and early twentieth centuries, there were numerous instances of declarations of independence, often strenuously opposed by the State from which independence was being declared. Sometimes a declaration resulted in the creation of a new State, at others it did not. In no case, however, does the practice of States as a whole suggest that the act of promulgating the declaration was regarded as contrary to international law. On the contrary, State practice during this period points clearly to the conclusion that international law contained no prohibition of declarations of independence. During the second half of the twentieth century, the international law of self-determination developed in such a way as to create a right to independence for the peoples of non-self-governing territories and peoples subject to alien subjugation, domination and exploitation. A great many new States have come into existence as a result of the exercise of this right. There were, however, also instances of declarations of independence outside this context. The practice of States in these latter cases does not point to the emergence in international law of a new rule prohibiting the making of a declaration of independence in such cases.

81. Several participants have invoked resolutions of the Security Council condemning particular declarations of independence: see, *inter alia*, Security Council resolutions 216 (1965) and 217 (1965), concerning Southern Rhodesia; Security Council resolution 541 (1983), concerning northern Cyprus; and Security Council resolution 787 (1992), concerning the Republika Srpska. [I]n all of those instances the Security Council was making a determination as regards the concrete situation existing at the time that those declarations of independence were made; the illegality attached to the declarations of independence thus stemmed not from the unilateral character of these declarations as such, but from the fact that they were, or would have been, connected with the unlawful use of force or other egregious violations of norms of general international law, in particular those of a peremptory character *(jus cogens)*. In the context of Kosovo, the Security Council has never taken this position. . . . [N]o general prohibition against unilateral declarations of independence may be inferred from the practice of the Security Council.

82. A number of participants in the present proceedings have claimed . . . that the population of Kosovo has the right to create an independent State. . . . Whether, outside the context of non-self-governing territories and peoples subject to alien subjugation, domination and exploitation, the international law of self-determination confers upon part of the population of an existing State a right to separate from that State is, however, a subject on which radically different views were expressed by those taking part in the proceedings and expressing a position on the question. . . .

83. The Court considers that it is not necessary to resolve these questions in the present case. [T]he Court need only determine whether the declaration of independence violated either general international law or . . . Security Council resolution 1244 (1999).

84. [T]he Court considers that general international law contains no applicable prohibition of declarations of independence. Accordingly, it concludes that the declaration of independence of 17 February 2008 did not violate general international law.

Accordance with International Law of the Unilateral Declaration of Independence in Respect of Kosovo, 2010 ICJ 403 (Advisory Opinion of 22 July).

Finally, Montenegro, which had remained tied to Serbia during the various wars in the region, eventually sought independence. On May 21, 2006, Montenegro's voters passed a pro-independence referendum by 55.4 percent. Serbia had agreed it would accept such a result, and Montenegro thereafter became an independent state.

Notes and Questions

1. In light of the many precedents where the absence of a government was not regarded as eliminating statehood, should the EC arbitration commission have regarded Yugoslavia as dissolving due to the weakness of its federal government? How might Opinion No. 1 actually encourage secessions?

2. The arbitration commission does not state in Opinion No. 2 that the Serbs in Bosnia and Croatia were collectively entitled to self-determination. Why might it avoid that term in light of the audience for the opinion?

3. Does the arbitration commission opinion reflect the norms in the Friendly Relations Declaration? Are minority rights a substitute for self-determination, or a form of it? Does the arbitration commission's solution—a right to choose one's nationality—offer a satisfactory response to the minorities in Bosnia?

4. Did the ICJ take an unduly narrow approach to answering the question posed to it by the General Assembly? What are the advantages and disadvantages—for resolving the Kosovo dispute, and for the Court's reputation—of issuing a narrow opinion?

5. What do the wars and secessions in Yugoslavia and their outcomes suggest about the views of the actors involved regarding the right to self-determination?

E. Other Practice on the Legality of Secession

1. Quebec

For many years, many French-speaking residents of Quebec have called for greater independence, and even secession, from Canada. Referenda among Quebec's citizens on this question have not shown a majority in favor of secession. In 1998, the Supreme Court of Canada, in response to a request by the Canadian Parliament, issued a lengthy opinion addressing the legality of unilateral secession under both the Canadian Constitution and international law. The opinion offers one of the clearest statements of the contemporary rules on self-determination.

Reference re Secession of Quebec
[1998] 2 S.C.R. 217

(ii) Scope of the Right to Self-Determination

The recognized sources of international law establish that the right to self-determination of a people is normally fulfilled through *internal* self-determination—a people's pursuit of its political, economic, social and cultural development within the framework of an existing state. A right to *external* self-determination (which in this case potentially takes the form of the assertion of a right to unilateral secession) arises in only the most extreme of cases and, even then, under carefully defined circumstances. . . .

The international law principle of self-determination has evolved within a framework of respect for the territorial integrity of existing states. The various international documents that support the existence of a people's right to self-determination also contain parallel statements supportive of the conclusion that the exercise of such a right must be sufficiently limited to prevent threats to an existing state's territorial integrity or the stability of relations between sovereign states. . . .

There is no necessary incompatibility between the maintenance of the territorial integrity of existing states, including Canada, and the right of a "people" to achieve a full measure of self-determination. A state whose government represents the whole of the people or peoples resident within its territory, on a basis of equality and without discrimination, and respects the principles of self-determination in its own internal arrangements, is entitled to the protection under international law of its territorial integrity. . . .

Accordingly, the general state of international law with respect to the right to self-determination is that the right operates within the overriding protection granted to the territorial integrity of "parent" states. . . .

A number of commentators have further asserted that the right to self-determination may ground a right to unilateral secession in a third circumstance [other than colonialism or foreign conquest]. Although this third circumstance has been described in several ways, the underlying proposition is that, when a people is blocked from the meaningful exercise of its right to self-determination internally, it is entitled, as a last resort, to exercise it by secession. . . .

Clearly, such a circumstance parallels the other two recognized situations in that the ability of a people to exercise its right to self-determination internally is somehow being totally frustrated. While it remains unclear whether this third proposition actually reflects an established international law standard, it is unnecessary for present purposes to make that determination. Even assuming that the third circumstance is sufficient to create a right to unilateral secession under international law, the current Quebec context cannot be said to approach such a threshold. As stated by the *amicus curiae* . . .

> [TRANSLATION] 15. The Quebec people is not the victim of attacks on its physical existence or integrity, or of a massive violation of its fundamental rights. The Quebec people is manifestly not, in the opinion of the *amicus curiae*, an oppressed people.
>
> 16. For close to 40 of the last 50 years, the Prime Minister of Canada has been a Quebecer. During this period, Quebecers have held from time to time all the most important positions in the federal Cabinet. During the 8 years prior to June 1997, the Prime Minister and the Leader of the Official Opposition in the House of Commons were both Quebecers. At present, the Prime Minister of Canada, the Right Honourable Chief Justice and two other members of the Court, the Chief of Staff of the Canadian Armed Forces and the Canadian ambassador to the United States, not to mention the Deputy Secretary-General of the United Nations, are all Quebecers. . . .

The population of Quebec cannot plausibly be said to be denied access to government. Quebecers occupy prominent positions within the government of Canada. Residents of the province freely make political choices and pursue economic, social and cultural development within Quebec, across Canada, and throughout the world. The population of Quebec is equitably represented in legislative, executive and judicial institutions. In short, to reflect the phraseology of the international documents that address the right to self-determination of peoples, Canada is a "sovereign and independent state conducting itself in compliance with the principle of equal rights and self-determination of peoples and thus possessed of a government representing the whole people belonging to the territory without distinction."

The continuing failure to reach agreement on amendments to the Constitution, while a matter of concern, does not amount to a denial of self-determination. In the absence of amendments to the Canadian Constitution, we must look at the constitutional arrangements presently in effect, and we cannot conclude under current circumstances that those arrangements place Quebecers in a disadvantaged position within the scope of the international law rule.

The Quebec secession debate has also included much discussion of the future of groups physically located in Quebec who oppose and fear a separate Quebec. The James Bay Crees are a nation of 12,000 aboriginal people who have lived in the area of the James and Hudson Bays for several thousand years. The Crees' homelands are primarily in Quebec, and they have been concerned that the independence of Quebec would not take into account their concerns for self-government. The Crees submitted a brief to the Canadian Supreme Court during its consideration of the legality of Quebec's secession. The brief argued:

> 84. Presently, the province of Quebec is made up of numerous peoples, including distinct Aboriginal peoples. It cannot be said by the National Assembly or government of Quebec that there is a single "people" within the province that is synonymous with the province or government of Quebec. Nor can it be suggested . . . that there is a single "people" in Canada under international law which can exercise rights of self-determination.
>
> 85. For purposes of self-determination and secession, it would appear that a "people" can be constituted of different peoples or different ethnic, linguistic, or religious groups—if there is a common will to constitute as a people. However, "common will" connotes an essential voluntariness among the different individuals and peoples involved. [T]here is clearly no such common will by the James Bay Cree people to identify, for purposes of self-determination or for secession, with Quebecers as a single "Quebec people." . . .
>
> 87. To force the James Bay Cree . . . to identify as a single people with Quebecers for the purposes of secession would effectively deny Aboriginal peoples not only their right to self-identification but also their right to self-determination. . . .
>
> 95. The James Bay Crees in Quebec are not claiming a right to secede. . . . However, the Crees reserve the right to claim a right to secede, in conformance with international law, should the Cree people and Cree territory be forcibly included in a sovereign Quebec, in violation of their fundamental rights.

2. South Ossetia and Abkhazia

South Ossetia and Abkhazia are small regions in Georgia along Russia's border, heavily populated by groups who do not ethnically identify themselves as Georgian. Both have declared independence from Georgia, and since the mid-1990s, Georgia's control over each territory has been minimal. In August 2008, the Russian army invaded South Ossetia and since then has remained firmly in control of the enclave. A European Union expert commission stated with respect to South Ossetia's claim of independence:

> [I]nternational law does not grant an unqualified right to external self-determination in the form of secession in the event of violations of the internal right to self-determination.

Even if an extraordinary allowance to secede were accepted under extreme circumstances, such an exception was not applicable to South Ossetia. The international community (including Russia) consistently emphasised the territorial integrity of Georgia, both before and after the outbreak of the armed conflict of 2008. This was expressed notably in numerous Security Council resolutions, and also in resolutions of other international organisations. These statements indicate the denial of any allowance to secede based on self-determination.

2 Report of the International Fact-Finding Commission on the Conflict in Georgia 144-145 (2009), *www.ceeig.ch/report.html.*

Notes and Questions

1. The Canadian Supreme Court's distinction between internal and external self-determination is a particularly clear restatement of the law and has been respected by the parties. Do courts and international law play a different role in the secession of entities from a stable state like Canada than from a dissolving one like Yugoslavia?

2. If Quebec were to secede, should it be able to take along with it the lands of the Crees, who oppose Quebec independence?

F. Evaluating the Arguments for Crimea's Secession

The actors in the Crimean secession made ample reference to international law in their claims. For example, the declaration of the Crimean parliament adopted before the referendum began as follows:

> We, members of the Supreme Council of the Autonomous Republic of Crimea and Sevastopol City Council, based on the provisions of the Charter of the United Nations and many other international instruments, as well as taking into account the confirmation of the status of Kosovo by the United Nations International Court of Justice on July 22, 2010 . . . , which says that the unilateral declaration of independence by a part of the state does not violate any rules of international law, decide together:

In a March 18, 2014 speech to the Russian Duma, President Vladimir Putin justified Crimea's separation from Ukraine as follows:

> As it declared independence and decided to hold a referendum, the Supreme Council of Crimea referred to the United Nations Charter, which speaks of the right of nations to self-determination. Incidentally, I would like to remind you that when Ukraine seceded from the USSR it did exactly the same thing, almost word for word. Ukraine used this right, yet the residents of Crimea are denied it. Why is that?

> Moreover, the Crimean authorities referred to the well-known Kosovo precedent – a precedent our western colleagues created with their own hands in a very similar situation, when they agreed that the unilateral separation of Kosovo from Serbia, exactly what Crimea is doing now, was legitimate and did not require any permission from the country's central authorities. Pursuant to Article 2, Chapter 1 of the United Nations Charter, the UN International Court agreed with this approach and made the following comment in its ruling of July 22, 2010, and I quote: "No general prohibition may be inferred from the practice of the Security Council with regard to declarations of independence," and "General international law contains no prohibition on declarations of independence." Crystal clear, as they say.

I do not like to resort to quotes, but in this case, I cannot help it. Here is a quote from another official document: the Written Statement of the United States of America of April 17, 2009, submitted to the same UN International Court in connection with the hearings on Kosovo. Again, I quote: "Declarations of independence may, and often do, violate domestic legislation. However, this does not make them violations of international law." End of quote. They wrote this, disseminated it all over the world, had everyone agree and now they are outraged. Over what? The actions of the Crimean people completely fit in with these instructions, as it were. For some reason, things that Kosovo Albanians (and we have full respect for them) were permitted to do, Russians, Ukrainians and Crimean Tatars in Crimea are not allowed. Again, one wonders why.

In its March 27 resolution, the UN General Assembly stated that it:

1. Affirms its commitment to the sovereignty, political independence, unity and territorial integrity of Ukraine within its internationally recognized borders;

2. Calls upon all States to . . . refrain from actions aimed at the partial or total disruption of the national unity and territorial integrity of Ukraine, including any attempts to modify Ukraine's borders through the threat or use of force or other unlawful means; . . . .

5. Underscores that the referendum held in the Autonomous Republic of Crimea . . . on 16 March 2014, having no validity, cannot form the basis for any alteration of the status of the Autonomous Republic of Crimea. . . .

Notes and Questions

1. In light of the legal instruments you have read, was Crimea's decision to secede from Ukraine and Russia's subsequent absorption of the territory lawful? Was the Crimean parliament's and Putin's analysis of international law correct, or was the General Assembly right?

2. What sorts of options remain for Ukraine and other states seeking to restore Crimea's status within Ukraine? What use is the law regarding other cities in Ukraine that are seeking unification with Russia?

G. Recognition of New States by Outside Actors: Does It Matter?

While the existence of a state and the entitlement of a people to its own state are in theory different legal questions, states' views on the former are often influenced by their views on the latter. Thus, at times, states may formally recognize an entity as a state even if the entity does not meet the four Montevideo criteria for statehood because they believe it is entitled to statehood, or even as a gesture of political support. At other times, they may refrain from recognizing an entity as a state even if it meets the Montevideo criteria. Under international law, is statehood purely a matter of meeting objective criteria, or does it depend upon the views of other states?

International law's characterization of this practically metaphysical question has come under the rubric of the doctrine of recognition. Under one theory, the *declaratory view*, recognition is a purely political act that states undertake, for example, to show support for a new state, but it is irrelevant for the legal determination of statehood. An entity that meets the criteria of statehood immediately enjoys all the rights and duties of a state regardless of the views of other states. States supporting this view codified it in the Montevideo Convention, which declares in Article 3: "The political existence of the state is independent of recognition by the other states." Recognition by one state of a new state is thus merely a declaration by the former of what is already the case; and if the entity is not yet a new state, recognition does not make it one.

The contrary position, known as the *constitutive view*, regards recognition as one of the elements of statehood—that is, regardless of its satisfaction of the objective criteria, a claimant to statehood is not itself a state until it has been recognized by others. Thus, the refusal by states to afford recognition would mean that the entity claiming statehood would not be entitled to the rights of a state. Indeed, the fear that powerful states, for political reasons, would refuse to recognize an entity meeting the criteria of statehood and thereby cut it off from interstate relations led the Latin American states to explicitly adopt the declaratory view in the Montevideo Convention.

Most scholars regard the declaratory view as more consistent with the practice of states, which have viewed recognition as a discretionary and political act and treated many entities meeting the formal criteria as states without formally recognizing them. Thus, although most Arab states have not recognized the existence of Israel, they have not, for example, ignored rules prohibiting unauthorized overflight by civilian aircraft.

Yet the determination whether a state has met the criteria of statehood is still made by other states, not by some independent body. Thus, if states refuse to acknowledge that an entity meets these criteria (even if it clearly does), they might continue to treat the claimant as something less than a state. For example, a state that is unrecognized may find that its passports are not accepted by immigration authorities in other states. This lends some credence to the constitutive view. As a leading treatise states, "Recognition, while declaratory of an existing fact, is constitutive in nature, at least so far as concerns relations with the recognising state." 1 Oppenheim's International Law 133 (Robert Jennings & Arthur Watts eds., 9th ed. 1992).

As support for the constitutive view, consider the 1965 decision of the UN Security Council following the unilateral declaration of independence from Britain by the white-dominated minority government of Southern Rhodesia (now Zimbabwe). Although the territory met all four criteria in the Montevideo Convention, the Security Council "[c]ondemn[ed] the usurpation of power by a racist settler minority in Southern Rhodesia and regard[ed] the declaration of independence by it as having no legal validity." S.C. Res. 217, Nov. 20, 1965. As a result, nearly all states refused to conclude treaties with Rhodesia. (The situation was resolved only in 1978 following a peace accord that led to a majority government in Zimbabwe.)

More recently, in 2011, the Palestinian authorities filed an application for admission as a member state of the United Nations. UN membership is open only to states. Palestine's territory consists of land on the West Bank of the Jordan River as well as the Gaza Strip, areas occupied by Israel since its 1967 war with its neighbors. Today, much of the West Bank, and all entry and exit from it, is still under Israeli military control, with large tracts occupied by Israeli settlers. Israel also controls air and sea access to the Gaza Strip. The result is a patchwork of territory controlled by the Palestinian authorities, suggesting that Palestine would not seem to meet the Montevideo criteria. Nonetheless, Palestine declared independence in 1988 and has been recognized as a state by most UN members.

Under the UN Charter, the Security Council must recommend membership before the General Assembly can approve it. Due to opposition by the United States and a few other states to Palestinian UN membership, the Security Council did not approve Palestine's request. In response, in 2012, Palestine sought and achieved the status of a "non-member observer state"—a status that can be granted by the General Assembly alone—by a vote of 138 to 9, with 41 abstentions. Palestine subsequently joined the United Nations Educational, Scientific, and Cultural Organization as a full member and has joined a number of human rights and humanitarian law treaties. In 2015, it became a party to the Statute of the International Criminal Court, which triggers the Court's jurisdiction over Israeli activities on Palestinian territory.

States have also sometimes imposed criteria for recognition beyond those in the Montevideo Convention. In 1991, European foreign ministers issued a set of guidelines for recognizing states emerging from Yugoslavia and the USSR. The guidelines for the latter included the following:

DECLARATION ON THE "GUIDELINES ON THE RECOGNITION OF NEW STATES IN EASTERN EUROPE AND IN THE SOVIET UNION"

31 I.L.M. 1486 (1992)

The Community and its Member States confirm their attachment to the principles of the Helsinki Final Act and the Charter of Paris [two important political declarations concluded among all European states in 1975 and 1990], in particular the principle of self-determination. They affirm their readiness to recognise, subject to the normal standards of international practice and the political realities in each case, those new states which . . . have constituted themselves on a democratic basis, have accepted the appropriate international obligations and have committed themselves in good faith to a peaceful process and to negotiations.

Therefore, they adopt a common position on the process of recognition of these new states, which requires:

- respect for the provisions of the Charter of the United Nations and the commitments subscribed to in the Final Act of Helsinki and in the Charter of Paris, especially with regard to the rule of law, democracy and human rights;

- guarantees for the rights of ethnic and national groups and minorities . . . ;

- respect for the inviolability of all frontiers which can only be changed by peaceful means and by common agreement. . . .

In the following months, European states jointly recognized all the states of the former USSR and of Yugoslavia as new states. Greece's opposition to Macedonian independence (Greece argued that the name Macedonia belonged exclusively to an area of northern Greece) led to recognition of that state under the name of The Former Yugoslav Republic of Macedonia (alphabetically listed in the UN's list of states under "T").

With respect to Kosovo, as of 2015, Kosovo's government reports that 96 states had recognized it as a state, including the United States, Japan, most EU members, Malaysia, Saudi Arabia, Senegal, and Colombia. However, states who fear secessionist groups at home, notably Russia, Spain, Cyprus, and China, have not. As for South Ossetia, after the invasion of Georgia by Russia, Russian President Medvedev signed a decree recognizing the independence of that entity and Abkhazia. Only Nicaragua, Venezuela, and Nauru (the last of these apparently after a payment from Russia) had recognized South Ossetia.

Notes and Questions

1. Did states recognizing Palestine as a state or voting to allow Palestine non-member-state status in the UN violate international law if Palestine does not meet the Montevideo criteria? Assuming Kosovo meets the Montevideo criteria, are states not recognizing it as a state violating international law?

2. Was it consistent with international law for the European states to inject other criteria into their decision to recognize new states?

3. If a state is not recognized by most states but still meets the criteria for statehood, should the non-recognizing states have a duty to treat it as a state nonetheless? Consider the case of Taiwan, which meets the Montevideo criteria and is not formally recognized by most states, yet other states treat it like a state by accepting its passports and maintaining separate trading relations with it.

II. THE PROCESS OF GOVERNMENTAL CHANGE: NEW GOVERNMENTS IN CAMBODIA

Despite the many legal questions arising from the formation and transformation of states, the far more common phenomenon in international relations is the change of government or ruling elites within a state. Many such changes are routine matters according to constitutional procedures following an election. For instance, the government (in the continental sense, meaning the head of government and his or her cabinet) might change from Social Democrats to Christian Democrats in Germany. Others, however, result from extraconstitutional situations, whether revolution, military coup, or civil war. When such changes take place, new governments are often tempted to renounce international commitments made by their predecessors. Moreover, external actors need to decide upon their attitude toward the new government—whether to approve it through, for instance, a formal act of recognition; disapprove it by, for example, continuing to deal only with the prior regime; transact interstate business with it without taking such a stance; or otherwise.

The goals for this Problem include:

- to understand international law's approach to the effect of a change of government on a state's international obligations; and
- to understand international law's approach to the effect of such changes on the ability of the new regime to represent the state in its external relations, including in international organizations.

As a starting point, international law provides a clear rule regarding the effect of governmental change on a state's duties: a change in government does not affect a states' international obligations. Moreover, traditional law also had strong views on the relevance of two other factors to the rights and duties of states with new governments: (1) the way in which the new government took power, and (2) the views of other states as to their legitimacy—often expressed in their decisions whether to recognize the new government.

American Chief Justice William Howard Taft put forth the position of international law on these issues while he was acting as arbitrator in a dispute between Great Britain and Costa Rica. The issue was whether Costa Rica could nullify the financial obligations incurred by the previous government, led by Frederico Tinoco, which had come to power extraconstitutionally and not been recognized by the United Kingdom or the United States.

> . . . [W]hen recognition . . . of a government is by such nations determined by inquiry, not into its *de facto* sovereignty and complete governmental control, but into its illegitimacy or irregularity of origin, their non-recognition loses something of evidential weight on the issue with which those applying the rules of international law are alone concerned. . . . Such non-recognition for any reason . . . cannot outweigh the evidence disclosed by this record before me as to the *de facto* character of Tinoco's government, according to the standard set by international law. . . . The issue is not whether the new government assumes power or conducts its administration under constitutional limitations established by the people during the incumbency of the government it has overthrown. The question is, has it really established itself in such a way that all within its influence recognize its control, and that there is no opposing force assuming to be a government in its place? Is it discharging its functions as a government usually does, respected within its own jurisdiction?

Tinoco Arbitration (U.K. v. Costa Rica), 1 U.N.R.I.A.A. 369, 381-382 (1923).

The legal irrelevance of recognition of governments received further support in the so-called Estrada Doctrine, enunciated by the Mexican Foreign Minister in 1930:

> [T]he Mexican government is issuing no declarations in the sense of grants of recognition, since that nation considers that such a course is an insulting practice and one which, in addition to the fact that it offends the sovereignty of other nations, implies that judgment of some sort may be passed upon the internal affairs of those nations by other governments, inasmuch as the latter assume, in effect, an attitude of criticism, when they decide, favorably or unfavorably, as to the legal qualifications of foreign régimes.

Marjorie Whiteman, 2 Digest of International Law 85 (1963).

Thus, international law regards a change in government by coup or revolution as no different from, for example, the transfer of power from the Republican Party to the Democratic Party in the United States after an election. The state's obligations continue, regardless of the mode of change or the reaction of outside actors.

The Tinoco and Estrada positions were not completely unopposed at the time. Woodrow Wilson, for instance, had endorsed the so-called Tobar Doctrine, named for the Ecuadoran foreign minister. To promote democratic transfers of power, the Tobar Doctrine would deny recognition to governments resulting from extraconstitutional power struggles; the United States even applied it in the first part of the twentieth century to a handful of recognition decisions regarding Latin America and the Soviet Union.

But if governmental change does not alter a state's international obligations as a general matter, such change clearly affects other aspects of its international relations, as demonstrated in the following materials about Cambodia's changing governments.

A. The Problem

Cambodia, a country of some 12 million people in Southeast Asia, has undergone significant governmental change since securing its independence from France in 1953. The first change took place in 1970, when Cambodia's long-serving monarch, Norodom Sihanouk, was overthrown in a coup backed by the United States (which saw him as an adversary in the Vietnam War). The ouster of Sihanouk led over time to full civil war between the new regime and the Khmer Rouge, a Communist insurgency.

The second change took place in 1975, when the Khmer Rouge defeated the pro-U.S. regime and began governing the state under the name Democratic Kampuchea. The new leaders engaged in horrific violations of human rights, including the evacuation of Cambodia's cities, extermination of perceived political opponents, and subjection of much of the population to forced agrarian work under abysmal conditions. Some one-fifth of Cambodia's 1975 population of 7.3 million perished under the Khmer Rouge.

The third change of regimes began in December 1978, when Vietnam invaded Cambodia and ousted the Khmer Rouge. Vietnam installed a pro-Vietnamese government, which renamed the state the People's Republic of Kampuchea (PRK). The Khmer Rouge fled to western Cambodia, and from there they fought the new government with aid from China and other opponents of Vietnam.

Many states responded to the Khmer Rouge's victory in 1975 by breaking diplomatic relations. Democratic Kampuchea's principal diplomatic ally was China. When the new government took over in 1979, most Western states remained at a distance, although the Soviet-bloc states, in solidarity with Vietnam and some others, resumed ties. Beyond the practice of individual states, the UN General Assembly had to decide who would occupy Cambodia's seat in the organization. The Khmer Rouge had quickly assumed Cambodia's seat upon its victory in 1975, but the PRK proved less successful at the UN after its conquest in 1979.

B. The China Precedent

The change in governments in Cambodia was not the first time the United Nations had to address the consequences of extraconstitutional change. The first significant challenge had come decades earlier, in 1949, when Communist forces in China achieved victory in a long civil war over the Nationalist Government, which fled to Taiwan. The Nationalist leaders declared that they remained the government of all of China and promised to liberate the mainland. The United States and many of its Western friends continued to recognize it as China's government.

Faced with a decision about which government would represent China in the UN, Secretary-General Trygve Lie made public his views in a memorandum.

Legal Aspects of Problems of Representation in the United Nations
U.N. Doc. S/1466 (1950)

The recognition of a new State, or of a new government of an existing state, is a unilateral act which the recognizing government can grant or withhold. [I]t is still regarded as essentially a political decision, which each State decides in accordance with its own free appreciation of the situation. . . .

. . . [D]espite the fairly large number of revolutionary changes of government and the larger number of instances of breach of diplomatic relations among members, there was not one single instance of a challenge of credentials of a representative in the many thousands of [UN]meetings . . . .

The practice which has been thus followed in the United Nations is not only legally correct but conforms to the basic character of the Organization. The United Nations is not an association limited to like-minded States and governments of similar ideological persuasion (as in the case in certain regional associations). As an Organization which aspires to universality, it must of necessity include States of varying and even conflicting ideologies.

The Chinese case is unique in the history of the United Nations . . . because it is the first in which two rival governments exist. It is quite possible that such a situation will occur again in the future. . . .

It is submitted that the proper principle can be derived by analogy from Article 4 of the Charter. This Article requires that an applicant for membership must be able and willing to carry out the obligations of membership. The obligations of membership can be carried out only by governments which in fact possess the power to do so. Where a revolutionary government presents itself as representing a State, in rivalry to an existing government, the question at issue should be which of these two governments in fact is in a position to employ the resources and direct the people of the State in fulfillment of the obligations of membership. In essence, this means an inquiry as to whether the new government exercises effective authority within the territory of the State and is habitually obeyed by the bulk of the population.

If so, it would seem to be appropriate for the United Nations organs, through their collective action, to accord it the right to represent the State . . . , even though the individual Members of the Organization refuse . . . to accord it recognition as the lawful government for reasons which are valid under their national policies.

On December 14, 1950, the General Assembly, by a vote of 36-6-9, adopted a resolution stating that "whenever more than one authority claims to be the government entitled to represent a Member State in the United Nations and this question becomes the subject of controversy in the United Nations, the question should be considered in the light of the Purposes and Principles of the Charter and the circumstances of each case." G.A. Res. 396 (1950).

The United States continued to muster enough support in the General Assembly for its position to block the seating of the PRC delegation throughout the 1950s and 1960s. In 1971, as US policy on China changed, the United States agreed to the seating of the PRC delegation. In 1979, the United States recognized the PRC regime as the sole legal government of China. The United States and other states maintain unofficial relations with Taiwan through government-controlled private bodies.

Notes and Questions

1. What would the UN's position on the seating of China call for with respect to the seating of a Cambodian delegation after the Vietnamese invasion and takeover in 1979?

2. The Secretary-General argues that international law requires seating the government with effective power, regardless of any decisions by individual member states to

recognize one regime or another. Does the UN Secretary-General's reliance on the language of the UN Charter resolve the question of which governmental claimants should represent states at the United Nations?

    3. What sort of arguments could the United States have made to the General Assembly to promote the continued seating of the delegation from Taiwan? How did law and politics interact to affect the outcome?

C. The 1979 Credentials Fight

    Following the PRK's ouster of the Khmer Rouge in 1979, the new government sought to represent Cambodia in the General Assembly. The issue first fell to the Assembly's Credentials Committee. By a vote of 6 (Belgium, China, Ecuador, Pakistan, Senegal, United States) to 3 (Congo, Panama, USSR), it accepted the credentials of the ousted government of Democratic Kampuchea and thereby rejected those of the PRK. When the full General Assembly debated the issue, various legal and political positions and options emerged:

26. Mr. MISHRA (India): . . .

31. It is our conviction that the General Assembly should not take a definitive position at this moment. . . . If we were to accept the report of the Credentials Committee as it stands, I have no doubt that we would get involved in a very acrimonious debate which might spill over from this meeting to other meetings of the Assembly. . . . We would like to try to have a solution, a temporary one, which would give this Assembly the opportunity to take stock of the situation, and if necessary, to reopen the question. . . .

33. [T]oday we are again asked to choose between two positions and we are not sure what the actual situation is. Is it correct for us to pronounce ourselves in a definitive manner? I submit that that would be unwise, not only for the sake of the Assembly, but for the sake of the situation which is involved in this procedural question. . . .

58. Mr. ZAITON (Malaysia): . . .

62. As we all know, Democratic Kampuchea has been legally accredited to the United Nations in all its previous meetings. Its credentials were accepted by the United Nations as its thirty-third session [in 1978] and it has been participating in all meetings of the United Nations and its various agencies and organs. Its credentials have now been challenged by none other than the party which has used force of arms to intervene in the internal affairs of Kampuchea, overthrow an established Government and set up in its place an alien Government, backed by the huge and immense military force of the Government which has intervened.

63. As we all know, one of the sacred principles of the United Nations is that of non-interference and non-intervention in the internal affairs of another State. . . . Were we to accept the draft resolution and seat the People's Republic of Kampuchea, it would mean that we would be condoning armed intervention and aggression that is in direct violation of the various principles we are supposed to uphold.

64. Furthermore, if we accept the draft resolution it will mean that qualification for membership in this Assembly will be measured by the yardstick of a Government's internal policies. This is an argument difficult to accept, for if it is valid then the Credentials

Committee will have to determine the credentials of all Member States on the basis of their internal policies.

65. It will be recalled that at the height of the atrocities committed by the Pol Pot Government [of Democratic Kampuchea], which we all deplore, no one in this Assembly voiced any objection to the credentials of Democratic Kampuchea. Yet now we are being asked to evaluate the credentials of a Government in the light of the record of its violations of human rights. . . . The very people who are today proposing that another delegation should be seated as the representative of that particular Government are performing a flagrant *volte-face* based not on any principle, but merely on political expediency.

8. Mr. TROYANOVSKY (Union of Soviet Socialist Republics) (interpretation from Russian): . . .

14. . . . If any delegation should vote in favour of the Committee's report . . . then the position adopted by that delegation would be tantamount to support for the criminal Pol Pot clique, which has been condemned by the Kampuchean people.

15. The whole world knows the facts of the bloody misdeeds of the [Khmer Rouge], which has slain 3 million Kampucheans—in other words, it is openly carrying out a policy of genocide vis-à-vis its own people. As representatives know, the crime of genocide, according to the Convention on the Prevention and Punishment of the Crime of Genocide . . . is severely condemned, and by no means can it be supposed that there is support in the United Nations for people who have committed that crime.

16. The only legitimate representative of Kampuchea is the [PRK]. That Government is exercising full and stable control over the whole territory of the country and is effectively exercising State power. [It] is implementing energetic measures to bring the country back to normal . . . . That policy conducted by the Government is supported by the absolute majority of the Kampuchean people. . . .

General Assembly Official Records, Thirty-Fourth Session, Records of the 3rd and 4th Plenary Meetings (1979).

    After a long debate, the General Assembly voted with 71 in favor, 35 against, 34 abstaining, with 12 absences, to accept the Credentials Committee's report and thereby retain the seating of the delegation from the ousted Democratic Kampuchea government. The states voting yes were principally developing world states and Western states; those opposed were principally the Soviet Union and its allies. At the end of the debate, the DK delegate, Ieng Thirith (the wife of Khmer Rouge leader Pol Pot), stated:

> Democratic Kampuchea would like to express . . . its deep gratitude to this honourable Assembly and to the peoples that love peace and justice, who by their vote just now have done an act of justice. They did this by saying "No" to aggression and "No" to violation of the United Nations Charter. . . .

Notes and Questions

    1. Which of the three delegates had the best legal argument?

    2. The divided vote over Cambodia suggests uncertainty over whether the 1950 Lie formula should still be the rule of international law. Should recognition decisions be made to protect other values, such as the ban on the use of force, or a state's human rights policies? What happened to the Lie formula?

3. The PRK's supporters were all members of the Soviet bloc. Those calling for the continued seating of the DK were states in the Southeast Asian region fearful of Vietnam's power, as well as their Western allies. Why would these groups want to make their arguments in legal terms? Who were the targets of these legal arguments?

4. Note the voting tally for seating of the DK delegation. Did it receive the support of a majority of the UN's members?

5. The United States favored continued seating of the Khmer Rouge regime out of opposition to Vietnam's invasion and solidarity with China. Robert Rosenstock, the U.S. delegate to the committee, later recalled that, after the vote, someone had grabbed his hand and shaken it in congratulations. "I looked up and saw it was Ieng Sary [the Khmer Rouge's number two official]. I felt like washing my hand." Gareth Porter, *Kampuchea's UN Seat: Cutting the Pol Pot Connection*, Indochina Issues, No. 8, July 1980, at 1.

D. The Next Stages

In 1991, Cambodia's warring factions accepted an internationally brokered peace treaty, leading to UN-run elections in 1993. The result was Cambodia's next change of government, when a multiparty coalition assumed power. The new regime, formally led by a son of Sihanouk, was broadly accepted as Cambodia's legitimate government.

But in 1997, Cambodia's prime minister was ousted in a coup led by the PRK's former leader (who had placed second in the elections). Both the elected regime and the coup-installed regime sought to represent Cambodia at the UN. The Credentials Committee, instead of voting to approve one delegation's seating, decided to leave the seat vacant at the UN. The following year, Cambodia held elections again, this time without UN oversight. The election was marked by significant irregularities, and the coup-installed regime won. Without any debate, the UN accepted the credentials of this government.

Notes and Questions

1. What factors do you think caused the Credentials Committee to act as it did at the UN's 1997 General Assembly?

2. Should the fairness of an election determine whether the United Nations will seat a delegation or whether foreign states should interact with it?

E. Integration of Human Rights Concerns: The Haiti Episode and Beyond

For the last several decades, UN members have faced periodic challenges regarding recognition of governments.

1. Extraconstitutional Changes of Power

In Haiti, the overthrow of the state's longtime strongman led to UN-monitored multiparty elections in 1990. The winner was Jean-Bertrand Aristide, a Catholic priest. Aristide's election ended one of the region's oldest dictatorships; it also enabled the Organization of American States (OAS) to claim with pride that all its members, many of which had once been military regimes, were now elected governments. (Cuba was excluded from the organization in January 1962.) In June 1991, the OAS General Assembly adopted the following resolution to address any future attempts at military coups:

Representative Democracy

O.A.S. Res. AG/RES 1080 (1991)

WHEREAS: . . .

Under the provisions of the Charter, one of the basic purposes of the OAS is to promote and consolidate representative democracy, with due respect for the principle of non-intervention. . . .

THE GENERAL ASSEMBLY

RESOLVES:

1. To instruct the Secretary General to call for the immediate convocation of a meeting of the Permanent Council in the event of any occurrences giving rise to the sudden or irregular interruption of the democratic political institutional process or of the legitimate exercise of power by the democratically elected government in any of the Organization's member states, in order, within the framework of the Charter, to examine the situation, decide on and convene an ad hoc meeting of the Ministers of Foreign Affairs, or a special session of the General Assembly, all of which must take place within a ten-day period.

2. To state that the purpose of the ad hoc meeting of Ministers of Foreign Affairs or the special session of the General Assembly shall be to look into the events collectively and adopt any decisions deemed appropriate. . . .

Just under four months later, however, Aristide was ousted in a military coup. He fled to the United States, where, with U.S. support, he waged a lengthy diplomatic campaign to oust the military government. The OAS condemned the coup, and the UN General Assembly unanimously passed Resolution 46/7, which stated:

> Aware that, in accordance with the Charter of the United Nations, the Organization promotes and encourages respect for human rights and fundamental freedoms for all, and that the Universal Declaration of Human Rights states that the will of the people shall be the basis of the authority of government, . . .
> 1. Strongly condemns the attempted illegal replacement of the constitutional President of Haiti, the use of violence and military coercion and the violation of human rights in that country;
> 2. Affirms as unacceptable any entity resulting from that illegal situation and demands the immediate restoration of the legitimate Government of President

Jean-Bertrand Aristide, together with the full application of the National Constitution and hence the full observance of human rights in Haiti. . . .

───────────

Delegations from Aristide's government continued to represent Haiti in the United Nations and other international organizations. Indeed, the UN Security Council imposed severe economic sanctions on the new government, pressured the military regime to sign an agreement returning power to Aristide, and, when the regime failed to comply with it, even authorized the use of force to return President Aristide to power. Only at the last minute, in September 1994, with U.S. troops poised to invade under the cloak of UN authority, did the military agree to depart, allowing Aristide to return to power.

Developments regarding the effect of unconstitutional takeovers extend beyond the UN and OAS. In October 1991, the Conference (now Organization) for Security and Cooperation in Europe adopted a policy on extraconstitutional takeovers similar to that expressed in OAS Resolution 1080, although it has not yet had to employ its procedures. The Constitutive Act of the African Union (AU) lists the "condemnation and rejection of unconstitutional changes of governments" among its core principles and prohibits participation in Union activities of governments coming to power through such means.

Yet the diverse reactions of states to extraconstitutional changes suggests that no norm of international law precludes a state from continuing to do business with regimes resulting from them.

- In June 2009, the military forces of Honduras overthrew and removed from the country its elected president, Manuel Zelaya. Zelaya's ouster was quickly confirmed by the country's Congress. Condemnation of the coup was swift, as the OAS General Assembly and the UN General Assembly denounced it and urged states not to recognize the new regime. In July, the OAS suspended Honduras's membership in the organization. In November 2009, a rival of Zelaya was elected President. The U.S. soon favored engagement with the new government. When the new president accepted an OAS-brokered deal in 2011 to allow Zelaya to return from exile, the OAS reinstated Honduras's membership.

- In July 2013, Mohammed Morsi, Egypt's first freely elected president, was ousted by the country's military leadership. Morsi and his supporters were immediately imprisoned and put on trial and their political party banned. Morsi's ouster followed significant domestic turmoil in which he was accused by opponents of accumulating too much power for his supporters in the Muslim Brotherhood and thus undermining the 2011 popular revolution that had led to Hosni Mubarak's removal from power. The military eventually drafted a new constitution and its leader, Abdel al-Sisi, won a popular election in 2014. Most governments condemned the coup but maintained ties with the new government. Six months after the coup, in late 2013, Morsi supporters sent a notice to the International Criminal Court purporting to indicate Egypt's consent to the Court's jurisdiction over crimes committed in Egypt since Morsi's ouster (which would have enabled the ICC to investigate those acts). However, the Court's Registrar and Prosecutor rejected the documentation on the grounds that the Morsi government no longer had effective control over Egypt.

2. Civil Wars

The reaction of states to other civil wars has shown a further willingness to recognize or allow the seating of regimes that do not have effective control of territory.

- Afghanistan: The Taliban, which gained control of the country in the late 1990s, eventually controlled over 90 percent of the state's territory, but its delegation was never seated at the UN due to claims by Western states that it supported international terrorism and drug trafficking. Instead, the regime defeated by the Taliban, the Northern Alliance, which controlled little territory, was seated at the United Nations. In late 2001, after U.S. and British military action against the Taliban, a new "Interim Authority" was created as "the repository of Afghan sovereignty"; it gradually began taking over the reins of government in late 2001 and assumed the UN seat as well, with a new government installed in 2004 under the state's 2003 constitution.

- Libya: In early 2011, a rebellion broke out in several cities against the regime of Muammar Qadhafi. The insurgent leaders announced the formation of a 33-member Interim Transitional National Council, declaring itself the "only legitimate body representing the people of Libya and the Libyan state." Within several months, at least 30 states accorded the TNC some form of official recognition. The U.S. Secretary of State announced on July 15, 2011, that "until an interim authority is in place, the United States will recognize the TNC as the legitimate governing authority for Libya, and we will deal with it on that basis." With the fall of the Qadhafi regime in the fall of 2011, the TNC was accepted by states and international organizations as the legitimate government of Libya.

- Syria: The outbreak of civil conflict within Syria also led to questions of recognition. As the war worsened and President Assad's government resorted to targeting civilians, a number of governments began to extend a form of recognition to the Syrian National Council, a coalition of opposition groups fighting the Assad regime. In November and December 2012, about 20 Arab and Western states, including the United States, recognized the coalition as the "sole" or "sole legitimate" "representative of the Syrian people" and began direct talks with it on solutions to the crisis. Some of these states, particularly Qatar and other Arab states, also provided arms to the coalition or armed groups within it. The Syrian civil war is discussed further in Chapter 13, Problem III.

Notes and Questions

1. One interpretation of the developments within international organizations is that international law now allows these bodies to take into account in seating a delegation from a state the way that the government came to power. Correspondingly, a state with a government in control of the territory, but not accepted by the organization as legitimate, loses rights of participation. Can these new rules be reconciled with the Tinoco Doctrine concerning the centrality of effective control of territory, or are they a victory for the Tobar Doctrine?

2. International law continues to allow individual states to recognize or not recognize governments as they choose. If states increasingly take into account the internal legitimacy of a government in affording it recognition, and recognize rebel movements even if they lack full power, should they then be allowed to disregard treaties with oppressive or coup-created governments? What would be the consequences of such a rule?

3. Customary international law generally prohibits states from intervening in the internal affairs of other states, although the meaning of intervention has changed a great deal over time. Today, verbal condemnations of governments, and even many types of

economic sanctions to promote human rights or advance other goals—especially those approved by the UN Security Council—are not considered unlawful intervention. Do you think that the recognition of the NCS as the legitimate representative of the Syrian people is, or should be, an illegal intervention? How about the supply of weapons to that group? Should it matter whether the government is violating human rights on a massive scale?

F. Note on Consequences of State and Governmental Change in Domestic Law

State and governmental changes also affect private actors through the disruptions they create for those engaging in economic transactions in a territory undergoing such events. Contracts granting various enterprises rights to carry out business—from mineral extraction to service industries—become the subject of significant controversy if part of the affected territory becomes a new state. Another scenario is that in which a business seeks to work with a government that is unrecognized by other states.

These and other situations may eventually come before national courts adjudicating controversies between private entities or between such entities and foreign states. In such cases, courts will typically face issues similar to those that governments face in deciding whether to recognize states or governments for purposes of diplomatic intercourse. Courts may have to determine whether a state or government unrecognized by the forum's government can sue or be sued, whether a citizen of such a state can sue or be sued, or whether the acts of an unrecognized government should be given effect or ignored. Should the state's or government's status be determined solely in terms of its de facto control of territory, or should other criteria, such as its democratic credentials, make a difference? Or should the possibility to sue or be sued turn on the foreign policy preferences of the forum state?

The United States has frequently been the forum for litigation arising from governmental change. As a general matter, under U.S. law, governments and states not recognized by the United States may not themselves sue in U.S. courts. On the other hand, U.S. courts have not challenged the validity of acts of unrecognized governments solely because they were unrecognized: in *Salimoff & Co. v. Standard Oil Co.*, 262 N.Y. 220 (1933), for example, the New York State Court of Appeals refused to strip Standard Oil of title to oil it drilled from plaintiff's land, which had been seized by the then-unrecognized Soviet government.

At the same time, with respect to governmental change, the State Department's practice for the last several decades has generally been to avoid either affirmatively recognizing or refusing to recognize a new government, a policy undertaken for the same reasons the United Nations has based most of its recognition decisions on effective control. Rather, the United States either continues or discontinues diplomatic relations, depending on the state of the bilateral relationship with the new government. On occasion, the United States has affirmatively announced that it does not recognize a government resulting from a coup (such as Haiti's).

The effect of the Executive Branch's recognition policy on a government's ability to sue in U.S. courts was at issue in *National Petrochemical Co. of Iran v. M/T Stolt Sheaf*, 860 F.2d 551 (2d Cir. 1988). In that case, Iran's governmentally owned oil company had contracted with and paid several foreign companies to purchase chemicals that it could not buy in the United States due to a U.S. embargo on trade with Iran. The foreign companies actually procured the chemicals in the United States but did not reveal this to Iran. When the companies eventually did not deliver the chemicals (because the defendants did not wish to ship to Iran once the Iran-Iraq war began in 1980), Iran sued the companies for fraud in Manhattan federal court in 1986. The United States had severed diplomatic relations with Iran in 1980 as a result of the 1979-1981 seizure of American diplomats in Tehran and had not resumed relations, though the United States had not formally stated that it did not recognize Iran's government. Indeed, the Secretary of State had said that the United States accepted the reality of the Iranian revolution and had concluded an agreement with that government for the release of the American diplomats. In the court of appeals, the U.S. government filed a brief urging that National Petrochemical Company (NPC) be granted access to U.S. courts. The court concluded as follows:

> A break in diplomatic relations with another government does not automatically signify denial of access to federal courts. As the Supreme Court has observed, courts are hardly competent to assess how friendly or unfriendly our relationship with a foreign government is at any given moment, and absent some "definite touchstone for determination, we are constrained to consider any relationship, short of war, with a recognized sovereign power as embracing the privilege of resorting to United States courts." [*Quoting Banco Nacional de Cuba v. Sabbatino*, 376 U.S. 398, 410 (1964).]
>
> . . . [A]ppellees urge that NPC must be denied access to federal court based on the President's failure to extend formal recognition to the Khomeini government. We disagree . . . . First, as this century draws to a close, the practice of extending formal recognition to new governments has altered: The United States Department of State has sometimes refrained from announcing recognition of a new government because grants of recognition have been misinterpreted as pronouncements of approval. . . . As a result, the absence of formal recognition cannot serve as the touchstone for determining whether the Executive Branch has "recognized" a foreign nation for the purpose of granting that government access to United States courts.
>
> Second, the power to deal with foreign nations outside the bounds of formal recognition is essential to a president's implied power to maintain international relations. As part of this power, the Executive Branch must have the latitude to permit a foreign nation access to U.S. courts, even if that nation is not formally recognized by the U.S. government. . . . It is evident that in today's topsy-turvy world governments can topple and relationships can change in a moment. The Executive Branch must therefore have broad, unfettered discretion in matters involving such sensitive, fast-changing, and complex foreign relationships. . . .
>
> . . . The United States has submitted a Statement of Interest . . . stating that "it is the position of the Executive Branch that the Iranian government and its instrumentality should be afforded access to our courts for purposes of resolution of the instant dispute." . . . This is not a case where the Executive Branch is attempting to prohibit a formally recognized government from bringing a single suit in the United States courts, nor is it a case where the Executive is arbitrarily allowing some suits by an unrecognized nation while disallowing others. Rather, here the Executive Branch . . . expressly entered this case as Amicus requesting that Iran be given access to our courts. Under such circumstances, and as the sole branch authorized to conduct relations with foreign countries, the Executive clearly did not act arbitrarily. Accordingly, we hold that, for all the reasons stated, NPC must be permitted to proceed with its diversity suit in the Southern District of New York.

860 F.2d at 554-555.

Notes and Questions

1. Are there any circumstances in which a foreign government not recognized by the United States should not have access to U.S. courts?

2. Why should this question be solely a matter for the Executive Branch and not the judiciary applying principles of international law?

3. Why would the Executive Branch want to allow Iran to sue in this case? At the time, the United States and Iran were participating in arbitration at The Hague under the terms of the 1981 agreement between them that ended the 1979-1981 hostage crisis. The Iran-U.S. Claims Tribunal was adjudicating the claims of the nationals of each country against the government of the other for expropriations during the Iranian hostage crisis. (For further details, see Chapters 2, 5, and 12.) The majority of private claimants were American companies and individuals, though the Tribunal also had jurisdiction over counterclaims by Iran. Prevailing American claimants were paid from a "judgment fund" of monies contributed by Iran; if the counterclaim exceeded the claim, Iran would obtain its proceeds through a suit in U.S. courts; if the suit failed, the U.S. government would have to pay. To avoid having to pay these counterclaim judgments itself, the U.S. government needed to assure Iran and the Tribunal that Iran would be able to sue the American claimants in U.S. courts, and thus it filed a statement of interest on behalf of Iran each time it asserted a claim in U.S. courts.

4. In *Kuwait Airways Corporation v. Iraqi Airways Co. (Nos. 4 and 5)*, [2002] UKHL 19, Kuwait's national airline sued Iraq's national airline for its seizure of KAC airplanes following Iraq's 1990 invasion and purported annexation of Kuwait and the subsequent destruction of the planes in Iraq by coalition bombing. Under British choice of law rules, British courts would normally apply Iraqi law as the law of the situs of the damage. The House of Lords upheld a lower court ruling refusing to apply the Iraqi official decree that dissolved KAC and took over the planes. It noted that Iraq's attempted annexation had not been recognized internationally, indeed had been explicitly rejected by the UN Security Council as a violation of the UN Charter (see Chapter 13) and was thus clearly contrary to British public policy. Is this case consistent with U.S. case law?

III. INTERNATIONAL ORGANIZATIONS AS GLOBAL ACTORS: THE UNITED NATIONS AND APARTHEID

Over the past two centuries, states have formed hundreds of international organizations, from localized technical groups such as the Commission Internationale pour la Protection des Eaux du Léman (International Commission for the Protection of the Waters of Lake Geneva), through regional organizations such as the Association of Southeast Asian Nations or the AU, to global specialized institutions such as the World Health Organization (WHO) or the WTO, to the largest and broadest in scope, the United Nations. Each came about because governments and other international actors perceived a need to engage in some institutionalized form of cooperation. Their actions have changed the planet in ways large and small. The WHO took the leading role in organizing a massive vaccination against smallpox, eradicating the disease; the International Telecommunication Union develops standards that allow telephones around the world to communicate and ensure that radio signals do not conflict with one another; and the International Civil Aviation Organization sets rules of aircraft and airport safety.

What forces drive states to create international organizations? Consider the following account of three perspectives from political science:

Harold K. Jacobson, Networks of Interdependence: International Organizations and the Global Political System

60-67 (2d ed. 1984)

FEDERALISM

. . . Federalism can be concerned with the expansion of the territorial domain of political authority, which is also the purpose of international governmental organizations. . . .

. . . The word "bargain" provides an equally apt description of what must occur for an international organization to be established. In forming an international organization, the constituent units, be they individuals, national associations, or governments, agree to give up some of their autonomy to achieve some purpose that can only be gained by aggregating their authority. . . . For an international organization to be created, those involved must perceive that in the relatively near term the benefits to be gained from membership will outweigh the costs. . . .

FUNCTIONALISM

Functionalism argues that two basic and observable trends in modern history are crucially important in shaping the domain and scope of political authority; they are the growth of technology and the spread and intensification of the desire for higher standards of material welfare. Technological developments both bring peoples closer together and make possible higher standards of material welfare. . . .

Functionalists feel that governments will be pressured by their citizens to engage in international cooperation to take advantage of technological developments. They maintain that people everywhere desire better material conditions, and they postulate that increasingly literate and urbanized populations will more and more be able to make governments respond to this desire. . . .

Functionalists applauded the fact that the specific purpose institutions that had been created were staffed by specialists in substantive fields rather than diplomats. . . . The functionalist strategy was based on the assumption that governments were not unitary actors but rather organizations of departments and individuals that often had different, and sometimes conflicting, interests. When it came to staffing the secretariats of international organizations, functionalists wanted career officials, and they postulated the creation of "a detached international civil service." . . .

The Theory of Public Goods

. . . The theory deals with a seeming paradox: contrary to the assumption that rational self-interest would lead the members of a group having a common interest to organize and to act collectively to promote their common interest, this does not happen.

. . . If the group is large, individual efforts will seem inconsequential and incapable of achieving the overall objective; hence the individual will concentrate on more proximate objectives even though their achievement may be counterproductive toward the group goal. An example is the individual who increases immediate income by increasing production even though the long-run effect of all producers doing this is to drive prices down and reduce the aggregate profits of the group. In world politics an individual state temporarily may increase security by increasing armaments, but all states may be less secure at the end of the resulting arms race.

. . . [Moreover], [s]ome services have the character of being public goods; that is, if they are available to anyone, they must be available to everyone. Thus, with large organizations, individual efforts will have no noticeable effect on the organization, and the individual will receive the benefits of the organization with or without contributing to it. . . . [I]n world politics, the benefits of general disarmament cannot be denied to the state that ignores the overall agreement and increases its own armaments. These properties of public goods are particularly relevant to international organizations since they are largely in the business of providing such goods.

Several ancillary arguments flow from these basic postulates. One is that to insure wide participation, large organizations must utilize coercive sanctions or benefits other than the public good that can be allocated selectively. Compulsory membership tends to be a corollary of the efficient production of the collective good by a large organization.

Another argument is that small groups operate according to fundamentally different principles than do large groups. In a small group it is likely that there will be at least a few members who would be better off if the public good were provided even if they had to provide it themselves. This is because the smaller the number of members that share in the benefits of the public good, the greater the proportion going to any individual. If the size of the members of the group is unequal, there will be a tendency for smaller members to rely on voluntary, self-interested actions of larger members. The largest member would receive the largest benefit, and consequently would be willing to make the largest contribution. . . . Consequently, in small groups there is a tendency for small members to exploit large members, to seek a free ride. . . . But small groups are much more likely to organize to provide public goods than are large groups. The larger the group, the less adequate the rewards for individual action, the less likely that any subset or individual will be willing to bear the entire or a substantial proportion of the burden of providing the public good, and the greater the initial costs of creating an organization.

The critical role of international organizations in the world raises important questions of how international law treats them. The goals for this Problem include:

- to provide a basic introduction to the role of international organizations in international law, including their powers, international legal status, and internal structure;
- to explain the ways that international organizations make and influence international law, including by examining the legal powers of organs within an organization and the role of organizations as venues for negotiation of international instruments; and
- to explain the jurisdiction and operation of international courts and other adjudicative mechanisms that can make decisions that are legally binding on states, individuals, and others.

A. The Problem

Nelson Mandela described apartheid as "the color line that all too often determines who is rich and who is poor . . . who lives in luxury and who lives in squalor . . . who shall get food, clothing, and health care . . . and who will live and who die." Apartheid was the system of racial separation and discrimination that prevailed in South Africa as a matter of governmental policy from 1948 until its abolition in the early 1990s. It classified persons as white, Bantu (black), coloured (mixed race), or Asian. Manifestations of apartheid included the denial of the right to vote, limitations on employment, separate living areas and schools, limits on ownership of property, prohibitions on intermarriage, internal pass laws limiting domestic travel of nonwhites, and white control of the legal system. The result was the legally mandated separation of the races and denial of basic human rights to approximately 90 percent of the state's population.

Apartheid was administered through a complex legal system, as described by South Africa's Truth and Reconciliation Commission (a panel appointed by the post-apartheid government to examine the apartheid era) in 1998.

Final Report of the Truth and Reconciliation Commission
Vol. 1, ch. 2 (1998)

[The Population Registration Act of 1950] formed the very bedrock of the apartheid state in that it provided for the classification of every South African into one of four racial categories. To achieve this end, it came up with definitions of racial groupings which were truly bizarre:

> *A White person is one who is in appearance obviously white—and not generally accepted as Coloured—or who is generally accepted as White—and is not obviously Non-White, provided that a person shall not be classified as a White person if one of his natural parents has been classified as a Coloured person or a Bantu . . . A Bantu is a person who is, or is generally accepted as, a member of any aboriginal race or tribe of Africa . . . a Coloured is a person who is not a white person or a Bantu.*

Despite the crude and hopelessly imprecise wording of these definitions, the Act was imposed with vigour and determination.

President Nelson Mandela wrote:

> Where one was allowed to live and work could rest on such absurd distinctions as the curl of one's hair or the size of one's lips. . . .

The effects of apartheid legislation

Overall, what the National Party did in its first ten to twelve years of power amounted, in Leo Kuper's words, to "a white counter-revolution" to forestall the perceived . . . threat to white supremacy from both local forces and the rising tide of African nationalist sentiment on the continent. . . .

It was also a social engineering project of awesome dimensions through which, from about the mid-1950s and for the next thirty or so years, the inherited rural and urban social fabric of South Africa was torn asunder and recreated in the image of a series of racist utopias. In the process, as indicated earlier, millions of black people and a handful of mainly poor whites were shunted around like pawns on a chessboard. Forced to relocate to places that often existed only on the drawing boards of the architects of apartheid, entire communities were simply wiped out. These included urban suburbs and rural villages, traditional communities and homelands, schools, churches and above all people. . . .

During this period, South Africa maintained diplomatic relations with many states and was a UN member. During the Cold War, South Africa was allied with the West, though this alliance often proved embarrassing to Western governments. Indeed, the need to abolish apartheid was one of the few principles on which East and West could agree, though both sides took advantage of the South African situation for their own strategic ends. As a result of this basic consensus, as well as the increased control of the General Assembly by developing states as a result of decolonization, the United Nations engaged in a sustained and proactive policy of placing pressure on the South African government.

The efforts to end apartheid had a normative and legal dimension as well. Apartheid violated one of the most fundamental prescriptions in the UN Charter and the Universal Declaration of Human Rights—the duty on states to respect human rights without distinction as to race. As a result, the UN's work to end apartheid can be viewed as an effort by its members to secure the compliance of South Africa with that basic norm.

B. Background on the Structures of International Organizations

The multiplicity of forms of international organizations makes categorization somewhat elusive. In general, they might be organized along two axes—the breadth of their *participation*, from fairly regional (or subregional), to global; and the *issues* over which they have a mandate, from specialized (or highly technical), to those with a mandate to consider all issues. Examples of the combinations are:

Global and general: United Nations

Global and specialized: WTO, IMF, World Bank, International Telecommunication Union, and others. Some global organizations are only open to states with a common interest, such as the International Coffee Organization or the Commonwealth (comprised of Great Britain and most of its former colonies).

Regional and general: Organization of American States, AU, Gulf Cooperation Council, Commonwealth of Independent States.

Regional and specialized: European Union (though its mandate is very large), Association of South East Asian Nations, Arctic Council, Inter-American Development Bank.

Organizations also differ with respect to their powers: they can serve merely as fora for dialogue, or they can possess decisionmaking powers that bind their members (including those members that may not have participated in the decision or that did and opposed it).

Despite these many differences, most international organizations share several core aspects. These are described below, with particular emphasis on the United Nations, the most significant organization in terms of breadth of responsibilities and legal effect of some of its decisions—as well as the organization most actively involved in the anti-apartheid movement. (See chart of the UN's components).

Constitutive Instruments: International organizations are usually the creatures of treaties, though some, notably the Organization for Security and Cooperation in Europe, are the products of political instruments. The UN Charter is the most significant document in this respect. Constitutive instruments describe the membership policies, powers of the organization, roles for different organs, and decisionmaking procedures.

Assembly of Members: International organizations typically have one organ that includes all the members. These bodies are entrusted with broad policy questions and

Published by the United Nations Department of Public Information   DPI/2470 rev.3—13-38229—August 2013

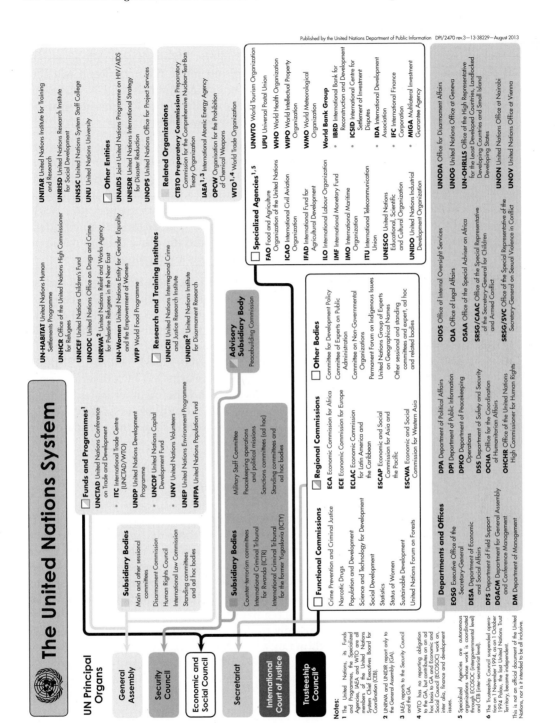

The United Nations System

UN Principal Organs

General Assembly

Security Council

Economic and Social Council

Secretariat

International Court of Justice

Trusteeship Council[6]

Subsidiary Bodies
Main and other sessional committees
Disarmament Commission
Human Rights Council
International Law Commission
Standing committees and ad hoc bodies

Subsidiary Bodies
Counter-terrorism committees
International Criminal Tribunal for Rwanda (ICTR)
International Criminal Tribunal for the former Yugoslavia (ICTY)
Military Staff Committee
Peacekeeping operations and political missions
Sanctions committees (ad hoc)
Standing committees and ad hoc bodies

☐ Funds and Programmes[1]
UNCTAD United Nations Conference on Trade and Development
• **ITC** International Trade Centre (UNCTAD/WTO)
UNDP United Nations Development Programme
• **UNCDF** United Nations Capital Development Fund
• **UNV** United Nations Volunteers
UNEP United Nations Environment Programme
UNFPA United Nations Population Fund
UN-HABITAT United Nations Human Settlements Programme
UNHCR Office of the United Nations High Commissioner for Refugees
UNICEF United Nations Children's Fund
UNODC United Nations Office on Drugs and Crime
UNRWA[2] United Nations Relief and Works Agency for Palestine Refugees in the Near East
UN-Women United Nations Entity for Gender Equality and the Empowerment of Women
WFP World Food Programme

☐ Research and Training Institutes
UNICRI United Nations Interregional Crime and Justice Research Institute
UNIDIR[2] United Nations Institute for Disarmament Research
UNITAR United Nations Institute for Training and Research
UNRISD United Nations Research Institute for Social Development
UNSSC United Nations System Staff College
UNU United Nations University

☐ Other Entities
UNAIDS Joint United Nations Programme on HIV/AIDS
UNISDR United Nations International Strategy for Disaster Reduction
UNOPS United Nations Office for Project Services

Related Organizations
CTBTO Preparatory Commission Preparatory Commission for the Comprehensive Nuclear-Test-Ban Treaty Organization
IAEA[1, 3] International Atomic Energy Agency
OPCW Organisation for the Prohibition of Chemical Weapons
WTO[1, 4] World Trade Organization

☐ Functional Commissions
Crime Prevention and Criminal Justice
Narcotic Drugs
Population and Development
Science and Technology for Development
Social Development
Statistics
Status of Women
Sustainable Development
United Nations Forum on Forests

☐ Regional Commissions
ECA Economic Commission for Africa
ECE Economic Commission for Europe
ECLAC Economic Commission for Latin America and the Caribbean
ESCAP Economic and Social Commission for Asia and the Pacific
ESCWA Economic and Social Commission for Western Asia

☐ Other Bodies
Committee for Development Policy
Committee of Experts on Public Administration
Committee on Non-Governmental Organizations
Permanent Forum on Indigenous Issues
United Nations Group of Experts on Geographical Names
Other sessional and standing committees and expert, ad hoc and related bodies

Advisory Subsidiary Body
Peacebuilding Commission

☐ Specialized Agencies[1, 5]
FAO Food and Agriculture Organization of the United Nations
ICAO International Civil Aviation Organization
IFAD International Fund for Agricultural Development
ILO International Labour Organization
IMF International Monetary Fund
IMO International Maritime Organization
ITU International Telecommunication Union
UNESCO United Nations Educational, Scientific and Cultural Organization
UNIDO United Nations Industrial Development Organization
UNWTO World Tourism Organization
UPU Universal Postal Union
WHO World Health Organization
WIPO World Intellectual Property Organization
WMO World Meteorological Organization
World Bank Group
• **IBRD** International Bank for Reconstruction and Development
• **ICSID** International Centre for Settlement of Investment Disputes
• **IDA** International Development Association
• **IFC** International Finance Corporation
• **MIGA** Multilateral Investment Guarantee Agency

Departments and Offices
EOSG Executive Office of the Secretary-General
DESA Department of Economic and Social Affairs
DFS Department of Field Support
DGACM Department for General Assembly and Conference Management
DM Department of Management
DPA Department of Political Affairs
DPI Department of Public Information
DPKO Department of Peacekeeping Operations
DSS Department of Safety and Security
OCHA Office for the Coordination of Humanitarian Affairs
OHCHR Office of the United Nations High Commissioner for Human Rights
OIOS Office of Internal Oversight Services
OLA Office of Legal Affairs
OSAA Office of the Special Adviser on Africa
SRSG/CAAC Office of the Special Representative of the Secretary-General for Children and Armed Conflict
SRSG/SVC Office of the Special Representative of the Secretary-General on Sexual Violence in Conflict
UNODA Office for Disarmament Affairs
UNOG United Nations Office at Geneva
UN-OHRLLS Office of the High Representative for the Least Developed Countries, Landlocked Developing Countries and Small Island Developing States
UNON United Nations Office at Nairobi
UNOV United Nations Office at Vienna

Notes:
1 The United Nations, its Funds and Programmes, the Specialized Agencies, IAEA and WTO are all members of the United Nations System Chief Executives Board for Coordination (CEB).

2 UNRWA and UNIDIR report only to the General Assembly (GA).

3 IAEA reports to the Security Council and the GA.

4 WTO has no reporting obligation to the GA, but contributes on an ad hoc basis to GA and Economic and Social Council (ECOSOC) work on, inter alia, finance and development issues.

5 Specialized Agencies are autonomous organizations whose work is coordinated through ECOSOC (intergovernmental level) and CEB (inter-secretariat level).

6 The Trusteeship Council suspended operation on 1 November 1994, as on 1 October 1994 Palau, the last United Nations Trust Territory, became independent.

This is not an official document of the United Nations, nor is it intended to be all-inclusive.

structural matters such as membership in the organization and in its sub-units, budget, personnel, and amendment of the constitutive instrument. Although generally each state has one vote in these organs, some institutions, typically in the financial arena, will allocate votes based on financial contributions. The General Assembly is the UN's assembly of all its members. The Assembly delegates many responsibilities to committees of states that study issues and draft resolutions for the General Assembly to adopt.

Specialized and Executive Organs: Organizations typically include entities composed of less than the entire membership to carry out key functions. In the case of the United Nations, the Charter establishes the Security Council (15 states), the Economic and Social Council (54 states), the Trusteeship Council (5 states, though it suspended operations in 1994 with the independence of the last trust territory created after World War II), and the International Court of Justice (15 judges). The Security Council's decisions are binding on all states, and the ICJ's judgments bind the states that are parties to a given case; the Economic and Social Council's resolutions are recommendations.

Secretariat: Because member states cannot undertake the work required for an organization to function, each institution has a professional staff, headed by a secretary-general or the equivalent. These international civil servants are, in theory, loyal only to the organization, not to the state of which they are a national. Their tasks include following issues in order to brief governments, staffing temporary missions, researching and preparing public reports, administering financial aid to states, and mediating disputes between governments. The presence of an effective secretariat led by a first-rate secretary-general gives an organization a life of its own beyond the member states. As long as they act within the terms of the constitutive instrument and are not challenged by too many member states, secretariat officials can significantly shape the agenda of the organization.

C. Modes of Decision Making in International Organizations

Much of the influence and power of any international organization turns upon the mechanisms it uses for making decisions, as well as the effect of those decisions upon member states. For example, the limited membership of the UN Security Council permits faster decisions than would be the case if the General Assembly had to agree on each issue. In addition, the International Civil Aviation Organization (with 191 members) delegates to its 36-member Council, which includes states with particular technical expertise on aviation matters, the authority to issue aviation regulations.

The constitutive instrument are usually quite explicit regarding the decisionmaking powers and processes within each organ. Consider the following articles of the UN Charter:

United Nations Charter
(1945)

Article 10

The General Assembly may discuss any questions or any matters within the scope of the present Charter or relating to the powers and functions of any organs provided for in the present Charter, and . . . make recommendations to the Members of the United Nations or to the Security Council or to both on any such questions or matters.

Article 11

1. The General Assembly may consider the general principles of co-operation in the maintenance of international peace and security . . . and may make recommendations with regard to such principles to the Members or to the Security Council or to both.

2. The General Assembly may discuss any questions relating to the maintenance of international peace and security brought before it by any Member of the United Nations, or by the Security Council [and] may make recommendations with regard to any such questions to the state or states concerned or to the Security Council or to both. . . .

Article 18

1. Each member of the General Assembly shall have one vote.

2. Decisions . . . on important questions shall be made by a two-thirds majority of the members present and voting. These questions shall include: recommendations with respect to the maintenance of international peace and security. . . .

3. Decisions on other questions . . . shall be made by a majority of the members present and voting.

Article 23

1. The Security Council shall consist of fifteen Members of the United Nations. The Republic of China [now the People's Republic of China], France, the Union of Soviet Socialist Republics [now Russia], the United Kingdom of Great Britain and Northern Ireland, and the United States of America shall be permanent members of the Security Council. The General Assembly shall elect ten other Members . . . to be non-permanent members of the Security Council, due regard being specially paid, in the first instance to the[ir] contribution . . . to the maintenance of international peace and security and to the other purposes of the Organization, and also to equitable geographical distribution.

2. The non-permanent members . . . shall be elected for a term of two years. . . .

Article 24

1. In order to ensure prompt and effective action by the United Nations, its Members confer on the Security Council primary responsibility for the maintenance of international peace and security, and agree that in carrying out its duties under this responsibility the Security Council acts on their behalf.

2. In discharging these duties the Security Council shall act in accordance with the Purposes and Principles of the United Nations. . . .

Article 25

The Members of the United Nations agree to accept and carry out the decisions of the Security Council in accordance with the present Charter.

Article 27

1. Each member of the Security Council shall have one vote.

2. Decisions of the Security Council on procedural matters shall be made by an affirmative vote of nine members.

3. Decisions of the Security Council on all other matters shall be made by an affirmative vote of nine members including the concurring votes of the permanent members. . . .

Article 48

1. The action required to carry out the decisions of the Security Council for the maintenance of international peace and security shall be taken by all the Members of the United Nations or by some of them, as the Security Council may determine.

———

Thus, the General Assembly's resolutions on matter of international peace and security are only recommendations. (Its votes on internal UN matters like the budget or membership on various bodies are binding on members.) On the other hand, the Security Council, depending on its choice of words in its resolutions, can make binding decisions or non-binding recommendations.

The drafters designated the states in Article 23 as permanent members because they were the principal World War II victors. (For discussion as to whether developments since 1945 suggest a different group of permanent members, or the elimination of the category, see Chapter 14.) Under a 1963 General Assembly resolution, the nonpermanent seats are allocated as follows: three to Africa, two to Asia, two to Latin America, two to Western Europe "and other states" (for instance, Australia), and one to Eastern Europe. A so-called gentlemen's agreement among the UN's members ensures that certain particularly populated, wealthy, or otherwise influential nonpermanent members, such as Japan, Germany, and India, rotate on the Council with greater frequency than other states.

By contrast, the Articles of Agreement of the IMF allocate votes based on each state's financial contribution to the IMF. The total number of votes as of 2015 was 2,519,762. Consider this sample of the number of votes of selected member states:

State	Number of votes	Percentage of total
Argentina	21,908	0.87
Botswana	1,615	.06
China	95,996	3.81
France	108,122	4.29
Germany	146,392	5.81
Indonesia	21,530	0.85
Japan	157,022	6.23
Russia	60,191	2.39
Saudi Arabia	70,592	2.80
United States	421,961	16.75

IMF Members' Quotas and Voting Power, and IMF Governors, *www.imf.org.*

As another example, the Organization for Security and Cooperation in Europe (OSCE) makes its decisions—none of which are legally binding on members—by consensus, either at summits of heads of government, meetings of foreign ministers, or meetings of diplomats. Each year one state serves as the Chairman-in-Office and convenes the various meetings and sets the agenda. The OSCE has established special procedures to make decisions by less than consensus: for example, if one state is committing gross violations of the OSCE's commitments, the others may make a decision on that question.

Notes and Questions

1. What factors would states creating an international organization consider in deciding which issues should be decided by the assembly of members and which should be delegated to smaller bodies?

2. Why do you think the UN's founders allowed only the Security Council to make binding decisions on matters of international peace and security? How does this decision relate to the structure and voting requirements of the Council?

3. What factors would states consider in deciding whether decisions should be made by unanimity, consensus, or other voting procedures? What type of system would you expect strong states to favor?

4. Do the articles of the Charter making five states permanent members of the Security Council and requiring that any nonprocedural decision of the Council have their assent violate the principle of the sovereign equality of states? How about the unequal voting in the Articles of Agreement of the IMF?

5. In response to the increased economic power of developing states, the members of the IMF agreed in the last decade to allocate a greater share of votes to fast-growing developing countries such as China, Korea, and India. Why would states that would lose proportionally in a reallocation agree to give other states more votes?

D. Legal "Personality"

The proliferation and power of international organizations leaves no doubt that they are major actors in the international legal process. Yet in the early years of the United Nations, some states and scholars still questioned just how much independent authority the United Nations and other organizations possessed in light of the traditional international law view that only states had rights and obligations. On the one hand, Article 104 of the Charter provided that the United Nations would have legal capacity within its member states (so that, for instance, it could hire plumbers and pay electricity bills); yet where the Charter was silent, what sorts of things could the organization do vis-à-vis its members, and who spoke for it—all of its members, some of them, or the Secretary-General? These questions are similar in a sense to questions faced in domestic systems long ago about the status of corporations as opposed to partnerships.

Decision makers within the United Nations faced this issue head on shortly after its creation. After the outbreak of war between Israel and the Arab states following Israel's declaration of independence in 1948, the Secretary-General appointed Count Folke Bernadotte of Sweden to mediate between the parties in the hopes of bringing about a cease-fire. That year, Bernadotte's car was blown up in Jerusalem, killing him and a French observer. While Jewish extremists were suspected, none was ever tried by Israel. In traditional international law, a state whose national is injured in the territory of another state has the right to bring a claim against the latter for damages. The General Assembly asked the ICJ whether the United Nations could make a claim for damages to the organization (e.g., expenses of returning and burying the body), and whether the United Nations could make a claim for damages to the victim's heirs. The Charter was silent on both questions.

obtaining promotions within the organization; some receive de facto instructions from their governments, who may hold sway over their post-UN careers. In peacekeeping operations, although soldiers officially serve under the UN flag and are paid by the United Nations, they are typically deployed in contingents by state of origin, and their governments play a central role in deciding where and how they will undertake their duties (with avoidance of danger a priority for most states donating troops). What tools do international organizations have to ensure that international civil servants are independent of governments?

E. Condemnations of Apartheid

The UN's first foray into the racial system in South Africa began in response to a complaint by the government of India in 1946 regarding the treatment of Indians in South Africa. In a mildly worded resolution, the General Assembly stated that Indians should be treated according to agreements concluded between the two governments and requested that the two parties consult. G.A. Res. 44 (1946). Four years after the legal establishment of apartheid in South Africa, a group of developing states requested that the Secretary-General put apartheid per se on the agenda of the Assembly. South Africa objected that the United Nations lacked the competence to consider the internal affairs of one of its members. The Assembly nonetheless passed the following resolution:

General Assembly Resolution 616 B (1952)

The General Assembly . . .

Considering that one of the purposes of the United Nations is to achieve international co-operation in promoting and encouraging respect for human rights and fundamental freedoms for all, without distinction as to race, sex, language or religion . . .

1. *Declares* that in a multi-racial society harmony and respect for human rights and freedoms and the peaceful development of a unified community are best assured when patterns of legislation and practice are directed towards ensuring equality before the law of all persons regardless of race, creed or colour, and when economic, social, cultural and political participation of all racial groups is on a basis of equality;

2. *Affirms* that governmental policies of Member States which are not directed towards these goals, but which are designed to perpetuate or increase discrimination, are inconsistent with the pledges of the Members under Article 56 of the Charter;

3. *Solemnly* calls upon all Member States to bring their policies into conformity with their obligation under the Charter to promote the observance of human rights and fundamental freedoms.

On March 21, 1960, in Sharpville, a township in northeastern South Africa, during a peaceful protest by blacks against the laws restricting their movement and habitations, government troops opened fire, killing 68 men, women, and children and injuring 180. Four days later, 29 states from Africa and Asia asked the UN Security Council to hold a meeting to discuss this issue. (See accompanying photo of the debate.) The Council's members agreed quickly (though Britain and France abstained) on the following resolution:

Security Council Resolution 134 (1960)

The Security Council . . .

Recognizing that such a situation has been brought about by the racial policies of the government of the Union of South Africa and the continued disregard by that Government of the resolutions of the General Assembly calling upon it to revise its policies and bring them into conformity with its obligations and responsibilities under the Charter of the United Nations . . .

1. *Recognizes* that the situation in the Union of South Africa is one that has led to international friction and if continued might endanger international peace and security;

2. *Deplores* that the recent disturbances in the Union of South Africa should have led to the loss of life of so many Africans and extends to the families of the victims its deepest sympathies; . . .

4. *Calls upon* the Government of the Union of South Africa to initiate measures aimed at bringing about racial harmony based on equality in order to ensure that the present situation does not continue or recur, and to abandon its policies of *apartheid* and racial discrimination. . . .

South African Representative Bernardus Fourie addresses the Security Council,
March 30, 1960
SOURCE: United Nations Photo 65121

Notes and Questions

1. Under what provisions of the UN Charter did the Security Council take these actions? Given the language of Resolution 134, is it binding on South Africa?

2. Article 2(7) of the Charter states that nothing in the Charter "shall authorize the United Nations to intervene in matters which are essentially within the domestic jurisdiction of any state" (except when the Council is undertaking enforcement measures, e.g., sanctions, under Chapter VII of the Charter). As early as 1946 the General Assembly had condemned the Spanish regime of Generalissimo Francisco Franco for its ties to the World War II Axis powers and not "represent[ing] the Spanish people." It recommended that the Security Council consider how to remedy the situation and urged states to withdraw their diplomats from Spain. With respect to South Africa, the vote on the 1952 resolution was 24 in favor, 1 opposed, and 34 abstentions; the abstentions included powerful Western states that opposed including apartheid on the UN's agenda as well as East bloc and developing states that favored stronger measures against South Africa. What does this practice suggest about member states' interpretation of Article 2(7)? Does the UN's refusal to condemn unrepresentative governments elsewhere change your answer?

3. What purpose do such condemnations serve? How do they differ from condemnations by individual states? What incentives might South Africa have to comply with the resolutions? How could they make a difference to those within South Africa?

F. The UN's Sanctioning Processes

During the apartheid years, the United Nations and its specialized agencies utilized a variety of sanctioning mechanisms. These efforts began in the General Assembly, whose powers under the Charter are limited to recommendations, but eventually included the Security Council as well. In November 1962, the Assembly passed the following resolution by a vote of 67-16-23; nearly all the opposing states were wealthy Western states.

General Assembly Resolution 1761 (1962)

The General Assembly . . .

1. *Deplores* the failure of the Government of the Republic of South Africa to comply with the repeated requests and demands of the General Assembly and of the Security Council and its flouting of world public opinion by refusing to abandon its racial policies;

2. *Strongly deprecates* the continued and total disregard by the Government of South Africa of its obligations under the Charter of the United Nations and, furthermore, its determined aggravation of racial issues by enforcing measures of increasing ruthlessness involving violence and bloodshed;

3. *Reaffirms* that the continuance of those policies seriously endangers international peace and security;

4. *Requests* Member States to take the following measures, separately or collectively, in conformity with the Charter, to bring about the abandonment of those policies:

(a) Breaking off diplomatic relations with . . . South Africa . . . ;

(b) Closing their ports to all vessels flying the South African flag;

(c) Enacting legislation prohibiting their ships from entering South African ports;

(d) Boycotting all South African goods and refraining from exporting goods . . . to South Africa;

(e) Refusing landing and passage facilities to all [South African] aircraft . . . ;

5. *Decides* to establish a Special Committee consisting of representatives of Member States [to review and report to the Assembly and Council on apartheid]; . . .

8. *Requests* the Security Council to take appropriate measures, including sanctions, to secure South Africa's compliance with the resolutions of the General Assembly and of the Security Council [and] to consider action under Article 6 of the Charter [concerning expulsion].

The Special Committee created by the General Assembly operated for over 31 years, until the end of the apartheid regime in 1994. Its work included elaborate reporting on apartheid; convening of conferences devoted to apartheid; and preparation and implementation of a program of action for the United Nations, its members, and other international organizations concerning South Africa (that included sports boycotts and other sanctions).

In 1963, Western nations, facing pressure from the developing world, announced that they would stop arms sales to South Africa. The Council then passed the first arms embargo by the United Nations against a member state. It was adopted with no opposition, with Britain and France again abstaining, the former asserting that Britain's military cooperation with South Africa for the protection of sea routes prevented support for a full arms embargo. The resolution was not, however, adopted under Chapter VII of the UN Charter and was not considered at the time to be a legally binding decision.

Security Council Resolution 181 (1963)

The Security Council,

Having considered the question of race conflict in South Africa resulting from the policies of *apartheid* of the Government of the Republic of South Africa, as submitted by the thirty-two African Member States . . .

Being convinced that the situation in South Africa is seriously disturbing international peace and security,

1. *Strongly deprecates* the policies of South Africa in its perpetuation of racial discrimination as being inconsistent with the principles contained in the Charter of the United Nations and contrary to its obligations as a Member of the United Nations;

2. *Calls upon* the Government of South Africa to abandon the policies of *apartheid* and discrimination . . . and to liberate all persons imprisoned, interned or subjected to other restrictions for having opposed the policy of *apartheid*;

3. *Solemnly calls upon* all States to cease forthwith the sale and shipment of arms, ammunition of all types and military vehicles to South Africa. . . .

———————

The U.S. delegate stated after the vote that U.S. support for the resolution was based on the resolution's sponsors' willingness to use the term "disturbing international peace and security" in the preamble, in lieu of the term "endangering international peace and security." He argued that the chosen language kept the embargo outside of Chapter VII, which he said was appropriate only to "a fully matured threat to, or breach of, the peace."

Yet South Africa continued to practice—and indeed strengthen—apartheid during the 1960s and 1970s. It obtained arms clandestinely from some states, such as Israel, and developed a domestic armaments industry. The Assembly, with its majority of developing world states, responded with numerous strongly worded resolutions.

In the early 1970s, a coalition of states opposed to apartheid sought to devise yet a new sanction—removal of South Africa from the United Nations itself. Article 6 of the Charter gives the General Assembly the right to expel a member that "has persistently violated the Principles" of the Charter, but only upon the recommendation of the Security Council; Article 5 allows the General Assembly to suspend any privileges of a member state that has been the subject of Security Council "preventive or enforcement action," but also only upon the Council's recommendation. These anti-apartheid states began this process in the Credentials Committee in September 1974.

First Report of the Credentials Committee

U.N. Doc. A/9779 (1974)

7. The representative of Senegal stated that his delegation objected to the acceptance of the credentials of the representatives of South Africa. . . . The representatives of South Africa to the General Assembly had been appointed by a Government which was the product of racial criteria and, as an institution, represented only a very small fraction of the South African population. . . . [T]hat country would certainly not have been admitted as a Member of the United Nations in 1945 had the policy of *apartheid* been put into law at the time. Furthermore, the question under consideration was to exclude not South Africa as a State Member of the United Nations, but solely the South African delegation, as it could not be considered that the latter represented the country. . . .

9. The representative of the United States of America declared that the Credentials Committee . . . was to examine whether the credentials of representatives had been issued in conformity with rules 27 and 28 of the rules of procedure. [Note: These rules address the form of the credentials submitted by governments.] The Committee's function was to verify the execution of the administrative duties that the Secretary-General had been entrusted with in relation to credentials, and was therefore much akin to that of a parliamentary body. . . . [T]he Committee was not in a position to make a decision in that matter. . . . [F]or the Committee to decide on the basis of domestic policies would constitute a dangerous precedent for all. Furthermore, there was much to be gained by the continued participation of South Africa in the activities of the United Nations. . . .

11. The representative of Costa Rica felt that the Committee should not go beyond its limited competence. As to the question of *apartheid* itself, the Government of Costa Rica was in complete agreement with the Government of Senegal. . . . However, the Committee

was not in a position to suspend or expel a Member State since that action, under Article 6 of the Charter, could be taken only by the General Assembly upon the recommendation of the Security Council. His delegation accepted the credentials submitted on behalf of South Africa as valid. . . .

––––––––––––

The Credentials Committee decided by a vote of 5-3-1 to accept the credentials of all states except South Africa. Two days later, the General Assembly approved the report of the Credentials Committee, as well as a resolution asking the Security Council to "review the relationship between the United Nations and South Africa in the light of the constant violation by South Africa of the principles of the Charter and the Universal Declaration of Human Rights." G.A. Res. 3207 (1974). When the Council took up the matter in October 1974, a resolution to expel South Africa was vetoed by France, the United Kingdom, and the United States. After this defeat for the states seeking South Africa's removal, the General Assembly decided the next month to consider the effect of the rejection of the credentials by the Credentials Committee.

Official Records of 2281st Plenary Meeting of the General Assembly

U.N. Doc. A/PV.2281 (1974)

53. Mr. RICHARD (United Kingdom): . . .

55. . . . We are either a law-abiding, law-respecting body or we are nothing, a mere talking shop. If we put aside the Charter whenever its provisions may seem to a majority of us—even, indeed, to a preponderant majority of us—to be inconvenient, then we lose all claim to authority and to credence. . . .

56. The Charter requires . . . that certain decisions have to be taken by the Security Council. Sometimes the Security Council operates alone; sometimes it operates in conjunction with the Assembly in the sense that a decision by the Security Council to make a certain recommendation to the Assembly is the necessary pre-condition for the Assembly to take action.

57. The Charter also provides—and again this is no incidental provision but goes to the heart of the way in which this Organization was conceived and in which therefore it must function—that certain decisions of the Security Council require not merely the support of the prescribed majority of members of the Council, but also the concurrence of all the permanent members. By concurrence we mean of course the absence of a negative vote. This in turn casts a heavy responsibility on those permanent members. . . .

58. We must therefore reject . . . any argument that in discharging this important function under the Charter we ought to abandon our own judgement in deference to the views urged upon us by other delegations, even a majority of them, or indeed by other organs of the United Nations. . . . The Charter imposes a responsibility on each of the members of the Security Council, and each of them in turn must discharge it as it sees fit, conscientiously, honourably and in good faith. . . .

59. I turn now to the . . . argument that, despite the fact that the Security Council has not made a recommendation to the Assembly under Article 5 or Article 6 of the Charter, it is

nevertheless open to the Assembly today by its own decision to exclude the delegation of a Member State.

60. . . . [This argument] flies in the face of the Charter. . . . That Charter provides explicitly and exhaustively in Article 5 how a Member State may be suspended from the exercise of its rights and privileges of membership. . . .

62. It seems to me to be unarguable, therefore, as a matter of law—as a matter of the fundamental constitutional law of this Organization—that if we purport to exclude the delegation of a Member State . . . from participating in our proceedings, and if we do so by a simple decision of the Assembly itself and not in the circumstances and in the manner provided for in Article 5, we are acting improperly, unconstitutionally and illegally. . . .

64. Mr. JAIPAL (India): . . .

67. No amount of pressure, influence and persuasion has so far deflected the white régime from its chosen doctrine of racial supremacy over the blacks, the browns and the Coloured people. . . .

68. . . . What, then, are the options open to us? The expulsion of the white régime in terms of Article 6 of the Charter is certainly one of the options; but, unfortunately, three permanent members of the Security Council have vetoed such a course of action. One may expect a similar decision in regard to action to suspend South Africa in terms of Article 5 of the Charter.

69. In vetoing expulsion, those three Member States have . . . condemned those policies, and yet they remain hopeful of bringing about a change in the policy of the Pretoria régime. This is a hope which we do not share. In our opinion, there is little evidence in support of such a hopeful posture. . . .

74. . . . [I]t is anomalous—that the representatives of a Member State whose credentials have been rejected should be allowed to participate in the work of this session. . . . Surely this decision is within our competence. . . .

76. In rejecting the credentials of the representatives of South Africa, we are in fact acting in accordance with our rules of procedure and also in conformity with the Charter; . . . we shall certainly not be acting contrary to the Charter, because we shall not be expelling or suspending South Africa. We shall only be deciding not to allow the representatives of South Africa to participate in this session of the General Assembly. . . .

153. The PRESIDENT [of the General Assembly, Abdelaziz Bouteflika of Algeria] *(interpretation from French)* . . .

155. . . . [T]he absence of a decision by the Security Council [due to the veto] in no way affects the General Assembly's rejection of the credentials of the delegation of South Africa. Since its twenty-fifth session the General Assembly has been regularly rejecting, each year, the credentials of that delegation. It did so until last year by adopting an amendment to the report of the Credentials Committee. . . .

159. It would therefore be a betrayal of the clearly and repeatedly expressed will of the General Assembly to understand this to mean that it was merely a procedural method of expressing its rejection of the policy of *apartheid*. On the basis of the consistency with which the General Assembly has regularly refused to accept the credentials of the South African delegation, one may legitimately infer that the General Assembly would in the same way reject the credentials of any other delegation authorized by the Government

of the Republic of South Africa to represent it, which is tantamount to saying . . . that the General Assembly refuses to allow the South African delegation to participate in its work.

160. Thus it is, as President of the twenty-ninth session of the General Assembly, that I interpret the decision of the General Assembly, leaving open the question of the status of the Republic of South Africa as Member of the United Nations which, as we all know, is a matter requiring a recommendation from the Security Council. . . .

———————

Compared to the actions in the General Assembly, the Security Council, by virtue of the veto power of three states with economic ties to South Africa, adopted far fewer and much narrower resolutions; these urged South Africa to cease specific policies, such as imprisonment and execution of political opponents, and emphasized the need for dialogue between the races. Yet in November 1977, the Security Council unanimously tightened the arms embargo on South Africa. It took action under Chapter VII of the Charter, the first time the Council had imposed such sanctions against a UN member state.

Security Council Resolution 418 (1977)

The Security Council, . . .

Recognizing that the military build-up by South Africa and its persistent acts of aggression against the neighbouring States seriously disturb the security of those States. . . .

Acting therefore under Chapter VII of the Charter of the United Nations,

1. *Determines* . . . that the acquisition by South Africa of arms and related *matériel* constitutes a threat to the maintenance of international peace and security;

2. *Decides* that all States shall cease forthwith any provision to South Africa of arms and related *matériel* of all types, including the sale or transfer of weapons and ammunition, military vehicles and equipment, [and] paramilitary police equipment. . . .

———————

In 1985, the Council urged member states to suspend new investment, prohibit the sale of South African gold coins, restrict sport and cultural relations, and prohibit sales of nuclear and computer technology and equipment.

Ultimately, domestic and international pressure led the Nationalist Party to select F. W. DeKlerk, a moderate party member, as President of South Africa in 1989. DeKlerk began a four-year process that led to the end of apartheid. Following free and open elections in April 1994, a nonracial government, led by Nelson Mandela, took office. In a speech to the General Assembly in October 1994, President Mandela stated:

> We stand here today to salute the United Nations Organization and its Member States, both singly and collectively, for joining forces with the masses of our people in common struggle that has brought about our emancipation and pushed back the frontiers of racism. The millions of our people say "thank you" and "thank you again" because the respect for your own dignity as human beings inspired you to act to ensure the restoration of our dignity as well.

Notes and Questions

1. The arms embargo began in the General Assembly with a recommendation to states, then moved into the Security Council, whose first resolution (181) did not seem to be a binding decision under Article 25 but whose later resolution (418) was—note the word "decides" in Resolution 418. What would explain this progression?

2. What are the respective roles of the General Assembly and the Security Council in sanctioning South Africa for apartheid? Did their actions appear to complement or conflict with one another? Should they act together or separately? How might the different legal effects of their decisions account for the outcomes in each body?

3. Which side had the better legal argument in the 1974 credentials battle? How much do you think law influenced the decision making of the General Assembly?

4. Are there legal limits on what sanctions the Security Council can impose? Could the Council have ordered states to block or seize the assets of leading apartheid officials without due process? These issues arose in the last 15 years as the Security Council imposed sanctions on individuals and organizations that the U.S. and other Council members said were affiliated with al Qaeda or the Taliban. For a discussion of this issue, see Chapter 14, Problem I.

5. The Irish author and sometime diplomat Conor Cruise O'Brien wrote the following about the United Nations in a compelling 1968 book titled *United Nations, Sacred Drama* (pp. 9-11). Consider its relevance to the role of the United Nations in South Africa.

> Why, men often ask, does the United Nations not *act?* The answer is that it seldom does anything else: it is acting all the time. . . . It has no power except the actor's power: the power to move, emotionally and morally. It has no *role* except a *role*; it plays the part of what men take it for. Its Council Chambers and Assembly Hall are stage sets for a continuous dramatisation of world history.
>
> . . . Since the United Nations makes its impression on the imagination of mankind through a spectacle presented in an auditorium with confrontations of opposing personages, it may be said to belong to the category of *drama*. Since the personages . . . symbolise mighty forces . . . the drama may rightly be called *sacred*. . . .
>
> . . . The "satisfaction" derived from the public offering of the "glowing phrases" [is] the same as that derived by the faithful from the public offering of a prayer: the sense of common aspiration; the appeal to a higher power, symbolised in this case by the Security Council and the General Assembly; the implied promise to meet again in continued acts of faith; the feeling that the thing feared may be averted, and the thing hoped for be won, by the solemn and collective use of appropriate words. . . .

G. The United Nations as a Forum for Other Law Making

The United Nations and international organizations are also key fora for preparation of legal instruments, from treaties to soft law. In the case of the UN, it will typically delegate preparatory work for a treaty to the International Law Commission, a 34-member body of independent legal experts created in 1947, or an intergovernmental conference process composed of numerous committees. Both will usually take a matter of years to complete their work. At times, the first process will flow into the second. The ILC's work has been critical to many conventions, such as the Vienna Convention on the Law of Treaties. Among the many treaties to emerge principally from the conference process is the 1982 Convention on the Law of the Sea.

In the case of apartheid, in 1973, a group of strong opponents of South Africa drafted a multilateral treaty through the UN to criminalize apartheid, i.e., make individual officials criminally liable. In a matter of weeks, states had negotiated and concluded a new convention, the International Convention on the Suppression and Punishment of the Crime of Apartheid. It gained the support of developing states, but was opposed by Western states for its broad language that could potentially inculpate anyone doing business with South Africa.

The drafting of treaties under the auspices of international organizations is no guarantee that states will in fact become parties to them. In many cases, when national governments closely consider agreements that their delegations to international conferences have voted to adopt, they do not in the end become parties to them. This has proven a particular problem with the conventions of the International Labor Organization (ILO). Although it has served as an arena for governments, business, and labor groups to develop global labor standards, only a relatively small number of the treaties negotiated under its auspices have garnered widespread ratification. For more on the ILO, see Chapter 4, Problem II.

Beyond treaties, international organizations routinely adopt decisions that their members accept as having certain legal effects. This process represents a form of international *administrative law making*, as members of the organization delegate responsibility to bodies within it to make decisions that carry more weight than mere expressions of government sentiments. One example is the International Whaling Commission, discussed in Chapter 2, Problem I.

Another important institution is the International Civil Aviation Organization (ICAO). It delegates much authority to its 36-member Council, which alone is empowered to pass International Civil Aviation Standards. These govern issues of civil aviation, from airport safety to airplane communications to search-and-rescue operations. Under the ICAO's constitutive instrument, after the Council passes a standard (a two-thirds majority is required), ICAO states can register their objection; if a majority do so, it will not enter into force. This, however, has never happened in the ICAO's history. In addition, individual states can object to a new standard because compliance would be "impracticable"; if they do not, the prevalent view among states and scholars is that the standard is binding on that state. Opt-outs tend to be unusual, and compliance with ICAO standards is very high. (Consider why a state would avoid opting out of an ICAO Standard, for example, on the required length of a runway to accept long-range aircraft.)

H. Judicial and Quasi-Judicial Settlement of Disputes

The UN's involvement in the apartheid issue demonstrate how international organizations can play an active role in the settlement of disputes between global actors, whether states, international organizations, or non-state actors. Chapter VI and other parts of the Charter specify the role of the Security Council, the General Assembly, and other organs in facilitating settlements of disputes between states. Chapter VI's first provision, Article 33, calls on all states whose disputes might create international friction to settle them by peaceful means, offering an illustrative list of techniques:

— negotiation: direct discussion between the parties
— enquiry: neutral fact-finding by a third party

— mediation: third-party attempts to bridge differences with its own proposals and possibly incentives
— conciliation: a combination of enquiry and mediation
— arbitration: a binding solution devised by a third party
— judicial settlement: a binding solution devised by an international court
— resort to regional agencies or arrangements.

Though disputes can be resolved through many techniques, many international law texts use the term "dispute settlement" to mean only arbitration and judicial settlement—and only of disputes between states—and sometimes only judicial settlement. This usage remains even though the vast majority of disputes among international actors never reach international tribunals.

Arbitral and judicial settlement began long before the United Nations, e.g., in bilateral commissions resolving economic claims between states or in third-party heads of states serving as arbitrators in boundary disputes. A major impetus toward institutionalization of arbitration was the creation in 1900 of the Permanent Court of Arbitration, which, despite its name, is not a court but rather a mechanism for the creation of ad hoc arbitral tribunals to resolve disputes that states wish to send to arbitration. A second major impetus was the establishment in 1921 of the Permanent Court of International Justice. The PCIJ was based in The Hague, Netherlands, and its jurisdiction resembled that of the International Court of Justice, discussed below. Its jurisprudence remains relevant for international lawyers, though neither it nor the League could prevent the catastrophes that soon overwhelmed Europe.

When the UN Charter was drafted at San Francisco, the founding states created the International Court of Justice (ICJ), which, like its predecessor, is a permanent court that sits in The Hague. Its Statute is appended to and part of the UN Charter. It is comprised of 15 permanent judges of different nationalities, elected by the General Assembly and the Security Council for nine-year renewable terms. In cases where a national of a litigating party is not on the Court, that party may appoint a judge *ad hoc*, a process meant to ensure that that state's views will receive ample consideration in the ICJ's deliberations. By informal agreement, a national from each of the five permanent members of the Security Council is always on the Court.

The Court hears two kinds of cases:

• *advisory proceedings*, where it provides nonbinding but authoritative answers to specific legal questions posed to it by a UN organ or agency; and
• *contentious cases* between states that are parties to the Statute (and only states), where it rules on a dispute between them.

Contentious cases often begin with a request to the Court by one state for provisional measures (i.e., a temporary injunction) pending its determination of the merits. Provisional measures and judgments of the Court are binding on the parties to a contentious case, the latter explicitly so under Article 94 of the Charter and the former as a result of recent ICJ jurisprudence (see Chapter 5, Problem III). The Security Council has the authority to enforce decisions of the ICJ, though it has rarely taken measures to do so.

Unlike domestic courts, the ICJ is not a court of mandatory jurisdiction with the ability to hear a case simply because a state is party to its Statute or a member of the United Nations. It is critical to remember that the ICJ can only hear cases where the states have consented in advance through some other instrument—not just ratification of the Charter—to its jurisdiction. The details of this jurisdictional regime are spelled out in its Statute.

Statute of the International Court of Justice, Art. 36 (1945)

1. The jurisdiction of the Court comprises all cases which the parties refer to it and all matters specially provided for in the Charter of the United Nations or in treaties and conventions in force.

2. The states parties to the present Statute may at any time declare that they recognize as compulsory ipso facto and without special agreement, in relation to any other state accepting the same obligation, the jurisdiction of the Court in all legal disputes concerning:

a. the interpretation of a treaty;

b. any question of international law;

c. the existence of any fact which, if established, would constitute a breach of an international obligation;

d. the nature or extent of the reparation to be made for the breach of an international obligation.

3. The declarations referred to above may be made unconditionally or on condition of reciprocity on the part of several or certain states, or for a certain time. . . .

In effect, Article 36 means that the ICJ can hear three sorts of contentious cases:

- those arising from treaties to which both states are parties that provide for settlement of disputes in the ICJ;
- those arising from a special agreement of the parties to send a dispute to the ICJ (a *compromis*); and
- those covered by declarations given by both parties in which they accept the compulsory jurisdiction of the Court. As of 2015, 70 states had consented to such jurisdiction, many with various qualifications and exceptions to their consent. (The United States withdrew its declaration, originally filed in 1946, in 1985, after Nicaragua instituted proceedings against it arising out of U.S. aid to the *contras*. See Chapter 13.)

Yet, except in contentious cases where both parties have signed a *compromis*, the state against which a suit is brought typically will contest the jurisdiction of the Court or, somewhat relatedly, the admissibility of the case. The ICJ may thus need to rule on (1) whether both states were parties to a treaty conferring jurisdiction under Article 36(1) before the dispute arose; (2) whether both states had filed declarations under Article 36(2) before the dispute arose; (3) whether the dispute fits within the description of cases for which the parties accept the Court's jurisdiction under those treaties or declarations; and (4) whether there is an ongoing legal dispute between the parties, e.g., whether it is moot, and whether the parties have a legal interest in the dispute (i.e., standing). As a result, the ICJ frequently avoids ruling on the merits of a contentious case.

In the case of apartheid, the ICJ was quite involved with respect to South Africa's western neighbor, Namibia (South West Africa). Namibia had been a German colony before World War I; after the war, the victorious powers placed it under the League of Nations' Mandates system. Despite an agreement with the League containing various commitments, South Africa extended racially discriminatory policies to Namibia. After World War II, South Africa asserted that the Mandate had expired with the League. The General Assembly asked the ICJ for an advisory opinion, and the Court replied in 1950 that the Mandate and South Africa's duties continued in force. South Africa rejected the opinion.

In 1960, Ethiopia and Liberia sued South Africa in the ICJ for violating the Mandate. The ICJ rejected South Africa's preliminary objections concerning the applicant states' standing and jurisdiction in an 8-7 opinion in 1962; but in 1966, it essentially reversed itself and ruled by 8-7 (due to changes in membership) that the applicants did not have a legal interest in the claims. The decision proved the low point for the ICJ's international reputation. For many years thereafter, developing states were reluctant to include ICJ dispute settlement clauses in treaties, conclude *compromis* sending disputes to the ICJ, or issue declarations under Article 36(2).

The UN's political actors eventually took stronger measures. In 1970, the Security Council declared South Africa's presence illegal and "call[ed] upon" all states to "refrain from any dealings" with South Africa that suggested otherwise. A 1970 ICJ advisory opinion clarified that these actions were within the Council's power and binding on member states, even though they were not taken under Chapter VII of the Charter. South Africa's grip on Namibia loosened only in the late 1980s, when the United States and the Soviet Union oversaw the negotiation of a complex transition agreement, leading to UN-overseen elections and independence in 1990.

The Namibia case demonstrates the many barriers to a major role for the ICJ in the settlement of disputes between states. Most states are unwilling to entrust major matters of foreign policy to international judges; as a result, most bilateral and multilateral treaties do not include clauses in which the parties consent to ICJ jurisdiction over disputes under Article 36(1). Most states also do not conclude a *compromis* on matters they view as of vital interest unless they are pressured from outside to do so. And declarations under Article 36(2) are the exception, and many are highly conditioned. On top of all this, jurisdiction is typically contested by the respondent state. Moreover, the pace of ICJ proceedings is slow, as the Court can do nothing to require states to file pleadings on time. Though it can issue provisional measures very quickly, cases can drag on for years, or even more than a decade. As a result, on matters of great urgency, the ICJ can only have a limited role.

The largest single type of case decided by the ICJ has been land and maritime boundary disputes, like the Libya-Chad *Territorial Dispute* in Chapter 1 or maritime cases discussed in Chapter 10, where the parties seek the political cover of a third-party decision maker to avoid painful concessions to the other side. Compliance with such decisions has generally been high. When states have attempted to use the ICJ for more controversial issues, in particular, the use of force, jurisdiction has been hotly contested, the ICJ itself has sought ways to avoid offending states, and compliance has been more problematic. This pattern can be seen in the *Avena* case on consular notification in Chapter 5, the *NATO Use of Force* and *Nicaragua* cases in Chapter 13, and the *Lockerbie Incident* case in Chapter 14. In the last twenty years, the ICJ's caseload has significantly increased from earlier years, with some 15 on the docket in early 2015. And the Court has issued some significant advisory opinions, including the *Legality of the Threat or Use of Nuclear Weapons* and the *Israeli Wall* opinions, discussed in Chapter 8.

Even with its limitations, the ICJ's pronouncements on the content of the rules of international law, even in an advisory opinion not binding on any state, are highly influential in shaping global actors' views of the law. Governments, international and domestic courts, and NGOs will frequently cite ICJ opinions as the most authoritative interpretations of the law. So even though it may rule on only a fraction of international disputes, and its rulings are not always observed, its opinions remain important for international lawyers to parse.

Despite, or perhaps because of, the limitations on the ICJ, the last fifty years have been marked by an increased willingness of states to entrust certain issues—not merely interstate disputes—to highly specialized tribunals. These include:

— human rights courts in Europe, Latin America, and Africa, which hear individual complaints against states
— the WTO's Dispute Settlement Body
— ad hoc tribunals for investment disputes, which hear business complaints against governments, usually for violations of treaties granting protections to foreign investors
— the International Tribunal for the Law of the Sea
— international criminal courts, where a prosecutor institutes cases against individuals
— numerous regional courts, such as the European Court of Justice and the Court of Justice of the Economic Community of West African States.

The caseload of these courts has greatly increased, indeed exploded in the case of the European Court of Human Rights, suggesting that judicial settlement is on the rise, even if the ICJ itself is not the major actor in this process. The significant increase in the number of tribunals and the frequency of their use has challenged decision makers regarding the relationships among international courts, an issue explored in the pages that follow. Nevertheless, it would be misleading to overemphasize the extent to which states use adjudication compared to other methods of dispute resolution. Hence, most international law disputes are still—and will likely always be—resolved outside any international court.

4

The Challenge of Non-State Actors

The international legal process has never been the province of states alone. Actors unaffiliated with governments have long played a role in the prescription, invocation, and application of international norms. Non-governmental actors range from large, territorially organized communities without state status, to organized religions, to groups of individuals sharing a dedication to a particular political cause, to business entities seeking a profit, to individual human beings. Men and women organized themselves into tribes millennia before any notion of a state; and religious institutions, such as the Catholic Church, have long had a global presence. These non-state actors are capable of action at the international level, action that inevitably affects the functioning of international law.

Traditional international lawyers and scholars rejected the notion that these actors could ever be true subjects of international law, for only states enjoyed rights and duties directly under international law. This mythical construct never really corresponded with the way non-state actors and states interacted. Instead, non-state actors have repeatedly made claims under international law. States have long endorsed many of these claims, whether by granting groups special rights in international agreements (as was done for the Catholic Church or ethnic minorities), including them in law making (as was done with antislavery groups), or even defending their interests militarily (as was done for domestic business interests operating abroad).

In this chapter, we explore three of the most significant non-state actors: non-governmental organizations, corporations, and states of the United States. A fourth — the individual — is the subject of Part IV of this book. This list of non-state actors is hardly exhaustive — one might also include special territories and organized communities within states, organized crime syndicates, sporting federations, organized religions, and international terrorists (the last of which are discussed in Chapter 14). In focusing on these three actors in this chapter, we hope to provide an understanding of their place in the international legal process in several senses: whether international norms recognize rights and duties for such entities; what sort of capacity they can and do enjoy to act independently of states in global arenas; and what sorts of effects they have had upon the international legal process.

I. NON-GOVERNMENTAL ORGANIZATIONS AS PARTICIPANTS IN INTERNATIONAL ARENAS: THE UNAIDS PROGRAM

Non-governmental organizations (NGOs) are groups of individuals or private entities united to advocate a particular agenda on the domestic or international stage. The majority of NGOs are national in their composition and goals; indeed, most are hardly known outside their home state. Others, however, are transnational in their membership, agenda, or both. As much as some might think that the telecommunications revolution is responsible for such transnational NGOs, they long predate it. One of the most significant NGOs in the nineteenth century was the Anti-Slavery League, which lobbied governments to eliminate the African slave trade. Today, NGOs have so proliferated that new acronyms have sprung up to describe them, including GONGOs (government-organized NGOs), BINGOs (business and industry NGOs), and DONGOs (donor-organized NGOs).

The era where NGOs focused on lobbying only their own governments to take positions in international legal fora is long gone. Today, NGOs actively participate in such arenas in multiple ways. As Peter Spiro writes,

> NGOs have levers and targets of influence. That is, in some contexts they aim to influence an actor to influence other actors in turn (levers). In other contexts, they may seek to influence actors with respect to their own conduct (targets). NGOs interact with states, IOs [international organizations], firms, and other NGOs in both respects.

Peter Spiro, *Nongovernmental Organizations in International Relations (Theory)*, in Interdisciplinary Perspectives on International Law and International Relations: The State of the Art (Dunoff and Pollack eds., 2013).

In carrying out these interactions, NGOs prepare studies for wide dissemination, engage the media in an attempt to influence public opinion, attend international conferences as observers or lobbyists, contribute expertise to governmental delegations and thereby gain a seat at intergovernmental negotiations, or even co-opt delegations through promises of assistance. The power of these groups, whose memberships can be anonymous or whose internal decision making may lack transparency or accountability compared to that of governments—both democratic and nondemocratic—has become one of the central issues in understanding the international legal process.

The goals for this Problem include:

- to understand the reasons behind increased NGO participation in law making;
- to understand the ways that international institutions and fora regulate the participation of NGOs; and
- to understand the debates about whether NGOs are legitimate participants in law making for a traditionally dominated by states.

A. *The Problem*

In the years following the outbreak of HIV/AIDS, the United Nations undertook a major effort to coordinate international responses to the pandemic. It first designated the World Health Organization as the UN's lead agency and created a coordination committee of UN and other institutions working on the issue. Because of WHO's longstanding work with NGOs advocating for the needs of persons with or highly at risk of HIV/AIDS, NGOs played an active role in the coordinating committee's work. In 1994, the UN

Economic and Social Council (ECOSOC) created a new agency, UNAIDS, putting the various participating entities under one institutional umbrella.

UNAIDS is headed by an executive director in conjunction with a board of directors called the Programme Coordinating Board (PCB). The PCB is comprised of 22 UN member states, 11 cosponsor organizations, and five NGOs, all allocated by region. UNAIDS was the first UN organization to provide a formal role for NGOs in its governance. Although NGOs have five delegates, in practice NGOs have also selected five alternates who are treated equally to primary delegates. Only the member states have formal voting rights. However, in practice the PCB makes decisions by consensus and without a formal vote.

Though the basic idea of including NGOs in the governance of UNAIDS was not especially controversial given prior NGO involvement on the issue, ECOSOC's members could not agree on all the details of NGO participation. The unresolved issues included the precise privileges that the NGO delegates would have in PCB deliberations as well as the selection process for the NGOs. It was also unclear what sort of impact the states on the PCB would allow the NGO delegates to have on the overall work of UNAIDS. NGOs represented on the PCB also faced some challenges regarding their accountability to those with HIV/AIDS or others advocating on their behalf at the national level. Over time, the PCB and the NGOs themselves would make policy on some of these matters through a series of important decisions.

B. *Evolving Modes of NGO Participation*

International law does not have any general rules requiring, permitting, or prohibiting participation by NGOs in the making or enforcement of international law. Although NGOs have long lobbied governments behind the scenes, their direct involvement in international negotiations has been in many ways limited. Article 71 of the UN Charter authorizes ECOSOC to make "suitable arrangements for consultation" with NGOs. ECOSOC has a special 19-member Committee on Non-Governmental Organizations, which considers applications from NGOs for so-called consultative status. That status gives them access to UN documents and public meetings and limited privileges to speak or circulate statements in ECOSOC. Some 3,900 NGOs had such status as of 2015. But beyond this participation, states generally expected NGOs to stay in the background during actual negotiations over new international agreements or other instruments. NGOs, for their part, have continually sought ways to have a seat at the table of conferences, a more influential role behind the scenes, or both.

In the case of UNAIDS, a 1995 ECOSOC resolution addressing details of the PCB's functions set forth the role of NGOs in an annex that summarized informal consultations among ECOSOC members.

Arrangements for the participation of non-governmental organizations in the work of the Programme Coordination Board: Report on the Informal Consultation of the Economic and Social Council

ECOSOC Res. 1995/2 (Annex)

(a) Non-governmental organizations would be invited to take part in the work of the Programme Coordination Board. Such invitations would need to be reviewed periodically. Non-governmental organizations invited should be those either in consultative status with [ECOSOC] or in relationship with one of the six co-sponsoring organizations or on the roster of non-governmental organizations dealing with matters pertaining to HIV/AIDS, in accordance with the rules, procedures and well-established practice of the United Nations system;

(b) The process of identification of the non-governmental organizations that sought to participate in the work of the Board would be determined by the non-governmental organizations themselves. The Board would formally approve the nomination of those organizations;

(c) There would be five such non-governmental participants, three from developing countries and two from developed countries and countries with economies in transition;

(d) In making the selection, non-governmental organizations would be encouraged to seek competent and relevant representatives, for example participation by groups concerned with economic and social development and groups representing people affected by HIV/AIDS;

(e) The need for rotation among non-governmental organizations was recognized; the appointment of an individual organization should not exceed three years;

(f) Non-governmental organizations would be advised of the terms and conditions of their participation. It would be made clear to them that such participation would include:

A seat at the table with 6 representatives of the Committee of Co-sponsoring Organizations and the 22 Member States;

Non-governmental organizations would be able to speak;

Non-governmental organizations would have no negotiating role;

Non-governmental organizations would not participate in any part of the formal decision-making process, including the right to vote, which is reserved for representatives of Governments;

(g) These arrangements for the participation of non-governmental organizations are not to be regarded as setting a precedent;

(h) Funding would be made available for the representatives of developing countries and for each of the three non-governmental organizations from developing countries to cover the costs of one representative each to attend Board meetings. Such funds would cover the cost of daily subsistence allowance and travel only and would be based on existing eligibility criteria.

Over time, the NGOs' role within the PCB increased. According to an independent review commissioned by UNAIDS, until 2007, members of the NGO delegation had to wait to speak until after member state delegates had spoken. Since 2007, NGO and member state delegates are treated equally in the speaking order. The NGO delegation also successfully pressed the UNAIDS Secretariat to fund an office with permanent staff to provide logistical support to the delegation. Efforts to provide NGOs with a formal voting role have been unsuccessful. However, given the ability of NGOs to participate equally in deliberations, voting rights no longer seem to be a key demand of NGOs.

Notes and Questions

1. How much participation did the ECOSOC allow NGOs? Could or should ECOSOC have provided for more? How can NGOs advance their concerns best within an organization controlled by states?

2. UNAIDS is primarily concerned with implementing UN programs, not making or interpreting international law, although it does issue guidelines to states on various HIV/AIDS-related issues. Does and should states' willingness to involve NGOs depend upon the purpose of the international forum, e.g., whether it is operational or lawmaking? Does it turn on the output, e.g., a treaty versus a softer instrument?

3. Since UNAIDS's founding in 1994, as new health organizations are founded, they have consistently included NGOs as participants in their governance. Both the GAVI Alliance, which funds immunizations in developing countries, and the Global Fund to Fight AIDS, Tuberculosis, and Malaria have given NGOs voting rights on their governing boards. Why might health-related institutions be particularly amenable to active NGO participation in their governance? Are other issues particularly susceptible to or resistant to such involvement?

C. *Representativeness of NGOs*

Among the most difficult issues for international organizations and the NGOs working with or within them is the selection of those NGOs that will be allowed to participate. In the case of a large international conference where NGO participation might be limited to holding an alternative set of meetings at a different venue, any NGO might be allowed to attend. But where NGOs will be closely involved in the institution's work, only some will be able to participate.

In the case of UNAIDS, the NGO delegation to the PCB itself addressed many of these questions. In October 2012, it issued a document entitled the "Terms of Reference of the UNAIDS PCB NGO Delegation." The Terms of Reference defined the delegation's mission as follows:

> To bring to the PCB the perspectives and expertise of people living with, most affected by, and most at risk of, vulnerable to, marginalized by, and affected by HIV and AIDS, as well as civil society and nongovernmental entities actively involved in HIV work, in order to ensure that their human rights and equitable, gender-sensitive access to comprehensive HIV prevention, treatment, care and support are reinforced by the policies, programmes, strategies and actions of the PCB and UNAIDS.

Regarding the selection of NGO delegation members, as noted above, ECOSOC required that three NGOs originate in the developing world and two in the developed world. The Terms of Reference state that one NGO shall come from Africa, Asia/Pacific, Latin America, Europe, and North America. It also sets forth the criteria for the selection of NGO representatives to the PCB. Applicants must:

> (1) be actively and principally involved with HIV work in the country and/or region for which the applicant is applying;

> (2) maintain a comprehensive understanding of the health, political and social consequences and needs of the AIDS pandemic, particularly as it relates to the region;

> (3) be strongly connected to and actively liaise with national and regional [civil society] networks; and

> (4) have extensive experience in national, regional and/or international policy-making and advocacy.

The Terms of Reference also include the following:

> Among the ten Delegates, the Delegation makes every effort to ensure that, unless impossible or not the best candidate is nominated during recruitment, the entire Delegation meets these overall representational balance considerations in priority order:
>
> **PLHIV** [People Living with AIDS/HIV]: [P]reference is given to qualified openly declared PLHIV applicants. As a rule, there should be a minimum of 3 PLHIV Delegates;
>
> **Constituency**: A balance among Delegates who possess the expertise to represent and advocate for specific key constituencies including: men who have sex with men (MSM), people who use drugs, sex workers, and young people;
>
> **Gender:** A balance of male and female Delegates is also taken into account; and
>
> **Organizations:** A balance among the Delegates' organization types: networks of PLHIV and PLHIV organizations, AIDS service organizations, community-based organizations, Human Rights organizations, development organizations, global networks, etc.

While the NGO delegation does not seem to have experienced significant differences in selecting its members, the independent study of the NGO delegation commissioned by UNAIDS noted that several member states on the PCB "question whether key aspects of civil society (notably faith-based organizations (FBOs) and AIDS service organizations) are fully welcomed or incorporated within the Delegation." In addition, the study reported:

> [S]ome people within wider civil society debate whether—despite the NGO Delegation's good intentions – selection is truly open to all within their sector, rather than just the "usual suspects". . . . [This] highlight[s] a common tension within the NGO Delegation (as well as other civil society Delegations to global institutions)—between the need to have high quality members (with appropriate seniority, knowledge and contacts) and the desire to move beyond the "usual suspects".

Notes and Questions

1. Do the criteria developed by the NGO Delegation help ensure diversity of viewpoints among its members? Or is such diversity not desirable in the case of global health? Should the PCB's member states take a more active role in the selection of the NGO representatives?

2. One enormously important non-state actor is the Holy See—the supreme organ of the Catholic Church. Though not legally a state itself, the Holy See enjoys diplomatic relations with over 100 states, has membership or observer status in international organizations, and has signed treaties. (Under a 1929 treaty between Italy and the Holy See, the latter has territorial sovereignty over the tiny State of Vatican City within Rome, but it is the Holy See, rather than Vatican City, that engages in diplomatic relations.) Moreover, it has been accorded the status of a "non-member observer state" at the United Nations (the same status afforded Palestine as of 2012) and has participated extensively at many UN conferences. If the Church had experience working on HIV/AIDS issues, would it be appropriate for it be chosen as the European NGO to serve on the PCB?

D. NGO Influence and Accountability

Beyond the selection of NGOs to participate in international institutions and conferences, a far broader question arises regarding the legitimate role for NGOs in law making and implementation. International law has no rules limiting the modes of participation of NGOs or their influence, but the rise of NGO power has raised the question of exactly whom they represent—a question that arises with respect to some governments as well but that has not prevented authoritarian regimes from representing their states.

According to the independent review commissioned by UNAIDS, the NGO delegation has taken an increasingly active role in shaping the PCB's agenda, rather than merely providing input on agenda items set by member states. NGOs are often influential in selecting the theme for PCB meetings or suggesting speakers. The NGO delegation has consistently used thematic sessions and their own speaking time to raise the profile of marginalized groups, such as sex workers.

That role has not come without some controversy. The independent review found that some member states felt that NGO delegates take an inappropriate activist tone and focus on issues that are culturally sensitive, rather than on global issues like access to treatment. However, most member states agreed that the NGO delegation's focus on key populations affected by the disease was an important contribution to UNAIDS's work. Indeed, some observers, including UN Secretariat staff, believed that the NGO delegation "has become overly diplomatic and lost touch with what they regard as its activist roots."

The involvement of NGOs within UNAIDS is part of a much larger trend, as NGO involvement in different facets of international law making has now become routine. They observe and participate in major international and regional conferences, lobbying governments behind the scenes. Adept with technology, they report on proceedings of the conferences, including official drafts of treaties and other documents, along with their commentary, and urge their members to lobby governments to take various positions.

For example, the International Campaign to Ban Landmines (ICBL), which began with six NGOs and grew to include over 1,200 NGOs from 60 countries, lobbied governments intensively in the 1990s to enact a global prohibition on landmines. When a UN conference reached an impasse in 1995-1996, ICBL, other NGOs, and some mid-size states collaborated to create an alternative negotiating forum, which came to be known as the Ottawa process. With strong NGO support, in just over a year the Ottawa process produced a new Landmines Treaty. The treaty, with 161 parties by 2015, prohibits the production or use of landmines and requires parties to destroy stockpiled and buried landmines. It represents the first time that an active weapons system has been banned outright (and not simply regulated) since poison gas was outlawed after World War I. NGOs were also major players during the negotiations for the Statute of the International Criminal Court, which is discussed in Chapter 9.

In the wake of these NGO successes, UN Secretary-General Kofi Annan stated to an NGO forum in 1999, "I see a United Nations which recognizes that the non-governmental organizations revolution—the new global people-power, or whatever else you wish to call this explosion of citizens' concern at the global level—is the best thing that has happened to our Organization in a long time."

NGOs also play an active role in judicial processes. They represent individuals before human rights tribunals in Europe and Latin America. The International Court of Justice's (ICJ's) important advisory opinion on the legality of nuclear weapons, discussed in Chapter 8, resulted from a ten-year effort by an NGO, the World Court Project, to persuade the members of the WHO and the General Assembly to request the ICJ for an opinion. The Project lobbied national leaders and collected 3.8 million signatures from citizens opposed to nuclear weapons. Another NGO provided pro bono legal assistance to the Solomon Islands, Samoa, and the Marshall Islands, allowing them to participate fully before the ICJ.

NGOs are also critical players in the making of soft law. Working with or apart from governments and corporations, they have set standards that other actors cannot ignore. They have set up codes in areas ranging from responsible investing to dolphin-safe tuna to labeling of rugs to demonstrate that they are not made with child labor. While these standards are not binding on governments, they can exert an enormous influence on consumers and shareholders that businesses ignore at their peril.

And NGOs have demonstrated the ability to complicate or disrupt lawmaking processes instituted by governments. One notable victory took place in 1998, when environmental and anti-corporate NGOs convinced governments in the Organization for Economic Co-operation and Development, the 30-nation organization of mostly rich states, to abandon negotiations on a Multilateral Agreement on Investment (MAI) that aimed at safeguarding foreign investment against discriminatory practices by host states. The NGOs accomplished this after they obtained a confidential copy of the draft agreement, posted it on the Internet along with their commentary, and mobilized members to urge their governments to change course.

Yet who is behind these increasingly powerful actors in the international arena? NGOs may be formed and funded by individuals, corporations, religious organizations, or even governments. Some have worldwide memberships in the tens of thousands; others are just a handful of volunteer activists dedicated to a particular cause. Some work by lobbying governments or corporations directly or through their members; others take direct action to advance their cause, such as Greenpeace's dispatch of dinghies to separate whales from whaling ships, or Médecins Sans Frontières' provision of doctors to war-torn areas of the world. Members of NGOs even serve on governmental delegations —perhaps as a way of co-opting the NGO to cooperate with the government—or because the government itself lacks expertise on a particular issue. Several Pacific Island nations have staffed their delegations to environmental conferences with experts from Western environmental NGOs.

In the absence of any international legal rules on the appropriate level of participation of these entities in the international legal process, states differ dramatically on the degree to which they believe NGOs should be accepted in lawmaking or implementation processes, given their vastly different constituencies and relationships with constituencies.

Consider the following academic commentary on the issue:

Steven Charnovitz, *The Illegitimacy of Preventing NGO Participation*

36 Brook. J. Intl. L. 891, 905-909 (2011)

The arena of modern governance is more horizontal than vertical and de-emphasizes status and hierarchy. . . .

Individuals join with likeminded colleagues, forming NGOs to influence global plural legal orders. Using NGOs makes it possible for an individual to delegate the function of representing himself. Social and economic NGOs are also efficient in that an individual interested in, say, environment and peace, can join two different NGO social networks, both of which will be specialized in its own area. Because NGOs are so important in allowing individuals to form and present their views, one might say that the core principle of international community is freedom of association.

A robust norm of freedom of association would forbid IOs or states from interfering with the legal capacity of an NGO to lobby for its interests. . . . Although traditional democratic theory imagines that individuals delegate their will to elected representatives, a more realistic view is that the individual is born into legal orders, such as family, church, local government, national government, and international government, and then in the process of socialization learns how to obey, evade, and/or to work to change such legal orders. To argue that the elected official is the better representative of the individual than the NGO is to miss the point that the individual voluntarily chooses what NGO she joins but does not, merely by voting, get to choose the elected officials that make decisions for her. One should not assume that on any particular issue, such as climate change, an individual has delegated more decisionmaking to an elected politician rather than to an NGO. Indeed, the individual may have voted against the politician who claims to represent her in Congress.

Although international action can be promoted by nongovernmental individuals . . . the more common methodology is that reform proposals from individuals get taken up by a group. As Professor Feilchenfeld explained in 1938: "The most common reform method in world affairs in our age has been this: Individuals advance suggestions for a particular reform. These suggestions, quite frequently, are then taken up by organisations concerned with reform work of various kinds. . . ."

The core activity in the IO as a community is deliberation. Lawmaking too may occur, but it does so only as an end product of cosmopolitan conversation. While NGOs can be kept on the sidelines when so-called lawmaking occurs within an IO, there can hardly be any grounds for excluding NGOs from the conversation that precedes lawmaking.

Kenneth Anderson, *What NGO Accountability Means—and Does Not Mean*

103 Am. J. Intl. L. 170, 176-177 (2009)

[T]o ask about accountability is really to ask whether NGOs are representative of those they claim (or once claimed) to represent and whether they merit the legitimacy that they claim such representativeness confers. In this sense, to ask about accountability is not merely to ask whether NGOs "responsibly" exercise their power but instead whether a basis exists for them to be invested with such power in the first place. . . . [I]f it is on the basis of representing "people" or "peoples" or "the world's Peoples," then we should not . . . presume the quite radical conclusion that they have a legitimate claim to "represent" and account for the interests and desires and values of all these "people" in the first place. NGOs helped themselves to this legitimacy by making otherwise unsubstantiated claims of representation . . . .

Critique of international and transnational NGOs is thus only partly about accountability in the fiduciary sense or even the single-issue sense versus social trade-offs sense. Rather, the critique centers on the NGOs' assertion of a legitimating role in global governance. The implication is that they hold a position—simultaneously adopted *by* NGOs as a means of gaining admission to officialdom and assigned *to* them by international organization bureaucracies in search of legitimacy for themselves—on that most highly contested of issues, global governance. . . . [P]owerful incentives for international and transnational NGOs to claim representativeness—as part of a mutually reinforcing dynamic in which global civil society offers legitimacy to international organizations in a notably undemocratic vision of global governance and takes back recognition, access, and legitimacy in their turn—are as present as ever.

[In comparing NGO lobbying of a government with NGO lobbying of international organizations,] NGO lobbying in the NGO's domestic (democratic) society must contend with an electorate, a ballot box, and the checks upon the legitimacy claims of the NGO because it exists within a democratic structure and process against which its advocacy can be tested. . . . Lobbying international organizations, however, is *not* the same as lobbying "groups of governments," even if the international organizations are somehow in principle the servants of their member-states. . . . NGOs in the international arena do not have to contend with the appurtenances of democracy that would confront (and often confound) them in a national democratic society. Moreover, for a decade or so, international NGOs came perilously close, or more, to claiming to *be* that democratic, or at least representative, structure in the international arena. These structural concerns about global governance have been relieved to some extent today by outside criticism, but the incentives that lead to such claims have not gone away.

Notes and Questions

1. What is the rationale for direct NGO participation in international law making if they can participate in domestic debates on international issues? Do you agree with Kofi Annan and Steven Charnovitz that NGOs foster the democratization of international processes or with Anderson's rejection of this claim?

2. What models of participation by NGOs address the need for inclusion of nongovernmental perspectives but take account of the need for some accountability? How does UNAIDS fare on this score?

3. Though the majority of NGOs in UNAIDS come from developing states, at many lawmaking conferences only NGOs from wealthy countries—or funded by donors from wealthy countries—can afford to show up. Does the influence of U.S. and European NGOs mean that NGO participation can exacerbate North-South tensions or prevent the expression of developing world perspectives?

4. Do concerns about NGO legitimacy disappear if the NGO makes its funding and governance structures transparent? One NGO represented in the PCB, the European AIDS Treatment Group, reports its income and expenses in an annual report and is also registered with the EU's Transparency Register, which allows NGOs to make public key aspects of their activities. And in 2008, a number of leading international NGOs (INGOs) created the INGO Accountability Charter, which sets forth ten commitments for members—including transparency, good governance, independence, and ethical fundraising—and requires periodic public reporting and review of NGO performance. *www. ingoaccountability.org*. Should NGOs have to make public their sources of funding in order to be able to participate in international conferences and institutions?

5. NGOs have, at times, used troubling tactics. For example, in order to obtain the three-fourths majority vote of states party to the International Convention for the Regulation of Whaling (IWRC) necessary to adopt a moratorium on commercial whaling, discussed in Chapter 2, NGOs mounted a "membership drive" to get developing states, many with little interest in whales, to join the IWC. NGOs paid the annual dues and expenses of attending IWC meetings and even drafted and submitted the membership documents for some states to join the IWC.

II. CORPORATIONS AS INTERNATIONAL ACTORS: WORKER SAFETY IN BANGLADESHI APPAREL FACTORIES

Corporations have long been major actors on the international scene. During the colonial era, charter companies, such as the Dutch East India Company, served as proxies for governments in gaining European domination over overseas territories and were given significant powers in governing certain colonies. The twentieth century brought the rise of the multinational corporation (MNC). The economic power of business enterprises has given them great influence over governmental policy on international issues such as trade, investment, antitrust, intellectual property, and telecommunications. They prod governments to make claims against each other regarding treatment of businesses—leading to diplomatic negotiations, new international agreements, or invocation of formal dispute resolution procedures such as those in the WTO. Corporations can also provide experts to sit on governmental teams at intergovernmental negotiations. NGOs have learned from the success of corporations in shaping the international legal process.

It is now common for international legal instruments to effectively grant business entities certain *rights*. For example, bilateral investment treaties and regional economic agreements, such as the North American Free Trade Agreement (NAFTA) and the treaties establishing the European Union, require states to allow foreign corporations to set up investments on a nondiscriminatory basis; some also require countries hosting foreign corporations to accede to international arbitration if the corporation prefers that option to the host state's local courts in the event of a dispute.

As for *duties* on corporations, for many years black-letter international law doctrine posited that only domestic law could place duties on corporations because corporations were not "international legal persons." International law instead imposed duties on states to regulate corporate behavior under domestic law. International labor treaties emerging from the International Labor Organization (ILO) have long required governments to enact domestic legislation affecting private businesses; and some environmental treaties require that states impose civil liability on corporations for accidents in the course of certain dangerous activities, such as transportation of hazardous wastes.

Whatever the significance of such doctrinal disagreements, serious disagreements remain about the proper role for international law in regulating corporate behavior and the proper role for corporations in prescribing international law.

The goals of this Problem include:

- to demonstrate how different international legal instruments, whether hard or soft law, have attempted to place duties on corporations;
- to address the ways that corporations are currently permitted to participate in the process of making international law; and
- to consider the relevance to international law of self-regulation of corporate behavior through codes of conduct.

A. The Problem

One of the most significant trends in international commerce in the past 50 years has been the shift in production of many different products from rich, Northern states to developing states. Today's global economy is characterized by global supply chains in which both finished and intermediate goods are traded in fragmented and internationally dispersed production processes. These processes are typically coordinated by MNCs through networks of affiliates, contractual partners, and suppliers. MNCs place enormous pressures on suppliers to cut costs and demand quick turnaround times. Suppliers, who fiercely compete with each other, have little incentive to invest in costly safety upgrades or invest in training workers. And lengthy supply chains of retailers, owners, importers, exporters, agents, contractors, and subcontractors complicate traditional, domestic law-oriented efforts to regulate each actor and raise complex questions of responsibility.

Bangladesh's role in the global garment manufacturing industry is typical of this process. Garment manufacturing constitutes 80 percent of Bangladesh's exports. Five thousand garment factories employ 4 million Bangladeshis and make the country second in clothing exports only to China. Bangladesh's extremely low wages make it an attractive country for garment production—despite the country's poor infrastructure and political instability. At least 10 percent of Bangladeshi members of parliament are garment factory owners, and many others have close ties to factory owners. These legislators have an interest in keeping wages low to retain manufacturing contracts with major international retailers. The industry has long resisted efforts to increase workers' wages or enforce legislation protecting workers from unsafe conditions.

In 2006, the Bangladesh government issued a building permit for a six-story shopping mall called Rana Plaza. Instead, the owner of the land built an eight-story garment factory with inadequate support for factory machinery and electricity generators. On April 23, 2013, the building began to show significant cracks. Workers rushed out of the building, but the owner insisted that the damage was superficial. The workers were ordered to return to work the next day, and the building collapsed. Over 1,100 people, almost all young women and girls, were killed. It was the worst accident in the industry's history. Just months previously, 112 people died in a fire in another Bangladeshi garment factory. The Bangladeshi government initially downplayed the Rana Plaza incident as an unforeseeable accident, but eventually announced criminal charges against dozens of individuals involved in the operation and design of Rana Plaza.

B. Attempts at Multilateral Regulation of Corporate Conduct

Despite the traditional principle that only states can bear duties under international law, states have used various international legal instruments to regulate corporate behavior. Here we examine several instruments in the area of worker health and safety.

1. ILO Treaties

The oldest regime governing employment conditions is that of the International Labor Organization, which has been developing a vast international labor code, composed of treaties and recommendations, since the 1920s. As of 2015, the ILO had promulgated over 180 conventions and over 190 recommendations. In creating the ILO, states sought to develop international standards for laborers and thereby avoid a situation where each state would cut back on worker protections in order to make its exports more competitive—the so-called race to the bottom.

The ILO has sought to regulate the activities at issue in the apparel industry controversy. Among the treaties on workplace conditions is the following agreement from 1981:

Convention Concerning Occupational Safety and Health and the Working Environment

ILO Convention No. 155 (1981), www.ilo.org

Article 4

1. Each Member shall, in the light of national conditions and practice, and in consultation with the most representative organisations of employers and workers, formulate, implement and periodically review a coherent national policy on occupational safety, occupational health and the working environment. . . .

Article 8

Each Member shall, by laws or regulations . . . take such steps as may be necessary to give effect to Article 4 of this Convention. . . .

Article 13

A worker who has removed himself from a work situation which he has reasonable justification to believe presents an imminent and serious danger to his life or health shall be protected from undue consequences in accordance with national conditions and practice. . . .

Article 16

1. Employers shall be required to ensure that, so far as is reasonably practicable, the workplaces, machinery, equipment and processes under their control are safe and without risk to health. . . .

Article 19

There shall be arrangements at the level of the undertaking [i.e., company] under which—

(a) workers, in the course of performing their work, co-operate in the fulfilment by their employer of the obligations placed upon him;

(b) representatives of workers in the undertaking co-operate with the employer in the field of occupational safety and health;

(c) representatives of workers in an undertaking are given adequate information on measures taken by the employer to secure occupational safety . . . ;

(d) workers and their representatives in the undertaking are given appropriate training in occupational safety and health. . . .

As of 2015, this treaty had only 62 parties. Indeed, most of the ILO conventions have relatively few ratifications. In an effort to encourage states to ratify the most important conventions, the ILO's Governing Body identified eight so-called fundamental conventions, covering freedom of association, forced labor, equal pay, and child labor. Each of these conventions has been ratified by well over 100 countries. (Convention 155 is not one of the fundamental conventions.)

2. Standard-Setting Outside of Treaties: Three Approaches

During the 1970s and 1980s, many UN members were concerned about corporate interference in a state's governance, following disclosures of corporate involvement in

U.S. government efforts to destabilize regimes in Iran, Guatemala, and Chile in the 1950s and 1970s. The General Assembly created a Commission on Transnational Corporations (CTC). Over the objections of many Western states, the CTC issued the following draft in June 1990, hoping for formal adoption by the General Assembly:

Draft Code of Conduct on Transnational Corporations

U.N. Conference on Trade and Development, U.N. Doc. E/1990/94 (1990)

The General Assembly . . .

Convinced that a universally accepted, comprehensive and effective Code of Conduct on Transnational Corporations is an essential element in the strengthening of international economic and social co-operation . . .

Decides to adopt the following Code of Conduct on Transnational Corporations: . . .

7. Transnational corporations shall respect the national sovereignty of the countries in which they operate and the right of each State to exercise its permanent sovereignty over its natural wealth and resources.

8. An entity of a transnational corporation is subject to the laws, regulations and established administrative practices of the country in which it operates. . . .

10. Transnational corporations should carry out their activities in conformity with the development policies, objectives and priorities set out by the Governments of the countries in which they operate. . . .

14. Transnational corporations shall respect human rights and fundamental freedoms in the countries in which they operate. . . .

16. Without prejudice to the participation of transnational corporations in activities that are permissible under the laws . . . of host countries . . . transnational corporations shall not interfere in the internal affairs of host countries. . . .

The Draft Code of Conduct, which was not meant to be a treaty, was never adopted by the General Assembly. Instead, political support for attempted UN regulation of corporations dissipated with the end of the Cold War. Developing states, increasingly desperate for foreign investment, acceded to Western demands that the United Nations drop the Draft Code.

Nonetheless, the global interest in corporate conduct beginning in the 1970s prompted a response from rich nations through the Organization for Economic Co-operation and Development (OECD), the organization of economically wealthy states that offers a forum for discussion and coordination of economic policy. In 1976, the OECD promulgated a brief set of nonbinding guidelines for multinational corporations and in agreed in 2000 upon a fuller set of principles, the OECD Guidelines for Multinational Enterprises. According to the Guidelines' preface,

They provide voluntary principles and standards for responsible business conduct consistent with applicable laws. The Guidelines aim to ensure that the operations of these enterprises are in harmony with government policies, to strengthen the basis of mutual confidence between enterprises and the societies in which they operate, to help improve the foreign investment climate and to enhance the contribution to sustainable development made by multinational enterprises.

OECD Guidelines for Multinational Enterprises

(2000), www.oecd.org/daf/investment/guidelines

General Policies

Enterprises should take fully into account established policies in the countries in which they operate, and consider the views of other stakeholders. In this regard, enterprises should:

1. Contribute to economic, social and environmental progress with a view to achieving sustainable development.

2. Respect the human rights of those affected by their activities consistent with the host government's international obligations and commitments. . . .

10. Encourage, where practicable, business partners, including suppliers and sub-contractors, to apply principles of corporate conduct compatible with the *Guidelines*. . . .

IV. Employment and Industrial Relations

Enterprises should, within the framework of applicable law, regulations and prevailing labour relations and employment practices:

1.   (a) Respect the right of their employees to be represented by trade unions . . . ;

   (b) Contribute to the effective abolition of child labour;

   (c) Contribute to the elimination of all forms of forced or compulsory labour;

   (d) Not discriminate against their employees with respect to employment or occupation on such grounds as race, colour, sex, religion, political opinion, national extraction or social origin. . . .

4.   (a) Observe standards of employment and industrial relations not less favourable than those observed by comparable employers in the host country;

   (b) Take adequate steps to ensure occupational health and safety in their operations.

   [Other provisions address transparency, the environment, bribery, consumer interests, and competition.]

Because the Guidelines are not a treaty, they are not binding on member states or corporations. But because many would argue that they have received serious treatment by OCED member states, they now arguably fall into the realm of soft law. The Guidelines have been supplemented by other standards. Among them are Social Accountability 8000, a set of standards issued by Social Accountability International, an NGO that relies on authorized monitors to certify labor conditions worldwide; and the UN Global Compact, a joint project of the United Nations and various business leaders that sets forth nine basic principles of corporate practice and urges business leaders to adopt them.

   The third example of global regulation arises from the renewed involvement of the United Nations in issues of corporate responsibility in the 2000s, with a specific focus on human rights. In 2005, after a UN expert committee proposed a set of human rights norms to bind corporations that industrialized states saw as extending human rights law too far, the UN Commission on Human Rights (the predecessor to the UN Human Rights

human rights abuses? Is there some way that corporations could be directly liable for human rights violations under international law? For one possible means of effecting such liability, see the discussion of the U.S. Alien Tort Statute in Chapter 5, Problem V.

C. Corporate Self-Regulation: Codes of Conduct

Corporations have responded to attempts at regulation by states by engaging in self-regulation through enactment of codes of conduct. These codes are voluntary commitments made by companies, business associations, or other entities that put forth standards and principles for the conduct of business. Although they date back at least to the beginning of the twentieth century, they have proliferated in the last 20 years due to shareholder, consumer, and NGO interest in corporate behavior. International law does not formally govern these private codes, although corporations sometimes try to incorporate international law and standards into them.

In the area of worker safety, Walmart, which purchased many clothes made in Bangladesh, has a "Statement of Ethics" (*www.ethics.walmartstores.com*) that has been translated into the language of numerous states, including Bangladesh. It includes the following:

Who's covered by the Statement of Ethics? . . .

This Statement of Ethics applies to all associates worldwide, and all members of the board of directors of Wal-Mart Stores, Inc. [and] to the associates and directors of all Walmart-controlled subsidiaries. . . . . Walmart expects its suppliers . . . contractors, and other service providers to act ethically and in a manner consistent with this Statement of Ethics. If you hire a service provider, you should take reasonable steps to make sure the service provider is aware of our Statement of Ethics, has a reputation for integrity, and acts in a responsible manner consistent with our standards.

What law applies

Walmart conducts business in many countries around the world. Our associates are citizens of many countries and, as a result, our operations are subject to many different laws, customs, and cultures. . . . When it's possible, this Statement of Ethics will be modified to conform to changes in laws and customs. In some instances, the laws of two or more countries will conflict. When you encounter a conflict, contact the Global Ethics Office or your in-country Ethics Committee to understand how to resolve the conflict. . . .

Environmental, health and safety in the workplace . . .

We're committed to the health and safety of our customers, members, and associates, because we care for one another. Conducting our business in compliance with all health and safety laws is crucial to protecting each other from harm. As an associate of Walmart, always comply with all relevant health and safety laws and policies. By following these, we can create and maintain a safe shopping and working environment for our customers, members, and associates.

In the aftermath of the Rana Plaza catastrophe, Western retailers announced their own actions to prevent future disasters. A group of primarily European retailers, including H&M, agreed on the Accord on Fire and Building Safety in Bangladesh. This initiative provides for increased safety inspections and training under an independent safety inspector, a means for workers to report unsafe conditions, and the right of workers to refuse to work in conditions they believe to be unsafe. As of 2015, it had 150 corporate signatories, as well as ten union signatories (mostly Bangladeshi) and four NGOs.

Accord on Fire and Safety in Bangladesh

www.bangladeshaccord.org (2013)

The undersigned parties are committed to the goal of a safe and sustainable Bangladeshi Ready-Made Garment ("RMG") industry in which no worker needs to fear fires, building collapses, or other accidents that could be prevented with reasonable health and safety measures.

The signatories to this Agreement agree to establish a fire and building safety program in Bangladesh for a period of five years. . . .

SCOPE:

The agreement covers all suppliers producing products for the signatory companies. The signatories shall designate these suppliers as falling into the following categories, according to which they shall require these supplier to accept inspections and implement remediation measures in their factories according to the following breakdown: [The plan sets up three categories of factories, with those producing the most goods subject to regular inspections, remediation, and fire safety training.] . . .

GOVERNANCE:

4. The signatories shall appoint a Steering Committee (SC) with equal representation chosen by the trade union signatories and company signatories (maximum 3 seats each) and a representative from and chosen by the International Labour Organization (ILO) as a neutral chair. The SC shall have responsibility for the selection, contracting, compensation and review of the performance of a Safety Inspector and a Training Coordinator; oversight and approval of the programme budget; oversight of financial reporting and hiring of auditors. . . .

REMEDIATION:

12. Where corrective actions are identified by the Safety Inspector as necessary to bring a factory into compliance with building, fire and electrical safety standards, the signatory company or companies . . . shall require that factory to implement these corrective actions, according to a schedule that is mandatory and time-bound, with sufficient time allotted for all major renovations. [The Accord also requires that workers receive up to six months' salary if the factory is closed for renovations and requires that suppliers respect the right of a worker "to refuse work that he or she has reasonable justification to believe is unsafe, without suffering discrimination or loss of pay."]

SUPPLIER INCENTIVES:

21. Each signatory company shall require that its suppliers in Bangladesh participate fully in the inspection, remediation, health and safety and, where applicable, training activities, as described in the Agreement. If a supplier fails to do so, the signatory will promptly implement a notice and warning process leading to termination of the business relationship if these efforts do not succeed.

22. In order to induce . . . factories to comply with upgrade and remediation requirements of the program, participating brands and retailers will negotiate commercial terms

with their suppliers which ensure that it is financially feasible for the factories to maintain safe workplaces and comply with . . . remediation requirements instituted by the Safety Inspector. Each signatory company may . . . use alternative means to ensure factories have the financial capacity to comply with remediation requirements, including . . . joint investments, providing loans, accessing donor or government support, through offering business incentives or through paying for renovations directly.

The Accord goes on to describe in detail the inspection and remediation regime, funding of the program, and other responsibilities of the signatory companies. The Accord's website states that the Accord is a "legally binding agreement" among the signatories, and it contains provisions for resolving disputes through arbitrations whose awards would be enforced in domestic courts.

A group of primarily U.S.-based suppliers, including Gap, Macy's, and Walmart, refused to sign the Accord and instead launched their own initiative, the Alliance for Bangladesh Worker Safety. Although the Alliance, now comprising 26 companies, is also based on a legally binding document among its corporate members, it differs from the Accord in key respects. It does not contain the commitment in Article 22 of the Accord to pay for remediation of unsafe factors, although it does require companies to contribute to a fund part of which is supposed to share the cost of displaced workers' salaries. In addition, the Alliance lacks the Accord's guarantee of six months of wages to employees displaced by renovations and the guarantee that employees refusing to work in unsafe factories will not be penalized. It also does not include worker representatives in its governing structure. The Clean Clothes Campaign, an international NGO, criticized the Alliance as "a company-developed and company-controlled scheme."

By late 2014, some progress had been achieved through both systems, as many hundreds of factories were inspected under the respective procedures. At the same time, fewer than half of Bangladesh's 5,000 apparel factories were covered under either document, and observers said these included the worst factories. Further, the question of who would pay for repairs and workers' wages during factory shutdowns remained unresolved. At least one factory owner covered under the Accord threatened to sue the Accord for not paying for orders lost during renovations. Leaders of the Accord and the Alliance insist that they are not competing with each other and are working toward the same goal, but press reports, industry representatives, and NGOs often compare each plan's inspections, financial schemes of compensation, and overall effectiveness. Most important, the new responsibilities of corporations do not seem to be addressing the core issues of corruption and lack of capacity that have prevented Bangladesh from enforcing its own laws.

Notes and Questions

1. Compare the Walmart statement of ethics with the Bangladesh Accord. What might explain the differences between them?

2. Does a legally binding code among corporations contribute to or disrupt the international lawmaking process of setting standards for worker safety? Does such a code shift too much responsibility from the host state—in this case, Bangladesh—to the corporations?

3. The overall effectiveness of corporate codes of conduct in changing corporate behavior is the subject of much debate. Consider the following argument:

> In the end, for optimal effect, corporations will need to internalize [human rights] norms in their decisionmaking. This point resonates with the key insight from international relations theorists and others that internalization is critical to successful implementation of international norms, whether in human rights or other areas of the law. . . .
>
> . . . The overall impact of such codes on corporate behavior is . . . unclear, with different companies and industries adopting stronger or weaker codes, each of which is observed with varying degrees of seriousness. The route of corporate-initiated codes of conduct nonetheless seems useful in the process of addressing violations of human rights, as it will at least raise corporate awareness of these issues and permit the possibility of monitoring (either by independent monitors paid by the industry or by NGOs). Undoubtedly, corporations will adopt various, even inconsistent, codes as a substantive matter, and human rights NGOs will object to that inconsistency. But the process of international lawmaking often begins with such private codes, which create expectations of appropriate conduct among diverse actors and can lead over time to other forms of lawmaking.

Steven R. Ratner, *Corporations and Human Rights: A Theory of Legal Responsibility*, 111 Yale L.J. 443, 531, 532-533 (2001).

4. For a more skeptical view, consider the views of a former U.S. Secretary of Labor:

> It is easy to understand why big business has embraced corporate social responsibility with such verve. It makes for good press and reassures the public. A declaration of corporate commitment to social virtue may also forestall government legislation or regulation in an area of public concern where one or more companies have behaved badly, such as transporting oil carelessly and causing a major spill or flagrantly failing to respect human rights abroad. The soothing promise of responsibility can deflect public attention from the need for stricter laws and regulations or convince the public that there's no real problem to begin with. Corporations that have signed codes of conduct promising good behavior appear to have taken important steps toward social responsibility, but the pressures operating on them to lure and keep consumers and investors haven't eased one bit. . . .

Robert B. Reich, The Case Against Corporate Social Responsibility (Goldman Sch. Working Paper Series, Aug. 1, 2008). Does the involvement of non-corporate groups in drafting codes of conduct alleviate any of his concerns?

D. Coda: Options for Direct Participation of Corporations in Law Making

Corporate involvement in lawmaking extends beyond the preparation of voluntary codes of conduct. In some situations, corporations, like NGOs, are involved directly in lawmaking by international organizations. As in the case of NGOs, international law does not have any general rules regarding corporate participation in lawmaking, leaving it up to each international organization to set up its own system. Consider the following two examples.

First, the ILO, the UN agency responsible for drafting Convention No. 155, quoted above, places businesses squarely within its governance structure, as seen in this description.

How the ILO Works

www.ilo.org

The ILO accomplishes its work through three main bodies . . . which comprise governments', employers' and workers' representatives.

International Labour Conference

The broad policies of the ILO are set by the International Labour Conference, which meets once a year in June, in Geneva, Switzerland. This annual Conference brings together governments', workers' and employer's delegates of the ILO member States. . . .

Each member State is represented by a delegation consisting of two government delegates, an employer delegate, a worker delegate, and their respective advisers. Many of the government representatives are cabinet ministers responsible for labour affairs in their own countries. Employer and Worker delegates are nominated in agreement with the most representative national organizations of employers and workers.

Every delegate has the same rights, and all can express themselves freely and vote as they wish. Worker and employer delegates may sometimes vote against their government's representatives or against each other. This diversity of viewpoints, however, does not prevent decisions being adopted by very large majorities or in some cases even unanimously.

Governing Body

The Governing Body is the executive body of the International Labour Organization. . . . It takes decisions on ILO policy, decides the agenda of the International Labour Conference, adopts the draft Programme and Budget of the Organization for submission to the Conference, and elects the Director-General.

It is composed of 56 titular members (28 Governments, 14 Employers and 14 Workers) and 66 deputy members (28 Governments, 19 Employers and 19 Workers). . . . The Employer and Worker members are elected in their individual capacity.

International Labour Office

The International Labour Office is the permanent secretariat of the International Labour Organization. . . . .

The second example is the International Telecommunication Union (ITU), the UN agency responsible for the regulation of global telecommunications. The ITU is divided into three sectors—one that sets technical standards for telecommunications equipment, one that allocates use of the radio-frequency spectrum, and one that assists developing nations. These Sectors work through periodic conferences and assemblies of all states, as well as smaller "study groups" composed of experts. The first sector, known as the Telecommunication Standardization Sector, has study groups that issue recommendations on telecommunications equipment. While not legally binding on states, the recommendations from the study groups become industry standards that companies follow.

Unlike the ILO, the ITU does not directly incorporate business entities into the main governance bodies. But as explained on the ITU's Web site, *www.itu.int*, companies can participate within the sectors as "members," and some 209 private enterprises are members of the Sectors. The web site includes the following information regarding membership by companies in the Telecommunication Standardization Sector ("ITU-T"):

implementation of the South African divestment statute would require no investigation by state officials into the operation of South African law and require no assessment of the credibility of South African officials. Second, the statute would fall directly on American companies and only indirectly on South Africa. . . .

Finally, in evaluating the impact of state investment decisions on foreign policy, it should be noted that a state is necessarily involved in the investment of state funds. . . . A state for instance, may decide not to invest in a company doing business in South Africa because it believes that there is a large risk of revolution and, thus, of expropriation in that country. The decision would have an impact on South Africa and on national policy toward that country identical to a decision to divest on the basis of moral opposition to South Africa's system of apartheid. But surely no one would suggest that states are constitutionally forbidden from making such investment decisions. . . . If state investment decisions are subject to invalidation for intrusion into foreign policy, we perceive no limiting principle to prevent constant judicial scrutiny of those decisions for consistency with some perceived foreign policy.

Congress eventually imposed sanctions on South Africa in the Comprehensive Anti-Apartheid Act of 1986. The law prohibited the importation of arms, minerals, and other commodities and the exportation of fuel, computers, most nuclear-related materials, and munitions for the police forces. It included financial sanctions but did not prohibit U.S investment—new or old—in South Africa. In the only court case to address the consistency of local sanctions with the 1986 federal law, the Maryland Court of Appeals upheld Baltimore's city statute requiring public pension funds to divest from companies doing significant business in South Africa. The court found no evidence that Congress meant to preempt local sanctions; the Maryland court further found that the law did not unconstitutionally impinge on the federal government's power over foreign affairs and did not violate the Commerce Clause. *Board of Trustees of the Employees' Retirement System of the City of Baltimore v. Mayor and City Council of Baltimore City*, 562 A.2d 720 (Md. Ct. App. 1989).

Notes and Questions

1. Is there a difference in the extent to which the federal government—or other nations—should tolerate sister-city relationships as compared to disinvestment of public pension funds or selective purchasing laws by localities?

2. Does the Justice Department effectively make the case that local anti-apartheid sanctions do not intrude on federal power over foreign affairs? What would be the perspective of a foreign governmental official on this question?

3. Does the type of human rights violations distinguish the South African case from the Myanmar case in terms of the extent to which subnational actors should be able to participate in the legal process?

C. International Reactions

U.S. allies, principally the European Union (EU) and Japan, protested the Massachusetts law, as it resulted in the exclusion from bidding of many European and Japanese companies (or their subsidiaries) that conducted business in Burma, a practice perfectly permissible in Europe and Japan. Indeed, many European companies without any business in Massachusetts were sent questionnaires by the state regarding their ties to Burma; if they responded that they did business with Burma, Massachusetts put their names on its public blacklist.

The EU and Japan based much of their legal argument on the view that the Massachusetts law violated a multilateral agreement on government procurement concluded in 1994 as part of the so-called Uruguay Round of trade talks that created the World Trade Organization (WTO). Under the Government Procurement Agreement (GPA), WTO members are supposed to ensure that governmental entities procure goods and services on a nondiscriminatory basis vis-à-vis companies of the other parties. During the negotiations for the Agreement, the U.S. delegation proposed that subnational units such as U.S. states be able to submit voluntarily to the new code. Eventually 37 states, including Massachusetts, agreed to abide by the provisions with respect to some or all of their government procurement.

Japanese and EU officials raised the Massachusetts law repeatedly with U.S. federal officials as well as with Massachusetts authorities. On September 8, 1998, the EU asked for the formation of a panel of the WTO's Dispute Settlement Body to adjudicate the responsibility of the United States for noncompliance with the Government Procurement Agreement.

Request for Establishment of a Panel by the European Communities

www.wto.org

The [Massachusetts] Law forbids State agencies, State authorities and other State entities from procuring goods and services from any person currently doing business with the Union of Myanmar . . . . In practice, this is achieved by applying an automatic price penalty of 10% on bids from companies which are deemed to be doing business in or with the Union of Myanmar. . . .

In doing so, the Law attaches conditions for the participation of suppliers in tendering procedures which violate the requirement set out in Article VIII(b) of the GPA [which requires government entities engaged in procurement to limit any conditions on participation in procurement to those "essential to ensure the firm's capability to fulfil the contract in question"]. Furthermore, by imposing a 10% price increase on the basis of whether or not a company does business in or with Myanmar, the Law violates the basic GPA requirement embodied inter alia in Article XIII.4(b) [which generally requires procuring entities to award contracts to the qualified bidder with the lowest offer]. . . .

On October 21, 1988, the WTO's Dispute Settlement Body established a panel to consider the EU's complaint and a similar complaint filed by Japan.

Notes and Questions

1. The above petition assumes, correctly, that the United States is legally responsible for the actions of U.S. states. Is there some way by which the United States might distance itself from the activities of its states? In 1994, the UN's Human Rights Committee, which monitors compliance with the International Covenant on Civil and Political Rights

(ICCPR), considered a complaint brought against Australia by Nicholas Toonen, a gay rights advocate from the state of Tasmania. Toonen asserted that a Tasmanian law criminalizing male homosexual sex violated the ICCPR's prohibition against "arbitrary or unlawful interference with . . . privacy, family, home or correspondence." Australia appeared before the Committee to respond to the complaint but essentially conceded that the Tasmanian law violated the ICCPR. The Committee ruled for Toonen and requested that Australia rescind the Tasmanian law, but Tasmanian authorities refused to comply. In response, the federal government enacted a new privacy law in 1994 meant to override the Tasmanian law. After Tasmanian advocates sued Tasmania in Australia's High Court to enforce the new law, the Tasmanian legislature finally repealed the offending law in 1997.

2. Why do you think U.S. states would have an interest in becoming party to the GPA?

3. What should the federal government do vis-à-vis Massachusetts in response to a claim of illegal action by foreign governments? Should it matter that the complaining states are political or military allies of the United States or major economic partners?

D. Domestic Reactions

In 1998, the National Foreign Trade Council (NFTC), an industry group that included companies on Massachusetts's no-purchase list, sued Massachusetts in federal district court, arguing that the statute unconstitutionally infringed on the federal government's foreign affairs power. The district court agreed and the U.S. Court of Appeals for the First Circuit affirmed. Massachusetts appealed to the U.S. Supreme Court.

The EU filed amicus briefs in support of the NFTC, alleging that the law had created a significant irritant in EU-U.S. relations. The U.S. Executive Branch debated the domestic political costs to challenging the Massachusetts law compared to the constitutional and foreign policy arguments against that law and in the end filed a brief that supported the NFTC 78 members of Congress filed an amicus brief urging reversal, arguing that Congress did not intend to preempt the Massachusetts law, while 20 members filed a brief urging affirmance.

Crosby, Secretary of Administration and Finance of Massachusetts v. National Foreign Trade Council

530 U.S. 363 (2000)

SOUTER, J., delivered the opinion of the Court, in which REHNQUIST, C.J., and STEVENS, O'CONNOR, KENNEDY, GINSBURG, and BREYER, JJ., joined. SCALIA, J., filed an opinion concurring in the judgment, in which THOMAS, J., joined.

III

A fundamental principle of the Constitution is that Congress has the power to preempt state law. Art. VI, cl. 2; *Gibbons v. Ogden*, 9 Wheat. 1 [1824]. . . . Even without an express provision for preemption, we have found that state law must yield to a congressional Act in at least two circumstances. When Congress intends federal law to "occupy the field," state law in that area is preempted. . . . And even if Congress has not occupied the field, state law is naturally preempted to the extent of any conflict with a federal statute. . . . We will find preemption where it is impossible for a private party to comply with both state and federal law . . . and where "under the circumstances of [a] particular case, [the challenged state law] stands as an obstacle to the accomplishment and execution of the full purposes and objectives of Congress." [Hines v. Davidowitz, 312 U.S. 52, 67 (1941)]. . . .

A

First, Congress clearly intended the federal Act to provide the President with flexible and effective authority over economic sanctions against Burma. Although Congress immediately put in place a set of initial sanctions prohibiting bilateral aid . . . , support for international financial assistance . . . , and entry by Burmese officials into the United States . . . , it authorized the President to terminate any and all of those measures upon determining and certifying that there had been progress in human rights and democracy in Burma. . . . It invested the President with the further power to ban new investment by United States persons. . . . And, most significantly, Congress empowered the President "to waive, temporarily or permanently, any sanction [under the federal act] . . . if he determines and certifies to Congress that the application of such sanction would be contrary to the national security interests of the United States."

This express investiture of the President with statutory authority to act for the United States in imposing sanctions with respect to the Government of Burma, augmented by the flexibility to respond to change by suspending sanctions in the interest of national security, recalls Justice Jackson's observation in *Youngstown Sheet & Tube Co. v. Sawyer*, 343 U.S. 579, 635 (1952): "When the President acts pursuant to an express or implied authorization of Congress, his authority is at its maximum, for it includes all that he possesses in his own right plus all that Congress can delegate." . . . Within the sphere defined by Congress, then, the statute has placed the President in a position with as much discretion to exercise economic leverage against Burma, with an eye toward national security, as our law will admit. And it is just this plenitude of Executive authority that we think controls the issue of preemption here. The President has been given this authority not merely to make a political statement but to achieve a political result. . . . It is simply implausible that Congress would have gone to such lengths to empower the President if it had been willing to compromise his effectiveness by deference to every provision of state statute or local ordinance that might . . . blunt the consequences of discretionary Presidential action.

And that is just what the Massachusetts Burma law would do in imposing a different, state system of economic pressure against the Burmese political regime. As will be seen, the state statute penalizes some private action that the federal Act (as administered by the President) may allow, and pulls levers of influence that the federal Act does not reach. [T]he state sanctions are immediate . . . and perpetual. . . . This unyielding application undermines the President's intended statutory authority by making it impossible for him to restrain fully the coercive power of the national economy. . . .

B

Congress manifestly intended to limit economic pressure against the Burmese Government to a specific range. The federal Act confines its reach to United States persons, . . . imposes limited immediate sanctions, . . . places only a conditional ban on a carefully defined area of "new investment," . . . and pointedly exempts contracts to sell or purchase goods, services, or technology. . . .

The State has set a different course, and its statute conflicts with federal law at a number of points by penalizing individuals and conduct that Congress has explicitly exempted or excluded from sanctions. . . . It restricts all contracts between the State and companies doing business in Burma . . . even though those transactions are explicitly exempted from the ambit of new investment prohibition when the President exercises his discretionary authority to impose sanctions under the federal Act. . . .

[T]he state Act's generality stands at odds with the federal discreteness. . . . The state Act . . . penalizes companies with pre-existing affiliates or investments, all of which lie beyond the reach of the federal Act's restrictions on "new investment" in Burmese economic development. . . . The state Act, moreover, imposes restrictions on foreign companies as well as domestic, whereas the federal Act limits its reach to United States persons.

The conflicts are not rendered irrelevant by the State's argument that there is no real conflict between the statutes because they share the same goals and because some companies may comply with both sets of restrictions. . . . The fact of a common end hardly neutralizes conflicting means, . . . and the fact that some companies may be able to comply with both sets of sanctions does not mean that the state Act is not at odds with achievement of the federal decision about the right degree of pressure to employ. . . . "'[C]onflict is imminent'" when "'two separate remedies are brought to bear on the same activity,'" *Wisconsin Dept. of Industry v. Gould Inc.*, 475 U.S. 282, 286 (1986). . . . Sanctions are drawn not only to bar what they prohibit but to allow what they permit, and the inconsistency of sanctions here undermines the congressional calibration of force.

C

Finally, the state Act is at odds with the President's intended authority to speak for the United States among the world's nations in developing a "comprehensive, multilateral strategy to bring democracy to and improve human rights practices and the quality of life in Burma." . . . Congress's express command to the President to take the initiative for the United States among the international community invested him with the maximum authority of the National Government . . . in harmony with the President's own constitutional powers, U.S. Const., Art. II, §2, cl. 2 ("[The President] shall have Power, by and with the Advice and Consent of the Senate, to make Treaties" and "shall appoint Ambassadors, other public Ministers and Consuls"); §3 ("[The President] shall receive Ambassadors and other public Ministers"). . . .

Again, the state Act undermines the President's capacity, in this instance for effective diplomacy. It is not merely that the differences between the state and federal Acts in scope and type of sanctions threaten to complicate discussions; they compromise the very capacity of the President to speak for the Nation with one voice. . . .

[T]he record is replete with evidence to answer any skeptics. First . . . a number of this country's allies and trading partners filed formal protests with the National Government, see [the court of appeals opinion] (noting protests from Japan, the European Union (EU), and ASEAN). . . . EU officials have warned that the state Act "could have a damaging effect on bilateral EU-US relations." [*Citing* a 1997 letter from the EU to the Massachusetts governor.]

Second, the EU and Japan have gone a step further in lodging formal complaints against the United States in the [WTO]. . . . EU officials point to the WTO dispute as threatening relations with the United States . . . and note that the state Act has become the topic of "intensive discussions" with officials of the United States at the highest levels, those discussions including exchanges at the twice yearly EU-U.S. Summit.

Third, the Executive has consistently represented that the state Act has . . . proven an impediment to accomplishing objectives assigned it by Congress. Assistant Secretary of

State Larson, for example, has directly addressed the mandate of the federal Burma law in saying that the imposition of unilateral state sanctions under the state Act "complicate[s] efforts to build coalitions with our allies" to promote democracy and human rights in Burma. . . .

IV

The State's remaining argument is unavailing. It contends that the failure of Congress to preempt the state Act demonstrates implicit permission. The State points out that Congress has repeatedly declined to enact express preemption provisions aimed at state and local sanctions, and it calls our attention to the large number of such measures passed against South Africa in the 1980s. . . . The State stresses that Congress was aware of the state Act in 1996, but did not preempt it explicitly when it adopted its own Burma statute. . . .

The argument is unconvincing on more than one level. A failure to provide for preemption expressly may reflect nothing more than the settled character of implied preemption doctrine that courts will dependably apply, and in any event, the existence of conflict cognizable under the Supremacy Clause does not depend on express congressional recognition that federal and state law may conflict. . . . The State's inference of congressional intent is unwarranted here, therefore, simply because the silence of Congress is ambiguous. . . .

V

Because the state Act's provisions conflict with Congress's specific delegation to the President of flexible discretion, with limitation of sanctions to a limited scope of actions and actors, and with direction to develop a comprehensive, multilateral strategy under the federal Act, it is preempted, and its application is unconstitutional, under the Supremacy Clause.

Notes and Questions

1. Does the Massachusetts statute conflict with federal law? Do not both seek to put pressure on Burma to improve its human rights practices?

2. What sorts of participation by states in foreign policy would the Supreme Court tolerate under the reasoning in *Crosby*? How does the Massachusetts law differ from the anti-apartheid statutes that the Office of Legal Counsel found constitutional in 1986?

3. How important to the Court's reasoning was the position of the Executive Branch that the law complicated multilateral efforts on Burma? What does this suggest about the Court's approach to the role of states?

4. Which was the better forum for the resolution of this matter—the WTO (through its three-person dispute resolution panel) or the U.S. Supreme Court? Should America's trading partners be satisfied with the Supreme Court's decision in light of their complaint to the WTO? After *Crosby*, Japan and the EU dropped their WTO case. In 2012, in response to major changes within Burma, the President used his authorities to begin removing sanctions.

E. State Prerogatives in the Absence of Congressional Action

In many situations where states seek an independent voice, Congress has not passed legislation addressing the same general area. As discussed in the 1986 Department of Justice opinion excerpted above, this was the issue in *Zschernig v. Miller.* It falls under the U.S. constitutional law doctrines on "dormant preemption." In 2003, it reached the Supreme Court again in litigation over California's response to claims by Holocaust survivors that European insurance companies had failed to pay survivors who were beneficiaries of pre-war insurance policies.

In the mid-1990s, the U.S. and German governments negotiated the German Foundation Agreement, whereby Germany and German companies set up a $7 billion foundation to compensate Holocaust victims. That foundation worked with a private organization, the International Commission on Holocaust Era Insurance Claims (ICHEIC), comprised of Holocaust survivor groups, European insurance companies, U.S. state insurance commissioners, and the government of Israel. ICHEIC negotiated with European insurance companies to get access to information on unpaid policies and settled claims of some survivors. The United States subsequently concluded similar agreements with Austria and France. As part of these undertakings, it promised to use its "best efforts" to ensure that U.S. state and local governments would allow the foundation to serve as the exclusive mechanism for resolution of these claims.

In 1999, California passed the Holocaust Victim Insurance Relief Act (HVIRA), which requires any insurer doing business there to disclose information about insurance policies issued "to persons in Europe, which were in effect between 1920 and 1945." This covers policies by any "related company," including parents, subsidiaries, and affiliates. If a company refuses to do so, it cannot do business in California. The legislature claimed the Act was needed "to protect the claims and interests of California residents." Federal officials claimed the action undermined the ICHEIC process, and an insurance industry association sued the state.

American Insurance Association v. Garamendi, Insurance Commissioner, State of California

539 U.S. 396 (2003)

SOUTER, J., delivered the opinion of the Court, in which REHNQUIST, C.J., and O'CONNOR, KENNEDY, and BREYER, JJ., joined. GINSBURG, J., filed a dissenting opinion, in which STEVENS, SCALIA, and THOMAS, JJ., joined.

The issue here is whether HVIRA interferes with the National Government's conduct of foreign relations. We hold that it does, with the consequence that the state statute is preempted. . . .

III

The principal argument for preemption made by petitioners and the United States as amicus curiae is that HVIRA interferes with foreign policy of the Executive Branch, as expressed principally in the executive agreements with Germany, Austria, and France. . . . There is, of course, no question that at some point an exercise of state power that touches on foreign relations must yield to the National Government's policy, given the "concern for uniformity in this country's dealings with foreign nations" that animated the Constitution's allocation of the foreign relations power to the National Government in the first place. *Banco Nacional de Cuba v. Sabbatino*, 376 U.S. 398, 427, n. 25 (1964). . . .

[The Court discusses the President's constitutional authority to make executive agreements settling the claims of Americans—see Chapter 5, Problem I. Relying on precedent, it reaffirms that such agreements can override state law if they expressly state so. But it finds that the agreements here did not expressly override state law and thus the Court needs to consider the question of HVIRA's interference with foreign policy.]

[After discussing the facts in *Zschernig*, the Court states:] The *Zschernig* majority relied on statements in a number of previous cases open to the reading that state action with more than incidental effect on foreign affairs is preempted, even absent any affirmative federal activity in the subject area of the state law, and hence without any showing of conflict. . . . Justice Harlan . . . disagreed with the *Zschernig* majority on this point, arguing that . . . "the States may legislate in areas of their traditional competence even though their statutes may have an incidental effect on foreign relations." . . . He would, however, have found preemption in a case of "conflicting federal policy." . . . [E]ven on Justice Harlan's view, the likelihood that state legislation will produce something more than incidental effect in conflict with express foreign policy of the National Government would require preemption of the state law. And since on his view it is legislation within "areas of . . . traditional competence" that gives a State any claim to prevail, it would be reasonable to consider the strength of the state interest, judged by standards of traditional practice, when deciding how serious a conflict must be shown before declaring the state law preempted. . . .

IV

A

. . . The exercise of the federal executive authority means that state law must give way where, as here, there is evidence of clear conflict between the policies adopted by the two. The foregoing account of negotiations toward the three settlement agreements is enough to illustrate that the consistent Presidential foreign policy has been to encourage European governments and companies to volunteer settlement funds in preference to litigation or coercive sanctions. . . .

California has taken a different tack. . . . The situation created by the California legislation calls to mind the impact of the Massachusetts Burma law [in] *Crosby v. National Foreign Trade Council*, 530 U.S. 363 (2000). HVIRA's economic compulsion to make public disclosure, of far more information about far more policies than ICHEIC rules require, employs "a different, state system of economic pressure," and in doing so undercuts the President's diplomatic discretion and the choice he has made exercising it. *Id.*, at 376. Whereas the President's authority to provide for settling claims in winding up international hostilities requires flexibility in wielding "the coercive power of the national economy" as a tool of diplomacy, *id.*, at 377, HVIRA denies this, by making exclusion from a large sector of the American insurance market the automatic sanction for noncompliance with the State's own policies on disclosure. "Quite simply, if the [California] law is enforceable the President has less to offer and less economic and diplomatic leverage as a consequence." *Ibid.* The law thus "compromise[s] the very capacity of the President to speak for the Nation with one voice in dealing with other governments" . . . 530 U.S., at 381.

Crosby's facts are replicated again in the way HVIRA threatens to frustrate the operation of the particular mechanism the President has chosen. The letters from [the State Department] to California officials show well enough how the portent of further litigation and sanctions has in fact placed the Government at a disadvantage in obtaining practical results from persuading "foreign governments and foreign companies to participate voluntarily in organizations such as ICHEIC." . . . California's indiscriminate disclosure provisions [also] place a handicap on the ICHEIC's effectiveness (and raise a further irritant to the European allies) by undercutting European privacy protections. . . .

B

The express federal policy and the clear conflict raised by the state statute are alone enough to require state law to yield. If any doubt about the clarity of the conflict remained, however, it would have to be resolved in the National Government's favor, given the weakness of the State's interest, against the backdrop of traditional state legislative subject matter, in regulating disclosure of European Holocaust-era insurance policies in the manner of HVIRA. . . .

[T]he state interest actually underlying HVIRA is concern for the several thousand Holocaust survivors said to be living in the State. . . . [T]he very same objective dignifies the interest of the National Government in devising its chosen mechanism for voluntary settlements, there being about 100,000 survivors in the country, only a small fraction of them in California. As against the responsibility of the United States of America, the humanity underlying the state statute could not give the State the benefit of any doubt in resolving the conflict with national policy.

C

. . . California seeks to use an iron fist where the President has consistently chosen kid gloves. We have heard powerful arguments that the iron fist would work better. . . . But our thoughts on the efficacy of the one approach versus the other are beside the point, since our business is not to judge the wisdom of the National Government's policy; dissatisfaction should be addressed to the President or, perhaps, Congress. . . .

JUSTICE GINSBURG, with whom JUSTICE STEVENS, JUSTICE SCALIA, and JUSTICE THOMAS join, dissenting. . . .

Although the federal approach differs from California's, no executive agreement or other formal expression of foreign policy disapproves state disclosure laws like the HVIRA. Absent a clear statement aimed at disclosure requirements by the "one voice" to which courts properly defer in matters of foreign affairs, I would leave intact California's enactment. . . .

At least until very recently . . . ICHEIC's progress has been slow and insecure. . . . Initially, ICHEIC's insurance company members represented little more than one-third of the Holocaust-era insurance market. . . . Moreover, ICHEIC has thus far settled only a tiny proportion of the claims it has received. Evidence submitted in a series of class actions filed against Italian insurer Generali indicated that by November 2001, ICHEIC had resolved only 797 of 77,000 claims. . . . Finally, although ICHEIC has directed its members to publish lists of unpaid Holocaust-era policies, that non-binding directive had not yielded significant compliance at the time this case reached the Court. . . .

We have not relied on *Zschernig* since it was decided, and I would not resurrect that decision here. The notion of "dormant foreign affairs preemption" with which *Zschernig* is associated resonates most audibly when a state action "reflect[s] a state policy critical of foreign governments and involve[s] 'sitting in judgment' on them." L. Henkin, Foreign Affairs and the United States Constitution 164 (2d ed. 1996); *see* Constitutionality of South African Divestment Statutes Enacted by State and Local Governments, 10 Op. Off. Legal Counsel 49, 50 (1986) ("[W]e believe that [*Zschernig*] represents the Court's reaction to a particular regulatory statute, the operation of which intruded extraordinarily deeply into foreign affairs."). The HVIRA . . . takes no position on any contemporary foreign government and requires no assessment of any existing foreign regime. It is directed solely at private insurers doing business in California, and it requires them solely to disclose information. . . .

[N]one of the executive agreements extinguish any underlying claim for relief. The United States has agreed to file precatory statements advising courts that dismissing Holocaust-era claims accords with American foreign policy, but the German Foundation Agreement confirms that such statements have no legally binding effect. It remains uncertain, therefore, whether even *litigation* on Holocaust-era insurance claims must be abated in deference to the German Foundation Agreement. . . . If it is uncertain whether insurance *litigation* may continue given the executive agreements on which the Court relies, it should be abundantly clear that those agreements leave *disclosure* laws like the HVIRA untouched. . . . Here, the Court invalidates a state disclosure law on grounds of conflict with foreign policy "embod[ied]" in certain executive agreements, although those agreements do not refer to state disclosure laws. . . . To fill the agreements' silences, the Court points to statements by individual members of the Executive Branch. . . . [N]o authoritative text accords such officials the power to invalidate state law simply by conveying the Executive's views on matters of federal policy. . . .

[B]y declining to invalidate the HVIRA in this case, we would reserve foreign affairs preemption for circumstances where the President, acting under statutory or constitutional authority, has spoken clearly to the issue at hand. . . . As I see it, courts step out of their proper role when they rely on no legislative or even executive text, but only on inference and implication, to preempt state laws on foreign affairs grounds.

Notes and Questions

1. After *Garamendi*, what sorts of international relations may U.S. states practice without fear of preemption? How can state and local officials determine whether their policies conflict with federal policy?

2. Does the slow pace of proceedings under the German Foundation agreement provide a justification for California's actions? Are the objections of the State Department and foreign governments a sufficient ground for preemption in the absence of federal law?

3. In December 2007, President George W. Bush signed the Sudan Accountability and Divestment Act, whose main provision states, "[A] State or local government may adopt and enforce measures . . . to divest [its] assets from, or prohibit investment of [its assets] in, persons that [it] determines . . . are conducting or have direct investments in business operations . . . [in Sudan concerning] power production activities, mineral extraction activities, oil-related activities, or the production of military equipment." States must provide targets of sanctions with notice and an opportunity to comment and to limit sanctions to those involved in the industries noted; it also urges states to take all efforts to avoid erroneously targeting persons. About two dozen states have such sanctions. How should the Supreme Court rule if the President objected to one of the state or local Sudan divestment laws?

PART III

International Law and Domestic Law

Having studied the ways international law is made and the participants in the international legal system, we now turn to the relationships between international and domestic law. This topic is of particular importance because, as discussed in Parts I and II above, the international system lacks a central lawmaking body, an executive to enforce the law, and a centralized judiciary to interpret the law and adjudicate disputes. As a result, international law is frequently interpreted, applied, and enforced in domestic political and legal systems. For example, executive branch officials may invoke international law to augment their power, or to limit the power of other branches or actors, and legislatures may pass statutes specifically designed to implement, change, or violate international legal norms.

Domestic courts, as well, frequently address the relationships between international and domestic law. Private parties often ask courts to decide whether the jurisdictional reach of domestic statutes violates international legal norms, to enforce treaty or customary international law obligations, and to resolve conflicts between international and domestic legal obligations. In these actions, courts often look to both international and domestic legal norms; in addition, domestic or foreign political actors may ask courts to consider the laws and public policies of foreign states, and to minimize judicial interference with the conduct of national foreign relations by the political branches.

Part III begins with a short overview of theoretical debates over the relationship between international and domestic law. These debates provide a useful framework for approaching the materials in Chapters 5 and 6. However, as a former World Court judge explains, how a domestic legal system treats the relationships between international and domestic law turns, in part, on that system's particular "legal culture":

> In some jurisdictions international law will be treated as a familiar topic, . . . the introduction of which occasions no special comment or interest. . . . But there is another culture that exists, in which it is possible to become a practising lawyer [or judge] without having studied international law. . . . Psychologically that disposes both counsel and judge to treat international law as some exotic branch of the law . . . to be looked upon as if it is unreal, of no practical application in the real world.

Rosalyn Higgins, Problems and Process: International Law and How We Use It 206 (1995).

Chapters 5 and 6 are an exploration of the ways that political actors and courts incorporate — or fail to incorporate — international law into domestic law and activities. While many national constitutions address the status of international law on the domestic plane, these provisions are often phrased at a sufficiently high level of generality that they fail to resolve concrete controversies, and many international law questions are resolved through domestic political processes or through domestic court litigation. In Chapter 5, we focus on these processes—on how domestic systems create rules regarding the hierarchy of international law sources, particularly treaty and custom, in relation to domestic law; and on how these systems make and apply rules concerning the ways that states can enter into—or violate—international legal obligations. We also look at how and when courts and legislatures enable private parties to rely upon international legal norms in domestic litigation.

Chapter 6 addresses the issues raised when domestic law reaches beyond national borders. As we will see, international law provides general principles that purport to govern the ability of states to regulate conduct and persons outside their borders, as well as their ability to enforce their laws outside their borders. Nevertheless, controversies over the extraterritorial reach of domestic jurisdiction arise with some frequency. These controversies are, at times, resolved in international fora, but more frequently are settled in domestic arenas. In Chapter 6, we explore the resolution of such jurisdictional conflicts, as well as the various types of jurisdiction recognized by international law.

A number of important themes that build on the materials presented in Parts I and II run through all of the problems in Part III. Chapter 1 introduced the idea of the *dédoublement fonctionnel*, the dual function of state authorities as representatives of specific states and, at times, as agents of the broader international community. Chapters 5 and 6 provide a series of case studies that test whether this is an accurate characterization of the role that domestic actors play, or whether it conceals the tensions between the policy and legal orientations (and obligations) of domestic political actors and judges, on the one hand, and the political and legal pull of international legal norms, which frequently require some degree of subordination of national policies to international law, on the other. The problems that follow also explore the ways that national bias and interests affect the resolution of international legal problems on the domestic plane, and permit you to test the various approaches to international law discussed in Chapter 1. In addition, the problems in this part show how the various actors described in Part II—states, international organizations, non-governmental organizations and multinational corporations—participate in a dynamic process of interpreting and applying international law on the domestic plane. Moreover, each of the problems reveals how the relationships between international and domestic law are complex and subtle, and blur what were once considered to be the bright lines that distinguish international from domestic law.

Finally, the problems in this part of the book raise the larger question of whether international legal norms addressing the relationships between international and domestic law strike an appropriate "balance between the inclusive competence of the general community of states and the exclusive competence [that is, jurisdiction] of particular states which best promotes the greatest total production, at least cost, of their shared values." Myres S. McDougal, *The Impact of International Law Upon National Law: A Policy-Oriented Perspective, in* International Law Essays 437, 438 (Myres S. McDougal & W. Michael Reisman eds., 1981). In considering whether the right balance has been struck, Professor McDougal identified the following "important questions" :

[H]ow, and with what access to decision by interested participants, are [international legal norms], purporting to express a common interest, actually prescribed . . . for regulating the practices of states and the exclusive competence of particular states; what balance between the inclusive competence of the general community of states and the exclusive competence of particular states . . . is in fact established by such prescription; in what degree, and by what practices, are [internationally] prescribed practices effectively applied in action . . . to regulate states both in their external strategies and in their internal policies; and, finally, how compatible are the aggregate effects achieved, by the impact of international upon national processes of authority, with shared values of human dignity?

Id. at 447.

   At bottom, norms governing the role of international law in the domestic plane (Chapter 5), and norms governing the exercise of jurisdiction (Chapter 6), are really norms governing the exercise of state power. Thus, the materials that follow are, in part, an examination of the international and domestic processes for defining and limiting state power and, in part, an inquiry into whether current international norms appropriately define and limit the exercise of state power.

5

International Law in the Domestic Arena

International law frequently says little about how governments should implement their international legal obligations. As a result, domestic actors, including legislatures, courts, and individuals, confront a number of complex conceptual and doctrinal questions regarding the role and status of international law on the domestic plane. In many states the constitution addresses the relationships between international and domestic law and allocates authority over specific international legal issues to one or another branch of government. Nevertheless, many international legal questions are resolved in the United States and other domestic legal systems through the interactions of different branches of government.

In this chapter, we will explore a variety of ways that domestic courts and political actors address international legal issues, including the ways that international law is incorporated into and made part of domestic law, whether and when international legal norms are judicially enforceable by individuals, and whether domestic law treats treaties and customary international law the same or differently. Stated less formally, in this chapter we explore many of the techniques and doctrines that domestic courts and political actors use to make, break, interpret, incorporate, or fail to incorporate international law. While our focus will be on the U.S. legal system, similar issues arise in virtually all domestic legal systems. From time to time, reference will be made to some of these other systems.

I. THE MONIST-DUALIST DEBATE

Understanding the relationships between domestic and international law often begins with the question of whether these legal systems are part of a single, universal legal order (the "monist" position) or form two distinct systems of law (the "dualist" position). For monists, international law is automatically part of a state's domestic legal system and is just as much domestic law as is contract or tax law. In addition, international law is superior to domestic law (as a constitution is superior to a statute) in the case of a conflict. Under the monist view, the national legislature is bound to respect international law when passing legislation; the executive is obliged to follow international law, even in the face of contrary domestic law; and the judiciary is bound to give effect to international law.

For dualists, as Professor Lassa Oppenheim explained, "International Law and Municipal Law are in fact two totally and essentially different bodies of law which have nothing in common except that they are both branches—but separate branches—of the tree of law." That is, for dualists, international and domestic law govern different actors and issues. International law governs relations among states, while domestic law governs relations between a state and its citizens and among citizens. Under the dualist view, each state determines for itself whether, when, and how international law is "incorporated" into domestic law, and the status of international law in the domestic system is determined by domestic law. In part, the monist-dualist debate turns on how to determine the status of international law in the domestic legal system. Monists would argue that international law provides the answer to this question; dualists counter that domestic legal norms answer this question. Of course, as is true of many idealized analytic dichotomies, pure forms of monism or dualism are rarely encountered in practice. Instead, different states tend to fall along a continuum between pure monism and total dualism in their approach to international law. The constitutional provisions reproduced below illustrate the diversity of approaches that states can take regarding the relationships between international and domestic law.

France

Article 54

If the Constitutional Council, on a reference from the President of the Republic, from the Prime Minister, from the President of one or the other Assembly, or from sixty deputies or sixty senators, has declared that an international commitment contains a clause contrary to the Constitution, authorization to ratify or approve the international commitment in question may be given only after amendment of the Constitution.

Article 55

Treaties or agreements duly ratified or approved upon publication, prevail over Acts of Parliament, subject, in regard to each agreement or treaty, to its application by the other party.

Haiti

Article 276

The National Assembly may not ratify any international treaty, convention or agreement containing clauses contrary to this Constitution. . . .

Article 276-2

Once international treaties or agreements are approved and ratified in the manner stipulated by the Constitution, they become part of the legislation of the country and abrogate any laws in conflict with them.

The Netherlands

Article 91

(1) The Kingdom shall not be bound by treaties, nor shall such treaties be denounced, without the prior approval of the Parliament. The cases in which approval is not required shall be specified by Act of Parliament.

(2) The manner in which approval shall be granted shall be laid down by Act of Parliament, which may provide for the possibility of tacit approval.

(3) Any provisions of a treaty that conflict with the Constitution or which lead to conflicts with it may be approved by the Chambers of the Parliament only if at least two-thirds of the votes cast are in favor.

Article 94

Statutory regulations in force within the Kingdom shall not be applicable if such application is in conflict with provisions of treaties that are binding on all persons or of resolutions by international institutions.

South Africa

Section 231 International Agreements

(4) Any international agreement becomes law in the Republic when it is enacted into law by national legislation; but a self-executing provision of an agreement that has been approved by Parliament is law in the Republic unless it is inconsistent with the Constitution or an Act of Parliament.

Section 232 Customary International Law

Customary international law is law in the Republic unless it is inconsistent with the Constitution or an Act of Parliament.

Section 233 Application of International Law

When interpreting any legislation, every court must prefer any reasonable interpretation of the legislation that is consistent with international law over any alternative interpretation that is inconsistent with international law.

United States of America

Article VI

[2] This Constitution, and the Laws of the United States which shall be made in Pursuance thereof; and all Treaties made, or which shall be made, under the Authority of the United States, shall be the supreme Law of the Land; and the Judges in every State shall be bound thereby, any Thing in the Constitution or Laws of any State to the Contrary notwithstanding.

The European Union (EU) provides an important example of how international law can be directly applicable on the domestic plane. The Union is a unique, treaty-based institutional framework that defines and manages economic and political cooperation among its 28 member states. The Union is the result of a process that began in the wake of World War II. At that time, as a devastated Western Europe sought ways to rebuild its economy and prevent future wars, Jean Monnet and Robert Schuman proposed placing German and French coal and steel production under a common high authority. The integration of these two industries was intended to make future war on the continent impossible, and to set the stage for future forms of economic and political integration. The 1951 Treaty of Paris, establishing the European Coal and Steel Community, was signed by the three Benelux countries, France, Germany, and Italy. Coal and steel trade among these six nations increased by 129 percent in the first five years that this treaty was in force.

Encouraged by this success, European leaders decided to pursue additional efforts at economic integration. In 1957, the two so-called Rome treaties were ratified. One created the European Economic Community to merge the separate national markets into a single market that would ensure the free movement of goods, people, capital, and services. The other created the European Atomic Energy Community (Euratom) to further the peaceful use of nuclear energy.

Progress in European integration slowed considerably in the 1970s and early 1980s. The Single European Act, signed in 1986, amended the three original treaties by, inter alia, changing the Community's decisionmaking processes and bringing new areas, such as the environment, within the scope of Community law. The Treaty on European Union, signed in Maastricht, Netherlands, in December 1991, created the European Union, which encompasses the existing European Community and two new "pillars"—Common Foreign and Security Policy as well as Justice and Home Affairs (addressing, inter alia, crime and immigration issues). The June 1997 Treaty of Amsterdam paved the way for the introduction of the single currency and the enlargement of EU membership. In May 2004, ten states joined the EU; Bulgaria and Romania followed in 2007, and Croatia joined in 2013, bringing EU membership to 28. In 2007, EU leaders signed the Treaty of Lisbon. This treaty included provisions democratizing EU processes, streamlining EU decision making, and attempting to enhance the EU's power in world affairs. Following ratification by all EU member states, the Lisbon Treaty entered into force on December 1, 2009.

Through a variety of processes, the EU produces several different types of legislation. The Rome Treaty creating the Community provides that regulations "are binding in their entirety and directly applicable in all Member States." They can be analogized to federal laws in the United States. Directives are binding with respect to "the results to be achieved." They are addressed to the member states, which are free to choose the best "form and methods" of implementation. Decisions are binding in their entirety upon those to whom they are addressed. Recommendations and opinions are not binding.

The development of a substantial body of Community law gave rise to a number of questions about the relationship between Community and national law. Does Community law create rights that private parties can enforce against member states or that member states can enforce against private parties? When is a member state adequately enforcing or implementing Community law? Who makes this determination? As the relevant treaties did not expressly address many of the fundamental questions involving the relationship between Community and member state law, the European Court of Justice (ECJ), the EU's judicial organ, took the initiative in defining this relationship.

In *Van Gend en Loos v. Nederlandse Administratie Der Belastingen,* [1963] E.C.R. 3, the court considered whether provisions of the Rome Treaty "have direct application within the territory of a Member State, in other words, whether nationals of such State can, on the basis of the Article in question, lay claim to an individual right which the courts must protect."

The Court reasoned that:

> The objective of the EEC [Rome] Treaty, which is to establish a Common Market, the functioning of which is of direct concern to interested parties in the Community, implies that this Treaty is more than an agreement which merely creates mutual obligations between the contracting states. This view is confirmed by the preamble to the Treaty which refers not only to governments but to peoples. It is also confirmed more specifically by the establishment of institutions endowed with sovereign rights, the exercise of which affects Member States and also their citizens. . . .

> . . . The Community constitutes a new legal order of international law for the benefit of which the states have limited their sovereign rights, albeit within limited fields, and the subjects of which comprise not only the Member States but also their nationals. Independently of the legislation of Member States, Community law therefore not only imposes obligations on individuals but is also intended to confer upon them rights which become part of their legal heritage.

The Court held that the treaty provision at issue had a "direct effect" in domestic law that individuals could rely upon in national courts.

A year after *Van Gend en Loos*, the ECJ considered whether a directly applicable treaty provision prevails over conflicting domestic law in national courts. In *Costa v. Ente Nazionale per l'Energia Ellettrica*, [1964] E.C.R. 585, plaintiffs challenged an Italian law nationalizing the electric industry as inconsistent with the Italian Constitution and the Rome Treaty. The Italian Corte Costituzionale (constitutional court) ruled that, as the nationalization law was adopted after the law approving the Rome Treaty, the domestic law was "last in time" and therefore controlling. The ECJ disagreed:

> By contrast with ordinary international treaties, the [Rome Treaty] has created its own legal system which, on the entry into force of the Treaty, became an integral part of the legal systems of the Member States and which their courts are bound to apply.
>
> By creating a Community of unlimited duration, having its own institutions, its own personality, its own capacity and capacity of representation on the international plane, and more particularly, real powers stemming from a limitation of sovereignty or a transfer of powers from the States to the Community, the Member States have limited their sovereign rights, albeit within limited fields, and have thus created a body of law which binds both their nationals and themselves.
>
> The integration into the laws of each Member State of provisions which derive from the Community and more generally the terms and the spirit of the Treaty, make it impossible for the States, as a corollary, to accord precedence to a unilateral and subsequent measure over a legal system accepted by them on a basis of reciprocity. . . .
>
> The obligations undertaken under the Treaty establishing the [European] Community would not be unconditional, but merely contingent, if they could be called in question by subsequent legislative acts of the signatories. . . .
>
> The precedence of Community law is confirmed by Article 189 [of the Rome Treaty], whereby a regulation "shall be binding" and "directly applicable in all Member States". This provision, which is subject to no reservation, would be quite meaningless if a State could unilaterally nullify its effects by means of a legislative measure which could prevail over Community law.
>
> It follows from all these observations that the law stemming from the Treaty, an independent source of law, could not, because of its special and original nature, be overriden by domestic legal provisions, however framed, without being deprived of its character as Community law and without the legal basis of the Community itself being called into question.

In later cases, the Court expanded these principles. First, the court applied the direct effects principle not only in cases where an individual invokes Community law against a member state (the "vertical" dimension) but also to cases where Community law is invoked by one individual against another (the "horizontal" dimension). Second, the court applied the principle not only in the context of treaty law but also in the context of secondary community legislation, such as directives and decisions.

It is difficult to overestimate the impact of these cases on the development of the Community. The following extract captures something of this impact:

The implications of [the judicial doctrine of direct effect] were and are far reaching. The European Court reversed the normal presumption of public international law whereby international legal obligations are result-oriented and addressed to states. Public international law typically allows the internal constitutional order of a state to determine the method and extent to which international obligations may, if at all, produce effects for individuals within the legal order of the state. Under the normal canons of international law, even when the international obligation itself . . . is intended to bestow rights (or duties) on individuals within a state, if the state fails to bestow the rights, the individual cannot invoke the international obligation before national courts, unless [domestic law] provides for such a remedy. The typical remedy under public international law in such a case would be an inter-state claim. The main import of the Community doctrine of direct effect was not simply the conceptual change it ushered forth. In practice direct effect meant that Member States violating their Community obligations could not shift the locus of dispute to the inter-state or Community plane. They would be faced with legal actions before their own courts at the suit of individuals within their own legal order.

Individuals (and their lawyers) noticed this practical implication, and the number of cases brought on the basis of this doctrine grew exponentially. Effectively, individuals in real cases and controversies (usually against state public authorities) became the principal "guardians" of the legal integrity of Community law within Europe similar to the way that individuals in the United States have been the principal actors in ensuring the vindication of the Bill of Rights and other federal law.

. . . The full impact of direct effect is realized in combination with the second "constitutionalizing" doctrine, supremacy. Unlike some federal constitutions, the Treaty does not include a specific "supremacy clause." However, in a series of cases starting [with *Costa*] the Court has pronounced an uncompromising version of supremacy: in the sphere of application of Community law, any Community norm, be it an article of the Treaty (the Constitutional Charter) or a minuscule administrative regulation enacted by the Commission, "trumps" conflicting national law whether enacted before or after the Community norm. . . .

In light of supremacy the full significance of direct effect becomes transparent. Typically, in monist or quasi-monist states . . . [treaties are] equivalent to national legislation. Thus the normal rule of "later in time" (*lex posteriori derogat lex anteriori*) governs the relationship between the treaty provision and conflicting national legislation. A national legislature unhappy with an internalized treaty norm simply enacts a conflicting national measure . . . . By contrast, in the Community, because of the doctrine of supremacy, the E.C. norm, which by virtue of the doctrine of direct effect must be regarded as part of the Law of the Land, will prevail even in these circumstances. The combination of the two doctrines means that Community norms that produce direct effects are not merely the Law of the Land but the "Higher Law" of the Land. Parallels to this kind of constitutional architecture may, with very few exceptions, be found only in the internal constitutional order of federal states.

J.H.H. Weiler, *The Transformation of Europe*, 100 Yale L.J. 2403, 2413-2415 (1991).

It is thus clear that, as a matter of Community law, European law trumps inconsistent domestic law. But, assuming that the European Union is a monist legal community, what should happen if a European law norm conflicts with an international law obligation arising out of a different treaty regime? The ECJ addressed the relationship between European Union law and international law in the *Kadi* case, discussed in Chapter 14.

II. MAKING INTERNATIONAL LAW: A JILTED LOVER, CHEMICAL WEAPONS, AND THE LIMITS OF THE TREATY POWER

The United States uses at least three different methods to enter into international agreements. Article II of the United States Constitution provides that the President "shall have power, by and with the advice and consent of the Senate to make treaties, provided that two thirds of the Senate present concur. . . ." These agreements are often called "Article II treaties." While the U.S. Constitution does not explicitly grant Presidents the power to conclude international agreements other than by an Article II treaty, since the early days of the republic the United States has also entered into congressional-executive agreements. The Executive Branch enters into these agreements with either the prior authorization or the subsequent approval of a simple majority of both Houses of Congress. Finally, Presidents from George Washington onward have entered into sole executive agreements, or agreements without congressional participation, on the basis of inherent constitutional authority. Since World War II, the use of such congressional-executive and sole executive agreements has greatly expanded. At various times in the nation's history, controversy has raged over the nature and scope of the government's power to enter into international agreements.

The goals for this Problem include:

- to understand the limits of the federal government's power to enter into international agreements on matters that the Constitution otherwise entrusts to the states;
- to understand whether the federal government is constitutionally obligated to use a particular method for entering into international agreements in different circumstances; and
- to understand the limits on the President's power to enter into international agreements.

A. *The Problem*

Carol Anne Bond was thrilled to learn in 2006 that Myrlinda Haynes, her closest friend, was pregnant. But when Bond learned that her husband was the child's father, her feelings of elation quickly turned to rage. Bond, a trained microbiologist, vowed to make Haynes's life "a living hell." Bond stole a quantity of an arsenic-based compound from her employer, a chemical manufacturer, and ordered a vial of potassium dichromate over the Internet. Both chemicals can cause toxic harm through minimal contact and, in large enough doses, are potentially fatal. Between November 2006 and June 2007, Bond went to Haynes's home on at least 24 separate occasions and spread the chemicals on her car door, mailbox, and door knob. However, because these chemicals are generally easy to see, Haynes was usually able to avoid them. Haynes repeatedly called the local police to report the suspicious substances; they suggested that she clean her car and door handles on a regular basis but took no further action. Haynes then complained to local postal officials about the chemicals on her mailbox, and U.S. postal inspectors placed surveillance cameras at her home. The cameras caught Bond opening Haynes's mailbox and placing chemicals inside the muffler of her car.

Federal prosecutors charged Bond with two counts of possessing and using a chemical weapon, in violation of 18 U.S.C. §229, which forbids knowing possession or use of any chemical that can "cause death, temporary incapacitation or permanent harm to humans or animals" where not intended for "a peaceful purpose." Section 229 is part of the Chemical Weapons Implementation Act, a federal statute enacted in 1998 to implement the Chemical Weapons Convention (CWC), a multilateral treaty the United States had signed a year earlier. The CWC's purpose, according to its preamble, is to achieve "the complete and effective prohibition of the development, . . . stockpiling, . . . transfer and use of chemical weapons." The treaty, now ratified by 190 states, prohibits the retention or use of chemical weapons and requires parties to destroy all existing stockpiles of chemical weapons, subject to international verification. It also provides that "[e]ach State Party shall, in accordance with its constitutional processes, adopt the necessary measures to implement its obligations under this Convention." The CWC also states that each party shall "[p]rohibit natural and legal persons . . . under its jurisdiction . . . from undertaking any activity prohibited to a State Party under this Convention, including enacting penal legislation with respect to such activity."

Bond moved to dismiss the §229 charges on the grounds that the statute exceeded Congress's constitutional authority and thus impermissibly interfered with the powers reserved to the states under the Tenth Amendment. The motion was denied. She then entered a conditional plea of guilty, reserving the right to appeal the validity of the statute, and was sentenced to six years in prison. On appeal, the Third Circuit held that Bond lacked standing to raise the Tenth Amendment claim. The Supreme Court unanimously found that Bond had standing to challenge the statute on Tenth Amendment grounds, and reversed. On remand, the Third Circuit rejected Bond's substantive challenge to her conviction, and the Supreme Court granted certiorari to consider whether applying the statute implementing the CWC to Bond's actions would exceeded Congress's constitutional powers.

B. Treaties and Federalism: Are There Limits to the U.S. Government's Power to Make and Implement International Agreements?

Article VI of the U.S. Constitution declares that, along with the Constitution and federal law, "all Treaties made, or which shall be made, under the Authority of the United States, shall be the supreme Law of the Land," and that they prevail over inconsistent state laws. However, neither the Supremacy Clause nor any other constitutional provisions define or limit the scope of the treaty power. As a result, since the founding there has been debate among politicians and scholars over the appropriate limits to this power. The following two cases address these issues.

Missouri v. Holland

252 U.S. 416 (1920)

MR. JUSTICE HOLMES delivered the opinion of the court.

This is a bill in equity brought by the State of Missouri to prevent a game warden of the United States from attempting to enforce the Migratory Bird Treaty Act of July 3, 1918, and the regulations made by the Secretary of Agriculture in pursuance of the same. The ground of the bill is that the statute is an unconstitutional interference with the rights reserved to the States by the Tenth Amendment, and that the acts of the defendant done and threatened under that authority invade the sovereign right of the State and contravene its will manifested in statutes. . . .

On December 8, 1916, a treaty between the United States and Great Britain was proclaimed by the President. It recited that many species of birds in their annual migrations traversed certain parts of the United States and of Canada . . . but were in danger of extermination through lack of adequate protection. It therefore provided for specified closed seasons and protection in other forms, and agreed that the two powers would take or propose to their law-making bodies the necessary measures for carrying the treaty out. The . . . Act of July 3, 1918 . . . prohibited . . . killing, capturing or selling any of the migratory birds included in the terms of the treaty. . . . [T]he question raised is the general one whether the treaty and statute are void as an interference with the rights reserved to the States.

To answer this question it is not enough to refer to the Tenth Amendment, reserving the powers not delegated to the United States, because by Article II, Section 2, the power to make treaties is delegated expressly, and by Article VI treaties made under the authority of the United States, along with the Constitution and laws of the United States made in pursuance thereof, are declared the supreme law of the land. If the treaty is valid there can be no dispute about the validity of the statute under Article I, Section 8, as a necessary and proper means to execute the powers of the Government. The language of the Constitution as to the supremacy of treaties being general, the question before us is narrowed to an inquiry into the ground upon which the present supposed exception is placed.

It is said that a treaty cannot be valid if it infringes the Constitution, that there are limits, therefore, to the treaty-making power, and that one such limit is that what an act of Congress could not do unaided, in derogation of the powers reserved to the States, a treaty cannot do. An earlier act of Congress that attempted . . . to regulate the killing of migratory birds within the States had been held bad in the District Court. *United States v. Shauver*, 214 Fed. Rep. 154. *United States v. McCullagh*, 221 Fed. Rep. 288. Those decisions were supported by arguments that migratory birds were owned by the States in their sovereign capacity for the benefit of their people, and that . . . this control was one that Congress had no power to displace. The same argument is supposed to apply now with equal force.

Whether the two cases cited were decided rightly or not they cannot be accepted as a test of the treaty power. Acts of Congress are the supreme law of the land only when made in pursuance of the Constitution, while treaties are declared to be so when made under the authority of the United States. It is open to question whether the authority of the United States means more than the formal acts prescribed to make the convention. We do not mean to imply that there are no qualifications to the treaty-making power; but they must be ascertained in a different way. It is obvious that there may be matters of the sharpest exigency for the national well being that an act of Congress could not deal with but that a treaty followed by such an act could, and it is not lightly to be assumed that, in matters requiring national action, "a power which must belong to and somewhere reside in every civilized government" is not to be found. . . . [W]e may add that when we are dealing with words that also are a constituent act, like the Constitution of the United States, we must realize that they have called into life a being the development of which could not have been foreseen completely by the most gifted of its begetters. It was enough for them to realize or to hope that they had created an organism; it has taken a century and has cost their successors much sweat and blood to prove that they created a nation. The case before us must be considered in the light of our whole experience and not merely in that of what was said a hundred years ago. The treaty in question does not contravene any prohibitory words to be found in the Constitution. The only question is whether it is forbidden by some invisible radiation from the general terms of the Tenth Amendment. We must consider what this country has become in deciding what that Amendment has reserved.

The State as we have intimated founds its claim of exclusive authority upon an assertion of title to migratory birds, an assertion that is embodied in statute. No doubt it is true that as between a State and its inhabitants the State may regulate the killing and sale of such birds, but it does not follow that its authority is exclusive of paramount powers. To put the claim of the State upon title is to lean upon a slender reed. . . . The whole foundation of the State's rights is the presence within their jurisdiction of birds that yesterday had not arrived, tomorrow may be in another State and in a week a thousand miles away. If we are to be accurate we cannot put the case of the State upon higher ground than that the treaty deals with creatures that for the moment are within the state borders, that it must be carried out by officers of the United States within the same territory, and that but for the treaty the State would be free to regulate this subject itself. . . .

Here a national interest of very nearly the first magnitude is involved. It can be protected only by national action in concert with that of another power. The subject-matter is only transitorily within the State and has no permanent habitat therein. But for the treaty and the statute there soon might be no birds for any powers to deal with. We see nothing in the Constitution that compels the Government to sit by while a food supply is cut off and the protectors of our forests and our crops are destroyed. . . . We are of the opinion that the treaty and statute must be upheld.

Notes and Questions

1. Does *Missouri* mean that Congress can, if acting to implement a treaty, pass a statute otherwise in excess of its constitutional authority?

2. Justice Holmes states that the limits to the treaty-making power "must be ascertained in a different way." Does he identify that "different way"? Does this opinion impose any limits on the treaty-making power?

———————————

Missouri has proved to be one of the most important, and controversial, decisions in the foreign affairs area. In the 1950s in particular there were efforts to amend the Constitution, in effect to overrule *Missouri*. These efforts, collectively known as the Bricker Amendment after Senator John Bricker of Ohio, grew out of conservative senators' concerns over the UN Charter and early human rights treaties, such as the Genocide Convention. Some Bricker Amendment supporters feared that the Charter's human rights provisions would give Congress power to enact civil rights legislation otherwise beyond its constitutional powers. In addition, many amendment supporters, including conservative Southern Democrats, believed that the Genocide Convention and other human rights treaties could be interpreted in a way that could override racially discriminatory state laws. Other amendment supporters argued that the Charter and human rights treaties would intrude upon domestic jurisdiction and diminish U.S. sovereignty, expand the power of the federal government at the expense of states' rights, and enhance the prospects of world government.

The most widely debated version of the Bricker Amendment was that reported out by the Senate Judiciary Committee in 1953. It provided:

1. A provision of a treaty which conflicts with this Constitution shall not be of any force or effect.

2. A treaty shall become effective as internal law in the United States only through legislation which would be valid in the absence of a treaty.

3. Congress shall have power to regulate all executive and other agreements with any foreign power or international organization. All such agreements shall be subject to the limitations imposed on treaties by this article.

The Eisenhower Administration strongly opposed the Bricker Amendment on the grounds that it would encroach on the President's foreign affairs powers. To help defeat the amendment, the administration stated that it would not seek to become a party to any additional human rights treaties. The Secretary of State testified, in 1953, that

> [t]he present administration intends to encourage the promotion everywhere of human rights and individual freedoms, but to favor methods of persuasion, education and example rather than formal undertakings. . . . Therefore, while we shall not withhold our counsel from those who seek to draft a treaty or covenant on human rights, we do not ourselves look upon a treaty as the means which we would now select as the proper and most effective way to spread throughout the world the goals of human liberty to which this Nation has been dedicated since its inception. We therefore do not intend to become a party to any such covenant or present it as a treaty for consideration by the Senate.

Treaties and Executive Agreements: Hearings Before a Subcomm. of the Senate Judiciary Comm. on S.J. Res. 1, and S.J. Res. 43, 83d Cong. 824 (1953).

For many years thereafter, Presidents did not submit major human rights treaties to the Senate (although they did continue to seek the Senate's advice and consent to the Genocide Convention submitted by President Truman to the Senate in 1949). This changed under President Carter, who submitted several major human rights treaties to the Senate in 1978. However, each was accompanied by a package of reservations, understandings, and declarations (RUDs) that, in effect, provided that adherence to these treaties would not effect changes in U.S. law or practice. We examine the use of RUDs to human rights treaties in more detail in Chapter 7.

The Supreme Court's next major discussion of the treaty power helped to defuse some of the political pressure in support of the Bricker Amendment.

Reid v. Covert

354 U.S. 1 (1957)

Mr. Justice Black announced the judgment of the Court and delivered an opinion, in which The Chief Justice, Mr. Justice Douglas, and Mr. Justice Brennan join.

These cases raise basic constitutional issues of the utmost concern. . . . Mrs. Clarice Covert killed her husband, a sergeant in the United States Air Force, at an airbase in England. . . . She was tried by a court-martial for murder under Article 118 of the Uniform Code of Military Justice (UCMJ). . . . The court-martial asserted jurisdiction over Mrs. Covert under Article 2(11) of the UCMJ, which provides:

> The following persons are subject to this code:
> (11) Subject to the provisions of any treaty or agreement to which the United States is or may be a party or to any accepted rule of international law, all persons serving with, employed by, or accompanying the armed forces without the continental limits of the United States. . . .

[Mrs. Covert was found guilty and sentenced to life imprisonment. She sought a writ of habeas corpus to set her free on the ground that the Constitution forbade her trial by military authorities.]

I

At the beginning we reject the idea that when the United States acts against citizens abroad it can do so free of the Bill of Rights. The United States is entirely a creature of the Constitution. Its power and authority have no other source. It can only act in accordance

and that upholding federal power in this case would "provide a roadmap for circumventing nearly every limitation on federal power [the Supreme] Court has ever recognized."

On June 2, 2014, the Supreme Court unanimously overturned Bond's conviction. Justice Roberts, writing for a majority including Justices Kennedy, Ginsburg, Breyer, Sotomayor, and Kagan, found that the Act did not reach her conduct. Given this conclusion, Justice Roberts found it unnecessary to reach the constitutional questions presented. Justices Scalia, Thomas, and Alito found that if the statute does reach her conduct, it exceeds Congress's constitutional authority.

Bond v. United States
134 S. Ct. 2077 (2014)

Chief Justice Roberts delivered the opinion of the Court.

II

In our federal system, the National Government possesses only limited powers; the states and the people retain the remainder. The States have broad authority to enact legislation for the public good—what we have often called a "police power." The Federal Government, by contrast, has no such authority and "can exercise only the powers granted to it," *McCulloch v. Maryland*, 4 Wheat. 316, 405 (1819), including the power to make "all Laws which shall be necessary and proper for carrying into Execution" the enumerated powers, U.S. Const., Art. I, §8, cl. 18. For nearly two centuries it has been "clear" that . . . [a] criminal act committed wholly within a State "cannot be made an offence against the United States, unless it have some relation to the execution of a power of Congress, or to some matter within the jurisdiction of the United States." *United States v. Fox*, 95 U.S. 670, 672 (1878). . . . [I]n this Court the parties have devoted significant effort to arguing whether section 229, as applied to Bond's offense, is a necessary and proper means of executing the National Government's power to make treaties. . . .

III

A

Part of a fair reading of statutory text is recognizing that "Congress legislates against the backdrop" of certain unexpressed presumptions. *EEOC v. Arabian American Oil Co.*, 499 U.S. 244, 248 (1991). . . . For example, we presume that a criminal statute derived from the common law carries with it the requirement of a culpable mental state—even if no such limitation appears in the text—unless it is clear that the Legislature intended to impose strict liability. . . . The notion that some things "go without saying" applies to legislation just as it does to everyday life.

Among the background principles of construction that our cases have recognized are those grounded in the relationship between the Federal Government and the States under our Constitution. . . .

Closely related to these [principles] is the well-established principle that " 'it is incumbent upon the federal courts to be certain of Congress' intent before finding that federal law overrides' " the "usual constitutional balance of federal and state powers." *Gregory v. Ashcroft*, 501 U.S. 452, 460 (1991). . . . [A]s explained by Justice Marshall, when legislation "affect[s] the federal balance, the requirement of clear statement assures that the legislature has in fact faced, and intended to bring into issue, the critical matters involved in the judicial decision." . . .

[Our] precedents make clear that it is appropriate to refer to basic principles of federalism embodied in the Constitution to resolve ambiguity in a federal statute. In this case, the ambiguity derives from the improbably broad reach of the key statutory definition given the term—"chemical weapon"—being defined; the deeply serious consequences of adopting such a boundless reading; and the lack of any apparent need to do so in light of the context from which the statute arose—a treaty about chemical warfare and terrorism. We conclude that, in this curious case, we can insist on a clear indication that Congress meant to reach purely local crimes, before interpreting the statute's expansive language in a way that intrudes on the police power of the States.

B

We do not find any such clear indication in section 229. "Chemical weapon" is the key term that defines the statute's reach, and it is defined extremely broadly. But that general definition does not constitute a clear statement that Congress meant the statute to reach local criminal conduct.

In fact, a fair reading of section 229 suggests that it does not have as expansive a scope as might at first appear. To begin, as a matter of natural meaning, an educated user of English would not describe Bond's crime as involving a "chemical weapon." Saying that a person "used a chemical weapon" conveys a very different idea than saying the person "used a chemical in a way that caused some harm." . . . More to the point, the use of something as a "weapon" typically connotes "[a]n instrument of offensive or defensive combat," Webster's Third New International Dictionary 2589 (2002). . . . But no speaker in natural parlance would describe Bond's feud-driven act of spreading irritating chemicals on Haynes's door knob and mailbox as "combat." . . .

The Government would have us brush aside the ordinary meaning and adopt a reading of section 229 that would sweep in everything from the detergent under the kitchen sink to the stain remover in the laundry room. . . . Any parent would be guilty of a serious federal offense—possession of a chemical weapon—when, exasperated by the children's repeated failure to clean the goldfish tank, he considers poisoning the fish with a few drops of vinegar. We are reluctant to ignore the ordinary meaning of "chemical weapon" when doing so would transform a statute passed to implement the international Convention on Chemical Weapons into one that also makes it a federal offense to poison goldfish. . . .

The Government's reading of section 229 would "'alter sensitive federal-state relationships,'" convert an astonishing amount of "traditionally local criminal conduct" into "a matter for federal enforcement," and "involve a substantial extension of federal police resources." It would transform the statute from one whose core concerns are acts of war, assassination, and terrorism into a massive federal anti-poisoning regime that reaches the simplest of assaults. . . .

In sum, the global need to prevent chemical warfare does not require the Federal Government to reach into the kitchen cupboard, or to treat a local assault with a chemical irritant as the deployment of a chemical weapon. There is no reason to suppose that Congress—in implementing the Convention on Chemical Weapons—thought otherwise.

Justice Scalia, joined by Justices Thomas and Alito, concurred in the result, but sharply disagreed with the majority's reading of the statute. These Justices concluded that Bond plainly violated a statue prohibiting the use of "chemical weapons," including "any chemical which . . . can cause death, temporary incapacitation, or permanent harm to humans." Justice Scalia, joined by Justice Thomas, continued:

Since the Act is clear, the *real* question this case presents is whether the Act is constitutional as applied to petitioner. An unreasoned and citation-less sentence from our opinion in *Missouri v. Holland*, purported to furnish the answer: "If the treaty is valid"—and no one argues that the Convention is not—"there can be no dispute about the validity of the statute under Article I, §8 , as a necessary and proper means to execute the powers of the Government." Petitioner and her *amici* press us to consider whether there is anything to this *ipse dixit*. The Constitution's text and structure show that there is not.

[As a textual matter, Justice Scalia noted that the Treaty Clause provides that the President "shall have Power, by and with the Advice and Consent of the Senate, to make Treaties." The Necessary and Proper Clause grants Congress the power "[t]o make all Laws which shall be necessary and proper for carrying into Execution" all powers vested by the Constitution in the federal government. "Read together, the two Clauses empower Congress to pass laws 'necessary and proper for carrying into Execution . . . [the] Power . . . to make Treaties.'" Justice Scalia continued: "It is obvious what the Clauses, read together, do *not* say. They do not authorize Congress to enact laws for carrying into execution 'Treaties.'" In other words, "[a] power to help the President *make* treaties is not a power to *implement* treaties already made." Justice Scalia then addressed the holding in *Missouri v. Holland*.]

"[T]he Constitutio[n] confer[s] upon Congress . . . not all governmental powers, but only discrete, enumerated ones." *Printz v. United States*, 521 U.S. 898, 919 (1997). And, of course, "enumeration presupposes something not enumerated." *Gibbons v. Ogden*, 9 Wheat. 1, 195 (1824).

But in *Holland*, the proponents of unlimited congressional power found a loophole: "By negotiating a treaty and obtaining the requisite consent of the Senate, the President . . . may endow Congress with a source of legislative authority independent of the powers enumerated in Article I." L. Tribe, American Constitutional Law §4-4, pp. 645-646 (3d ed. 2000). . . .

If that is true, then the possibilities of what the Federal Government may accomplish, with the right treaty in hand, are endless and hardly farfetched. It could begin, as some scholars have suggested, with abrogation of this Court's constitutional rulings. For example, the holding that a statute prohibiting the carrying of firearms near schools went beyond Congress's enumerated powers, *United States v. Lopez*, 514 U.S. 549, 551 (1995), could be reversed by negotiating a treaty with Latvia providing that neither sovereign would permit the carrying of guns near schools. . . .

But reversing some of this Court's decisions is the least of the problem. Imagine the United States' entry into an Antipolygamy Convention, which called for—and Congress enacted—legislation providing that, when a spouse of a man with more than one wife dies intestate, the surviving husband may inherit no part of the estate. Constitutional? The Federalist answers with a rhetorical question: "Suppose by some forced constructions of its authority (which indeed cannot easily be imagined) the Federal Legislature should attempt to vary the law of descent in any State; would it not be evident that . . . it had exceeded its jurisdiction and infringed upon that of the State?" The Federalist No. 33, at 206 (A. Hamilton). Yet given the Antipolygamy Convention, *Holland* would uphold it. Or imagine that, to execute a treaty, Congress enacted a statute prohibiting state inheritance taxes on real property. Constitutional? Of course not. Again, The Federalist: "Suppose . . . [Congress] should undertake to abrogate a land tax imposed by the authority of a State, would it not be equally evident that this was an invasion of that concurrent jurisdiction in respect to this species of tax which its constitution plainly supposes to exist in the State governments?" No. 33, at 206. *Holland* would uphold it. As these examples show, *Holland* places Congress only one treaty away from acquiring a general police power. . . .

We have here a supposedly "narrow" opinion which, in order to be "narrow," sets forth interpretive principles never before imagined that will bedevil our jurisprudence (and proliferate litigation) for years to come. . . . All this to leave in place an ill-considered *ipse dixit* that enables the fundamental constitutional principle of limited federal powers to be set aside by the President and Senate's exercise of the treaty power. We should not have shirked our duty and distorted the law to preserve that assertion; we should have welcomed and eagerly grasped the opportunity—nay, the obligation—to consider and repudiate it.

Notes and Questions

1. Are you persuaded by Justice Roberts's reading of the statutory language at issue? What factors persuaded the majority that the statutory language at issue was ambiguous?

2. Are you persuaded by Justice Scalia's claim that the Necessary and Proper Clause authorizes legislation related to the *making* of treaties but does not authorize legislation for their *implementation*?

3. In a separate opinion, Justice Thomas, joined by Justices Scalia and Alito, argues that "treaties by their nature relate to intercourse with other nations (including their people and property) rather than to purely domestic affairs," although he concedes that "the distinction between matters of international intercourse and matters of purely domestic regulation may not be obvious in all cases." As an institutional matter, should determining whether a particular issue is "a proper subject[] of negotiation" be vested with the courts, or the political branches? As a substantive matter, would Justice Thomas's proposed distinction invalidate human rights treaties, many of which govern the relationship of a state to its own citizens?

4. The *Bond* majority carefully avoids reaching constitutional questions. Reading between the lines, is *Missouri v. Holland* more secure, or less secure, following the *Bond* decision?

D. *Are There Limits to the Use of Congressional-Executive Agreements?*

In addition to any limits imposed by principles of federalism, the power of the United States to enter into international agreements may also be shaped by other constitutional principles, prominently including separation of powers. The next two sections of this Problem explore constitutional challenges to the ability of the United States to make and implement international law through congressional-executive and sole executive agreements. These issues are of particular relevance as the United States frequently uses these processes to make and implement its international obligations, as the chart below indicates.

Years	Article II Treaties	Sole Executive and Congressional-Executive Agreements
1789-1839	60	27
1839-1889	215	238
1889-1939	524	917
1940-1949	116	919
1950-1959	138	2,229
1960-1969	114	2,324
1970-1979	173	3,039
1980-1989	166	3,524
1990-1999	249	2,857
Totals	1,755	16,074

Figures derived from Committee on Foreign Relations, Treaties and Other International Agreements: The Role of the United States Senate, S. Rpt. 106-71, 106th Congress, 2d Sess. (2001).

The decline in the use of Article II treaties relative to the use of other processes continues in the early twenty first century. However, this trend is not uniform across all issue areas. For example, every arms control agreement since 1972 has been approved as a treaty, and human rights conventions have only been submitted as treaties. However, the political branches increasingly use congressional-executive agreements for many of the nation's most important international agreements, particularly in the economic area. For example, both the North American Free Trade Agreement (NAFTA) and the Uruguay Round Agreements creating the World Trade Organization were approved via congressional-executive agreements. It is therefore important to examine whether there are constitutional limitations on their use.

For much of the twentieth century, conventional wisdom held that congressional-executive agreements were legally equivalent to Article II treaties and that one was interchangeable with the other. This so-called "interchangeability thesis" is reflected in a comment to the Restatement (Third) of the Foreign Relations Law of the United States §303(e):

> Since any agreement concluded by Congressional-Executive Agreement could also be concluded by treaty . . . [t]he prevailing view is that the Congressional-Executive agreement can be used as an alternative to the treaty method in every instance. Which procedure should be used is a political judgment, made in the first instance by the President, subject to the possibility that the Senate might refuse to consider a joint resolution of Congress to approve an agreement, insisting that the President submit the agreement as a treaty.

For many decades, the interchangeability thesis was largely unquestioned in Congress. However, during the NAFTA debate in the 1990s, NAFTA opponents argued that this agreement could not properly be treated as a congressional-executive agreement and had to be submitted to the Senate as an Article II treaty. The ensuing debate raised the more general question of whether congressional-executive agreements were interchangeable with Article II treaties.

Harvard Law School Professor Laurence Tribe summarized the arguments against the interchangeability thesis in Senate testimony:

> In the leading Supreme Court case on treaties, *Missouri v. Holland*, the Court made clear—as everyone understands—that the treaty power and Congress's legislative power are not coextensive. The Constitution permits treaties to accomplish things that cannot be achieved through mere legislation. It necessarily follows that the treaty form and the congressional-executive agreement are not wholly interchangeable. . . .
>
> Those who would read the Treaty Clause out of the Constitution by appealing to past congressional practice (no matter how questionable that practice) essentially suggest that a period of disregard for constitutional text and structure may suffice in large part to erase the disregarded constitutional text or structure from the Constitution. If this becomes the accepted wisdom, then the Constitution will have failed in its central mission—to establish a framework for government that would outlast those who hold office at any given time. . . .
>
> State sovereignty concerns find special protection in the Treaty Clause because the Senate is the only body that represents the states as states, and the only body in which every state, from the smallest to the largest, is guaranteed equal representation. It is the only national body in which all members are politically accountable to all the voters in their respective states. . . . [T]he Treaty Clause's provision for supermajority approval is an independent guarantee that particularly important international agreements—those that very significantly constrain U.S. sovereignty by seriously implicating normal state and federal lawmaking process—will be subject to especially serious deliberation and will be based upon especially strong national consensus.

GATT Implementing Legislation: Hearings Before the Senate Comm. on Commerce, Science, and Transportation on S. 2467, 103d Cong. 285 (1994).

The Clinton Administration responded to these arguments in a memorandum prepared by the Justice Department:

As Secretary of State Dulles explained in testimony before the Senate Judiciary Committee in 1953, there is an

undefined, and probably undefinable, borderline between international agreements which require two-thirds Senate [c]oncurrence, but no House concurrence, as in the case of treaties, and agreements which should have the majority concurrence of both Chambers of Congress. . . . This is an area to be dealt with by friendly cooperation between the three departments of Government which are involved, rather than by attempts at constitutional definition, which are futile, or by the absorption, by one branch of Government, of responsibilities which are presently and properly shared.

. . . [T]he Constitution on its face permits foreign commerce to be regulated either through the Treaty Clause or through the Foreign Commerce Clause [which grants Congress power "to regulate Commerce with foreign Nations"]. Nothing in the language of the Constitution privileges the Treaty Clause as the "sole" or "exclusive" means of regulating such activity. In actual practice, Congress and the President, understanding that nothing in the Constitution constrained them to choose one procedure rather than the other, have followed different procedures on different occasions. . . .

In general, these inter- and intra-branch disputes over the scope of the Treaty Clause have been resolved through the political process, occasionally with marked departures from prior practices. . . .

The existence of such recurring disputes over the scope and meaning of the Treaty Clause undermines any dogmatic claim that a major trade agreement such as the Uruguay Round Agreements, which stands at the intersection of the foreign affairs, revenue raising and commerce powers, *must* be ratified as a treaty and *cannot* be implemented by the action of both Houses of Congress. The distinctions between the Federal government's treaty power and the other constitutional powers in play are simply too fluid and dynamic to dictate the conclusion that one method must be followed to the complete exclusion of the other. Here, if anywhere, is an area where the sound judgment of the political branches, acting in concert and accommodating the interests and prerogatives of one another, should be respected. . . .

18 Opinions of the Office of Legal Counsel 232, 237, 239, 240 (1994).

After NAFTA was implemented as a congressional-executive agreement, a coalition of labor organizations and an NGO that promotes the purchase of American-made products filed a constitutional challenge. The appellate court decision in this action is one of the few to address when international agreements must be ratified as Article II treaties.

Made in the USA Foundation v. United States

242 F.3d 1300 (11th Cir. 2001)

The Constitution confers a vast amount of power upon the political branches of the federal government in the area of foreign policy—particularly foreign commerce. The breadth of the President's inherent powers in foreign affairs arises from his role as Chief Executive, U.S. Const. Art. II, §1, cl. 1, and as Commander in Chief, U.S. Const. Art. III, §2, cl. 1. In addition to his power to "make Treaties" with the advice and consent of two-thirds of the Senators present, the President's authority in foreign affairs is further bolstered by his power to "appoint Ambassadors . . . and Consuls," U.S. Const. Art. II, §2,

One action then pending in a United States court involved Dames & Moore, a U.S. company that had sued the government of Iran in federal district court and, shortly after the Algiers Accords were signed, had obtained summary judgment. Dames & Moore then filed an action for declaratory and injunctive relief against the United States and the Secretary of the Treasury to prevent enforcement of the executive orders implementing the Algiers Accords. The case quickly made its way to the Supreme Court, which, eight days after oral argument, issued a unanimous opinion addressing the President's ability to suspend pending litigations against Iran.

Dames & Moore v. Regan

453 U.S. 654 (1981)

JUSTICE REHNQUIST delivered the opinion of the Court.

The questions presented by this case touch fundamentally upon the manner in which our Republic is to be governed. . . .

The parties and the lower courts . . . have all agreed that much relevant analysis is contained in *Youngstown Sheet & Tube Co. v. Sawyer*, 343 U.S. 579 (1952). . . . Justice Jackson's concurring opinion elaborated in a general way the consequences of different types of interaction between the two democratic branches in assessing Presidential authority to act in any given case. When the President acts pursuant to an express or implied authorization from Congress, he exercises not only his powers but also those delegated by Congress. In such a case the executive action "would be supported by the strongest of presumptions and the widest latitude of judicial interpretation, and the burden of persuasion would rest heavily upon any who might attack it." When the President acts in the absence of congressional authorization he may enter "a zone of twilight in which he and Congress may have concurrent authority, or in which its distribution is uncertain." In such a case the analysis becomes more complicated, and the validity of the President's action, at least so far as separation-of-powers principles are concerned, hinges on a consideration of all the circumstances which might shed light on the views of the Legislative Branch toward such action, including "congressional inertia, indifference or quiescence." Finally, when the President acts in contravention of the will of Congress, "his power is at its lowest ebb," and the Court can sustain his actions "only by disabling the Congress from acting upon the subject."

Although we have in the past found and do today find Justice Jackson's classification of executive actions into three general categories analytically useful, we should be mindful of Justice Holmes' admonition . . . that "[t]he great ordinances of the Constitution do not establish and divide fields of black and white." . . . [I]t is doubtless the case that executive action in any particular instance falls, not neatly in one of three pigeonholes, but rather at some point along a spectrum running from explicit congressional authorization to explicit congressional prohibition. . . .

IV

[T]here remains the question of the President's authority to suspend claims pending in American courts. . . . In terminating these claims through Executive Order, the President purported to act under authority of both the [International Emergency Economic Powers Act (IEEPA)] and . . . the so-called "Hostage Act."

We conclude that . . . the IEEPA . . . cannot be read to authorize the suspension of the claims. [IEEPA grants the President authority over "property" in which foreign states have an interest.] The claims of American citizens against Iran are not in themselves transactions involving Iranian property . . . . An *in personam* lawsuit, although it might eventually be reduced to judgment and that judgment might be executed upon, is an effort to establish liability and fix damages and does not focus on any particular property within the jurisdiction. The terms of the IEEPA therefore do not authorize the President to suspend claims in American courts. . . .

[The Court also analyzes the Hostage Act, which provides that when "any citizen of the United States has been unjustly deprived of his liberty by or under the authority of any foreign government, . . . the President shall use such means . . . as he may think necessary and proper to obtain or effectuate [their] release." Relying upon legislative history, the Court concludes that this Act also does not authorize the President to suspend the claims.]

Concluding that neither the IEEPA nor the Hostage Act constitutes specific authorization of the President's action suspending claims, however, is not to say that these statutory provisions are entirely irrelevant to the question of the validity of the President's action. We think both statutes highly relevant in the looser sense of indicating congressional acceptance of a broad scope for executive action in circumstances such as those presented in this case. . . . [T]he IEEPA delegates broad authority to the President to act in times of national emergency with respect to property of a foreign country. The Hostage Act similarly indicates congressional willingness that the President have broad discretion when responding to the hostile acts of foreign sovereigns. . . .

Although we have declined to conclude that the IEEPA or the Hostage Act directly authorizes the President's suspension of claims for the reasons noted, we cannot ignore the general tenor of Congress' legislation in this area in trying to determine whether the President is acting alone or at least with the acceptance of Congress. As we have noted, Congress cannot anticipate and legislate with regard to every possible action the President may find it necessary to take or every possible situation in which he might act. Such failure of Congress specifically to delegate authority does not, "especially . . . in the areas of foreign policy and national security," imply "congressional disapproval" of action taken by the Executive. On the contrary, the enactment of legislation closely related to the question of the President's authority in a particular case which evinces legislative intent to accord the President broad discretion may be considered to "invite" "measures on independent presidential responsibility," *Youngstown*, 343 U.S., at 637 (Jackson, J., concurring). At least this is so where there is no contrary indication of legislative intent and when, as here, there is a history of congressional acquiescence in conduct of the sort engaged in by the President. It is to that history which we now turn.

Not infrequently in affairs between nations, outstanding claims by nationals of one country against the government of another country are "sources of friction" between the two sovereigns. To resolve these difficulties, nations have often entered into agreements settling the claims of their respective nationals. . . . Consistent with that principle, the United States has repeatedly exercised its sovereign authority to settle the claims of its nationals against foreign countries. Though those settlements have sometimes been made by treaty, there has also been a longstanding practice of settling such claims by executive agreement without the advice and consent of the Senate. Under such agreements, the President has agreed to renounce or extinguish claims of United States nationals against foreign governments in return for lump-sum payments or the establishment of arbitration procedures. . . . It is clear that the practice of settling claims continues today. Since 1952, the President has entered into at least 10 binding settlements with foreign nations, including an $80 million settlement with the People's Republic of China.

Crucial to our decision today is the conclusion that Congress has implicitly approved the practice of claim settlement by executive agreement. This is best demonstrated by Congress' enactment of the International Claims Settlement Act of 1949. The Act had two purposes: (1) to allocate to United States nationals funds received in the course of an executive claims settlement with Yugoslavia, and (2) to provide a procedure whereby funds resulting from future settlements could be distributed. To achieve these ends Congress created [a commission] and gave it jurisdiction to make final and binding decisions with respect to claims by United States nationals against settlement funds. By creating a procedure to implement future settlement agreements, Congress placed its stamp of approval on such agreements. . . .

Over the years Congress has frequently amended the International Claims Settlement Act to [implement settlement agreements with other states] thus demonstrating Congress' continuing acceptance of the President's claim settlement authority. . . .

In light of all of the foregoing—the inferences to be drawn from the character of the legislation Congress has enacted in the area, such as the IEEPA and the Hostage Act, and from the history of acquiescence in executive claims settlement—we conclude that the President was authorized to suspend pending claims pursuant to Executive Order No. 12294. As Justice Frankfurter pointed out in *Youngstown*, "a systematic, unbroken, executive practice, long pursued to the knowledge of the Congress and never before questioned . . . may be treated as a gloss on 'Executive Power' vested in the President by §1 of Art. II." Past practice does not, by itself, create power, but "long-continued practice, known to and acquiesced in by Congress, would raise a presumption that the [action] had been [taken] in pursuance of its consent. . . ." *United States v. Midwest Oil Co.*, 236 U.S. 459, 474 (1915). Such practice is present here and such a presumption is also appropriate. In light of the fact that Congress may be considered to have consented to the President's action in suspending claims, we cannot say that action exceeded the President's powers. . . .

Just as importantly, Congress has not disapproved of the action taken here. Though Congress has held hearings on the Iranian Agreement itself, Congress has not enacted legislation, or even passed a resolution, indicating its displeasure with the Agreement. Quite the contrary, the relevant Senate Committee has stated that the establishment of the Tribunal is "of vital importance to the United States." We are thus clearly not confronted with a situation in which Congress has in some way resisted the exercise of Presidential authority.

Finally, we re-emphasize the narrowness of our decision. We do not decide that the President possesses plenary power to settle claims, even as against foreign governmental entities. . . . But where, as here, the settlement of claims has been determined to be a necessary incident to the resolution of a major foreign policy dispute between our country and another, and where, as here, we can conclude that Congress acquiesced in the President's action, we are not prepared to say that the President lacks the power to settle such claims.

Notes and Questions

1. Was the President's action upheld as part of his inherent foreign affairs power, or on the basis of congressional authorization? Could a sole executive agreement override an earlier federal statute?

2. Is the Court correct to read congressional silence as acquiescence? Is the Court in effect granting the President plenary discretion over foreign affairs as long as Congress lacks the votes to override a presidential veto of restrictive legislation?

3. *Dames & Moore* involves questions of whether executive agreements can override earlier federal statutes. More recently, courts have addressed whether a federal statute can override an executive agreement. The plaintiffs in *Roeder v. Islamic Republic of Iran*, 646 F.3d 56 (D.C. Cir. 2011), *cert. denied*, 132 S. Ct. 2680 (2012), included several American citizens taken hostage in Iran in 1979. Plaintiffs sued Iran under a 2008 provision of the Foreign Sovereign Immunities Act that removed sovereign immunity for states listed by the State Department as sponsors of terrorism. Plaintiffs claimed that the new statutory provision trumped the promises the United States made in the Algiers Accords. However, the court determined that neither a treaty nor an executive agreement will be considered abrogated or modified by a subsequent statute unless Congress "clearly expressed" an intention to do so. The court noted that legislators in four consecutive Congresses had "tried—and failed—to enact legislation that would explicitly abrogate the provision of the Algiers Accords barring the hostages' suit." Since the new provisions did not, on their face, say anything about the Algiers Accords or otherwise manifest a clear expression to modify them, the action was dismissed.

The Foreign Sovereign Immunities Act is considered in more detail in Chapter 6.

III. BREAKING INTERNATIONAL LAW: CONSULAR NOTIFICATION AND THE ARREST OF FOREIGN NATIONALS

What should happen if a state's domestic law conflicts with its international legal obligations? Article 27 of the Vienna Convention on the Law of Treaties provides that a state "may not invoke the provisions of its internal law as justification for its failure to perform a treaty." Domestic law may, however, suggest different approaches to conflicting domestic and international legal obligations. While the Supremacy Clause of the U.S. Constitution states that both statutes and treaties are the supreme law of the land, it is silent on how to resolve a conflict between these two sources of law (and on the status of custom as domestic law). In the treaty context, the Supreme Court has long applied the "later in time" rule, meaning that "[a] treaty may supersede a prior act of Congress, and an act of Congress may supersede a prior treaty." *The Cherokee Tobacco*, 78 U.S. (11 Wall.) 616, 621 (1870).

Of course, a subsequent federal statute does not extinguish the nation's international legal obligation. As Secretary of State Charles Evans Hughes wrote, "Congress has the power to violate treaties, but if they are violated, the Nation will be none the less exposed to all the international consequences of such a violation because the action is taken by the legislative branch of the Government." As a result, courts have often sought to minimize the conflict between U.S. law and international law. Over two centuries ago, the Supreme Court stated that, "an Act of Congress ought never to be construed to violate the law of nations if any other possible construction remains." *Murray v. Schooner Charming Betsy*, 6 U.S. (2 Cranch) 64, 118 (1804). In the materials that follow, we examine various ways that U.S. courts respond when confronted with international legal norms and apparently inconsistent domestic law.

The goals for this Problem include:

- to understand different strategies U.S. courts use when considering apparently conflicting domestic and international legal norms;
- to understand the significance of the distinction between self-executing and non-self-executing treaties; and
- to understand the status of international tribunal decisions in U.S. courts.

A. The Problem

On the evening of June 24, 1993, Jose Ernesto Medellín participated in the brutal rape and murder of two teenage girls in Houston, Texas. Shortly thereafter, Medellín, a Mexican citizen, was arrested by Texas police. Mexico, the United States, and 165 other states are parties to the 1963 Vienna Convention on Consular Relations, 596 U.N.T.S. 261, which expressly provides that foreign nationals have the right, upon arrest, to contact their consulate and to have consular officials notified of the arrest. (Consular officials are employed by foreign governments to provide assistance on behalf of that government to that government's citizens in a foreign country.) Medellín was not advised of his Vienna Convention rights at the time of his arrest.

Medellín was convicted of capital murder and sentenced to death. In March 1997, the Texas Court of Criminal Appeals affirmed Medellín's conviction and sentence. Medellín did not raise a claim based on Texas's failure to advise him of his treaty rights at trial or on appeal. In April 1997, some six weeks after the affirmance of his death sentence on direct appeal, Mexican consular officials first learned of Medellín's arrest, detention, trial, conviction, and sentence.

Medellín filed a state habeas corpus petition in March 1998, alleging for the first time the violation of his Vienna Convention rights. The Texas Court of Criminal Appeals rejected Medellín's Vienna Convention claims on the ground that they had not been raised at trial.

In November 2001, Medellín filed a federal habeas corpus petition, again raising a Vienna Convention claim. In June 2003, the district court denied relief; the court held that Medellín had defaulted his Vienna Convention claim under the procedural default rule* used by the Texas state system and, in any event, that the Vienna Convention did not create judicially enforceable rights.

On January 9, 2003, while Medellín's federal habeas petition was pending, Mexico filed suit against the United States in the International Court of Justice (ICJ), alleging violations of the Vienna Convention in the cases of Medellín and 53 other Mexican nationals who had been sentenced to death in state criminal proceedings in the United States. *Avena and Other Mexican Nationals (Mexico v. United States of America)*. ICJ jurisdiction was based upon Article I of the Optional Protocol to the Vienna Convention, which provides that "[d]isputes arising out of the interpretation or application of the [Vienna Convention on Consular Relations] shall lie within the compulsory jurisdiction of the [ICJ]." Both Mexico and the United States were parties to the Optional Protocol at the time Mexico initiated this suit.

Mexico requested, among other relief, the annulment of the convictions and sentences of the 54 Mexicans and a declaration that procedural default rules may not be applied to prevent redress of Vienna Convention violations. Mexico also sought provisional measures, a form of interim relief akin to a preliminary injunction, preventing the execution of Mexican nationals pending the Court's final judgment.

---

*Under procedural default rules applied in state and federal courts, a criminal defendant who could have raised, but fails to raise, a legal issue at trial will generally not be permitted to raise it in future proceedings, including on appeal or in a habeas corpus petition.

B. *Addressing Conflicts Between International and Domestic Legal Obligations*

Mexico's suit was the third in a trilogy of ICJ cases involving U.S. breaches of the Vienna Convention. Domestic court litigations involving U.S. breaches of the Vienna Convention squarely raise questions regarding conflicting domestic and international legal norms, the ability of private parties to invoke treaty norms in domestic courts, and the domestic law status of ICJ orders.

1. The Execution of Angel Breard

The first ICJ action against the United States for noncompliance with the Vienna Convention involved Angel Breard, a Paraguayan citizen who was convicted of capital murder. At the time of his arrest, Virginia authorities failed to advise Breard of his Vienna Convention rights. Breard testified at his trial, against the advice of his court-appointed attorneys. Breard admitted that he committed the murder, but claimed he did so under the influence of a satanic curse placed on him by his ex-wife's father. The jury found Breard guilty of capital murder and attempted rape, and Breard was sentenced to death.

Breard did not raise his Vienna Convention claim at trial, on appeal, or in state habeas corpus proceedings. He raised his treaty claim for the first time in a federal habeas petition filed three years after his conviction. His petition was denied, and Virginia set an execution date of April 14, 1998.

On April 3, 1998, Paraguay filed suit against the United States in the ICJ, requesting that Breard's conviction and sentence be voided. Paraguay also requested that the Court indicate provisional measures directing the United States to ensure that Breard not be executed pending the Court's determination of the case. Six days later, the ICJ unanimously indicated that "[t]he United States should take all measures at its disposal to ensure that [Breard] is not executed pending the final decision in these proceedings. . . ." Immediately thereafter, both Breard and Paraguay sought relief from the U.S. Supreme Court.

On April 13, the U.S. Secretary of State wrote to Virginia's governor, requesting that Virginia stay the execution. She argued that "[t]he immediate execution of Mr. Breard in the face of the Court's April 9 action could be seen as a denial by the United States of the significance of international law and the Court's processes in its international relations and thereby limit our ability to ensure that Americans are protected when living or traveling abroad."

At the same time, the Departments of State and Justice submitted an amicus brief to the Supreme Court urging the Court to deny Breard's petition. After arguing that provisional measures orders are not binding, the brief stated:

> Finally, even if [ICJ provisional measures are binding], the ICJ's order in this case does not require *this Court* to stop Breard's execution. That order states that the United States "should" take all measures "at its disposal" to ensure that Breard is not executed.
>
>   . . . [T]he "measures at [the Government's] disposal" are a matter of domestic United States law, and our federal system imposes limits on the federal government's ability to interfere with the criminal justice systems of the States. The "measures at [the United States's] disposal" under our Constitution may in some cases include only persuasion—such as the Secretary of State's request to the Governor of Virginia to stay Breard's execution—and not legal compulsion through the judicial system. That is the situation here. Accordingly, the ICJ's order does not provide an independent basis for this Court either to grant certiorari or to stay the execution.

In addition, the Court decided, for the first time ever, that an order indicating provisional measures is binding and, in this case, "created a legal obligation for the United States." The Court held that (1) the federal government's forwarding of the Court's order to Arizona's governor, "without even so much as a plea for a temporary stay," (2) the Executive Branch's argument to the Supreme Court that "an order of the [ICJ] indicating provisional measures is not binding," and (3) the Supreme Court's summary rejection of Germany's application for a stay of execution, constituted a failure by "the various competent United States authorities . . . to take all the steps they could have taken to give effect to the Court's Order."

3. *Avena* and Its Aftermath

On February 5, 2003, a unanimous ICJ granted Mexico's request for provisional measures and ordered the United States to "take all measures necessary" to prevent the executions of three Mexican nationals who were "at risk of execution in the coming months." On March 31, 2004, the Court issued a final judgment in *Avena*.

Case Concerning Avena and Other Mexican Nationals (Mexico v. United States of America)
2004 I.C.J. 1 (Mar. 31)

[The Court held that, in cases of 51 of the Mexican nationals, the United States had breached its obligation under Article 36(1)(b) of the Vienna Convention "to inform detained Mexican nationals of their rights under that paragraph" and in 49 of those cases "to notify the Mexican consular post of the[ir] detention." The ICJ also held that in 49 cases, the United States had breached its obligation under Article 36(1)(a) "to enable Mexican consular officers to communicate with and have access to their nationals, as well as its obligation under paragraph 1(c) of that Article regarding the right of consular officers to visit their detained nationals." Jose Ernesto Medellín was expressly included in each of these holdings of breach. The Court then discussed "what remedies are required in order to redress the injury done to Mexico and to its nationals by the United States."]

119. The general principle on the legal consequences of the commission of an internationally wrongful act was stated by the Permanent Court of International Justice . . . as follows: "It is a principle of international law that the breach of an engagement involves an obligation to make reparation in an adequate form." (*Factory at Chorzów, Jurisdiction, 1927, P.C.I.J., Series A, No. 9*, p. 21.) What constitutes "reparation in an adequate form" clearly varies depending upon the concrete circumstances surrounding each case and the precise nature and scope of the injury. . . .

121. . . . It should be clear from what has been observed above that the internationally wrongful acts committed by the United States were the failure of its competent authorities to inform the Mexican nationals concerned, to notify Mexican consular posts and to enable Mexico to provide consular assistance. It follows that the remedy to make good these violations should consist in an obligation on the United States to permit review and reconsideration of these nationals' cases by the United States courts . . . with a view to ascertaining whether in each case the violation of Article 36 . . . caused actual prejudice to the defendant in the process of administration of criminal justice.

123. It is not to be presumed, as Mexico asserts, that partial or total annulment of conviction or sentence provides the necessary and sole remedy. . . . [I]n the present case it is not the convictions and sentences of the Mexican nationals which are to be regarded

as a violation of international law, but solely certain breaches of treaty obligations which preceded them.

133. However, the Court wishes to point out that the current situation in the United States criminal procedure, as explained by the [U.S.] Agent at the hearings, is that . . . "*If the foreign national did not raise his Article 36 claim at trial, he may face procedural constraints* [i.e., the application of the procedural default rule] on raising that particular claim in direct or collateral judicial appeals" (emphasis added). As a result, a claim based on the violation of Article 36, paragraph 1, of the Vienna Convention, however meritorious in itself, could be barred in the courts of the United States by the operation of the procedural default rule. . . .

138. The Court would emphasize that the "review and reconsideration" prescribed by it . . . should be effective. Thus it should "tak[e] account of the violation of the rights set forth in [the] Convention" and guarantee that the violation and the possible prejudice caused by that violation will be fully examined and taken into account in the review and reconsideration process. . . .

140. As has been explained . . . the Court is of the view that, in cases where the [Vienna Convention has been breached], the legal consequences of this breach have to be examined and taken into account in the course of review and reconsideration. The Court considers that it is the judicial process that is suited to this task.

The *Avena* decision had a dramatic and substantial impact on several cases proceeding through courts in the United States. For example, Osbaldo Torres is one of the Mexicans covered by the ICJ's provisional measures. He was not advised of his Vienna Convention rights when he was arrested by Oklahoma police in July 1993; subsequently he was convicted of murder and sentenced to death.

On May 13, 2004, the Oklahoma Court of Criminal Appeals ordered that Torres's execution date be stayed pending an evidentiary hearing on "whether Torres was prejudiced by the State's violation of his Vienna Convention rights." *Torres v. Oklahoma*, No. PCD-04-442 (Okla. Crim. App. May 13, 2004). In a concurrence, Judge Charles S. Chapel wrote:

> At its simplest, this is a matter of contract. A treaty is a contract between sovereigns. The notion that contracts must be enforceable against those who enter into them is fundamental to the Rule of Law. This case is resolved by that very basic idea. The United States voluntarily and legally entered into a treaty, a contract with over 100 other countries. The United States is bound by the terms of the treaty and the State of Oklahoma is obligated by virtue of the Supremacy Clause to give effect to the treaty.
>
> As this Court is bound by the treaty itself, we are bound to give full faith and credit to the *Avena* decision. I am not suggesting that the International Court of Justice has jurisdiction over this Court—far from it. However . . . the issue of whether this Court must abide by [the ICJ's] opinion in [the *Avena*] case is not ours to determine. The United States Senate and the President have made that decision for us. . . .
>
> In order to give full effect to *Avena*, we are bound by its holding to review Torres's conviction and sentence in light of the Vienna Convention violation, without recourse to procedural bar. . . .

On the same day that this opinion was issued, Oklahoma's governor commuted Torres's death sentence to life imprisonment without the possibility of parole, citing the violation of Torres's Vienna Convention rights.

4. The Supreme Court Addresses the Domestic Effects of ICJ Judgments

The *Avena* judgment also sparked a complex series of events in the *Medellín* litigation. Shortly after *Avena* was decided, the Fifth Circuit denied Medellín's habeas corpus petition. Medellín then filed a petition for a writ of certiorari with the United States Supreme Court. The Court granted the writ; thereafter the Executive Branch submitted an amicus brief arguing that the Vienna Convention does not provide judicially enforceable private rights: "It is for the President, not the courts, to determine whether the United States should comply with the [ICJ] decision, and, if so, how." The brief went on to state that the United States has a treaty obligation to comply with the *Avena* decision and that, on February 28, 2004 (one day before the brief was filed), the President had issued a memorandum to the Attorney General making the following determination:

> I have determined . . . that the United States will discharge its international obligations under the [*Avena* decision] by having state courts give effect to the decision in accordance with general principles of comity in cases filed by the 51 Mexican nationals addressed in that decision.

Relying upon the President's memorandum and the *Avena* judgment as separate bases for relief that were not available at the time of his first state habeas corpus action, Medellín filed a new state habeas petition four days before oral argument at the Supreme Court. The Supreme Court then dismissed the writ as "improvidently granted," given the possibility that "Texas courts will provide Medellín with the review he seeks pursuant to the *Avena* judgment and the President's memorandum." However, the Texas courts rejected Medellín's petition, and the case returned to the Supreme Court. In considering Medellín's claims, the Court spent substantial time discussing whether and when treaties are self-executing within the domestic legal system. The roots of the distinction between self-executing and non-self-executing treaties are usually traced to Chief Justice Marshall's opinion in *Foster v. Neilson*, 27 U.S. (2 Pet.) 253 (1829). In that case, plaintiffs claimed title to property in Florida on the basis of a grant from Spain. The treaty that transferred the disputed land from Spain to the United States provided, according to the English-language text, that the Spanish grants "shall be ratified and confirmed to the persons in possession of the lands." Plaintiffs argued that the treaty confirmed their title to the property. The Court decided that the Spanish grants were not valid as domestic law until Congress passed legislation confirming the grants.

> A treaty is in its nature a contract between two nations, not a legislative act. It does not generally effect, of itself, the object to be accomplished, especially so far as its operation is infra-territorial; but is carried into execution by the sovereign power of the respective parties to the instrument.
>
> In the United States a different principle is established. Our constitution declares a treaty to be the law of the land. It is, consequently, to be regarded in courts of justice as equivalent to an act of the legislature, whenever it operates of itself without the aid of any legislative provision. But when the terms of the stipulation import a contract, when either of the parties engages to perform a particular act, the treaty addresses itself to the political, not the judicial department; and the legislature must execute the contract before it can become a rule for the Court.

The Court thus distinguished between treaties that "operate of themselves" and are therefore applicable by the courts without legislative action, and those that are not judicially applicable unless and until implementing legislation is enacted. However, this distinction has proved easier to state than to apply. For example, the treaty provision at issue in *Foster* was also central to a case decided by the Court only four years later. In that case,

United States v. Percheman, 32 U.S. (7 Pet.) 51 (1833), the Court relied upon the Spanish language version of the treaty, translated as stating that the land grants "shall remain ratified and confirmed to the persons in possession [of the lands]," and held that the treaty was self-executing.

The *Medellín* opinion is the Supreme Court's most recent statement on the doctrine of self-executing treaties.

Medellín v. Texas
552 U.S. 491 (2008)

CHIEF JUSTICE ROBERTS delivered the opinion of the court, in which JUSTICES SCALIA, KENNEDY, THOMAS, and ALITO joined.

II

No one disputes that the *Avena* decision . . . constitutes an international law obligation on the part of the United States. But not all international law obligations automatically constitute binding federal law enforceable in United States courts. The question we confront here is whether the *Avena* judgment has automatic domestic legal effect such that the judgment of its own force applies in state and federal courts.

This Court has long recognized the distinction between treaties that automatically have effect as domestic law, and those that—while they constitute international law commitments—do not by themselves function as binding federal law. . . . In sum, while treaties "may comprise international commitments . . . they are not domestic law unless Congress has either enacted implementing statutes or the treaty itself conveys an intention that it be 'self-executing' and is ratified on these terms." *Igartua-De La Rosa v. United States,* 417 F.3d 145, 150 (C.A.1 2005) (en banc) (Boudin, C.J.).[2]

A treaty is, of course, "primarily a compact between independent nations." *Head Money Cases,* 112 U.S. 580, 598 (1884). It ordinarily "depends for the enforcement of its provisions on the interest and the honor of the governments which are parties to it." *Ibid.* "If these [interests] fail, its infraction becomes the subject of international negotiations and reclamations. . . . It is obvious that with all this the judicial courts have nothing to do and can give no redress." *Head Money Cases,* 112 U.S. 580. Only "[i]f the treaty contains stipulations which are self-executing, that is, require no legislation to make them operative, [will] they have the force and effect of a legislative enactment." *Whitney [v. Robertson,* 124 U.S. 190, 194].

Medellín and his *amici* . . . contend that the Optional Protocol [to the Vienna Convention], United Nations Charter, and ICJ Statute supply the "relevant obligation" to give the *Avena* judgment binding effect in the domestic courts of the United States. . . .

A

The most natural reading of the Optional Protocol is as a bare grant of jurisdiction. It provides only that "[d]isputes arising out of the interpretation or application of the

---

[2] The label "self-executing" has on occasion been used to convey different meanings. What we mean by "self-executing" is that the treaty has automatic domestic effect as federal law upon ratification. Conversely, a "non-self-executing" treaty does not by itself give rise to domestically enforceable federal law. Whether such a treaty has domestic effect depends upon implementing legislation passed by Congress.

[Vienna] Convention shall lie within the compulsory jurisdiction of the International Court of Justice" and "may accordingly be brought before the [ICJ].". . . The Protocol says nothing about the effect of an ICJ decision and does not itself commit signatories to comply with an ICJ judgment. . . .

The obligation on the part of signatory nations to comply with ICJ judgments derives not from the Optional Protocol, but rather from Article 94 of the United Nations Charter . . . [which] provides that "[e]ach Member of the United Nations *undertakes to comply* with the decision of the [ICJ] in any case to which it is a party." (emphasis added). The Executive Branch contends that the phrase "undertakes to comply" is not "an acknowledgement that an ICJ decision will have immediate legal effect in the courts of U.N. members," but rather "a commitment on the part of U.N. Members to take future action through their political branches to comply with an ICJ decision." We agree with this construction of Article 94. The Article is not a directive to domestic courts. It does not provide that the United States "shall" or "must" comply with an ICJ decision. . . .

The remainder of Article 94 confirms that the U.N. Charter does not contemplate the automatic enforceability of ICJ decisions in domestic courts. Article 94(2) — the enforcement provision — provides the sole remedy for noncompliance: referral to the United Nations Security Council by an aggrieved state. . . .

If ICJ judgments were . . . regarded as automatically enforceable domestic law, they would be immediately and directly binding on state and federal courts pursuant to the Supremacy Clause. Mexico . . . would have no need to proceed to the Security Council to enforce the judgment in this case. Noncompliance with an ICJ judgment through exercise of the Security Council veto — always regarded as an option by the Executive and ratifying Senate during and after consideration of the U.N. Charter, Optional Protocol, and ICJ Statute — would no longer be a viable alternative. There would be nothing to veto. In light of the U.N. Charter's remedial scheme, there is no reason to believe that the President and Senate signed up for such a result. . . .

The pertinent international agreements, therefore, do not provide for implementation of ICJ judgments through direct enforcement in domestic courts, and "where a treaty does not provide a particular remedy, either expressly or implicitly, it is not for the federal courts to impose one on the States through lawmaking of their own." *Sanchez-Llamas*, 548 U.S., at 347.

B

The dissent faults our analysis because it "looks for the wrong thing (explicit textual expression about self-execution) using the wrong standard (clarity) in the wrong place (the treaty language)." Given our obligation to interpret treaty provisions to determine whether they are self-executing, we have to confess that we do think it rather important to look to the treaty language to see what it has to say about the issue. That is after all what the Senate looks to in deciding whether to approve the treaty.

The interpretive approach employed by the Court today — resorting to the text — is hardly novel. In two early cases involving an 1819 land-grant treaty between Spain and the United States, Chief Justice Marshall found the language of the treaty dispositive. In *Foster*, after distinguishing between self-executing treaties (those "equivalent to an act of the legislature") and non-self-executing treaties (those "the legislature must execute"), Chief Justice Marshall held that the 1819 treaty was non-self-executing. 2 Pet., at 314. Four years later, the Supreme Court considered another claim under the same treaty, but concluded that the treaty was self-executing. See *Percheman*, 7 Pet., at 87. The reason was not because the treaty was sometimes self-executing and sometimes not, but because "the language of" the Spanish translation (brought to the Court's attention for the first time) indicated the parties' intent to ratify and confirm the land-grant "by force of the instrument itself." *Id.*, at 89. . . .

. . . The dissent's novel approach to deciding which (or, more accurately, when) treaties give rise to directly enforceable federal law is arrestingly indeterminate. . . . The dissent's approach risks the United States' involvement in international agreements. It is hard to believe that the United States would enter into treaties that are sometimes enforceable and sometimes not. Such a treaty would be the equivalent of writing a blank check to the judiciary. Senators could never be quite sure what the treaties on which they were voting meant. Only a judge could say for sure and only at some future date. This uncertainty could hobble the United States' efforts to negotiate and sign international agreements. . . .

III

Medellín next argues that the ICJ's judgment in *Avena* is binding on state courts by virtue of the President's February 28, 2005 Memorandum. . . .

A

Justice Jackson's familiar tripartite scheme provides the accepted framework for evaluating executive action in this area. First, "[w]hen the President acts pursuant to an express or implied authorization of Congress, his authority is at its maximum, for it includes all that he possesses in his own right plus all that Congress can delegate." *Youngstown*, 343 U.S., at 635 (Jackson, J., concurring). Second, "[w]hen the President acts in absence of either a congressional grant or denial of authority, he can only rely upon his own independent powers, but there is a zone of twilight in which he and Congress may have concurrent authority, or in which its distribution is uncertain." *Id.*, at 637. In this circumstance, Presidential authority can derive support from "congressional inertia, indifference or quiescence." *Ibid.* Finally, "[w]hen the President takes measures incompatible with the expressed or implied will of Congress, his power is at its lowest ebb," and the Court can sustain his actions "only by disabling the Congress from acting upon the subject." *Id.*, at 637-638.

B

1

The President has an array of political and diplomatic means available to enforce international obligations, but unilaterally converting a non-self-executing treaty into a self-executing one is not among them. The responsibility for transforming an international obligation arising from a non-self-executing treaty into domestic law falls to Congress. As this Court has explained, when treaty stipulations are "not self-executing they can only be enforced pursuant to legislation to carry them into effect." *Whitney, supra*, at 194. Moreover, "[u]ntil such act shall be passed, the Court is not at liberty to disregard the existing laws on the subject." *Foster, supra*, at 315.

The requirement that Congress, rather than the President, implement a non-self-executing treaty derives from the text of the Constitution, which divides the treaty-making power between the President and the Senate. The Constitution vests the President with the authority to "make" a treaty. Art. II, §2. If the Executive determines that a treaty should have domestic effect of its own force, that determination may be implemented "in mak[ing]" the treaty, by ensuring that it contains language plainly providing for domestic enforceability. If the treaty is to be self-executing in this respect, the Senate must consent to the treaty by the requisite two-thirds vote, *ibid.*, consistent with all other constitutional restraints.

Once a treaty is ratified without provisions clearly according it domestic effect, however, whether the treaty will ever have such effect is governed by the fundamental constitutional principle that "'[t]he power to make the necessary laws is in Congress; the power to execute in the President.'" *Hamdan v. Rumsfeld*, 548 U.S. 557, 591 (2006). . . . [T]he terms of a non-self-executing treaty can become domestic law only in the same way as any other law—through passage of legislation by both Houses of Congress, combined with either the President's signature or a congressional override of a Presidential veto. . . .

A non-self-executing treaty, by definition, is one that was ratified with the understanding that it is not to have domestic effect of its own force. That understanding precludes the assertion that Congress has implicitly authorized the President—acting on his own—to achieve precisely the same result. . . .

Indeed, the preceding discussion should make clear that [w]hen the President asserts the power to "enforce" a non-self-executing treaty by unilaterally creating domestic law, he acts in conflict with the implicit understanding of the ratifying Senate. His assertion of authority, insofar as it is based on the pertinent non-self-executing treaties, is therefore within Justice Jackson's third category, not the first or even the second.

2

We thus turn to the United States' claim that—independent of the United States' treaty obligations—the Memorandum is a valid exercise of the President's foreign affairs authority to resolve claims disputes with foreign nations. The United States relies on a series of cases in which this Court has upheld the authority of the President to settle foreign claims pursuant to an executive agreement. . . .

The claims-settlement cases involve a narrow set of circumstances: the making of executive agreements to settle civil claims between American citizens and foreign governments or foreign nationals. They are based on the view that "a systematic, unbroken, executive practice, long pursued to the knowledge of the Congress and never before questioned," can "raise a presumption that the [action] had been [taken] in pursuance of its consent." *Dames & Moore*, [453 U.S. 654, 686 (1981)].

The President's Memorandum is not supported by a "particularly longstanding practice" of congressional acquiescence. . . . Indeed, the Government has not identified a single instance in which the President has attempted (or Congress has acquiesced in) a Presidential directive issued to state courts, much less one that reaches deep into the heart of the State's police powers and compels state courts to reopen final criminal judgments and set aside neutrally applicable state laws. The Executive's narrow and strictly limited authority to settle international claims disputes pursuant to an executive agreement cannot stretch so far as to support the current Presidential Memorandum. . . .

JUSTICE STEVENS, concurring in the judgment.

[Justice Stevens found that neither constitutional text nor precedent supports a presumption against self-execution, but concluded that the relevant treaties did not authorize the Court to enforce the *Avena* judgment. He continued:]

Even though the ICJ's judgment in *Avena* is not "the supreme Law of the Land," U.S. Const., Art. VI, cl. 2, no one disputes that it constitutes an international law obligation on the part of the United States. By issuing a memorandum declaring that state courts should give effect to the judgment in *Avena*, the President made a commendable attempt to induce the States to discharge the Nation's obligation. I agree with the Texas judges and the majority of this Court that the President's memorandum is not binding law. Nonetheless, the fact that the President cannot legislate unilaterally does not absolve the United States from its promise to take action necessary to comply with the ICJ's judgment.

Under the express terms of the Supremacy Clause, the United States' obligation to "undertak[e] to comply" with the ICJ's decision falls on each of the States as well as the Federal Government. One consequence of our form of government is that sometimes States must shoulder the primary responsibility for protecting the honor and integrity of the Nation. Texas' duty in this respect is all the greater since it was Texas that — by failing to provide consular notice in accordance with the Vienna Convention — ensnared the United States in the current controversy. Having already put the Nation in breach of one treaty, it is now up to Texas to prevent the breach of another.

The decision in *Avena* merely obligates the United States "to provide, by means of its own choosing, review and reconsideration of the convictions and sentences of the [affected] Mexican nationals," 2004 I.C.J., at 72, ¶153(9), "with a view to ascertaining" whether the failure to provide proper notice to consular officials "caused actual prejudice to the defendant in the process of administration of criminal justice," *id.*, at 60, ¶121. The cost to Texas of complying with *Avena* would be minimal, particularly given the remote likelihood that the violation of the Vienna Convention actually prejudiced José Ernesto Medellín. It is a cost that the State of Oklahoma unhesitatingly assumed [in the *Torres* case discussed at page 239].

On the other hand, the costs of refusing to respect the ICJ's judgment are significant. The entire Court and the President agree that breach will jeopardize the United States' "plainly compelling" interests in "ensuring the reciprocal observance of the Vienna Convention, protecting relations with foreign governments, and demonstrating commitment to the role of international law." When the honor of the Nation is balanced against the modest cost of compliance, Texas would do well to recognize that more is at stake than whether judgments of the ICJ, and the principled admonitions of the President of the United States, trump state procedural rules in the absence of implementing legislation.

JUSTICE BREYER, with whom JUSTICE SOUTER and JUSTICE GINSBURG join, dissenting.

. . .

The case law provides no simple magic answer to the question whether a particular treaty provision is self-executing. But the case law does make clear that, insofar as today's majority looks for language about "self-execution" in the treaty itself and insofar as it erects "clear statement" presumptions designed to help find an answer, it is misguided. . . .

Indeed, the majority does not point to a single ratified United States treaty that contains the kind of "clea[r]" or "plai[n]" textual indication for which the majority searches. . . . But that simply highlights how few of them actually do speak clearly on the matter. And that is not because the United States never, or hardly ever, has entered into a treaty with self-executing provisions. . . . Rather, it is because the issue whether further legislative action is required before a treaty provision takes domestic effect in a signatory nation is often a matter of how that Nation's domestic law regards the provision's legal status. And that domestic status-determining law differs markedly from one nation to another. . . . Britain, for example, taking the view that the British Crown makes treaties but Parliament makes domestic law, virtually always requires parliamentary legislation. . . . [In contrast,] the law of other nations, the Netherlands for example, directly incorporates many treaties concluded by the executive into its domestic law even without explicit parliamentary approval of the treaty.

The majority correctly notes that the treaties do not explicitly state that the relevant obligations are self-executing. But given the differences among nations, why would drafters write treaty language stating that a provision . . . is self-executing? How could those drafters achieve agreement when one signatory nation follows one tradition and a second follows another? . . .

In a word, for present purposes, the absence or presence of language in a treaty about a provision's self-execution proves nothing at all. At best the Court is hunting the snark. At worst it erects legalistic hurdles that can threaten the application of provisions in many existing commercial and other treaties and make it more difficult to negotiate new ones.

The case law also suggests practical, context-specific criteria that this Court has previously used to help determine whether, for Supremacy Clause purposes, a treaty provision is self-executing. . . .

In making this determination, this Court has found the provision's subject matter of particular importance. Does the treaty provision declare peace? Does it promise not to engage in hostilities? If so, it addresses itself to the political branches. Alternatively, does it concern the adjudication of traditional private legal rights such as rights to own property, to conduct a business, or to obtain civil tort recovery? If so, it may well address itself to the Judiciary. Enforcing such rights and setting their boundaries is the bread-and-butter work of the courts.

One might also ask whether the treaty provision confers specific, detailed individual legal rights. Does it set forth definite standards that judges can readily enforce? Other things being equal, where rights are specific and readily enforceable, the treaty provision more likely "addresses" the judiciary. . . .

Applying the approach just described, I would find the relevant treaty provisions self-executing as applied to the ICJ judgment before us (giving that judgment domestic legal effect) for the following reasons, taken together.

First, the language of the relevant treaties strongly supports direct judicial enforceability, at least of judgments of the kind at issue here. The Optional Protocol bears the title "Compulsory Settlement of Disputes," thereby emphasizing the mandatory and binding nature of the procedures it sets forth. . . . Thus, the Optional Protocol's basic objective is not just to provide a forum for *settlement* but to provide a forum for *compulsory* settlement.

Moreover, in accepting Article 94(1) of the Charter, "[e]ach Member . . . undertakes to comply with the decision" of the ICJ "in any case to which it is a party." And the ICJ Statute (part of the U.N. Charter) makes clear that, a decision of the ICJ between parties that have consented to the ICJ's compulsory jurisdiction has "*binding force* . . . between the parties and in respect of that particular case." (emphasis added). Enforcement of a court's judgment that has "binding force" involves quintessential judicial activity.

True, neither the Protocol nor the Charter explicitly states that the obligation to comply with an ICJ judgment automatically binds a party as *a matter of domestic law* without further domestic legislation. *But how could the language of those documents do otherwise?* The treaties are multilateral. . . . Why, given national differences, would drafters, seeking as strong a legal obligation as is practically attainable, use treaty language that requires all signatories to adopt uniform domestic-law treatment in this respect? . . .

Second, the Optional Protocol here applies to a dispute about the meaning of a Vienna Convention provision that is itself self-executing and judicially enforceable. The Convention provision is about an individual's "rights," namely, his right upon being arrested to be informed of his separate right to contact his nation's consul. . . . The dispute arises at the intersection of an individual right with ordinary rules of criminal procedure; it consequently concerns the kind of matter with which judges are familiar. The provisions contain judicially enforceable standards. And the judgment itself requires a further hearing of a sort that is typically judicial. . . .

Third, logic suggests that a treaty provision providing for "final" and "binding" judgments that "settl[e]" treaty-based disputes is self-executing insofar as the judgment in question concerns the meaning of an underlying treaty provision that is itself self-executing. . . .

Fifth, other factors, related to the particular judgment here at issue, make that judgment well suited to direct judicial enforcement. The specific issue before the ICJ concerned "'review and reconsideration'" of the "possible prejudice" caused in each of the 51 affected cases by an arresting State's failure to provide the defendant with rights guaranteed by the Vienna Convention. This review will call for an understanding of how criminal procedure works, including whether, and how, a notification failure may work prejudice. As the ICJ itself recognized, "it is the judicial process that is suited to this task." . . .

Seventh, neither the President nor Congress has expressed concern about direct judicial enforcement of the ICJ decision. To the contrary, the President favors enforcement of this judgment. Thus, insofar as foreign policy impact, the interrelation of treaty provisions, or any other matter within the President's special treaty, military, and foreign affairs responsibilities might prove relevant, such factors *favor,* rather than militate against, enforcement of the judgment before us.

For these seven reasons, I would find that the United States' treaty obligation to comply with the ICJ judgment in *Avena* is enforceable in court in this case without further congressional action beyond Senate ratification of the relevant treaties. The majority reaches a different conclusion because it looks for the wrong thing (explicit textual expression about self-execution) using the wrong standard (clarity) in the wrong place (the treaty language). . . .

Following the Supreme Court's ruling, Texas set an execution date for Medellín of August 5, 2008. In June, Mexico filed a "Request for Interpretation of the [*Avena*] Judgment" and a request for provisional measures at the ICJ. Article 60 of the ICJ Statute permits states to seek an interpretation of a judgment when a "dispute as to the meaning or scope" of a judgment exists. Before the ICJ could rule, the U.S. Secretary of State and Attorney General wrote to the governor of Texas to urge that Texas take the "steps necessary to give effect to the *Avena* decision." The governor responded that Texas was not bound by an ICJ judgment.

On July 16, by a vote of seven to five, the ICJ issued provisional measures stating that the United States "shall take all measures necessary to ensure that [named Mexican nationals including Medellín] are not executed pending judgment" on Mexico's request for interpretation. The following week, a federal court rejected Medellín's second federal habeas corpus petition. Two days later, the Inter-American Commission on Human Rights issued a preliminary report concluding that Medellín's rights had been violated by the failure to provide access to Mexican diplomats while Medellín's cases proceeded in Texas courts.

On August 1, 2008, Medellín filed a petition for a stay of execution with the U.S. Supreme Court. Just before 10:00 p.m. on August 5, 2008, the Supreme Court, by a 5-4 vote, refused to stay the execution. *Medellín v. Texas,* 129 S. Ct. 360 (2008). Shortly thereafter Medellín was given a lethal injection and pronounced dead.

On January 19, 2009, the ICJ issued a final judgment. It found that Mexico's request did not fall within the scope of an Article 60 proceeding. The Court nevertheless observed:

> considerations of domestic law which have so far hindered the implementation of the obligations incumbent upon the United States, cannot relieve it of its obligation. A choice of means was allowed to the United States in the implementation of its obligation and, failing success within a reasonable period of time through the means chosen, it must rapidly turn to alternative and effective means of attaining that result.

The Court unanimously found that the United States breached its obligations under the provisional measures order and reaffirmed, by a vote of 11-1, the continuing binding nature of U.S. obligations under the *Avena* judgment.

During the time that the cases discussed above were being litigated, the U.S. State Department provided hundreds of training classes, briefings, and meetings about consular notification across the country, and distributed more than one million pieces of instructional material regarding the Vienna Convention, including a Consular Notification and Access Reference Card with a script that law enforcement officers can use upon detaining a foreign national; a translation of consular notification requirements into 13 languages; and a flow chart that explains the Vienna Convention. More information on the State Department's efforts to promote compliance with the Vienna Convention can be found at *http://travel.state.gov/content/travel/english/consularnotification.html*.

Notes and Questions

1. Does the Supreme Court find that *Avena* is not self-executing, or that the Optional Protocol or Article 94 of the UN Charter is not self-executing? Does the majority provide a coherent approach to determining when treaties are self-executing? How persuasive is Justice Breyer's argument that, because states adopt very different approaches to the domestic effect of treaties, it is unrealistic to expect them to address the domestic effect of treaties in a treaty's text?

2. In what sense do non-self-executing treaties constitute domestic law? Does the judicial creation of the self-execution doctrine undermine the intent of the Framers who drafted the Supremacy Clause?

3. Cases involving Vienna Convention claims continue to work their way through the courts. Edgar Arias Tamayo was another Mexican national convicted of murder and sentenced to death. An execution date of January 22, 2014, was set. Secretary of State John Kerry wrote to Texas Governor Rick Perry requesting that Texas review Tamayo's case in light of *Avena* and noting that "the setting of an execution date for Mr. Tamayo would be extremely detrimental to the interests of the United States." Texas officials cited *Medellín* for the proposition that the state was not bound by the ICJ decision and denied a petition for clemency.

A week before the scheduled execution date, the Inter-American Commission on Human Rights (IACHR) adopted a report finding that the failure to advise Tamayo of his Vienna Convention rights deprived him of a criminal process that satisfied the minimum standards of due process and a fair trial. On the day of the scheduled execution, the U.S. Supreme Court denied Tamayo's application for a stay, over a dissent by Justices Ginsburg, Breyer, and Sotomayor. *Tamayo v. Stephens*, 134 S. Ct. 2022 (2014). Later that evening, Tamayo was executed.

The UK Ambassador to the United States, the Head of Delegation of the European Union in the United States, the Office of the High Commissioner for Human Rights, and other international actors strongly condemned the execution. The IACHR "deplore[d] the failure on the part of the United States and the state of Texas to comply with the recommendations issued by the IACHR in a merits report." The U.S. State Department called for the passage of legislation that would enable the U.S. to comply with its international obligations.

IV. OPENING AND CLOSING THE COURTHOUSE DOOR TO INTERNATIONAL LAW CLAIMS: SEEKING REDRESS FOR CORPORATE COMPLICITY IN HUMAN RIGHTS VIOLATIONS

States have a number of reasons for accepting and for rejecting international legal claims in their court systems. While many of the problems explored above can be understood in this light, we now turn to some specific statutes and doctrines that explicitly either open or close U.S. courts to international law claims. In particular, we focus on efforts to hold multinational corporations liable in U.S. courts for direct or indirect participation in human rights violations. As you read these materials, consider the political and institutional forces that tend to support or oppose the use of international law norms in U.S. courts. Consider also how courts explicitly struggle with the appropriate relationship between international and domestic law—and with the appropriate role of courts in determining this relationship. Finally, consider the gap between the transnational nature of corporate activity and the limited availability of either national or transnational regulatory regimes to govern corporate behavior, and the efficacy of domestic litigation in promoting higher corporate standards.

The goals for this Problem include:

- to understand the nature and territorial scope of the jurisdiction granted to United States courts by the Alien Tort Statute (ATS);
- to understand the nature and scope of the act of state doctrine; and
- to understand the policy debates surrounding the litigation of international legal claims, and particularly human rights claims, in domestic courts.

A. *The Problem*

Multinational corporations engaged in extractive industries in developing states are frequently accused of participating in human rights abuses. One high-visibility example arises out of oil exploration activities undertaken in the Ogoni region of Nigeria by the Shell Petroleum Development Company of Nigeria (SPDC), a subsidiary of two European corporations, the Royal Dutch Petroleum Company and the Shell Transport and Trading Company. These activities led to several lawsuits in various states, including one action filed by residents of the Ogoni region that was twice argued in the United States Supreme Court.

SPDC has been engaged in oil exploration and production in the Ogoni region since 1958. In response to widespread environmental damage caused by SPDC's operations, Ogoni residents formed the Movement for Survival of Ogoni People (MOSOP), an organization devoted to non-violent action to advance environmental justice, corporate social responsibility, and the rights of the Ogoni. In 1993, following a demand by MOSOP for royalties for the Ogoni people, Shell and SPDC officials allegedly collectively formulated a strategy to suppress MOSOP. In April 1993, SPDC called for assistance from government troops in suppressing Ogoni residents protesting the building of a new oil pipeline. The Nigerian government troops fired on Ogoni protesters, killing 11. Later, SPDC's divisional manager wrote to the Governor of Rivers State (in which Ogoni is located) and requested "the usual assistance" to protect the progress of SPDC's further work on the pipeline. From August through October 1993, the Nigerian military repeatedly attacked Ogoni villages, killing many civilians. SPDC allegedly assisted in several ways, including providing a helicopter and boats for reconnaissance, transporting Nigerian forces, allowing SPDC property to be used as a staging area for attacks, and giving food and compensation to soldiers involved in the attacks.

In December 1993, SPDC's managing director, with Shell's approval, asked the Nigerian Police to increase security in exchange for providing Nigerian forces with salary, housing, equipment, and vehicles. Shortly thereafter, the Nigerian government created a special Internal Security Task Force (ISTF). Shell and SPDC allegedly provided transportation, food, and ammunition to ISTF personnel. From May to August 1994, the ISTF engaged in numerous nighttime raids on Ogoni towns during which ISTF members broke into homes, allegedly shooting or beating anyone in their path, including the elderly, women, and children, raping, forcing villagers to abandon their homes, and destroying or looting property. At least fifty Ogoni residents were killed, and many were arrested and detained without formal charges in poor facilities. SPDC officials were said to regularly provide food and logistical support to the soldiers who worked at the detention facility.

In 1994, the Nigerian military created a "Special Tribunal" to try leaders of MOSOP, including Dr. Barinem Kiobel, a prominent politician who objected to the tactics of the ISTF and supported MOSOP. After a trial allegedly tainted by false testimony, the Special Tribunal condemned Dr. Kiobel and others, including the famed playwright Ken Saro-Wiwa, to death. The so-called Ogoni Nine were executed in November 1995.

In September 2002, Dr. Kiobel's wife and 11 other plaintiffs filed a class action in the United States District Court in Manhattan alleging torts in violation of the law of nations, pursuant to the Alien Tort Statute, which provides that "[t]he district courts shall have original jurisdiction of any civil action by an alien for a tort only, committed in violation of the law of nations or a treaty of the United States." With respect to each claim, plaintiffs alleged that Shell and SPDC aided and abetted or were otherwise complicit in the Nigerian military's violations of the law of nations.

B. Opening the Door to International Law Claims?
The Alien Tort Statute

Originally passed as part of the Judiciary Act of 1789, the ATS was rarely used for nearly 200 years. However, in 1980, the Second Circuit launched the modern era of ATS litigation with its landmark decision in *Filartiga v. Pena-Irala*, excerpted below.

Filartiga v. Pena-Irala

630 F.2d 876 (2d Cir. 1980)

I

The appellants, plaintiffs below, are citizens of the Republic of Paraguay. Dr. Joel Filartiga, [is] . . . a longstanding opponent of the government of President Alfredo Stroessner, which has held power in Paraguay since 1954. [Plaintiff Dolly Filartiga is his daughter.] . . . The Filartigas brought this action in the Eastern District of New York against Americo Norberto Pena-Irala (Pena), also a citizen of Paraguay, for wrongfully causing the death of Dr. Filartiga's seventeen-year old son, Joelito. . . .

[O]n March 29, 1976, Joelito Filartiga was kidnapped and tortured to death by Pena, who was then Inspector General of Police in Asuncion, Paraguay. . . . The Filartigas claim that Joelito was tortured and killed in retaliation for his father's political activities and beliefs.

[The Filartigas' efforts to obtain justice in Paraguay were unsuccessful. In 1978, Pena entered the United States on a visitor's visa. Dolly Filartiga learned that Pena was in Brooklyn and had a summons and complaint served on Pena. The complaint invoked the ATS as a basis for jurisdiction. The district court dismissed the complaint on the grounds that "the law of nations" as used in the ATS does not govern a state's treatment of its own citizens.]

II

[T]he Alien Tort Statute . . . provides: "The district courts shall have original jurisdiction of any civil action by an alien for a tort only, committed in violation of the law of nations or a treaty of the United States." Since appellants do not contend that their action arises directly under a treaty of the United States, a threshold question on the jurisdictional issue is whether the conduct alleged violates the law of nations. . . .

The Paquete Habana, 175 U.S. 677 (1900), reaffirmed that

> where there is no treaty, and no controlling executive or legislative act or judicial decision, resort must be had to the customs and usages of civilized nations; and, as evidence of these, to the works of jurists and commentators, who by years of labor, research and experience, have made themselves peculiarly well acquainted with the subjects of which they treat. . . .

Habana is particularly instructive for present purposes, for it held that the traditional prohibition against seizure of an enemy's coastal fishing vessels during wartime, a standard that began as one of comity only, had ripened over the preceding century into "a settled rule of international law" by "the general assent of civilized nations." Thus it is clear that courts must interpret international law not as it was in 1789, but as it has evolved and exists among the nations of the world today. . . .

The United Nations Charter . . . makes it clear that in this modern age a state's treatment of its own citizens is a matter of international concern. It provides:

> With a view to the creation of conditions of stability and well-being which are necessary for peaceful and friendly relations among nations . . . the United Nations shall promote . . . universal respect for, and observance of, human rights and fundamental freedoms for all. . . .

[A]lthough there is no universal agreement as to the precise extent of the "human rights and fundamental freedoms" guaranteed to all by the Charter, there is at present no dissent from the view that the guaranties include, at a bare minimum, the right to be free from torture. This prohibition has become part of customary international law, as evidenced and defined by the Universal Declaration of Human Rights, which states, in the plainest of terms, "no one shall be subjected to torture." The General Assembly has declared that the Charter precepts embodied in this Universal Declaration "constitute basic principles of international law." Particularly relevant is the [General Assembly] Declaration on the Protection of All Persons from Being Subjected to Torture . . . [which] expressly prohibits any state from permitting the dastardly and totally inhuman act of torture. . . . This Declaration, like the Declaration of Human Rights before it, was adopted without dissent by the General Assembly. . . .

Turning to the act of torture, we have little difficulty discerning its universal renunciation in the modern usage and practice of nations. The international consensus surrounding torture has found expression in numerous international treaties and accords. E.g., American Convention on Human Rights, Art. 5 ("No one shall be subjected to torture or to cruel, inhuman or degrading punishment or treatment"); International Covenant on Civil and Political Rights (identical language). The substance of these international agreements is reflected in modern municipal—*i.e.*, national—law as well. Although torture was once a routine concomitant of criminal interrogations in many nations, during the modern and hopefully more enlightened era it has been universally renounced. According to one survey, torture is prohibited, expressly or implicitly, by the constitutions of over fifty-five nations, including both the United States and Paraguay. . . .

We have been directed to no assertion by any contemporary state of a right to torture its own or another nation's citizens. Indeed, United States diplomatic contacts confirm the universal abhorrence with which torture is viewed:

> In exchanges between United States embassies and all foreign states with which the United States maintains relations, it has been the Department of State's general experience that no government has asserted a right to torture its own nationals. Where reports of torture elicit some credence, a state usually responds by denial or, less frequently, by asserting that the conduct was unauthorized or constituted rough treatment short of torture.[15]

Memorandum of the United States as *Amicus Curiae* at 16 n.34.

Having examined the sources from which customary international law is derived—the usage of nations, judicial opinions and the works of jurists—we conclude that official torture is now prohibited by the law of nations. The prohibition is clear and unambiguous, and admits of no distinction between treatment of aliens and citizens. Accordingly, we must conclude that the dictum in [earlier cases] to the effect that "violations of international law do not occur when the aggrieved parties are nationals of the acting state," is clearly out of tune with the current usage and practice of international law. . . .

Human rights activists hailed *Filartiga* and in the years that followed the number of ATS cases grew in number and expanded in scope. In particular, suits began to be filed against prominent foreign officials, U.S. and foreign companies, and U.S. government officials. For example, Chinese survivors of the Tiananmen Square crackdown filed suit against Li Peng, China's Premier at the time of the crackdown; Burmese plaintiffs sued Unocal for human rights abuses associated with the construction of a gas pipeline project in Burma; former detainees at the Abu Ghraib prison in Iraq sued Titan and other military contractors hired by the U.S. government in connection with the occupation of Iraq; and several Guantanamo Bay detainees filed ATS actions against the Secretary of Defense, Chairman of the Joint Chiefs of Staff, and other U.S. officials.These suits proved highly controversial, with many commentators arguing that ATS cases interfered

---

[15] The fact that the prohibition of torture is often honored in the breach does not diminish its binding effect as a norm of international law. As one commentator has put it, "The best evidence for the existence of international law is that every actual State recognizes that it does exist and that it is itself under an obligation to observe it. States often violate international law, just as individuals often violate municipal law; but no more than individuals do States defend their violations by claiming they are above the law." J. Brierly, The Outlook for International Law 4-5 (Oxford 1944).

with Executive Branch prerogatives in foreign affairs and threatened U.S. foreign policy interests. A more technical critique argued that the ATS is purely jurisdictional, and that ATS plaintiffs must rely upon the law of nations or legislation creating a cause of action before they can proceed with an action under §1350. Federal courts of appeal split over whether the ATS provided a cause of action, and the issue remained open until the *Sosa* opinion excerpted below.

Notes and Questions

1. What interest does the United States have in the adjudication in U.S. courts of claims by foreign plaintiffs against foreign defendants over events that happened outside the United States?

2. Could the *Filartiga* plaintiffs have sued Paraguay in addition to Pena? A later case established that plaintiffs cannot sue a foreign state under the ATS. In *Argentine Republic v. Amerada Hess*, 488 U.S. 428 (1989), the Supreme Court held that the Foreign Sovereign Immunities Act (FSIA) provides the sole basis for obtaining jurisdiction over foreign states and their instrumentalities in U.S. courts. The FSIA is explored in Chapter 6.

C. The Sosa Decision: "The Door Is Still Ajar"

In June 2004, the U.S. Supreme Court addressed the scope of the ATS for the first time. The case involved a Mexican national, Humberto Alvarez-Machain, whom the U.S. government believed to be an accomplice in the murder of an undercover Drug Enforcement Administration (DEA) agent. The DEA approved the abduction of Alvarez-Machain from Mexico to the United States to stand trial. As discussed in Chapter 6, the U.S. Supreme Court rejected the argument that the kidnapping divested U.S. courts of jurisdiction over Alvarez-Machain. After Alvarez-Machain was acquitted at his murder trial, he successfully sued his abductors under the ATS, and the Ninth Circuit affirmed.

Sosa v. Alvarez-Machain

542 U.S. 692 (2004)

Justice Souter delivered the Court's opinion; he wrote for a unanimous Court in Part III of his opinion, and was joined by Justices Stevens, O'Connor, Kennedy, Ginsburg and Breyer in Part IV of his opinion. Justice Scalia filed an opinion concurring in part and concurring in the judgment, in which Justices Rehnquist and Thomas joined.

III

A

Alvarez says that the ATS was intended not simply as a jurisdictional grant, but as authority for the creation of a new cause of action for torts in violation of international law. We think that reading is implausible. As enacted in 1789, the ATS gave the district courts "cognizance" of certain causes of action, and the term bespoke a grant of jurisdiction, not power to mold substantive law. The fact that the ATS was placed in §9 of the Judiciary Act, a statute otherwise exclusively concerned with federal-court jurisdiction, is itself support for its strictly jurisdictional nature. . . . In sum, we think the statute was intended as jurisdictional in the sense of addressing the power of the courts to entertain cases concerned with a certain subject.

But holding the ATS jurisdictional raises a new question, this one about the interaction between the ATS at the time of its enactment and the ambient law of the era. . . .

1

In the years of the early Republic, [the] law of nations comprised two principal elements, the first covering the general norms governing the behavior of national states with each other. . . . This aspect of the law of nations thus occupied the executive and legislative domains, not the judicial.

The law of nations included a second, more pedestrian element, however, that did fall within the judicial sphere, as a body of judge-made law regulating the conduct of individuals situated outside domestic boundaries and consequently carrying an international savor. To Blackstone, the law of nations in this sense was implicated "in mercantile questions, such as bills of exchange and the like; in all marine causes, relating to freight, average, demurrage, insurances, bottomry . . . ; [and] in all disputes relating to prizes, to shipwrecks, to hostages, and ransom bills." 4 W. Blackstone, Commentaries on the Laws of England 67 (1769). . . .

There was, finally, a sphere in which these rules binding individuals for the benefit of other individuals overlapped with the norms of state relationships. Blackstone referred to it when he mentioned three specific offenses against the law of nations addressed by the criminal law of England: violation of safe conducts, infringement of the rights of ambassadors, and piracy. An assault against an ambassador, for example, impinged upon the sovereignty of the foreign nation and if not adequately redressed could rise to an issue of war. It was this narrow set of violations of the law of nations, admitting of a judicial remedy and at the same time threatening serious consequences in international affairs, that was probably on the minds of the men who drafted the ATS with its reference to tort.

2

Before there was any ATS, a distinctly American preoccupation with these hybrid international norms had taken shape owing to the distribution of political power from independence through the period of confederation. The Continental Congress was hamstrung by its inability to "cause infractions of treaties, or of the law of nations to be punished," J. Madison, Journal of the Constitutional Convention 60. . . .

Appreciation of the Continental Congress's incapacity to deal with this class of cases was intensified by the so-called Marbois incident of May 1784, in which a French adventurer, Longchamps, verbally and physically assaulted the Secretary of the French Legion in Philadelphia. *See Respublica v. De Longchamps*, 1 Dall. 111 (O.T. Phila. 1784). Congress called again for state legislation addressing such matters. . . .

The Framers responded by vesting the Supreme Court with original jurisdiction over "all Cases affecting Ambassadors, other public ministers and Consuls." U.S. Const., Art. III, §2, and the First Congress followed through [by enacting the ATS]. . . .

3

[Although legislative history does not clarify legislative intent, nonetheless] there is every reason to suppose that the First Congress did not pass the ATS as a jurisdictional convenience to be placed on the shelf for use by a future Congress or state legislature that might, some day, authorize the creation of causes of action or itself decide to make some element of the law of nations actionable for the benefit of foreigners. The anxieties of the preconstitutional period cannot be ignored easily enough to think that the statute was not meant to have a practical effect. . . . It would have been passing strange for . . . Congress to vest federal courts expressly with jurisdiction to entertain civil causes brought by aliens alleging violations of the law of nations, but to no effect whatever until the Congress should take further action. . . .

IV

We think it is correct, then, to assume that the First Congress understood that the district courts would recognize private causes of action for certain torts in violation of the law of nations, though we have found no basis to suspect Congress had any examples in mind beyond . . . violation of safe conducts, infringement of the rights of ambassadors, and piracy. . . . Accordingly, we think courts should require any claim based on the present-day law of nations to rest on a norm of international character accepted by the civilized world and defined with a specificity comparable to the features of the 18th-century paradigms we have recognized. . . .

[The Court reviewed a series of reasons that "argue for judicial caution" when considering the claims that fall within the scope of the ATS:]

First, the prevailing conception of the common law has changed since 1789 in a way that counsels restraint in judicially applying internationally generated norms. When §1350 was enacted, the accepted conception was of the common law as "a transcendental body of law outside of any particular State but obligatory within it unless and until changed by statute." *Black and White Taxicab & Transfer Co. v. Brown and Yellow Taxicab & Transfer Co.*, 276 U.S. 518, 533 (1928) (Holmes, J., dissenting). Now, however, in most cases where a court is asked to state or formulate a common law principle in a new context, there is a general understanding that the law is not so much found or discovered as it is either made or created. . . .

Second, along with, and in part driven by, that conceptual development in understanding common law has come an equally significant rethinking of the role of the federal courts in making it. *Erie R. Co. v. Tompkins*, 304 U.S. 64 (1938), was the watershed in which we denied the existence of any federal "general" common law. . . .

[The Court also noted that the "decision to create a private right of action is one better left to legislative judgment in the great majority of cases," that "the potential implications for the foreign relations of the United States of recognizing such causes should make courts particularly wary of impinging on the discretion of the Legislative and Executive Branches in managing foreign affairs," and that Congress had given the courts "no congressional mandate to seek out and define new and debatable violations of the law of nations."]

C

. . . [W]e are persuaded that federal courts should not recognize private claims under federal common law for violations of any international law norm with less definite content and acceptance among civilized nations than the historical paradigms familiar when §1350 was enacted. . . . And the determination whether a norm is sufficiently definite to support a cause of action[20] should (and, indeed, inevitably must) involve an element of

---

[20] A related consideration is whether international law extends the scope of liability for a violation of a given norm to the perpetrator being sued, if the defendant is a private actor such as a corporation or individual.

judgment about the practical consequences of making that cause available to litigants in the federal courts.[21]

[The Court next considered whether Alvarez's claim is actionable under the ATS. Alvarez argued that his "arbitrary arrest" was prohibited by the Universal Declaration of Human Rights and the International Covenant on Civil and Political Rights.] But the Declaration does not of its own force impose obligations as a matter of international law. And, although the Covenant does bind the United States . . . , the United States ratified the Covenant on the express understanding that it was not self-executing and so did not itself create obligations enforceable in the federal courts. Accordingly, Alvarez cannot say that the Declaration and Covenant themselves establish the relevant and applicable rule of international law. He instead attempts to show that prohibition of arbitrary arrest has attained the status of binding customary international law.

[Alvarez's claim rests not on the cross-border feature of his abduction, but on the conclusion that U.S. law did not authorize Alvarez's arrest, because the DEA lacked extra-territorial authority under federal law.]

Alvarez thus invokes a general prohibition of "arbitrary" detention defined as officially sanctioned action exceeding positive authorization to detain under the domestic law of some government. . . . Alvarez cites little authority that a rule so broad has the status of a binding customary norm today. . . . His rule would support a cause of action in federal court for any arrest, anywhere in the world, unauthorized by the law of the jurisdiction in which it took place. . . . [A] single illegal detention of less than a day, followed by the transfer of custody to lawful authorities and a prompt arraignment, violates no norm of customary international law so well defined as to support the creation of a federal remedy.

JUSTICE SCALIA, with whom THE CHIEF JUSTICE and JUSTICE THOMAS join, concurring in part and concurring in the judgment.

III

The analysis in the Court's opinion departs from my own in this respect: After concluding in Part III that "the ATS is a jurisdictional statute creating no new causes of action," the Court addresses at length in Part IV the "good reasons for a restrained conception of the *discretion* a federal court should exercise in considering a new cause of action" under the ATS. By framing the issue as one of "discretion," the Court skips over the antecedent question of authority. This neglects the "lesson of *Erie*," that "grants of jurisdiction alone" (which the Court has acknowledged the ATS to be) "are not themselves

[21] This requirement of clear definition is not meant to be the only principle limiting the availability of relief in the federal courts for violations of customary international law, though it disposes of this case. For example, the European Commission argues as *amicus curiae* that basic principles of international law require that before asserting a claim in a foreign forum, the claimant must have exhausted any remedies available in the domestic legal system, and perhaps in other fora such as international claims tribunals. We would certainly consider this requirement in an appropriate case.

Another possible limitation that we need not apply here is a policy of case-specific deference to the political branches. For example, there are now pending in federal district court several class actions seeking damages from various corporations alleged to have participated in, or abetted, the regime of apartheid that formerly controlled South Africa. The Government of South Africa has said that these cases interfere with the policy embodied by its Truth and Reconciliation Commission, which [is] . . . "based on confession and absolution, informed by the principles of reconciliation, reconstruction, reparation and goodwill." The United States has agreed. In such cases, there is a strong argument that federal courts should give serious weight to the Executive Branch's view of the case's impact on foreign policy.

grants of law-making authority." On this point, the Court observes only that no development between the enactment of the ATS (in 1789) and the birth of modern international human rights litigation under that statute (in 1980) "has categorically *precluded* federal courts from recognizing a claim under the law of nations as an element of common law." This turns our jurisprudence regarding federal common law on its head. The question is not what case or congressional action *prevents* federal courts from applying the law of nations as part of the general common law; it is what *authorizes* that peculiar exception from *Erie*'s fundamental holding that a general common law *does not exist*. . . .

* * *

We Americans have a method for making the laws that are over us. We elect representatives to two Houses of Congress, each of which must enact the new law and present it for the approval of a President, whom we also elect. For over two decades now, unelected federal judges have been usurping this lawmaking power by converting what they regard as norms of international law into American law. Today's opinion approves that process in principle, though urging the lower courts to be more restrained. . . .

Notes and Questions

1. Are you persuaded by the Court's discussion of (a) congressional intent behind the passage of the ATS, (b) the judiciary's ability to recognize claims under common law, or (c) the role of the courts in cases involving foreign relations? Which seems most important to the Court?

2. The *Sosa* majority stated that "the door is still ajar [to further independent judicial recognition of actionable international norms] subject to vigilant doorkeeping, and thus [U.S. courts remain] open to a narrow class of international norms today." Compare the sources that the *Filartiga* court used to find the existence of a customary norm prohibiting official torture and the sources that the *Sosa* court found insufficient to establish a customary norm prohibiting arbitrary detention. What sources should future ATS plaintiffs rely upon to establish the existence of a customary norm actionable in ATS litigation?

After *Sosa*, courts struggled to determine which wrongs were actionable under the ATS as well as whether corporations could be sued under the statute for violations of international law (an issue alluded to in footnote 20 of the *Sosa* opinion but not resolved). For example, in *Sarei v Rio Tinto*, 671 F.3d 736 (9th Cir. 2011), the Ninth Circuit found that genocide and war crimes are actionable under the ATS, but that "the international norm prohibiting systemic racial discrimination" is not "sufficiently specific and obligatory to give rise to a cause of action under the ATS." The court noted that the United States's ratification of the Convention on the Elimination of All Forms of Racial Discrimination contained a declaration that the treaty was not self-executing, and that the treaty's norm against systematic racial discrimination "has been given no further content through international tribunals, subsequent treaties, or similar sources of customary international law."

D. Is the Door Still Ajar?

Relying upon the *Sosa* opinion, the Kiobel defendants moved to dismiss the complaint. The district court granted the motion in part and, on appeal, the Second Circuit dismissed the complaint on the grounds that the law of nations does not recognize corporate liability for human rights abuses. 621 F.3d 111 (2d Cir. 2010). Appellate courts in other circuits—including the Seventh, Ninth, and D.C. Circuits—meanwhile concluded that nothing in the ATS precludes corporate liability. The Supreme Court granted certiorari in *Kiobel* to consider the issue of corporate liability under the ATS.

Following oral argument, however, the Court directed the parties to file supplemental briefs on an additional question: "Whether and under what circumstances the [ATS] allows courts to recognize a cause of action for violations of the law of nations occurring within the territory of a sovereign other than the United States." This question raised the applicability of a long-standing presumption that, unless a contrary intent appears, legislation is meant to apply only within the territorial jurisdiction of the United States. The presumption, which rests on the perception that Congress ordinarily legislates with respect to domestic matters only, is explored in greater detail in Chapter 6.

Kiobel v. Royal Dutch Petroleum Co.

133 S. Ct. 1659 (2013)

ROBERTS, C. J., delivered the opinion of the Court, in which SCALIA, KENNEDY, THOMAS, and ALITO, JJ., joined.

II

The question here is not whether petitioners have stated a proper claim under the ATS, but whether a claim may reach conduct occurring in the territory of a foreign sovereign. Respondents contend that claims under the ATS do not, relying primarily on a canon of statutory interpretation known as the presumption against extraterritorial application. That canon provides that "[w]hen a statute gives no clear indication of an extraterritorial application, it has none," *Morrison v. National Australia Bank Ltd.*, 561 U.S. 247, 255 (2010), and reflects the "presumption that United States law governs domestically but does not rule the world," *Microsoft Corp. v. AT&T Corp.*, 550 U.S. 437, 454 (2007). . . . This presumption "serves to protect against unintended clashes between our laws and those of other nations which could result in international discord." *EEOC v. Arabian American Oil Co.*, 499 U.S. 244, 248 (1991) (*Aramco*). . . .

[T]he danger of unwarranted judicial interference in the conduct of foreign policy is magnified in the context of the ATS, because the question is not what Congress has done but instead what courts may do. This Court in *Sosa* repeatedly stressed the need for judicial caution in considering which claims could be brought under the ATS, in light of foreign policy concerns. These concerns, which are implicated in any case arising under the ATS, are all the more pressing when the question is whether a cause of action under the ATS reaches conduct within the territory of another sovereign. . . .

The principles underlying the presumption against extraterritoriality thus constrain courts exercising their power under the ATS.

III

Petitioners contend that even if the presumption applies, the text, history, and purposes of the ATS rebut it for causes of action brought under that statute. It is true that Congress, even in a jurisdictional provision, can indicate that it intends federal law to apply to conduct occurring abroad. But to rebut the presumption, the ATS would need to evince a "clear indication of extraterritoriality." *Morrison*, 561 U.S., at 265. It does not.

To begin, nothing in the text of the statute suggests that Congress intended causes of action recognized under it to have extraterritorial reach. The ATS covers actions by aliens for violations of the law of nations, but that does not imply extraterritorial reach—such violations affecting aliens can occur either within or outside the United States. Nor does the fact that the text reaches "*any* civil action" suggest application to torts committed abroad; it is well established that generic terms like "any" or "every" do not rebut the presumption against extraterritoriality. . . .

Nor does the historical background against which the ATS was enacted overcome the presumption against application to conduct in the territory of another sovereign. We explained in *Sosa* that when Congress passed the ATS, "three principal offenses against the law of nations" had been identified by Blackstone: violation of safe conducts, infringement of the rights of ambassadors, and piracy. The first two offenses have no necessary extraterritorial application. Indeed, Blackstone—in describing them—did so in terms of conduct occurring within the forum nation.

Two notorious episodes involving violations of the law of nations occurred in the United States shortly before passage of the ATS. Each concerned the rights of ambassadors, and each involved conduct within the Union. In 1784, a French adventurer verbally and physically assaulted Francis Barbe Marbois—the Secretary of the French Legion—in Philadelphia. The assault led the French Minister Plenipotentiary to lodge a formal protest with the Continental Congress and threaten to leave the country unless an adequate remedy were provided. And in 1787, a New York constable entered the Dutch Ambassador's house and arrested one of his domestic servants. At the request of Secretary of Foreign Affairs John Jay, the Mayor of New York City arrested the constable in turn, but cautioned that because "neither Congress nor our [State] Legislature have yet passed any act respecting a breach of the privileges of Ambassadors," the extent of any available relief would depend on the common law. . . .

These prominent contemporary examples—immediately before and after passage of the ATS—provide no support for the proposition that Congress expected causes of action to be brought under the statute for violations of the law of nations occurring abroad.

The third example of a violation of the law of nations familiar to the Congress that enacted the ATS was piracy. Piracy typically occurs on the high seas. . . . Petitioners contend that because Congress surely intended the ATS to provide jurisdiction for actions against pirates, it necessarily anticipated the statute would apply to conduct occurring abroad.

Applying U.S. law to pirates, however, does not typically impose the sovereign will of the United States onto conduct occurring within the territorial jurisdiction of another sovereign, and therefore carries less direct foreign policy consequences. Pirates were fair game wherever found, by any nation, because they generally did not operate within any jurisdiction. We do not think that the existence of a cause of action against them is a sufficient basis for concluding that other causes of action under the ATS reach conduct that does occur within the territory of another sovereign; pirates may well be a category unto themselves. . . .

We therefore conclude that the presumption against extraterritoriality applies to claims under the ATS, and that nothing in the statute rebuts that presumption. . . .

IV

On these facts, all the relevant conduct took place outside the United States. And even where the claims touch and concern the territory of the United States, they must do so with sufficient force to displace the presumption against extraterritorial application.

Corporations are often present in many countries, and it would reach too far to say that mere corporate presence suffices. If Congress were to determine otherwise, a statute more specific than the ATS would be required.

JUSTICE KENNEDY, concurring.

The opinion for the Court is careful to leave open a number of significant questions regarding the reach and interpretation of the Alien Tort Statute. In my view that is a proper disposition. Many serious concerns with respect to human rights abuses committed abroad have been addressed by Congress in statutes such as the Torture Victim Protection Act of 1991 (TVPA), and that class of cases will be determined in the future according to the detailed statutory scheme Congress has enacted. Other cases may arise with allegations of serious violations of international law principles protecting persons, cases covered neither by the TVPA nor by the reasoning and holding of today's case; and in those disputes the proper implementation of the presumption against extraterritorial application may require some further elaboration and explanation.

JUSTICE BREYER, with whom JUSTICE GINSBURG, JUSTICE SOTOMAYOR and JUSTICE KAGAN join, concurring in the judgment.

In my view the majority's effort to [rely upon] the "presumption against extraterritoriality" does not work well. That presumption "rests on the perception that Congress ordinarily legislates with respect to domestic, not foreign matters." *Morrison v. National Australia Bank Ltd.*, 561 U.S. 247, 255 (2010) The ATS, however, was enacted with "foreign matters" in mind. The statute's text refers explicitly to "alien[s]," "treat[ies]," and "the law of nations." The statute's purpose was to address "violations of the law of nations, admitting of a judicial remedy and at the same time threatening serious consequences in international affairs." *Sosa*, 542 U.S., at 715. And at least one of the three kinds of activities that we found to fall within the statute's scope, namely piracy, normally takes place abroad. . . .

In applying the ATS to acts "occurring within the territory of a[nother] sovereign," I would assume that Congress intended the statute's jurisdictional reach to match the statute's underlying substantive grasp. . . . And just as we have looked to established international substantive norms to help determine the statute's substantive reach, so we should look to international jurisdictional norms to help determine the statute's jurisdictional scope.

The Restatement (Third) of Foreign Relations Law is helpful. Section 402 recognizes that, subject to §403's "reasonableness" requirement, a nation may apply its law . . . not only (1) to "conduct" that "takes place [or to persons or things] within its territory" but also (2) to the "activities, interests, status, or relations of its nationals outside as well as within its territory," (3) to "conduct outside its territory that has or is intended to have substantial effect within its territory," and (4) to certain foreign "conduct outside its territory . . . that is directed against the security of the state or against a limited class of other state interests." In addition, §404 of the Restatement explains that a "state has jurisdiction to define and prescribe punishment for certain offenses recognized by the community of nations as of universal concern, such as piracy, slave trade," and analogous behavior.

Considering these jurisdictional norms in light of both the ATS's basic purpose (to provide compensation for those injured by today's pirates) and *Sosa's* basic caution (to avoid international friction), I believe that the statute provides jurisdiction where (1) the alleged tort occurs on American soil, (2) the defendant is an American national, or (3) the defendant's conduct substantially and adversely affects an important American national interest, and that includes a distinct interest in preventing the United States from becoming a safe harbor (free of civil as well as criminal liability) for a torturer or other common enemy of mankind. . . .

Applying these jurisdictional principles to this case, however, I agree with the Court that jurisdiction does not lie. The defendants are two foreign corporations. Their shares, like those of many foreign corporations, are traded on the New York Stock Exchange. Their only presence in the United States consists of an office in New York City (actually owned by a separate but affiliated company) that helps to explain their business to potential investors. The plaintiffs are not United States nationals but nationals of other nations. The conduct at issue took place abroad. And the plaintiffs allege, not that the defendants directly engaged in acts of torture, genocide, or the equivalent, but that they helped others (who are not American nationals) to do so.

Under these circumstances . . . it would be farfetched to believe, based solely upon the defendants' minimal and indirect American presence, that this legal action helps to vindicate a distinct American interest. . . . I consequently join the Court's judgment but not its opinion.

Notes and Questions

1. Note that in its *Kiobel* opinion, the Supreme Court did not address the question of corporate liability under the ATS. Thus the disagreement among the circuit courts on the issue of corporate liability remains unresolved.

2. Does *Kiobel* shut the door to ATS litigation? Applying the presumption against extraterritoriality to ATS actions, would *Filartiga* be decided the same way today? The presumption against extraterritoriality is examined in more detail in Chapter 6.

3. Does the last paragraph of the majority opinion impose an additional burden on plaintiffs beyond the requirement that the case "touch and concern" the United States? Some argue that, after *Kiobel*, foreign corporations are largely immune to ATS suits, while actions against U.S. corporations are far more likely to "touch and concern" the United States with "sufficient force." What rationale would justify a doctrine that treats foreign corporations more favorably than U.S. corporations?

4. To the extent *Kiobel* imposes new limits on ATS litigation in federal courts, what are the likely consequences? Will plaintiffs be more likely to pursue transnational tort claims in state courts? Or might plaintiffs pursue corporate human rights litigation in courts outside the United States? Note, in this respect, that an EU regulation opens EU member states' courts to tort claims against companies that are "domiciled" within the EU or by their foreign subsidiaries, based on their conduct outside the EU.

As Justice Kennedy's concurrence notes, the *Kiobel* opinion leaves open many questions, including particularly when "claims touch and concern the territory of the United States . . . with sufficient force to displace the presumption against extraterritoriality." The federal courts of appeals have begun to address this issue.

In *Cardona v. Chiquita*, 760 F.3d 1185 (11th Cir. 2014), over 4,000 Colombian plaintiffs filed an ATS action against Chiquita Brands International, a U.S. corporation, alleging that Chiquita aided and abetted and conspired with paramilitary forces in Colombia to torture and murder trade unionists, banana-plantation workers, social activists, and others. The court dismissed the complaint, noting that all of the relevant conduct took place outside the United States, and that defendant's U.S. corporate citizenship was not sufficient to displace the presumption. In a case alleging that corporate defendants aided and abetted South Africa's apartheid policy, the Second Circuit similarly concluded that a defendant's corporate citizenship in the United States was not sufficient to displace the *Kiobel* presumption. *Balintulo v. Daimler AG*, 727 F.3d 174 (2d Cir. 2013).

Cases with greater connections to the United States have been allowed to proceed. For example, *Al Shimari v. CACI*, 758 F.3d 516 (4th Cir. 2014), involves allegations by former Abu Ghraib detainees of torture, war crimes, and cruel, inhuman, or degrading treatment against a U.S. military contractor. The court held that the presumption was displaced because the defendant was a U.S. corporation; the employees who allegedly mistreated the plaintiffs were U.S citizens and were hired in the United States; the conduct occurred at a military facility operated by the U.S. government; the conduct occurred pursuant to a contract with the U.S. government entered into in the United States; and defendant's managers in the United States allegedly gave tacit approval to the mistreatment in Iraq.

E. Closing the Door to International Legal Claims? Judging the Acts of Foreign Governments

Plaintiffs seeking redress for violations of international law face another potential obstacle to the consideration of their claims. Courts in the United States, and elsewhere, have developed an "act of state" doctrine providing that domestic courts should generally refrain from judging the validity of another state's sovereign acts taken within its own territory, even if the acts violate international legal norms. Like the doctrine of foreign sovereign immunity discussed in Chapter 6, the act of state doctrine is premised, in part, upon the juridical equality of all states and the fear that having courts in one state judging the validity of another state's acts would likely "imperil the amicable relations between governments and vex the peace of nations." *Oetjen v. Central Leather Co.*, 246 U.S. 297 (1918). However, while foreign sovereign immunity can only be invoked by sovereigns and provides a jurisdictional immunity, the act of state doctrine can be invoked by private parties and constitutes a defense on the merits.

In the United States, judicial application of this doctrine has its origins in *Underhill v. Hernandez*, 168 U.S. 250 (1897). Underhill, a U.S. citizen, had built a waterworks project for the Venezuelan government. He was living in Venezuela when, in 1892, a revolution began. Revolutionary forces, later recognized by the United States as Venezuela's government, placed Underhill under house arrest during the insurrection. After he was released and returned to the United States, Underhill filed suit in federal court seeking damages for unlawful detention and assault and battery by the Venezuelan forces. The Supreme Court held that

> [e]very sovereign state is bound to respect the independence of every other sovereign state, and the courts of one country will not sit in judgment on the acts of the government of another, done within its own territory. Redress of grievances by reason of such acts must be obtained through the means open to be availed of by sovereign powers as between themselves.

The Supreme Court's seminal modern discussion of the act of state doctrine is found in the *Sabbatino* opinion.

However offensive to the public policy of this country and its constituent States an expropriation of this kind may be, we conclude that both the national interest and progress toward the goal of establishing the rule of law among nations are best served by maintaining intact the act of state doctrine in this realm of its application. . . .

Mr. Justice White, dissenting:

I am dismayed that the Court has, with one broad stroke, declared the ascertainment and application of international law beyond the competence of the courts of the United States in a large and important category of cases. I am also disappointed in the Court's declaration that the acts of a sovereign state with regard to the property of aliens within its borders are beyond the reach of international law in the courts of this country. However clearly established that law may be, a sovereign may violate it with impunity, except insofar as the political branches of the government may provide a remedy. This backward-looking doctrine, never before declared in this Court, is carried a disconcerting step further: not only are the courts powerless to question acts of state proscribed by international law but they are likewise powerless to refuse to adjudicate the claim founded upon a foreign law; they must render judgment and thereby validate the lawless act. . . . No other civilized country has found such a rigid rule necessary for the survival of the executive branch of its government; the executive of no other government seems to require such insulation from international law adjudications in its courts; and no other judiciary is apparently so incompetent to ascertain and apply international law. . . .

IV

The reasons for nonreview, based as they are on traditional concepts of territorial sovereignty, lose much of their force when the foreign act of state is shown to be a violation of international law. All legitimate exercises of sovereign power, whether territorial or otherwise, should be exercised consistently with rules of international law, including those rules which mark the bounds of lawful state action against aliens or their property located within the territorial confines of the foreign state. Although a state may reasonably expect that the validity of its laws operating on property within its jurisdiction will not be defined by local notions of public policy of numerous other states . . . , it cannot with impunity ignore the rules governing the conduct of all nations and expect that other nations and tribunals will view its acts as within the permissible scope of territorial sovereignty. . . .

The Court puts these considerations to rest with the assumption that the decisions of the courts "of the world's major capital exporting country and principal exponent of the free enterprise system" would hardly be accepted as impartial expressions of sound legal principle. The assumption, if sound, would apply to any other problem arising from transactions that cross state lines and is tantamount to a declaration excusing this Court from any future consequential role in the clarification and application of international law. This declaration ignores the historic role which this Court and other American courts have played in applying and maintaining principles of international law. . . .

Notes and Questions

1. Should the *Sabbatino* Court have applied the international legal norms on expropriation, discussed in Chapter 2? Does the Court rest its decision not to examine the international legality of the alleged expropriation on comity? Separation of powers? Or does the act of state doctrine act as a choice of law doctrine? If so, why should the validity

of Cuba's expropriation be governed by Cuban law, rather than by international (or U.S.) law?

2. The *Sabbatino* decision was extremely unpopular. It prompted Congress to pass what has become known as the Sabbatino or Second Hickenlooper Amendment to the Foreign Assistance Act of 1964. This amendment provides:

> Notwithstanding any other provision of law, no court in the United States shall decline on the ground of the federal act of state doctrine to make a determination on the merits giving effect to the principles of international law in a case in which a claim of title or other right to property is asserted by any party including a foreign state (or a party claiming through such state) based upon (or traced through) a confiscation or other taking after January 1, 1959, by an act of that state in violation of the principles of international law, including the principles of compensation. . . .
>
> *Provided*, That this subparagraph shall not be applicable . . . in any case with respect to which the President determines the application of the act of state doctrine is required in that particular case by the foreign policy interests of the United States and a suggestion to this effect is filed on his behalf in that case with the court.

22 U.S.C. §2370(e)(2). Courts have, in general, narrowly interpreted this Amendment. The Second Circuit, for example, held that the Amendment applies only when the expropriated property is found in the United States.

Cases following *Sabbatino* revealed considerable confusion over both the scope and underlying rationale for the act of state doctrine. Two sharply divided decisions, *First National City Bank v. Banco Nacional de Cuba*, 406 U.S. 759 (1972), and *Alfred Dunhill v. Republic of Cuba*, 425 U.S. 682 (1976), raised as many questions as they answered, as in neither case was any Justice's opinion able to garner a majority of the Court. For example, in *First National City Bank*, Justice Rehnquist's plurality opinion adopted the *Bernstein* exception to the act of state doctrine, although at least five Justices rejected the exception in a splintered series of opinions. Not surprisingly, lower courts have had difficulty determining whether a *Bernstein* exception exists and, if so, its scope.

In *Dunhill*, a four-Justice plurality held that the act of state doctrine applied only to "sovereign acts" and that "the concept of an act of state should not be extended to include the repudiation of a purely commercial obligation owed by a foreign sovereign or by one of its commercial instrumentalities." 425 U.S. at 695. Four other Justices rejected this so-called commercial activity exception, and one declined to address the issue. Lower courts have split on whether this exception exists, and the Supreme Court has not addressed the issue since *Dunhill*.

Finally, courts after *Sabbatino* also split over the question of whether to apply the act of state doctrine where the plaintiff's claim would require an examination of the motivations for a foreign state's act, as opposed to an inquiry into the validity of a foreign state's act. In its most recent act of state case, the Court addressed this question.

W. S. Kirkpatrick & Co. v. Environmental Tectonics Corp., International

493 U.S. 400 (1990)

In this case we must decide whether the act of state doctrine bars a court in the United States from entertaining a cause of action that does not rest upon the asserted invalidity of an official act of a foreign sovereign, but that does require imputing to foreign officials an unlawful motivation (the obtaining of bribes) in the performance of such an official act. . . .

[Plaintiff unsuccessfully sought a construction contract from the Republic of Nigeria. After the contract was awarded, the plaintiff learned that the defendants obtained the contract by paying a bribe to Nigerian officials. The plaintiff brought this information to the U.S. Attorney, who filed criminal charges against the defendants. After the defendants pleaded guilty to these charges, the plaintiff filed a civil action against the defendants in federal district court. The defendants argued that the act of state doctrine barred the suit.

The District Court held that the act of state doctrine applies "if the inquiry presented for judicial determination includes the motivation of a sovereign act which would result in embarrassment to the sovereign or constitute interference in the conduct of foreign policy of the United States." The court dismissed the complaint because, to prevail, the plaintiff would have to show bribery of a Nigerian governmental official. The Court of Appeals for the Third Circuit reversed, relying heavily upon a State Department letter stating that judicial inquiry into the purpose behind the act of a foreign sovereign would not produce the "unique embarrassment, and the particular interference with the conduct of foreign affairs, that may result from the judicial determination that a foreign sovereign's acts are invalid."]

II

This Court's description of the jurisprudential foundation for the act of state doctrine has undergone some evolution over the years. We once viewed the doctrine as an expression of international law, resting upon "the highest considerations of international comity and expediency," *Oetjen v. Central Leather*, 246 U.S. 297, 303-04 (1918). We have more recently described it, however, as a consequence of domestic separation of powers, reflecting "the strong sense of the Judicial Branch that its engagement in the task of passing on the validity of foreign acts of state may hinder" the conduct of foreign affairs, *Banco Nacional de Cuba v. Sabbatino*, 376 U.S. 398, 423 (1964). Some Justices have suggested possible exceptions to application of the doctrine . . . , for example, for acts of state that consist of commercial transactions, since neither modern international comity nor the current position of our Executive Branch accorded sovereign immunity to such acts, or an exception for cases in which the Executive Branch has represented that it has no objection to denying validity to the foreign sovereign act, since then the courts would be impeding no foreign policy goals.

The parties have argued at length about the applicability of these possible exceptions, and, more generally, about whether the purpose of the act of state doctrine would be furthered by its application in this case. We find it unnecessary, however, to pursue those inquiries, since the factual predicate for application of the act of state doctrine does not exist. Nothing in the present suit requires the Court to declare invalid, and thus ineffective as "a rule of decision for the courts of this country," *Ricaud v. American Metal Co.*, 246 U.S. 304, 310 (1918), the official act of a foreign sovereign.

In every case in which we have held the act of state doctrine applicable, the relief sought or the defense interposed would have required a court in the United States to declare invalid the official act of a foreign sovereign performed within its own territory. In *Underhill v. Hernandez*, holding the defendant's detention of the plaintiff to be tortious would have required denying legal effect to "acts of a military commander representing the authority of the revolutionary party as government, which afterwards succeeded and was recognized by the United States." . . . In *Sabbatino*, upholding the defendant's claim to the funds would have required a holding that Cuba's expropriation of goods located in Havana was null and void. In the present case, by contrast, neither the claim nor any asserted defense requires a determination that Nigeria's contract with Kirkpatrick International was, or was not, effective.

Petitioners point out . . . that in order to prevail respondent must prove that petitioner Kirkpatrick made, and Nigerian officials received, payments that violate Nigerian law, which would, they assert, support a finding that the contract is invalid under Nigerian law. Assuming that to be true, it still does not suffice. The act of state doctrine is not some vague doctrine of abstention but a "*principle of decision* binding on federal and state courts alike." *Sabbatino, supra,* at 427 (emphasis added). . . . Act of state issues only arise when a court *must decide*—that is, when the outcome of the case turns upon—the effect of official action by a foreign sovereign. When that question is not in the case, neither is the act of state doctrine. That is the situation here. Regardless of what the court's factual findings may suggest as to the legality of the Nigerian contract, its legality is simply not a question to be decided in the present suit, and there is thus no occasion to apply the rule of decision that the act of state doctrine requires. . . .

Petitioners insist, however, that the policies underlying our act of state cases—international comity, respect for the sovereignty of foreign nations on their own territory, and the avoidance of embarrassment to the Executive Branch in its conduct of foreign relations—are implicated in the present case because, as the District Court found, a determination that Nigerian officials demanded and accepted a bribe "would impugn or question the nobility of a foreign nation's motivations," and would "result in embarrassment to the sovereign or constitute interference in the conduct of foreign policy of the United States." The United States, as *amicus curiae*, favors the same approach to the act of state doctrine, though disagreeing with petitioners as to the outcome it produces in the present case. . . .

These urgings are deceptively similar to what we said in *Sabbatino*, where we observed that sometimes, even though the validity of the act of a foreign sovereign within its own territory is called into question, the policies underlying the act of state doctrine may not justify its application. We suggested that a sort of balancing approach could be applied—the balance shifting against application of the doctrine, for example, if the government that committed the "challenged act of state" is no longer in existence. But what is appropriate in order to avoid unquestioning judicial acceptance of the acts of foreign sovereigns is not similarly appropriate for the quite opposite purpose of expanding judicial incapacities where such acts are not directly (or even indirectly) involved. It is one thing to suggest, as we have, that the policies underlying the act of state doctrine should be considered in deciding whether, despite the doctrine's technical availability, it should nonetheless not be invoked; it is something quite different to suggest that those underlying policies are a doctrine unto themselves, justifying expansion of the act of state doctrine . . . into new and uncharted fields.

The short of the matter is this: Courts in the United States have the power, and ordinarily the obligation, to decide cases and controversies properly presented to them. The act of state doctrine does not establish an exception for cases and controversies that may embarrass foreign governments, but merely requires that, in the process of deciding, the acts of foreign sovereigns taken within their own jurisdictions shall be deemed valid. That doctrine has no application to the present case because the validity of no foreign sovereign act is at issue. . . .

Notes and Questions

1. Does the Court satisfactorily explain the distinction between an inquiry into the "motivation" for the acts of a foreign state and inquiry into the "validity" of the acts of a foreign state? Does the plaintiff's case require an inquiry into the validity of the Nigerian contract? Is "validity" the same as "legality"?

2. After *Kirkpatrick* (a unanimous opinion), does the act of state doctrine still rest upon a separation of powers rationale? What does the court mean when it says that the doctrine is not "some vague doctrine of abstention" but a "principle of decision"?

3. Do not virtually all ATS actions involve an inquiry into the validity of acts of a foreign state? Do the policy rationales supporting act of state — including international comity, respect for the acts of foreign sovereigns on their own territory, and concerns over judicial interference with foreign relations — counsel dismissal of most ATS actions?

6

The Reach of Domestic Law in the International Arena: Jurisdiction and Its Limits

I. LIMITING THE REACH OF DOMESTIC LAW

Many of the most difficult and controversial international legal disputes arise when states seek to assert authority over persons, property, or events abroad. These disputes often involve the extraterritorial application of domestic law in ways that affect the interests of other states and at times are contrary to international legal limits on the exercise of jurisdiction. Given the frequency with which these disputes arise, Rosalyn Higgins, a former judge of the International Court of Justice (ICJ), stated that "[t]here is no more important way to avoid conflict than by providing clear norms as to which state can exercise authority over whom, and in what circumstances. . . ." Rosalyn Higgins, Problems and Process: International Law and How We Use It 57 (1994).

Litigants often ask domestic courts to address the international legality of extraterritorial assertions of jurisdiction. In addition, Legislative and Executive Branches also address these issues as they consider whether and when to assert extraterritorial jurisdiction. The legal limits on a state's exercise of jurisdiction implicate both domestic and international legal norms—which may or may not be consistent with each other.

States assert their authority over people, things, and events in various ways. For international law purposes, these assertions of authority fall within one of three categories. The first is "jurisdiction to prescribe," which refers to a state's authority or competence to promulgate law applicable to persons or activities. As this jurisdiction is typically exercised by legislative bodies, it is sometimes called legislative jurisdiction. But because government authorities other than legislatures also prescribe laws and regulations, the broader term "prescriptive jurisdiction" is more accurate. International law limits on prescriptive jurisdiction can be analogized to domestic constitutional law limits on the scope of legislative authority. In Section II of this chapter, we explore various bases upon which states can exercise jurisdiction to prescribe. The second type of jurisdiction is "jurisdiction to adjudicate," which refers to a state's authority or competence to subject persons or things to its judicial processes. International law limits on adjudicative jurisdiction can be analogized to domestic law limits on a court's exercise of personal jurisdiction. The third type of jurisdiction is "jurisdiction to enforce," which refers to a state's authority or competence to induce or compel compliance with its law through its courts, as well as through executive, administrative, or police action. In Section III of this chapter, we explore these two types of jurisdiction. Finally, in Section IV, we examine an important immunity from jurisdiction, foreign sovereign immunity.

As you review the materials in this chapter, keep in mind that the norms governing jurisdiction are largely customary and hence not the result of deliberate and purposeful acts of assembled states at any one time. Consider why international law developed *any* limitations on the ability of autonomous states to exercise jurisdiction and why the particular limitations that exist were developed. What purposes are served, and what values are furthered, by these norms? Finally, consider how states deal with conflicting claims of jurisdiction and whether the "system" that exists provides clear norms regarding the exercise of jurisdiction.

A. *The* Lotus *Case*

On August 2, 1926, the *Lotus*, a French mail steamer, collided with the *Boz-Kourt*, a Turkish vessel, on the high seas. The collision sank the *Boz-Kourt* and caused the deaths of eight Turkish nationals. The accident was allegedly caused by the gross negligence of the *Lotus*'s watch officer, Lieutenant Demons. The day after the collision, the *Lotus* arrived in Constantinople, and Turkish authorities asked Lieutenant Demons to go ashore and provide evidence. Following his examination, Lieutenant Demons was placed under arrest and later charged with involuntary manslaughter by the Public Prosecutor of Stamboul (now Istanbul). The Criminal Court of Stamboul rejected Demons's argument that it lacked jurisdiction over him. Following a trial, Demons was found guilty and sentenced to 80 days' imprisonment and fined 22 Turkish pounds. By special agreement, France and Turkey asked the Permanent Court of International Justice to determine whether Turkey "acted in conflict with the principles of international law" by instituting criminal proceedings against Demons.

The S.S. "Lotus" (France/Turkey)
P.C.I.J., Ser. A, No. 10, p. 4 (1927)

The Court . . . is confronted in the first place by a question of principle which . . . has proved to be a fundamental one. The French Government contends that the Turkish Courts, in order to have jurisdiction, should be able to point to some title to jurisdiction recognized by international law in favor of Turkey. On the other hand, the Turkish Government takes the view that [it can exercise] jurisdiction whenever such jurisdiction does not come into conflict with a principle of international law.

The latter view seems to be in conformity with the special agreement itself . . . which asks the Court to say whether Turkey has acted contrary to the principles of international law and, if so, what principles. . . .

This way of stating the question is also dictated by the very nature and existing conditions of international law.

International law governs relations between independent States. The rules of law binding upon States therefore emanate from their own free will as expressed in conventions or by usages generally accepted as expressing principles of law and established in order to regulate the relations between these co-existing independent communities or with a view to the achievement of common aims. Restrictions upon the independence of States cannot therefore be presumed.

Now the first and foremost restriction imposed by international law upon a State is that—failing the existence of a permissive rule to the contrary—it may not exercise its power in any form in the territory of another State. In this sense jurisdiction is certainly territorial; it cannot be exercised by a State outside its territory except by virtue of a permissive rule derived from international custom or from a convention.

It does not, however, follow that international law prohibits a State from exercising jurisdiction in its own territory, in respect of any case which relates to acts which have taken place abroad, and in which it cannot rely on some permissive rule of international law. . . . Far from laying down a general prohibition to the effect that States may not extend the application of their laws and the jurisdiction of their courts to persons, property and acts outside their territory, [international law] leaves them in this respect a wide measure of discretion which is only limited in certain cases by prohibitive rules; as regards other cases, every State remains free to adopt the principles which it regards as best and most suitable. . . .

It follows from the foregoing that the contention of the French Government to the effect that Turkey must in each case be able to cite a rule of international law authorizing her to exercise jurisdiction, is opposed to the generally accepted international law. . . .

[France argues that] international law does not allow a state to take proceedings with regard to offenses committed by foreigners abroad, simply by reason of the nationality of the victim. . . .

. . . Even if that argument were correct generally speaking—and in regard to this the Court reserves its opinion—it could only be used in the present case if international law forbade Turkey to take into consideration the fact that the offense produced its effects on the Turkish vessel and consequently in a place assimilated to Turkish territory in which the application of Turkish criminal law cannot be challenged. . . . But no such rule of international law exists. . . . On the contrary . . . the courts of many countries . . . interpret criminal law in the sense that offenses, the authors of which at the moment of commission are in the territory of another state, are nevertheless to be regarded as having been committed in the national territory if one of the constituent elements of the offense, and more especially its effects, have taken place there. . . . Consequently, it becomes impossible to hold that there is a rule of international law which prohibits Turkey from prosecuting Lieutenant Demons because of the fact that . . . [Demons] was on board the French ship. . . .

The second argument put forward by the French Government is the principle that the State whose flag is flown has exclusive jurisdiction over everything which occurs on board a merchant ship on the high seas. . . .

. . . All that can be said is that . . . a ship is placed in the same position as national territory. . . . It follows that what occurs on board a vessel on the high seas must be regarded as if it occurred on the territory of the State whose flag the ship flies. If, therefore, a guilty act committed on the high seas produces its effects on a vessel flying another flag . . . the same principles must be applied as if the territories of two different States were concerned, and the conclusion must therefore be drawn that there is no rule of international law prohibiting the State to which the ship on which the effects of the offense have taken place belongs, from regarding the offense as having been committed in its territory. . . .

The offense . . . was an act . . . having its origin on board the *Lotus*, whilst its effects made themselves felt on board the *Boz-Kourt*. These two elements are, legally, entirely inseparable, so much so that their separation renders the offense nonexistent. Neither the exclusive jurisdiction of either State, nor the limitations of the jurisdiction of each of the occurrences which took place on the respective ships would appear calculated to satisfy the requirements of justice and effectively to protect the interests of the two States. It is only natural that each should be able to exercise jurisdiction and to do so in respect of the incident as a whole. It is therefore a case of concurrent jurisdiction. . . .

Notes and Questions

1. The Judges of the Permanent Court were evenly divided in *Lotus*; in these circumstances, the President of the Court breaks the tie by voting twice. In dissent, Judge Bernard Loder (Netherlands) argued:

> The fundamental consequence of the[] independence and sovereignty [of states] is that no municipal law, in the particular case under consideration no criminal law, can apply or have binding effect outside the national territory. . . .
> The criminal law of a State may extend to crimes and offenses committed abroad by its nationals, since such nationals are subject to the law of their own country; but it *cannot* extend to offenses committed by a foreigner in foreign territory, without infringing the sovereign rights of the foreign State concerned, since in that State the State enacting the law has no jurisdiction. . . .

2. Is *Lotus* about how to allocate the burden of proof on jurisdictional issues? Or does it stand for a more fundamental proposition about the international legal system? Is the Court suggesting, as Judge Loder charged elsewhere in his dissent, that "under international law everything which is not prohibited is permitted"? How could such a principle be justified?

3. How persuasive is the following critique:

> [T]he reasoning of the majority seems to imply that the process by which the international principles of penal jurisdiction have been formed is by the imposition of certain limitations on originally unlimited competence, and this is surely historically unsound. The original conception of law was personal, and it was only the rise of the modern territorial State that subjected aliens—even when they happened to be resident in a State not their own—to the law of that State. International law did not start as the law of a society of States each of omnicompetent jurisdiction, but of States possessing a personal jurisdiction over their own nationals and later acquiring a territorial jurisdiction over resident non-nationals. If it is alleged that they have now acquired a measure of jurisdiction over non-resident non-nationals, a valid international custom to that effect should surely be established by those who allege it.

J.L. Brierly, *The Lotus Case*, 44 L.Q. Rev. 154, 156 (1928).

4. What is the flaw in the following jurisdictional syllogism—(1) under international law, the extraterritorial exercise of jurisdiction is generally forbidden, save for a handful of exceptions; (2) Turkish jurisdiction in this case did not fall within any of these exceptions; (3) therefore, Turkey's exercise of jurisdiction violated international law norms.

B. Creating International Law on Jurisdiction

Lotus remains a landmark of twentieth-century international legal jurisprudence. But suppose that an individual, a trade association, a state, or a number of states disagreed with the Court's holding? What strategies might they pursue?

Shortly after the *Lotus* decision was rendered, the International Association of Mercantile Marine Officers expressed a concern that the Court's holding would permit masters (and shipowners) to be prosecuted by the state where the vessel put in as well as the flag state. The Association raised the issue before the League of Nations Advisory and Technical Committee for Communications and Transit. The Association also brought the issue to the Permanent Committee on Ports and Maritime Navigation, and to the International Labour Office's Bureau, Governing Body, and Joint Maritime Commission. Eventually, the issue was referred to the International Maritime Committee (IMC)—a private body organized by national groups of maritime lawyers in 1897—which considered the issue for many years. In 1933, the IMC unanimously adopted a resolution approving

the principle that in cases of a collision upon the high seas no criminal or disciplinary proceedings arising out of such collision should be permissible against [any person] in the service of the ship except in the ports of the State of which the [person] is a national or of which his ship was flying the flag at the moment of collision. . . .

Thereafter, the issue was raised in various regional and international negotiations. In March 1940 a number of Latin American states adopted an International Penal Law treaty, which provided that "crimes committed on the high seas . . . must be tried and punished according to the law of the State whose flag the vessel flies." Thereafter, the IMC's 1952 Brussels Conference adopted the International Convention for the Unification of Certain Rules Relating to Penal Jurisdiction in Matters of Collision or Other Incidents of Navigation, which provides in Article I that in the event of a collision at sea, criminal proceedings may be instituted only by the state whose flag the vessel was flying at the time of the collision.

Both the 1958 Convention on the High Seas, the first major effort to codify oceans law, and the 1982 United Nations Convention on the Law of the Sea, a treaty examined in detail in Chapter 10, provide that in the event of a high seas collision "involving the penal or disciplinary responsibility of [any person] in the service of the ship, no penal or disciplinary proceedings may be instituted against such persons except before the judicial or administrative authorities either of the flag State or of the State of which such person is a national."

These provisions, of course, effectively reverse the *Lotus* holding for the parties to these treaties. For current purposes, consider the law making process employed. International law was traditionally considered to be formed though state action, but here a complex legal process was set in motion by a high seas collision between vessels owned by two private parties. This was followed by a domestic court action, a bilateral agreement, and an authoritative pronouncement by an international tribunal. However, this judicial decision proved highly unsatisfactory to a directly affected group, which then sought to influence domestic and international law makers to adopt a rule other than that announced by the Court. After inconclusive consideration by several international bodies, the International Maritime Committee—a private body of shipowners, merchants, bankers, and other parties interested in the maritime trade—injected itself in the law making process. At IMC urging, states eventually adopted a jurisdictional rule preferred by IMC members.

Recalling the discussion of "public interest" NGOs and corporations in Chapter 4, consider whether it is appropriate to have "special interest" groups like the International Association of Mercantile Marine Officers and the IMC play such a central role in the law making process.

II. JURISDICTION TO MAKE AND APPLY LAW: THE EU DIRECTIVE ON AIRCRAFT EMISSIONS

States have claimed a number of bases for the exercise of jurisdiction to prescribe, with varying degrees of international acceptance. The most commonly used and accepted is the "territorial principle," under which a state has jurisdiction to make law applicable to all persons and property within its territory.

During the nineteenth century, many states also understood the territorial principle to strictly limit the ability of states to regulate conduct outside their territory. In *The Apollon*, 22 U.S. 362 (1824), the Supreme Court held that "[t]he laws of no nation can justly extend beyond its own territories, except so far as regards its own citizens." The Court observed that extraterritorial assertion of jurisdiction to prescribe would be "at variance with the independence and sovereignty of foreign nations," and that such extraterritorial claims had "never yet been acknowledged by other nations, and would be resisted by none with more pertinacity than by the American." Relying on this view of the "law of nations," the Court declared that "however general and comprehensive the phrases used in our municipal laws may be, they must always be restricted in construction, to places and persons, upon whom the Legislature have authority and jurisdiction." Despite its historic importance, the presumption that domestic statutes have only territorial reach and its underlying rationale have significantly eroded in the post-World War II era, as illustrated by the materials that follow.

The goals for this Problem include:

- to understand the evolution of the territorial principle and continuing debates over the international legal norms governing the extraterritorial reach of domestic legislation;
- to understand the other bases upon which states assert jurisdiction; and
- to understand different ways that conflicting claims over jurisdiction can be addressed.

A. The Problem

Climate change is a global problem. However, efforts to craft an effective global response have met with limited success. In the absence of a strong global regime, a wide variety of regional, national, and private efforts have emerged. The European Union has been particularly active in this area. For example, in 2005, the EU began implementing the world's first mandatory carbon dioxide trading program. The European Trading Scheme (ETS) limits greenhouse gas emissions by creating a "cap and trade" program which sets a mandatory "cap" on emissions in any year; the cap is lowered over time.

At present, aviation accounts for approximately 2 to 3 percent of global emissions of greenhouse gases. However, aviation is one of the most rapidly growing sources of carbon emissions; the International Civil Aviation Organization (ICAO) estimates that carbon dioxide emissions from aviation almost doubled between 1990 and 2006, and predicts that they will continue to grow rapidly over the next several decades.

Aviation is a particular concern to the EU; from 1990 to 2010, overall EU carbon emissions declined by roughly 5 percent, while aviation emissions grew by approximately

80 percent. However, aviation emissions are virtually unregulated at the international level. The Kyoto Protocol, a climate change treaty discussed in more detail in Chapter 11, states that aviation emissions should be addressed by the ICAO, but lengthy negotiations at ICAO have not produced a binding agreement on emissions targets.

As originally enacted, the ETS covered power plants and energy-intensive industrial sectors. In 2008, the EU adopted an Aviation Directive, EU Directive 2008/101/EC, which expanded the ETS to cover aviation as of January 1, 2012. The Aviation Directive covers flights arriving in or departing from an airport within the European Union. The Directive provides that emissions are calculated on the entire length of the flight. Under this approach, emissions calculations on international flights will include emissions while the aircraft is flying over third states or the high seas. For example, it is estimated that for a flight from San Francisco to London, 29 percent of emissions will occur in U.S. airspace, 37 percent in Canadian airspace, 25 percent over the high seas, and 9 percent over EU airspace. The airline would be assessed for all of the emissions associated with the flight, regardless of where they occurred. Under the Directive, airlines would have been required to report their 2012 emissions by March 31, 2013, and to surrender allowances to cover those emissions by April 31, 2013. Flights from states that have adopted measures to reduce aviation emissions could be exempted from the Directive.

A wide variety of international actors vigorously objected to the Aviation Directive. More than two dozen states met in India in September 2011 to denounce the Directive; China reportedly suspended some $4 billion worth of aircraft orders from Airbus, a manufacturer owned by European governments; and the ICAO adopted a nonbinding resolution calling on the EU to exempt international operators from the Directive. Moreover, in November 2012, U.S. President Barack Obama signed the "European Union Emissions Trading Scheme Prohibition Act," which authorized the U.S. Secretary of Transportation to forbid U.S. carriers from participating in the ETS.

The Directive also sparked a high-profile legal challenge. In December 2009, three U.S. airlines and the Air Transport Association of America, a trade group, filed an action in the High Court of Justice of England and Wales, Queen's Bench Division. They alleged that the UK regulations implementing the Directive were "not compatible with international law and [are] therefore invalid." Because the suit involved questions of EU law, the action was referred to the European Court of Justice to consider whether, to the extent the Directive applies to those parts of flights outside EU airspace, it violates international law limits on jurisdiction.

B. Prescribing Law Based on Territorial Links

Courts in the United States and elsewhere are frequently asked to rule upon the scope and limits of the exercise of jurisdiction pursuant to the territorial principle. As we will see in the materials that follow, the principle has undergone considerable evolution over the last century. We begin by examining how, over time, U.S. courts have treated extraterritorial assertions of jurisdiction. While many of the cases explored below involve antitrust issues, questions regarding the extraterritorial reach of domestic statutes arise in many other legal contexts as well.

In 1903, Sam McConnell, an American businessman, bought a banana plantation in what is now Panama but was then part of Colombia. McConnell soon realized that the United Fruit Company controlled both the local banana industry and the local military.

United Fruit threatened to put McConnell out of business if he did not sell his assets to United Fruit. McConnell refused. In November 1903, Panama became independent and, shortly thereafter, McConnell sold his plantation to American Banana, a U.S. corporation. Costa Rican soldiers invaded Panama, allegedly at the behest of United Fruit, and seized American Banana's plantation. Through *ex parte* proceedings in a Costa Rican court, the plantation was transferred to an individual who then sold the land to United Fruit. American Banana filed a complaint in a U.S. court alleging that United Fruit's activities violated the Sherman Antitrust Act, which prohibits "[e]very contract, combination . . . or conspiracy, in restraint of trade or commerce." Justice Holmes, writing for the Supreme Court in *American Banana Co. v. United Fruit Co.*, 213 U.S. 347, 355-357 (1909), discussed whether U.S. antitrust laws governed United Fruit's conduct in Panama:

> It is obvious that, however stated, the plaintiff's case depends on several rather startling propositions. In the first place, the acts causing the damage were done, so far as appears, outside the jurisdiction of the United States, and within that of other states. It is surprising to hear it argued that they were governed by the act of Congress.
>
> . . . [T]he general and almost universal rule is that the character of an act as lawful or unlawful must be determined wholly by the law of the country where the act is done. . . . For another jurisdiction, if it should happen to lay hold of the actor, to treat him according to its own notions rather than those of the place where he did the acts, not only would be unjust, but would be an interference with the authority of another sovereign, contrary to the comity of nations, which the other state concerned justly might resent. . . .
>
> The foregoing considerations would lead in case of doubt to a construction of any statute as intended to be confined in its operation and effect to the territorial limits over which the lawmaker has general and legitimate power. "All legislation is prima facie territorial." Words having universal scope, such as "every contract in restraint of trade," "every person who shall monopolize," etc., will be taken, as a matter of course, to mean only everyone subject to such legislation, not all that the legislator subsequently may be able to catch. In the case of the present statute, the improbability of the United States attempting to make acts done in Panama or Costa Rica criminal is obvious. . . . We think it entirely plain that what the defendant did in Panama or Costa Rica is not within the scope of the statute so far as the present suit is concerned. . . .

1. Extending the Reach of the Territorial Principle

As *American Banana* illustrates, the governing assumption in the early 1900s was that jurisdiction was territorial. However, with the increasing internationalization of economic activity, governments increasingly viewed the territorial test as overly restrictive. Courts in the United States and elsewhere replaced the territorial test with one that examined whether the foreign conduct had an effect in the forum state.

United States v. Aluminum Co. of America (Alcoa) remains a landmark in the U.S. development of the effects doctrine. The suit arose out of the government's attempts to break up Alcoa's aluminum holdings and to prohibit Alcoa and Aluminum Limited (Limited), a Canadian corporation, from engaging in an international cartel with several major European aluminum companies. The Second Circuit, sitting by certification as a court of final appeal because the Supreme Court lacked a quorum, addressed whether the Sherman Act reached Limited's participation in the cartel, even though most of Limited's cartel-related activities occurred outside the United States. The court, in an opinion by Judge Learned Hand, reasoned as follows:

United States v. Aluminum Co. of America (Alcoa)

148 F.2d 416 (2d Cir. 1945)

Whether "Limited" itself violated [the Sherman Act] depends upon the character of the "Alliance." It was a Swiss corporation, created [through an agreement among Limited and several European companies. The Alliance made agreements in 1931 and 1936 that governed the sale of aluminum by Limited and the European companies.] . . .

Did either the agreement of 1931 or that of 1936 violate §1 of the Act? . . . [We] are concerned only with whether Congress chose to attach liability to the conduct outside the United States of persons not in allegiance to it. That being so, the only question open is whether Congress intended to impose the liability, and whether our own Constitution permitted it to do so: as a court of the United States, we cannot look beyond our own law. Nevertheless, it is quite true that we are not to read general words, such as those in this Act, without regard to the limitations customarily observed by nations upon the exercise of their powers; limitations which generally correspond to those fixed by the "Conflict of Laws." We should not impute to Congress an intent to punish all whom its courts can catch, for conduct which has no consequences within the United States. *American Banana Co. v. United Fruit Co.* On the other hand, it is settled law—as "Limited" itself agrees—that any state may impose liabilities, even upon persons not within its allegiance, for conduct outside its borders that has consequences within its borders which the state reprehends; and these liabilities other states will ordinarily recognize. It may be argued that this Act extends further. Two situations are possible. There may be agreements made beyond our borders not intended to affect imports, which do affect them, or which affect exports. Almost any limitation of the supply of goods in Europe, for example, or in South America, may have repercussions in the United States if there is trade between the two. Yet when one considers the international complications likely to arise from an effort in this country to treat such agreements as unlawful, it is safe to assume that Congress certainly did not intend the Act to cover them. Such agreements may on the other hand intend to include imports into the United States, and yet it may appear that they have had no effect upon them. That situation might be thought to fall within the doctrine that intent may be a substitute for performance in the case of a contract made within the United States; or it might be thought to fall within the doctrine that a statute should not be interpreted to cover acts abroad which have no consequence here. We shall not choose between these alternatives; but for argument we shall assume that the Act does not cover agreements, even though intended to affect imports or exports, unless its performance is shown actually to have had some effect upon them. . . .

Both agreements would clearly have been unlawful, had they been made within the United States; and it follows from what we have just said that both were unlawful, though made abroad, if they were intended to affect imports and did affect them. . . . [The court finds that the 1936 agreement restricting production was intended to restrict imports into the United States, had such an effect, and therefore violated U.S. antitrust laws.]

The *Alcoa* effects test quickly gained wide acceptance in U.S. courts, and U.S. government agencies and courts repeatedly applied federal antitrust laws to conduct taking place partially or wholly outside the United States. However, the extraterritorial assertion of U.S. law gave rise to considerable friction between the United States and other states. These tensions arose, in part, out of disagreements over the appropriate substantive content of antitrust law and in part out of a belief by other states that foreign law ought to regulate conduct occurring on foreign territory. As the British Secretary of State for Trade stated during a 1979 parliamentary debate:

> [W]e do not dispute the right of the United States or any other nation to pass and enforce what economic laws it likes to govern business operating fully within its own country. Our objection arises only at the point when a country attempts to achieve the maximum beneficial regulation of its own economic environment by ensuring that all those having any contact with it abide by its laws and legal principles.
>
> [These U.S. efforts are] an attempt to export economic policy and law to persons domiciled in countries that may have different legal systems and priorities, without recognizing that those countries have the right to lay down the standards to be observed by those trading within their jurisdiction.

Dissatisfaction with the *Alcoa* test, along with uncertainties regarding the test's scope and limits, prompted judicial efforts to refine this test. Several courts invoked the principle of "comity"—the respect that sovereigns extend to one another—and developed a "jurisdictional rule of reason" which balanced the interests of the United States with those of foreign jurisdictions. However, foreign litigants and states continued to challenge extraterritorial application of the Sherman Act, and the Supreme Court addressed the question in *Hartford Fire v. California*.

Hartford Fire involved 19 U.S. states and numerous private plaintiffs, who alleged that certain London reinsurers, who sell insurance to primary insurers, conspired to coerce primary insurers in the United States to make certain changes in their insurance contracts that were advantageous to the reinsurers. Plaintiffs alleged that the reinsurers would boycott any insurance company that failed to make these changes, in violation of the Sherman Act. A central question was whether U.S. antitrust law governed British reinsurers concerning reinsurance written by them in London relating to primary insurance written by U.S. companies in the United States, where the British Parliament had established a comprehensive regulatory regime over the UK reinsurance market. Relevant portions of the Court's opinion follow:

Hartford Fire Insurance Co. v. California

509 U.S. 764 (1993)

[JUSTICE SOUTER, joined by JUSTICES WHITE, BLACKMUN, STEVENS, and REHNQUIST, delivered the opinion of the Court with respect to the extraterritorial reach of the Sherman Act.]

III

At the outset, we note that the District Court undoubtedly had jurisdiction of these Sherman Act claims. . . . Although the proposition was perhaps not always free from doubt, see *American Banana Co. v. United Fruit Co.*, it is well established by now that the Sherman Act applies to foreign conduct that was meant to produce and did in fact produce some substantial effect in the United States. Such is the conduct alleged here: that the London reinsurers engaged in unlawful conspiracies to affect the market for insurance in the United States and that their conduct in fact produced substantial effect.

According to the London reinsurers, the District Court should have declined to exercise such jurisdiction under the principle of international comity. . . . [However, w]e need not decide that question here, however, for even assuming that in a proper case a court may decline to exercise Sherman Act jurisdiction over foreign conduct . . . international comity would not counsel against exercising jurisdiction in the circumstances alleged here.

The only substantial question in this litigation is whether "there is in fact a true conflict between domestic and foreign law." *Société Nationale Industrielle Aérospatiale v. United States District Court for Southern Dist. of Iowa*, 482 U.S. 522, 555 (1987) (Blackmun, J., concurring in part and dissenting in part). The London reinsurers contend that applying the Act to their conduct would conflict significantly with British law, and the British Government, appearing before us as *amicus curiae*, concurs. They assert that Parliament has established a comprehensive regulatory regime over the London reinsurance market and that the conduct alleged here was perfectly consistent with British law and policy. But this is not to state a conflict. . . . No conflict exists, for these purposes, "where a person subject to regulation by two states can comply with the laws of both." Restatement (Third) Foreign Relations Law §403, Comment *e*. Since the London reinsurers do not argue that British law requires them to act in some fashion prohibited by the law of the United States, or claim that their compliance with the laws of both countries is otherwise impossible, we see no conflict with British law. We have no need in this litigation to address other considerations that might inform a decision to refrain from the exercise of jurisdiction on grounds of international comity. . . .

JUSTICE SCALIA, joined by JUSTICES O'CONNOR, KENNEDY, and THOMAS, dissenting. . . .

II

. . . It is important to distinguish two distinct questions raised by this petition: whether the District Court had jurisdiction, and whether the Sherman Act reaches the extraterritorial conduct alleged here. On the first question . . . Respondents asserted nonfrivolous claims under the Sherman Act, and 28 U.S.C. §1331 vests district courts with subject-matter jurisdiction over cases "arising under" federal statutes. As precedents . . . make clear, that is sufficient to establish the District Court's jurisdiction over these claims. . . .

The second question—the extraterritorial reach of the Sherman Act—has nothing to do with the jurisdiction of the courts. It is a question of substantive law turning on whether, in enacting the Sherman Act, Congress asserted regulatory power over the challenged conduct. If a plaintiff fails to prevail on this issue, the court does not dismiss the claim for want of subject-matter jurisdiction—want of power to adjudicate; rather, it decides the claim, ruling on the merits that the plaintiff has failed to state a cause of action under the relevant statute.

There is, however, a type of "jurisdiction" relevant to determining the extraterritorial reach of a statute; it is known as "legislative jurisdiction," or "jurisdiction to prescribe." . . . Congress has broad power . . . "[t]o regulate Commerce with foreign Nations," and this Court has repeatedly upheld its power to make laws applicable to persons or activities beyond our territorial boundaries where United States interests are affected. But the question in this litigation is whether, and to what extent, Congress *has* exercised that undoubted legislative jurisdiction in enacting the Sherman Act.

Two canons of statutory construction are relevant in this inquiry. The first is the "longstanding principle of American law 'that legislation of Congress, unless a contrary intent appears, is meant to apply only within the territorial jurisdiction of the United States.'" [*EEOC v. Arabian American Oil Co. [Aramco]*, 499 U.S. 244, 248 (1991).] Applying that canon in *Aramco*, we held that the version of Title VII of the Civil Rights Act of 1964 then in force [prohibiting discrimination in employment] did not extend outside the territory of the United States even though the statute contained broad provisions extending its prohibitions to, for example, "any activity, business, or industry in commerce." We held such "boilerplate language" to be an insufficient indication to override the presumption against extraterritoriality. The Sherman Act contains similar "boilerplate language," and if the question were not governed by precedent, it would be worth considering whether that presumption controls the outcome here. We have, however, found the presumption to be overcome with respect to our antitrust laws; it is now well established that the Sherman Act applies extraterritorially.

But if the presumption against extraterritoriality has been overcome or is otherwise inapplicable, a second canon of statutory construction becomes relevant: "[A]n act of congress ought never to be construed to violate the law of nations if any other possible construction remains." *Murray v. Schooner Charming Betsy*, 6 U.S. (2 Cranch) 64, 118 (1804) (Marshall, C.J.). This canon is "wholly independent" of the presumption against extraterritoriality. It is relevant to determining the substantive reach of a statute because "the law of nations," or customary international law, includes limitations on a nation's exercise of its jurisdiction to prescribe. Though it clearly has constitutional authority to do so, Congress is generally presumed not to have exceeded those customary international law limits on jurisdiction to prescribe.

Consistent with that presumption, this and other courts have frequently recognized that . . . statutes should not be interpreted to regulate foreign persons or conduct if that regulation would conflict with principles of international law. . . .

In proceeding to apply that practice to the present cases, I shall rely on the Restatement (Third) for the relevant principles of international law. . . . Whether the Restatement precisely reflects international law in every detail matters little here, as I believe this litigation would be resolved the same way under virtually any conceivable test that takes account of foreign regulatory interests.

Under the Restatement, a nation having some "basis" for jurisdiction to prescribe law should nonetheless refrain from exercising that jurisdiction "with respect to a person or activity having connections with another state when the exercise of such jurisdiction is unreasonable." Restatement (Third) §403(1). The "reasonableness" inquiry turns on a number of factors including, but not limited to: "the extent to which the activity takes place within the territory [of the regulating state]," *id.*, §403(2)(a); "the connections, such as nationality, residence, or economic activity, between the regulating state and the person principally responsible for the activity to be regulated," *id.*, §403(2)(b); "the character of the activity to be regulated, the importance of regulation to the regulating state, the extent to which other states regulate such activities, and the degree to which the desirability of such regulation is generally accepted," *id.*, §403(2)(c); "the extent to which another state may have an interest in regulating the activity," *id.*, §403(2)(g); and "the likelihood of conflict with regulation by another state," *id.*, §403(2)(h). Rarely would these factors point more clearly against application of United States law. The activity relevant to the counts at issue here took place primarily in the United Kingdom, and the defendants in these counts are British corporations and British subjects having their principal place of business or residence outside the United States. Great Britain has established a comprehensive regulatory scheme governing the London reinsurance markets, and clearly has a heavy "interest in regulating the activity," *id.*, §403(2)(g). . . . Considering these factors, I think it unimaginable that an assertion of legislative jurisdiction by the United States would be considered reasonable, and therefore it is inappropriate to assume, in the absence of statutory indication to the contrary, that Congress has made such an assertion.

It is evident from what I have said that the Court's comity analysis, which proceeds as though the issue is whether the courts should "decline to exercise . . . jurisdiction," rather than whether the Sherman Act covers this conduct, is simply misdirected. . . . In any event, if one erroneously chooses, as the Court does, to make adjudicative jurisdiction (or, more precisely, abstention) the vehicle for taking account of the needs of prescriptive comity, the Court still gets it wrong. It concludes that no "true conflict" counseling nonapplication of United States law (or rather, as it thinks, United States judicial jurisdiction) exists unless compliance with United States law would constitute a *violation* of another country's law. That breathtakingly broad proposition, which contradicts the many cases discussed earlier, will bring the Sherman Act and other laws into sharp and unnecessary conflict with the legitimate interests of other countries—particularly our closest trading partners. . . .

The Supreme Court revisited the extraterritorial reach of the Sherman Act in *F. Hoffman LaRoche v. Empagran*, 542 U.S. 155 (2004). *Empagran* involved a worldwide conspiracy to fix prices for vitamins that produced significant effects in the U.S. market and that independently harmed consumers outside the United States. Plaintiff was a foreign purchaser who brought suit in the United States based entirely on harm in foreign markets. In determining that the Sherman Act did not reach plaintiff's claim, the Court reasoned as follows:

> [T]his Court ordinarily construes ambiguous statutes to avoid unreasonable interference with the sovereign authority of other nations. This rule of construction reflects principles of customary international law—law that (we must assume) Congress ordinarily seeks to follow.
>
> This rule of statutory construction cautions courts to assume that legislators take account of the legitimate sovereign interests of other nations when they write American laws. It thereby helps the potentially conflicting laws of different nations work together in harmony—a harmony particularly needed in today's highly interdependent commercial world.
>
> No one denies that America's antitrust laws, when applied to foreign conduct, can interfere with a foreign nation's ability independently to regulate its own commercial affairs. But our courts have long held that application of our antitrust laws to foreign anticompetitive conduct is nonetheless reasonable, and hence consistent with principles of prescriptive comity, insofar as they reflect a legislative effort to redress *domestic* antitrust injury that foreign anticompetitive conduct has caused. *See United States v. Aluminum Co. of America*, 148 F.2d 416, 443-444 (C.A.2 1945). . . .
>
> But why is it reasonable to apply those laws to foreign conduct *insofar as that conduct causes independent foreign harm and that foreign harm alone gives rise to the plaintiff's claim?* Like the former case, application of those laws creates a serious risk of interference with a foreign nation's ability independently to regulate its own commercial affairs. But, unlike the former case, the justification for that interference seems insubstantial. . . .

Notes and Questions

1. Was there a conflict between U.S. antitrust laws and the English reinsurance regulations in *Hartford Fire*? How, if at all, does the test for a U.S.-foreign law conflict in *Hartford Fire* differ from the test for a federal-state law conflict in *Crosby*, discussed in Chapter 4?

2. Do *Hartford Fire* and *Empagran* shed light on the international legality of the EU's Aviation Directive?

The cases discussed above trace the trajectory of changing judicial interpretations of the Sherman Act over time. However, focusing only on antitrust cases conceals considerable variation in U.S. court willingness to exercise extraterritorial jurisdiction across different issue areas. In the course of deciding disputes over the extraterritorial reach of U.S. statutes, courts often refer to presumptions of statutory interpretation. One presumption, mentioned in Justice Scalia's *Hartford Fire* dissent, is that statutes are presumed to apply within the territory of the United States. Although this presumption was displaced in the antitrust area, courts have invoked it with increasing frequency over the past few decades.

For example, *Morrison v. National Australia Bank* involved Australian plaintiffs who purchased stock in an Australian banking company through transactions on the Australian stock market. The Australian investors sought compensation for injuries caused by the bank's allegedly misleading statements about its purchase in the United States of HomeSide Lending, a Florida business that serviced mortgages. The Supreme Court addressed whether §10(b) of the U.S. securities law, prohibiting fraud in the sale of securities, provided a cause of action to foreign plaintiffs in these circumstances.

Morrison v. National Australia Bank, Ltd.

561 U.S. 247 (2010)

SCALIA, J., delivered the opinion of the Court, in which ROBERTS, C.J., and KENNEDY, THOMAS, and ALITO, JJ., joined. SOTOMAYOR, J., took no part in the consideration or decision of the case.

III

A

It is a "longstanding principle of American law 'that legislation of Congress, unless a contrary intent appears, is meant to apply only within the territorial jurisdiction of the United States.'" *EEOC v. Arabian American Oil Co.*, 499 U.S. 244, 248 (1991) (*Aramco*). This principle . . . rests on the perception that Congress ordinarily legislates with respect to domestic, not foreign matters. *Smith v. United States*, 507 U.S. 197, 204, n. 5 (1993). . . .

[The Court considered the application of the presumption to §10(b) of the Securities Act of 1934, which provides: "It shall be unlawful for any person, directly or indirectly, by the use of any means or instrumentality of interstate commerce or of the mails, or of any facility of any national securities exchange . . . [t]o use or employ, in connection with the purchase or sale of any security registered on a national securities exchange or any security not so registered, . . . any manipulative or deceptive device or contrivance in contravention of such rules and regulations as the [Securities and Exchange] Commission may prescribe. . . ." 15 U.S.C. 78j(b). The Court determined that nothing in the statute's text or context provided an "affirmative indication that this provision applies extraterritorially."]

IV

A

Petitioners argue that the conclusion that §10(b) does not apply extraterritorially does not resolve this case. They contend that they seek no more than domestic application anyway, since Florida is where HomeSide and its senior executives engaged in the deceptive conduct of manipulating HomeSide's financial models; their complaint also alleged that [Homeside's executives] made misleading public statements there. This is less an answer to the presumption against extraterritorial application than it is an assertion—a quite valid assertion—that that presumption here (as often) is not self-evidently dispositive, but its application requires further analysis. For it is a rare case of prohibited extraterritorial application that lacks all contact with the territory of the United States. But the presumption against extraterritorial application would be a craven watchdog indeed if it retreated to its kennel whenever some domestic activity is involved in the case. . . . In *Aramco*, for example, [the plaintiff alleged that he had been fired in Saudi Arabia by a U.S. corporation in violation of U.S. antidiscrimination law. The plaintiff] had been hired in Houston, and was an American citizen. The Court concluded, however, that neither that territorial event nor that relationship was the "focus" of congressional concern, but rather domestic employment.

Applying the same mode of analysis here, we think that the focus of the Exchange Act is not upon the place where the deception originated, but upon purchases and sales of securities in the United States. Section 10(b) does not punish deceptive conduct, but only deceptive conduct "in connection with the purchase or sale of any security registered on a national securities exchange or any security not so registered." 15 U.S.C. §78j(b). Those purchase-and-sale transactions are the objects of the statute's solicitude. It is those transactions that the statute seeks to "regulate,"; it is parties or prospective parties to those transactions that the statute seeks to "protec[t]." And it is in our view only transactions in securities listed on domestic exchanges, and domestic transactions in other securities, to which §10(b) applies. . . .

. . . [W]e reject the notion that the Exchange Act reaches conduct in this country affecting exchanges or transactions abroad for the same reason that *Aramco* rejected overseas application of Title VII to all domestically concluded employment contracts or all employment contracts with American employers: The probability of incompatibility with the applicable laws of other countries is so obvious that if Congress intended such foreign application "it would have addressed the subject of conflicts with foreign laws and procedures." 499 U.S., at 256. Like the United States, foreign countries regulate their domestic securities exchanges and securities transactions occurring within their territorial jurisdiction. And the regulation of other countries often differs from ours as to what constitutes fraud, what disclosures must be made, what damages are recoverable, what discovery is available in litigation, what individual actions may be joined in a single suit, what attorney's fees are recoverable, and many other matters. The Commonwealth of Australia, the United Kingdom of Great Britain and Northern Ireland, and the Republic of France have filed *amicus* briefs in this case. So have (separately or jointly) such international and foreign organizations as the International Chamber of Commerce, the Swiss Bankers Association, the Federation of German Industries, the French Business Confederation, the Institute of International Bankers, the European Banking Federation, the Australian Bankers' Association, and the Association Française des Entreprises Privées. They all complain of the interference with foreign securities regulation that application of §10(b) abroad would produce, and urge the adoption of a clear test that will avoid that consequence. The transactional test we have adopted—whether the purchase or sale is made in the United States, or involves a security listed on a domestic exchange—meets that requirement.

Notes and Questions

1. Almost immediately after *Morrison* was decided, Congress passed legislation providing that the SEC and the Justice Department would have authority to enforce §10(b) in cases involving "conduct within the United States that constitutes significant steps in

furtherance of the violation, even if the securities transaction occurs outside the United States and involves only foreign investors." Does this response suggest that the Court misread the statute? Or does it confirm the wisdom of the Court requiring Congress to express clearly its intentions regarding extraterritorial application of federal statutes?

2. In *Morrison* and in the antitrust cases discussed above, the Supreme Court applied the presumption against extraterritoriality to a statutes that set out substantive rules of conduct. In *Kiobel v. Royal Dutch Petroleum*, 133 S. Ct. 1659 (2013), a case discussed in more detail in Chapter 5, the Court applied the presumption against extraterritoriality to the Alien Tort Statute, a statute that is "strictly jurisdictional."

Do the arguments in favor of applying the canon against extraterritorial application to substantive statutes that directly regulate conduct, such as the securities laws, apply with equal force to the Alien Tort Statute, which, according to the Court, "does not directly regulate conduct or afford relief," but "instead allows federal courts to recognize certain causes of action based on sufficiently definite norms of international law"?

2. A European Alternative?

European nations are often vocal critics of efforts to apply U.S. law to foreign conduct. The European Court of Justice has addressed whether EC laws apply to conduct outside the territory of the EC's member states. A leading case, *Wood Pulp*, involved alleged "concerted practices" by foreign wood pulp producers and trade associations outside of the EC that affected the prices for wood pulp within the EC. Defendants challenged the European Commission's attempt to assert jurisdiction over them. In a decision issued five years before the U.S. Supreme Court decided *Hartford Fire*, the European Court of Justice upheld the extraterritorial assertion of EC competition law.

Re Wood Pulp Cartel
[1988] E.C.R. 5193

[T]he Commission [has] set out the grounds which in its view justify the Community's jurisdiction to apply Article 85 of the Treaty [of Rome, prohibiting agreements and concerted practices that prevent, restrict, or distort competition] to the concentration in question. It stated first that all the addressees of the decision were either exporting directly to purchasers within the Community or were doing business within the Community through branches, subsidiaries, agencies or other establishments in the Community. It further pointed out that the concentration applied to the vast majority of the sales of those undertakings to and in the Community. Finally it stated that two-thirds of total shipments and 60 per cent of consumption of the product in question in the Community had been affected by such concentration. The Commission concluded that "the effect of the agreements and practices on prices announced and/or charged to customers and on resale of pulp within the EEC was therefore not only substantial but intended, and was the primary and direct result of the agreements and practices" . . . .

. . . The applicants have submitted that the decision is incompatible with public international law on the grounds that the application of the competition rules in this case was founded exclusively on the economic repercussions within the Common Market of conduct restricting competition which was adopted outside the Community.

. . . It should be observed that an infringement of Article 85, such as the conclusion of an agreement which has had the effect of restricting competition within the Common Market, consists of conduct made up of two elements, the formation of the agreement, decision or concerted practice and the implementation thereof. If the applicability of prohibitions laid down under competition law were made to depend on the place where the agreement, decision or concerted practice was formed, the result would obviously be to give undertakings an easy means of evading those prohibitions. The decisive factor is therefore the place where it is implemented.

. . . The producers in this case implemented their pricing agreement within the Common Market. It is immaterial in that respect whether or not they had recourse to subsidiaries, agents, sub-agents, or branches within the Community in order to make their contacts with purchasers within the Community.

. . . Accordingly the Community's jurisdiction to apply its competition rules to such conduct is covered by the territoriality principle as universally recognized in public international law. . . . As regards the argument based on the infringement of the principle of non-interference, it should be pointed out that the applicants who are members of KEA have referred to a rule according to which where two States have jurisdiction to lay down and enforce rules and the effect of those rules is that a person finds himself subject to contradictory orders as to the conduct he must adopt, each State is obliged to exercise its jurisdiction with moderation. . . .

. . . There is not, in this case, any contradiction between the conduct required by the United States and that required by the Community since [U.S. law] merely exempts the conclusion of export cartels from the application of United States antitrust laws but does not require such cartels to be concluded. . . .

Notes and Questions

1. Shortly after the *Wood Pulp* decision, the Assistant Attorney General in charge of the Antitrust Division of the U.S. Department of Justice argued that the *Wood Pulp* decision was, as a practical matter, "very close to, if not indistinguishable from, the so-called 'effects' test as applied by U.S. courts." However, the EC's Commissioner for Competition Policy sharply disagreed:

> [I]t is in my view unreasonable to assume unqualified espousal of a doctrine in a judgement which does not mention it by name, while those who urged its adoption accepted that it should be qualified. So the Court of Justice does not endorse the effects doctrine. . . . But the Court of Justice held the sale in the Community at a concerted price was implementation, and I find that conclusion thoroughly reasonable and appropriate. . . . Nevertheless, this specific use of the word "implementation" rather than "effects" suggests to me that implementing conduct perhaps has to be direct, substantial, and foreseeable for jurisdiction to be engaged.

As a doctrinal matter, which test makes more sense? In practice, would you expect the "implementation test" often to yield results different from the U.S. "effects test"?

2. Is the European Court of Justice more or less sensitive to the potential foreign policy implications of extraterritorial assertions of jurisdiction than the U.S. Supreme Court? Does the last paragraph of the excerpt from *Wood Pulp* decision suggest that the Court of Justice endorses the "true conflict" test that the *Hartford Fire* decision used?

3. Although European states, and others, challenged the legality and the legitimacy of the effects test, by the mid-1990s many states, including much of Western Europe, had adopted jurisdictional approaches similar to the effects doctrine. Can you reconcile European and other governments' protests against the assertion of extraterritorial jurisdiction by the United States under the Sherman Act while at the same time interpreting their own antitrust laws to permit prescriptive jurisdiction over foreign conduct?

C. Resolving the Dispute over the Aviation Directive

On December 21, 2011, the Grand Chamber of the European Court of Justice issued a decision on the Aviation Directive. After rejecting claims that the Directive violated the Convention on International Civil Aviation and the Kyoto Protocol, the Court considered whether the Directive exceeded customary international law limits on prescriptive jurisdiction.

Air Transport Association of America v. Secretary of State for Energy and Climate Change

Case C-366/10 (2011)

101 Under [its founding treaties], the European Union is to contribute to the strict observance and the development of international law. Consequently, when it adopts an act, it is bound to observe international law in its entirety, including customary international law, which is binding upon the institutions of the European Union.

102 Thus, it should be examined first whether the principles to which the referring court makes reference are recognised as forming part of customary international law. If they are, it should, secondly, then be determined whether and to what extent they may be relied upon by individuals to call into question the validity of an act of the European Union, such as Directive 2008/101. . . .

103 The referring court mentions a principle that each State has complete and exclusive sovereignty over its airspace and another principle that no State may validly purport to subject any part of the high seas to its sovereignty. It also mentions the principle of freedom to fly over the high seas.

104 These three principles are regarded as embodying the current state of customary international maritime and air law. . . .

105 Nor has the existence of those principles of international law been contested by the Member States, the institutions of the European Union, the Republic of Iceland or the Kingdom of Norway in their written observations or at the hearing.

110 However, since a principle of customary international law does not have the same degree of precision as a provision of an international agreement, judicial review must necessarily be limited to the question whether, in adopting the act in question, the institutions of the European Union made manifest errors of assessment concerning the conditions for applying those principles.

124 European Union legislation may be applied to an aircraft operator when its aircraft is in the territory of one of the Member States and, more specifically, on an aerodrome situated in such territory, since, in such a case, that aircraft is subject to the unlimited jurisdiction of that Member State and the European Union.

125 In laying down a criterion for Directive 2008/101 to be applicable to operators of aircraft registered in a Member State or in a third State that is founded on the fact that those aircraft perform a flight which departs from or arrives at an aerodrome situated in the territory of one of the Member States, Directive 2008/101 . . . does not infringe the principle of territoriality or the sovereignty which the third States from or to which such flights are performed have over the airspace above their territory, since those aircraft are physically in the territory of one of the Member States of the European Union and are thus subject on that basis to the unlimited jurisdiction of the European Union.

127 It is only if the operator of such an aircraft has chosen to operate a commercial air route arriving at or departing from an aerodrome situated in the territory of a

Member State that the operator, because its aircraft is in the territory of that Member State, will be subject to the allowance trading scheme.

128 As for the fact that the operator of an aircraft in such a situation is required to surrender allowances calculated in the light of the whole of the international flight that its aircraft has performed . . . , it must be pointed out that . . . the European Union legislature may in principle choose to permit a commercial activity . . . to be carried out in the territory of the European Union only on condition that operators comply with the criteria that have been established by the European Union and are designed to fulfil the environmental protection objectives which it has set for itself, in particular where those objectives follow on from an international agreement to which the European Union is a signatory, such as the [UN] Framework Convention [on Climate Change] and the Kyoto Protocol.

129 Furthermore, the fact that . . . certain matters contributing to the pollution of the air, sea or land territory of the Member States originate in an event which occurs partly outside that territory is not such as to call into question, in the light of the principles of customary international law . . . the full applicability of European Union law in that territory.

130 It follows that the European Union had competence, in the light of the principles of customary international law . . . to adopt Directive 2008/101 to all flights which arrive at or depart from an aerodrome situated in the territory of a Member State.

———————————

The ECJ decision did not end the dispute. The U.S. Secretary of State warned that the United States would take "appropriate action" if the EU did not abandon efforts to include foreign carriers in the ETS. In February 2012, 22 nations, including Brazil, China, India, Japan, Mexico, Russia, Saudi Arabia, South Africa, Thailand, and the United States, adopted a "Joint Declaration" stating their position that the EU "must cease operation [of the Directive] to airlines/aircraft operators registered in third States," and threatening to adopt a range of responses, including legislation prohibiting domestic carriers from participating in the ETS program, filing complaints at the World Trade Organization and/or the ICAO, and imposing fees on EU carriers. Responding on Twitter, the EU Commissioner for Climate Action asked, "what's your concrete, constructive alternative?" Nevertheless, international pressure continued to grow: in April 2012, several states, including the United States, signaled that the failure to change or postpone the ETS might derail global climate talks, and some thirty states publicly threatened noncompliance. In response, the EU indicated that it might "suspend" application of the Directive to foreign aircraft "if countries were to make clear progress this year toward establishing a global emissions control system."

In November 2012, in response to discussions at the ICAO, the EU proposed to suspend implementation of the ETS for flights into or out of Europe for a period of one year. The EU noted that "significant progress" had been made in efforts to craft a global approach to carbon emissions from aviation, and that agreement on a global "market-based mechanism" (i.e., cap and trade program) was expected at an ICAO meeting scheduled for fall of 2013. The EU stated that the proposal "demonstrates the EU's strong political commitment to facilitate and drive forward the successful conclusion of these ICAO processes." However, the EU made clear that if talks at ICAO did not succeed, it would implement the provisions of the Aviation Directive addressing flights into or out of Europe.

On October 4, 2013, the ICAO Assembly agreed on a roadmap for developing a global market-based mechanism to control aviation emissions. The mechanism is to be finalized at the next ICAO Assembly in 2016, and implemented by 2020. In April 2014, the EU formally amended the Aviation Directive, excluding from the program international flights into or out of the EU for the period from January 1, 2013, to December 31, 2016.

Notes and Questions

1. How does the European Court of Justice's approach to the extraterritorial reach of EU law differ from the U.S. Supreme Court's approach to the extraterritorial reach of U.S. statutes?

2. As a policy matter, should international rules on jurisdiction treat extraterritorial domestic measures to address global commons problems that have not been amenable to multilateral solutions differently from other extraterritorial assertions of jurisdiction? Do such measures make multilateral solutions more or less likely?

3. Who prevailed in this dispute? How do we know if international law made a difference to the outcome?

D. Note on Other Bases for Prescriptive Jurisdiction

States recognize several bases, in addition to territory, upon which to exercise jurisdiction. Some of the most important are outlined below.

1. The Nationality Principle

Under the nationality principle, states can exercise prescriptive jurisdiction over their own nationals, even when they are located outside national territory. A classic example of the exercise of nationality jurisdiction occurred in *Blackmer v. United States*, 284 U.S. 421 (1932), where the Supreme Court ruled that U.S. laws applied to a U.S. citizen resident in France: "By virtue of the obligations of citizenship, the United States retained its authority over him, and he was bound by its laws made applicable to him in a foreign country." The criminal laws of several states, including France, Germany, India, and the UK, cover the criminal acts of citizens committed while abroad.

While defining the nationality of natural persons is often relatively straightforward, determining the nationality of corporations and other legal entities raises a number of difficult problems. What is the nationality of a Polish subsidiary of a German multinational corporation? Or, more controversially, who can exercise nationality jurisdiction over, for example, a dollar-denominated bank account of a Korean citizen located in the Singapore branch of a London-based bank?

The United States has been relatively aggressive in asserting nationality jurisdiction in the corporate setting. For example, since 1996, U.S. law has prevented U.S. companies from engaging in trade with Iran. In August 2012, the United States enacted the Iran Threat Reduction and Syria Human Rights Act, which expands the jurisdictional reach of sanctions against Iran to foreign subsidiaries of U.S. firms. In particular, the law reaches foreign firms if a U.S. parent corporation has greater than 50 percent ownership, or if a U.S. firm "otherwise control[s] the actions, policies, or personnel decisions of the [foreign] entity." The law also provides that the U.S. parent corporations can be liable for Iran-related sanctions violations committed by their foreign subsidiaries. In November 2013, the United States lifted certain sanctions on Iran following an interim agreement on Iran's nuclear program; however, the prohibitions on essentially all trade by U.S. firms and their foreign subsidiaries remained in place.

At times, U.S. efforts to control behavior of foreign subsidiaries of U.S. firm have sparked vigorous objections. For example, in the early 1980s, in response to the imposition of martial law in Poland, the United States prohibited foreign subsidiaries of U.S. corporations from delivering oil and gas equipment to the Soviet Union. In response, the EC issued a legal opinion concluding that the pipeline controls "were not in conformity with well-recognized principles of international law," the British government prohibited British companies from complying with the U.S. law, and France directed its companies to honor their pipeline contracts. The United States eventually lifted the pipeline controls in exchange for a vague promise that the Europeans would study future limits on trade with the Soviets.

In the aftermath of this dispute, a former German diplomat offered the following observations:

> More in the United States than in any other country, international law in general and jurisdiction in particular is seen as a dynamic process rather than as a set of given rules. The view that rules of jurisdiction emanate from the process of action and reaction may be helpful as a political analysis of legal development. As a guide for national decision makers to assert jurisdictional powers, however, such an approach invites a disregard for existing rules in the hope that other nations may tolerate the assertion either freely or be forced to by the existing power balance. This may serve a powerful nation well, and it might not even damage the stability of the international community so long as the acting state shows moderation and does not judge the reasonableness of its assertion entirely and persistently on national interests alone. But generally, this approach implies a risk of international conflict and creates uncertainty and unpredictability for international business and trade. . . . Moreover, it appears to be an inherent aspect of this approach that an affected country considers retaliation in order to prevent a repetition of the extraterritorial application of jurisdiction. . . .

Extraterritorial Application of U.S. Export Controls—The Siberian Pipeline, Remarks by Werner Hein, 77 Proc. Am. Socy. Intl. L. 241, 247-278 (1983).

2. The Protective Principle

The French Napoleonic Code provided:

> Any foreigner who, outside the territory of France, shall be culpable, either as principal or as an accomplice, of a crime against the security of the state, or of counterfeiting the seal of the state or national moneys in circulation or national papers or bank notes authorized by law, shall be prosecuted and tried according to the provisions of French laws, if he is arrested in France or if the Government obtains his extradition.

This provision served as a model for the drafting of many criminal codes in Europe in the 1800s. Many Latin American nations have similar provisions in their domestic laws. More generally, states recognize the right to regulate conduct outside their territory by non-nationals that is directed against their security or a limited number of other important state interests. This is known as the "protective principle."

The House of Lords considered the protective principle for the first time in the *Joyce* case, which arose out of allegedly treasonous acts during World War II. William Joyce was born in Brooklyn, New York, in 1906, and moved to England in 1921. In 1933, he applied for a British passport, stating that he was a British subject by birth. Joyce received a British passport, which was renewed in 1939, ten days before the outbreak of World War II. He then left for Germany and, weeks after the war started, began broadcasting pro-German propaganda from Germany. Joyce broadcast until April 30, 1945. A month later, British officers arrested him near the Danish frontier.

Joyce was tried in September 1945 and was convicted and sentenced to death. He appealed on the grounds, inter alia, that "the Court wrongly assumed jurisdiction to try an alien for an offense against British law committed in a foreign country." On December 18, the House of Lords dismissed the appeal, and, three weeks later, William Joyce was hanged before a crowd of approximately 300 people. On February 1, 1946, the House of Lords issued an opinion containing the following passage:

> The second point of appeal . . . was that . . . no English court has jurisdiction to try an alien for a crime committed abroad . . . . There is, I think, a short answer to this point. The statute in question deals with the crime of treason committed within or . . . without the realm: it is general in its terms and I see no reason for limiting its scope. No principle of comity demands that a state should ignore the crime of treason committed against it outside its territory. On the contrary a proper regard for its own security requires that all those who commit that crime, whether they commit it within or without the realm should be amenable to its laws. . . . .

[1946] A.C. 347, 372 (per Lord Jowett, L.C.).

New technologies have given rise to new applications of criminal statutes grounded in the protective principle. For example, in June 2014, Germany's top prosecutor announced that he had opened a criminal investigation into the tapping of German Chancellor Angela Merkel's cell phone by the U.S. National Security Agency. The statement noted that any charges would most likely be filed under Article 99 of the German penal code, which provides that "[t]hose who carry out secret service activities for a foreign power against the German state are subject to up to five years or in extreme cases up to ten years in prison."

Despite its historic skepticism toward the protective principle, the United States has at times exercised jurisdiction based on the principle. For example, in *U.S. v. Saac*, 632 F.3d 1203 (11th Cir. 2011), the court upheld a conviction under the Drug Trafficking Vessel Interdiction Act, which prohibits the operation of a semi-submersible vessel (i.e., a narco-sub) without nationality in international waters with the intent to evade detection. Defendants, Colombian citizens, were arrested in the eastern Pacific Ocean near the Galapagos Islands as they abandoned a semi-submersible vessel, and later convicted and sentenced to serve nine-year terms. On appeal, the court reasoned that the application of U.S. criminal law did not violate international legal norms as semi-submersible vessels "pose a formidable security threat because they are difficult to detect and easy to scuttle or sink." It also found that, under the protective principle, there was no requirement "of an actual or intended effect inside the United States."

3. The Passive Personality Principle

Under the passive personality principle, a state may apply its law—particularly criminal law—to an act committed outside its territory by a person not its national when a national is a victim of the act. Although this form of jurisdiction was traditionally disfavored, over the past few decades, increasing numbers of countries began to incorporate the passive personality principle in domestic legislation, largely in response to increased terrorist activity. The United States, in particular, has moved away from its historic criticism of the principle and enacted a number of federal statutes that authorize passive personality jurisdiction. For example, in *United States v. Bin Laden*, 92 F. Supp. 2d 189 (S.D.N.Y. 2000), defendants were indicted, *inter alia*, for a conspiracy to kill U.S. nationals abroad. The court rejected a challenge to the indictment and noted, quoting the *Restatement*, that the passive personality principle is "increasingly accepted as applied to terrorist and other organized attacks on a state's nationals by reason of their nationality. . . ."

4. Universal Jurisdiction

Under the universal jurisdiction principle, any state may exercise jurisdiction over an individual who commits certain heinous and widely condemned offenses, even when no other recognized basis for jurisdiction exists. The traditional rationale for universal jurisdiction is that the prohibited acts are of an international character and are of serious concern to the international community as a whole. States accept that piracy, war crimes, genocide, and slave trade give rise to universal jurisdiction. Debate on the universal principle tends to center on whether to extend universal jurisdiction to other categories of acts, such as certain acts of terrorism, assaults on diplomatic personnel, or kidnapping.

The classic modern example of a state exercising universal jurisdiction is the Eichmann episode. Adolf Eichmann was the senior German official responsible for organizing the arrest, deportation, internment, and extermination of Jews during World War II, as discussed further in Section III below. After the war, Eichmann stood trial in Israel for his wartime actions. The Israeli Supreme Court rejected Eichmann's challenge to Israel's jurisdiction.

Attorney-General of the State of Israel v. Adolf Eichmann
36 I.L.R. 277 (1962)

1. The Appellant, Adolf Eichmann, was found guilty by the District Court of Jerusalem of offenses of the most extreme gravity against the Nazis and Nazi Collaborators (Punishment) Law 5710-1950 (hereinafter—"the Law") and was sentenced to death. . . .

6. Most of the legal contentions of Counsel for the Appellant concentrate on the argument that the District Court, in assuming jurisdiction to try the Appellant, acted contrary to the principles of international law. . . .

(2) The offenses for which the Appellant was tried are in the nature of "extra-territorial offenses," that is to say, offenses that were committed outside the territory of Israel by a citizen of a foreign state; and even though the above-mentioned Law confers jurisdiction in respect of such offenses, it conflicts, in so doing, with the principle of territorial sovereignty, which postulates that only the country within whose territory the offense was committed, or to which the offender belongs—in this case, Germany—has jurisdiction to punish therefor. . . .

12. . . . [I]t is the universal character of the crimes in question which vests in every state the power to try those who participated in the perpetration of such crimes and to punish them therefor. . . .

(a) One of the principles whereby states assume, in one degree or another, the power to try and punish a person for an offense he has committed, is the principle of universality. Its meaning is, in essence, that that power is vested in every state regardless of the fact that the offense was committed outside its territory by a person who did not belong to it, provided he is in its custody at the time he is brought to trial. This principle has wide support and is universally acknowledged with respect to the offense of piracy *jure gentium*. But while there exists general agreement as to its application to this offense, there is a difference of opinion as to the scope of its application. Thus one school of thought holds that it cannot be applied to any offense other than the one mentioned above, lest this entail excessive interference with the competence of the state in which the offense was committed. . . .

A second school of thought . . . considers [universal jurisdiction] to be no more than an auxiliary principle, to be applied in circumstances in which no resort can be had to the principle of territorial sovereignty or to the nationality principle, both of which are universally agreed to. . . . [Under this theory,] the state contemplating the exercise of the power in question must first offer the extradition of the offender to the state within whose territory the offense was committed. . . .

A third school of thought holds that the rule of universal jurisdiction, which is valid in cases of piracy, logically applies also to all such criminal acts of commission or omission which constitute offenses under the law of nations. . . .

(b) This brief survey of views . . . shows that, notwithstanding the differences between them, there is full justification for applying here the principle of universal jurisdiction, since the international character of the "crimes against humanity" (in the wide meaning of the term) is, in this case, not in doubt, and the unprecedented extent of their injurious and murderous effects is not open to dispute . . . . In other words, the basic reason for which international law recognizes the right of each state to exercise such jurisdiction in piracy offences—notwithstanding the fact that its own jurisdiction does not extend to the scene of the commission of the offense (the high seas) and the offender is a national of another state or is stateless—applies with all the greater force to the above-mentioned crimes. That reason is, it will be recalled, that the interest to prevent bodily and material harm to those who sail the seas, and to persons engaged in free trade between nations, is a vital interest, common to all civilized states and of universal scope. . . .

This means that it was not the recognition of the universal jurisdiction to try and punish the person who committed "piracy" that justified the viewing of such an act as an international crime *sui generis*, but it was the agreed vital interest of the international community that justified the exercise of the jurisdiction in question. . . .

It follows that the state which prosecutes and punishes a person for that offense acts solely as the organ and agent of the international community, and metes out punishment to the offender for his breach of the prohibition imposed by the law of nations. . . .

The above explanation of the substantive basis underlying the exercise of universal jurisdiction in respect of the crime of piracy also justifies its exercise in regard to the crimes with which we are dealing in this case. . . .

(d) This is the place to discuss the limitation imposed by most of those who support this principle upon the exercise of universal jurisdiction, namely, that the state which has apprehended the offender must first offer his extradition to the state in which the offense was committed (see sub-paragraph (a) above). This means that only if the second state does not respond to the offer of extradition may the first state arrogate to itself the jurisdiction to try and punish. The above limitation is based upon the approach implicit in the maxim *aut dedere aut punire* [extradite or prosecute]. . . .

As to the limitation itself in the sense explained above, we are of the opinion that it has no place in the circumstances of this case. First . . . Counsel for the Appellant has himself admitted that his application to the Government of Western Germany to demand the extradition of his client was refused, and therefore an offer in this sense by the Government of Israel could be of no practical use. Secondly—and this is the principal reason for the rejection of his submission—the idea behind the above-mentioned limitation is not that the requirement to offer the offender to the state in which the offense was committed was designed to prevent the violation of its territorial sovereignty. Its reason is rather a purely practical one: The great majority of the witnesses and the greater part of the evidence are concentrated in that state, and it becomes, therefore, the most convenient place (*forum conveniens*) for the conduct of the trial. . . . [I]t must be said that the great majority of the witnesses who gave evidence here on the grave crimes attributed to the Appellant, especially those against the Jews, were residents of Israel, and, moreover, the bulk of the vast mass of documents produced was previously gathered and preserved (through Yad Vashem) [a Holocaust museum and research center] in the State of Israel. . . . It is clear, therefore, that it is the State of Israel—not the State of Germany—that must be regarded as the *forum conveniens* for the trial.

. . . (f) We sum up our views on this subject as follows: Not only are all the crimes attributed to the Appellant of an international character, but they are crimes whose evil and murderous effects were so widespread as to shake the stability of the international community to its very foundations. The State of Israel, therefore, was entitled, pursuant to the principle of universal jurisdiction, and acting in the capacity of guardian of international law and agents for its enforcement, to try the Appellant. This being the case, it is immaterial that the State of Israel did not exist at the time the offenses were committed. . . .

Should universal jurisdiction reach acts of terrorism? In *United States v. Yousef*, defendant was charged, *inter alia*, with the bombing of a Philippines Airlines flight. He was indicted under the Aircraft Sabotage Act of 1984, which criminalizes certain offenses committed against non–U.S. flag aircraft. Defendant argued that because the airplane was not a U.S.-flag aircraft, the plane was flying between two destinations outside the United States, and there was no evidence that any U.S. citizens were on the flight or targets of the bombing, the extraterritorial application of U.S. criminal statutes in these circumstances was inconsistent with international law principles regarding jurisdiction to prescribe. The district court held that the exercise of jurisdiction was justified under the principles of universal jurisdiction. On appeal, the Second Circuit rejected this conclusion.

United States v. Yousef

327 F.3d 56 (2d Cir. 2003)

[The court reviews the expansion of crimes subject to universal jurisdiction from piracy to include war crimes and crimes against humanity.]

The historical restriction of universal jurisdiction to piracy, war crimes, and crimes against humanity demonstrates that universal jurisdiction arises under customary international law only where crimes (1) are universally condemned by the community of nations, and (2) by their nature occur either outside of a State or where there is no State capable of punishing, or competent to punish, the crime (as in a time of war).

Unlike those offenses supporting universal jurisdiction under customary international law—that is, piracy, war crimes, and crimes against humanity—that now have fairly precise definitions and that have achieved universal condemnation, "terrorism" is a term as loosely deployed as it is powerfully charged. Judge Harry T. Edwards of the District of Columbia Circuit stated eighteen years ago in *Tel-Oren v. Libyan Arab Republic*, 726 F.2d 774 (D.C. Cir. 1984), that "[w]hile this nation unequivocally condemns all terrorist acts, that sentiment is not universal. Indeed, the nations of the world are so divisively split on the legitimacy of such aggression as to make it impossible to pinpoint an area of harmony or consensus."

We regrettably are no closer now than eighteen years ago to an international consensus on the definition of terrorism or even its proscription; the mere existence of the phrase "state-sponsored terrorism" proves the absence of agreement on basic terms among a large number of States that terrorism violates public international law. Moreover, there continues to be strenuous disagreement among States about what actions do or do not constitute terrorism, nor have we shaken ourselves free of the cliché that "one man's terrorist is another man's freedom fighter." We thus conclude . . . that terrorism—unlike piracy, war crimes, and crimes against humanity—does not provide a basis for universal jurisdiction.

The court then found that because the U.S. statute at issue was passed to implement the country's obligations under the Montreal Convention for the Suppression of Unlawful Acts Against the Safety of Civil Aviation, the exercise of jurisdiction did not violate international law: "far from exceeding its jurisdictional competence . . . the United States merely met its non-discretionary obligation under the Convention to prosecute Yousef for the acts charged. . . ." The court also ruled that jurisdiction was proper under the protective principle, as Yousef's plan to destroy aircraft was intended to influence U.S. foreign policy.

Notes and Questions

1. In upholding the exercise of universal jurisdiction, the Israeli Supreme Court in *Eichmann* draws an analogy between war crimes and crimes against humanity, on the one hand, and piracy, on the other. Are you persuaded by this analogy? Is it relevant that piracy is typically defined to include private acts but to exclude state acts?

2. What factors does the *Eichmann* court use to distinguish between those criminal acts that give rise to universal jurisdiction and those that do not? Under the *Eichmann* court's reasoning, should terrorism give rise to universal jurisdiction?

3. While the *Eichmann* case was for many years the preeminent example of the exercise of universal jurisdiction, in recent years many states have revised their criminal law to permit the exercise of universal jurisdiction in certain circumstances. A 2012 survey by the human rights NGO Amnesty International found that 147 of the 193 UN member states (approximately 76 percent) have provided for universal jurisdiction over war crimes, crimes against humanity, genocide, and/or torture in their domestic laws. Many of these statutes implement treaties that permit or require parties to exercise universal jurisdiction in particular circumstances, although some provide for the exercise of universal jurisdiction under customary international law. In recent years, criminal complaints or investigations based on universal jurisdiction have been instituted in a number of European and African states. (A number of these cases are discussed in Chapter 9.) Why would a state devote resources to prosecuting foreign nationals for human rights atrocities committed against other foreign nationals outside its territory?

III. CAPTURING CRIMINALS ABROAD: THE ARREST OF SLAVKO DOKMANOVIC

We now turn our attention to jurisdiction to adjudicate and jurisdiction to enforce. States have long accepted the general norm that one state cannot exercise its judicial functions within the territory of another state without that state's consent. They have also accepted that international law prohibits the agents of one state from enforcing, without permission, their criminal law within the territory of another state. Nevertheless, from time to time, a state or some of its citizens may undertake to enforce its laws through direct actions in another state's territory. One dramatic example is the abduction or luring of a suspect from one state to another to stand trial.

The goals for this Problem include:

- to understand how international law bears on the permissibility and exercise of adjudicative jurisdiction by domestic courts after an abduction, luring, or other irregular rendition of a suspect from one state to another;
- to understand how domestic courts have treated claims that irregular renditions preclude them from exercising personal jurisdiction over defendants; and
- to understand the controversy over U.S. practices of irregular renditions of suspected terrorists.

A. The Problem

In June 1991, Croatia declared independence from the Federal Republic of Yugoslavia (FRY). Shortly thereafter, many Croatian Serbs, supported by the federal Yugoslav National Army (JNA), rose up against the Croatian government. By August 1991, the JNA had surrounded Vukovar, Croatia, and was laying siege to it. Vukovar is located on the bank of the Danube River, which marks the boundary between Serbia (part of the FRY) and Croatia.

In November 1991, several hundred people sought refuge at Vukovar Hospital. On November 18, the JNA and the Croatian government agreed that the hospital would be evacuated in the presence of international observers. The next day, JNA units took control of Vukovar Hospital. JNA soldiers hurriedly removed about 400 men from the hospital, including wounded patients, hospital staff, Croatian political activists, and other civilians. The men were loaded onto buses and driven to a site outside of Vukovar, where JNA soldiers beat the men for several hours. The men were then divided into groups, loaded onto trucks, and transported to the edge of a nearby ravine. There JNA and Serb paramilitary troops under the command of Slavko Dokmanovic, a Croatian Serb and President of the Vukovar Municipality, shot and killed approximately 260 men. A bulldozer pushed the bodies into a mass grave at the site. These events constituted the greatest single massacre of the 1991 war in Croatia.

In April 1996, Dokmanovic was secretly indicted by the Prosecutor of the International Criminal Tribunal for the Former Yugoslavia (ICTY) for his role in the Vukovar massacre. At the same time, an order for Dokmanovic's arrest was secretly transmitted to the UN Transitional Administration for Eastern Slavonia (UNTAES),* directing the UN forces to search for, arrest, and surrender Dokmanovic to the ICTY. However, by the time UNTAES received the order for Dokmanovic's arrest, he had moved from Eastern Slavonia to the Federal Republic of Yugoslavia.

In January 1997, ICTY investigators traveled to UNTAES headquarters in Vukovar to develop a plan to entice Dokmanovic to leave the FRY and enter the UNTAES region

---

*A UN Security Council Resolution had temporarily placed the administration of Eastern Slavonia, a part of Croatia that the Serbs occupied during the war, under UNTAES control, pending its return to Croatian control. The resolution also gave UN peacekeeping forces the right to exercise police powers in that region of Croatia.

where he could be arrested. United Nations Secretary-General Kofi Annan and UN legal authorities in New York approved the plan.

During the first half of 1997, investigators from the Office of the Prosecutor (OTP) made several attempts to arrange meetings with Dokmanovic. Finally, a meeting was held in Dokmanovic's home on June 24. The ostensible purpose of the meeting was for Dokmanovic to assist ICTY officials in their investigation of Croatian war crimes. During the meeting, Dokmanovic raised the issue of compensation for property in Croatia that he lost. The OTP investigator suggested that Dokmanovic raise this issue with Transitional Administrator Jacques Klein and offered to arrange a meeting between Dokmanovic and Klein. On June 25, the investigator urged Dokmanovic to call Klein's office to confirm a meeting time. Dokmanovic did so, and Klein's office offered to send an UNTAES vehicle to collect Dokmanovic from a bridge over the Danube river.

On the afternoon of June 27, Dokmanovic arrived at the border post on the FRY side of the Danube River. Walking onto the bridge and past the FRY checkpoint, he entered an UNTAES vehicle. Soon after crossing the bridge, the vehicle abruptly departed the road and sped into a secured area. UNTAES troops quickly removed Dokmanovic from the vehicle at gunpoint. Within minutes, ICTY agents appeared and placed Dokmanovic under arrest. The speed of the maneuver prevented Dokmanovic from removing a loaded .357 Magnum Zastafa hand pistol from his briefcase. Within an hour of his arrest, Dokmanovic was placed on an airplane bound for The Hague. On July 7, 1997, Dokmanovic filed a preliminary motion for release on the grounds that his arrest had been unlawful and that the ICTY therefore lacked jurisdiction over him.

B. Seizing War Criminals: The Eichmann Precedent

The Dokmanovic case was not the first time that a suspected war criminal argued that he had been unlawfully brought before a court. During World War II, Adolf Eichmann was in charge of Jewish Affairs and Evacuation in the Gestapo and was responsible for the arrest, deportation, internment, and extermination of Jews. After the war, Eichmann fled to Argentina, where he lived under an assumed name. In 1960, Israeli agents kidnapped Eichmann and forcibly brought him to Israel to stand trial for his actions during the war. Earlier in this chapter we explored Eichmann's challenge to Israel's jurisdiction to prescribe. Eichmann also argued that due to the kidnapping, the Israeli courts lacked jurisdiction to adjudicate. Excerpts from the Jerusalem district court's opinion follow.

Attorney-General of the Government of Israel v. Eichmann
36 I.L.R. 5 (1961)

1. Adolf Eichmann has been arraigned before this Court on charges of unsurpassed gravity—crimes against the Jewish people, crimes against humanity, and war crimes. . . .

40. . . . Counsel argued that the accused, who had resided in Argentina under an assumed name, was kidnaped on May 11, 1960, by agents of the State of Israel and forcibly brought . . . [to Israel] in violation of international law. He summed up his submission by contending that the Court ought not to lend its support to an illegal act of the State, and that in these circumstances the State of Israel has no jurisdiction to try the accused.

Eichmann in the dock at the district court in Jerusalem, 1961
SOURCE: Library of Congress

On the other hand, the learned Attorney-General pleaded that . . . it is the duty of
the Court simply to try such crimes; and that in accordance with established judicial
precedents in England, the United States and Israel, the Court is not to enter into the
circumstances of the arrest of the accused and of his transfer to the area of jurisdiction
of the State, these questions having no bearing on the jurisdiction of the Court to try the
accused for the offenses for which he is being prosecuted, but only on the foreign relations of the State. The Attorney-General added that, with reference to the circumstances
of the arrest of the accused and his transfer to Israel, the Republic of Argentina had
lodged a complaint with the Security Council of the United Nations, which resolved on
June 23, 1960, as follows (Doc. S/4349):

The Security Council,
    Having examined the complaint that the transfer of Adolf Eichmann to the terri-
tory of Israel constitutes a violation of the sovereignty of the Argentine Republic, . . .
    Noting that the repetition of acts such as that giving rise to this situation would
involve a breach of the principles upon which international order is founded, creating
an atmosphere of insecurity and distrust incompatible with the preservation of peace,
    Mindful of the universal condemnation of the persecution of the Jews under the
Nazis and the concern of people in all countries that Eichmann should be brought to
appropriate justice for the crimes of which he is accused,

Noting at the same time that this resolution should in no way be interpreted as condoning the odious crimes of which Eichmann is accused,

    1. *Declares* that acts such as that under consideration, which affect the sovereignty of a Member State and therefore cause international friction, may, if repeated, endanger international peace and security;

    2. *Requests* the Government of Israel to make appropriate reparation in accordance with the Charter of the United Nations and the rules of international law;

    3. *Expresses* the hope that the traditionally friendly relations between Argentina and Israel will be advanced.

Pursuant to this Resolution the two Governments reached agreement on the settlement of the dispute between them, and on August 3, 1960, issued the following joint communiqué:

> The Governments of Argentina and Israel, animated by a desire to give effect to the resolution of the Security Council of June 23, 1960, in so far as the hope was expressed that the traditionally friendly relations between the two countries will be advanced, resolve to regard as closed the incident which arose out of the action taken by citizens of Israel, which infringed the fundamental rights of the State of Argentina. . . .

    41. It is an established rule of law that a person being tried for an offense against the laws of a State may not oppose his trial by reason of the illegality of his arrest or of the means whereby he was brought within the jurisdiction of that State. The courts in England, the United States and Israel have constantly held that the circumstances of the arrest and the mode of bringing of the accused into the territory of the State have no relevance to his trial, and they have consistently refused in all instances to enter upon an examination of these circumstances. . . .

    42. That principle is also acknowledged in Palestine case law. . . .

    43. . . . The question which poses itself from this point of view is—whether the principle . . . that the accused may not challenge his trial by reason of the illegality of his arrest or of the means whereby he was brought into the jurisdiction, is limited to the illegality of those means in the sense of the municipal law of the country in question, or whether the principle is general and also applies to the use of means which are a violation of international law, namely, a violation of the sovereignty of a foreign State. . . .

    44. . . . American precedents expressly establish that it makes no difference whether or not the measures whereby the accused was brought into the jurisdiction were unlawful in point of municipal law or of international law and they are all unanimous that the Court will not enter into an examination of this question, which is not relevant to the trial of the accused. The *ratio* of this rule is that the right to plead violation of the sovereignty of a State is the exclusive right of that State. Only a sovereign State may raise the plea or waive it, and the accused has no right to take over the rights of that State. . . .

Considerable importance attaches to this [principle] in the present case, in view of the settlement of the dispute between Argentina and Israel. . . . The indictment in this case was filed after Argentina had exonerated Israel of violation of her sovereignty and there was no longer any breach of international law. In these circumstances the accused cannot presume to speak, as it were, on behalf of Argentina and claim rights which that sovereign State had waived. . . .

    48. The Anglo-Saxon rule has been accepted by Continental jurists as well. . . .

    50. Indeed, there is no escaping the conclusion that the question of the violation of international law by the manner in which the accused was brought into the territory of a country arises at the international level, namely, the relations between the two countries concerned alone, and must find its solution at such level. A violation of international law

of this order constitutes an "international tort" to which the usual rules of current international law apply. . . .

Notes and Questions

1. Immediately after learning of the abduction, Argentina demanded "the restitution of Eichmann" and "the punishment of the individuals guilty of the violation of Argentine territory" and recalled its ambassador to Israel. As noted above, the June 1960 Security Council resolution on this matter requested that Israel make "appropriate reparation" to Argentina. In response, Israel stated that "the expressions of regret which we have already made directly to the Argentine Government constitute adequate reparations." Two weeks later, Argentina declared itself "not satisfied" with Israel's expressions of regret, and reserved the right to take appropriate action. Argentina then expelled the Israeli Ambassador to Argentina. In August 1960, the two states issued their joint communiqué declaring the incident "closed."

What, if anything, does the Security Council's failure to demand Eichmann's return suggest about international attitudes toward kidnapping? Might the international community react differently if the kidnapped person was not a notorious war criminal? Should it?

In considering what would constitute "appropriate reparation," note that in the *Rainbow Warrior* affair, an arbitral panel stated that "the condemnation of the French Republic for its breaches of its treaty obligations to New Zealand, made public by the decision of the Tribunal, constitutes in the circumstances appropriate satisfaction for the legal and moral damage caused to New Zealand." In the *Corfu Channel* case, 1949 I.C.J. 4, the ICJ held that the entry of British minesweepers into Albanian territorial waters to remove undersea mines violated Albania's sovereignty. It then stated that "this declaration by the Court constitutes in itself appropriate satisfaction." Is the Security Council statement that Israel had violated Argentina's sovereignty "appropriate reparation" in this case?

2. In her controversial report on the Eichmann trial, Hannah Arendt argued that the kidnapping was justified:

> Its justification was the unprecedentedness of the crime and the coming into existence of a Jewish State. There were, however, important mitigating circumstances in that there hardly existed an alternative if one indeed wished to bring Eichmann to justice. . . . In short, the realm of legality offered no alternative to kidnaping. Those who are convinced that justice, and nothing else, is the end of law will be inclined to condone the kidnaping act, though not because of precedents.

Hannah Arendt, Eichmann in Jerusalem: A Report on the Banality of Evil 264-265 (1963).

However, Arendt went on to argue that the Israeli Attorney General's explicit use of the trial as a pedagogic device to educate Israelis and the world about the Holocaust undermined its legal function: "the purpose of a trial is to render justice, and nothing else; even the noblest of ulterior purposes . . . can only detract from the law's main business: to weigh the charges brought against the accused, to render judgment, and to mete out due punishment." *Id.* at 233.

The *Eichmann* court stated:

> In this maze of insistent questions, the path of the Court was and remains clear. It must not allow itself to be enticed to stray into provinces which are outside its sphere. The judicial process has ways of its own, laid down by law and immutable, whatever the subject-matter of the trial. . . . The purpose of every criminal trial is to investigate the

truth of the prosecutor's charges against the accused who is on trial, and, if the accused is convicted, to mete out due punishment to him.

Is it appropriate for the prosecution to pursue extralegal goals through the vehicle of a criminal trial? May the prosecution avoid doing so in cases involving events as momentous as those at issue in the Eichmann case? Do such extralegal goals undermine the court's legal role?

C. Kidnapping or Extradition?: The Alvarez-Machain Case

One way that states can avoid disputes like those arising out of the *Eichmann* case is by entering into extradition treaties. These treaties set forth the procedures by which one state can request another state to send it individuals charged with a crime in the first state. However, extradition treaties do not solve all problems in this area, as the case of *United States v. Alvarez-Machain* illustrates.

Humberto Alvarez-Machain is a Mexican citizen and a medical doctor. He was indicted in the United States for his alleged participation in the February 1985 torture and murder of a U.S. Drug Enforcement Agency (DEA) agent who was working in Mexico. On April 2, 1990, Alvarez-Machain was forcibly kidnapped from his office in Mexico and flown by private plane to Texas, where he was arrested by DEA agents. The DEA approved the use of Mexican nationals to apprehend Alvarez-Machain. Alvarez-Machain moved to dismiss the complaint on the grounds that the abduction violated an extradition treaty between the United States and Mexico and divested the court of jurisdiction over him.

United States v. Alvarez-Machain

504 U.S. 655 (1992)

CHIEF JUSTICE REHNQUIST delivered the opinion of the Court.

Although we have never before addressed the precise issue raised in the present case, we have previously considered proceedings in claimed violation of an extradition treaty and proceedings against a defendant brought before a court by means of a forcible abduction. We addressed the former issue in *United States v. Rauscher,* 119 U.S. 407 (1886); more precisely, the issue whether the Webster-Ashburton Treaty of 1842, which governed extraditions between England and the United States, prohibited the prosecution of defendant Rauscher for a crime other than the crime for which he had been extradited. Whether this prohibition, known as the doctrine of specialty, was an intended part of the treaty had been disputed between the two nations for some time. [After reviewing the treaty's terms and history, and the practice of nations, the *Rauscher* court held:]

[A] person who has been brought within the jurisdiction of the court *by virtue of proceedings under an extradition treaty,* can only be tried for one of the offenses described in that treaty, and for the offense with which he is charged in the proceedings for his extradition, until a reasonable time and opportunity have been given him, after his release or trial upon such charge, to return to the country from whose asylum he had been forcibly taken under those proceedings. . . .

In *Ker v. Illinois,* 119 U.S. 436 (1886), . . . decided the same day as *Rauscher,* we addressed the issue of a defendant brought before the court by way of a forcible abduction. Frederick Ker had been tried and convicted in an Illinois court for larceny; his presence before the court was procured by means of forcible abduction from Peru. . . . We distinguished Ker's case from *Rauscher*, on the basis that Ker was not brought into the United States by virtue of the extradition treaty between the United States and Peru, and rejected Ker's argument that he had a right under the extradition treaty to be returned to this country only in accordance with its terms. We rejected Ker's due process argument more broadly, holding . . . that "such forcible abduction is no sufficient reason why the party should not answer when brought within the jurisdiction of the court which has the right to try him for such an offense, and presents no valid objection to his trial in such court." . . .

The only differences between *Ker* and the present case . . . are that *Ker* was decided on the premise that there was no governmental involvement in the abduction, and Peru, from which Ker was abducted, did not object to his prosecution. Respondent finds these differences to be dispositive, as did the Court of Appeals . . . contending that they show that respondent's prosecution, like the prosecution of Rauscher, violates the implied terms of a valid extradition treaty. . . . [O]ur first inquiry must be whether the abduction of respondent from Mexico violated the Extradition Treaty between the United States and Mexico. If we conclude that the Treaty does not prohibit respondent's abduction, the rule in *Ker* applies, and the court need not inquire as to how respondent came before it.

In construing a treaty, as in construing a statute, we first look to its terms to determine its meaning. The Treaty says nothing about the obligations of the United States and Mexico to refrain from forcible abductions of people from the territory of the other nation, or the consequences under the Treaty if such an abduction occurs. . . .

. . . Article 9 of the Treaty . . . provides:

> 1. Neither Contracting Party shall be bound to deliver up its own nationals, but the executive authority of the requested Party shall, if not prevented by the laws of that Party, have the power to deliver them up if, in its discretion, it be deemed proper to do so.
> 2. If extradition is not granted pursuant to paragraph 1 of this Article, the requested Party shall submit the case to its competent authorities for the purpose of prosecution. . . .

According to respondent, Article 9 embodies the terms of the bargain which the United States struck: If the United States wishes to prosecute a Mexican national, it may request that individual's extradition. Upon a request from the United States, Mexico may either extradite the individual or submit the case to the proper authorities for prosecution in Mexico. In this way, respondent reasons, each nation preserved its right to choose whether its nationals would be tried in its own courts or by the courts of the other nation. This preservation of rights would be frustrated if either nation were free to abduct nationals of the other nation for the purposes of prosecution. More broadly, respondent reasons, as did the Court of Appeals, that all the processes and restrictions on the obligation to extradite established by the Treaty would make no sense if either nation were free to resort to forcible kidnaping to gain the presence of an individual for prosecution in a manner not contemplated by the Treaty.

We do not read the Treaty in such a fashion. Article 9 does not purport to specify the only way in which one country may gain custody of a national of the other country for the purposes of prosecution. In the absence of an extradition treaty, nations are under no obligation to surrender those in their country to foreign authorities for prosecution. Extradition treaties exist so as to impose mutual obligations to surrender individuals in certain defined sets of circumstances, following established procedures. The Treaty thus provides a mechanism which would not otherwise exist, requiring, under certain circumstances, the United States and Mexico to extradite individuals to the other country, and establishing the procedures to be followed when the Treaty is invoked.

The history of negotiation and practice under the Treaty also fails to show that abductions outside of the Treaty constitute a violation of the Treaty. As the Solicitor General notes, the Mexican Government was made aware, as early as 1906, of the *Ker* doctrine, and the United States' position that it applied to forcible abductions made outside of the terms of the United States-Mexico Extradition Treaty. Nonetheless, the current version of the Treaty, signed in 1978, does not attempt to establish a rule that would in any way curtail the effect of *Ker*. . . .

Respondent contends that the Treaty must be interpreted against the backdrop of customary international law, and that international abductions are "so clearly prohibited in international law" that there was no reason to include such a clause in the Treaty itself. The international censure of international abductions is further evidenced, according to respondent, by the United Nations Charter and the Charter of the Organization of American States. Respondent does not argue that these sources of international law provide an independent basis for the right respondent asserts not to be tried in the United States, but rather that they should inform the interpretation of the Treaty terms. . . .

[T]he difficulty with the support respondent garners from international law is that none of it relates to the practice of nations in relation to extradition treaties. In *Rauscher*, we implied a term in the Webster-Ashburton Treaty because of the practice of nations with regard to extradition treaties. In the instant case, respondent would imply terms in the Extradition Treaty from the practice of nations with regards to international law more generally. Respondent would have us find that the Treaty acts as a prohibition against a violation of the general principle of international law that one government may not "exercise its police power in the territory of another state." There are many actions which could be taken by a nation that would violate this principle, including waging war, but it cannot seriously be contended that an invasion of the United States by Mexico would violate the terms of the Extradition Treaty between the two nations.

. . . In *Rauscher*, the implication of a doctrine of specialty into the terms of the Webster-Ashburton Treaty, which, by its terms, required the presentation of evidence establishing probable cause of the crime of extradition before extradition was required, was a small step to take. By contrast, to imply from the terms of this Treaty that it prohibits obtaining the presence of an individual by means outside of the procedures the Treaty establishes requires a much larger inferential leap, with only the most general of international law principles to support it. The general principles cited by respondent simply fail to persuade us that we should imply in the United States-Mexico Extradition Treaty a term prohibiting international abductions.

Respondent and his *amici* may be correct that respondent's abduction was "shocking," and that it may be in violation of general international law principles. Mexico has protested the abduction of respondent through diplomatic notes, and the decision of whether respondent should be returned to Mexico, as a matter outside of the Treaty, is a matter for the Executive Branch. We conclude, however, that respondent's abduction was not in violation of the Extradition Treaty between the United States and Mexico, and therefore the rule of *Ker v. Illinois* is fully applicable to this case. The fact of respondent's forcible abduction does not therefore prohibit his trial in a court in the United States for violations of the criminal laws of the United States.

JUSTICE STEVENS, with whom JUSTICE BLACKMUN and JUSTICE O'CONNOR join, dissenting.

I

The extradition treaty with Mexico is a comprehensive document containing 23 articles and an appendix listing the extraditable offenses covered by the agreement. The parties announced their purpose in the preamble: The two governments desire "to cooperate more closely in the fight against crime and, to this end, to mutually render better assistance in matters of extradition." From the preamble, through the description of the parties' obligations with respect to offenses committed within as well as beyond the territory of a requesting party, the delineation of the procedures and evidentiary requirements for extradition, the special provisions for political offenses and capital punishment, and other details, the Treaty appears to have been designed to cover the entire subject of extradition. . . . Article 9 expressly provides that neither contracting party is bound to deliver up its own nationals, although it may do so in its discretion, but if it does not do so, it "shall submit the case to its competent authorities for purposes of prosecution."

The Government's claim that the Treaty is not exclusive, but permits forcible governmental kidnaping, would transform these, and other, provisions into little more than verbiage. For example, provisions requiring "sufficient" evidence to grant extradition (Art. 3), withholding extradition for political or military offenses (Art. 5), withholding extradition when the person sought has already been tried (Art. 6), withholding extradition when the statute of limitations for the crime has lapsed (Art. 7), and granting the requested country discretion to refuse to extradite an individual who would face the death penalty in the requesting country (Art. 8), would serve little purpose if the requesting country could simply kidnap the person. . . . In addition, all of these provisions "only make sense if they are understood as *requiring* each treaty signatory to comply with those procedures whenever it wishes to obtain jurisdiction over an individual who is located in another treaty nation."

It is true, as the Court notes, that there is no express promise by either party to refrain from forcible abductions in the territory of the other nation. Relying on that omission, the Court, in effect, concludes that the Treaty merely creates an optional method of obtaining jurisdiction over alleged offenders, and that the parties silently reserved the right to resort to self-help whenever they deem force more expeditious than legal process. If the United States, for example, thought it more expedient to torture or simply to execute a person rather than to attempt extradition, these options would be equally available because they, too, were not explicitly prohibited by the Treaty. That, however, is a highly improbable interpretation of a consensual agreement, which on its face appears to have been intended to set forth comprehensive and exclusive rules concerning the subject of extradition. In my opinion, "the manifest scope and object of the treaty itself," *Rauscher*, 119 U.S. at 422, plainly imply a mutual undertaking to respect the territorial integrity of the other contracting party. . . .

Notes and Questions

1. The *Alvarez-Machain* ruling provoked a strong international reaction. China, Colombia, Costa Rica, Cuba, Denmark, Ecuador, Guatemala, Honduras, Jamaica, Malaysia, and Venezuela all filed formal diplomatic protests with the United States in the months following the decision. The opinion also prompted actions in several multilateral fora. For example, in 1992, the UN Working Group on Arbitrary Detention determined that "the object and purpose of the Treaty, and an analysis of the context, lead to the unquestionable conclusion that abduction for the purpose of bringing someone in Mexico or in the United States before a court of the requesting party is a breach of the 1978 Treaty." Similarly, the Inter-American Juridical Committee, an Organization of American States advisory body, found that "the abduction in question was a serious violation of public international law since it was a transgression of the territorial sovereignty of Mexico." It noted that "any state that violates an international obligation must make

reparations for the consequences of the violation," with the "purpose of returning, to the extent possible, the situation to the way it was before the transgression occurred." The Committee concluded that the United States was therefore obliged to repatriate Alvarez-Machain. Legal Opinion on the Decision of the Supreme Court of the United States of America, CJI/Res. II-15/92.

Why did the international community react so differently to the abductions of Eichmann and Alvarez-Machain?

2. After the Supreme Court's ruling, Alvarez-Machain was tried in federal district court in Los Angeles. After the prosecution concluded its case, the trial judge granted Alvarez-Machain's motion for acquittal and stated that the case against Alvarez-Machain had been based on "hunches" and the "wildest speculation." After the acquittal, Alvarez-Machain filed suit in federal district court against the United States, several DEA agents, and several individuals who participated in his abduction. Alvarez-Machain's suit eventually reached the U.S. Supreme Court, and is discussed in Chapter 5.

D. Challenging Irregular Renditions in Other Jurisdictions

Domestic courts in several other states have considered whether to exercise jurisdiction over criminal defendants who were irregularly brought into the territory of the prosecuting state. For example, in *R. v. Horseferry Road Magistrates' Court, Ex Parte Bennett*, [1993] 3 All E.R. 138, the English police located the defendant, a New Zealand citizen, in South Africa. After consulting with the Crown Prosecution Service, the police decided not to seek formal extradition. Instead, they persuaded the South African police to arrest the defendant and return him forcibly to England under the pretext of deporting him to New Zealand via London's Heathrow Airport. The defendant was arrested by the English police upon arrival at Heathrow.

By a 4-1 vote, the Law Lords held that English courts have discretion not to exercise jurisdiction over a criminal defendant where English police disregarded the protections of formal extradition procedures and had the defendant seized abroad by illegal means.

Lord Griffiths wrote:

> Extradition procedures are designed not only to ensure that criminals are returned from one country to another but also to protect the rights of those who are accused of crimes by the requesting country. . . . If a practice developed in which the police or prosecuting authorities of this country ignored extradition procedures and secured the return of an accused by a mere request to police colleagues in another country they would be flouting the extradition procedures and depriving the accused of the safeguards built into the extradition process for his benefit. It is to my mind unthinkable that in such circumstances the court should declare itself to be powerless and stand idly by. . . .

Lord Lowry wrote:

> [I]f British officialdom at any level has participated in or encouraged the kidnaping, it seems to represent a grave contravention of international law, the comity of nations and the rule of law generally if our courts allow themselves to be used by the executive to try an offense which the courts would not be dealing with if the rule of law had prevailed.

In dissent, Lord Oliver argued that courts should not concern themselves with pretrial police impropriety that does not affect the fairness of the trial itself. In his view, the proper remedy for Executive Branch unlawfulness is civil or criminal proceedings against the wrongdoers, not the denial of criminal jurisdiction. Lord Oliver rejected the argument that English courts should act to protect the rights of foreign states, as such matters "can only properly be pursued on a diplomatic level between the government of the United Kingdom and the government of that state."

Courts in New Zealand and Australia have also held that judges have discretion to refuse to exercise jurisdiction over defendants who have been irregularly brought into the jurisdiction. For example, in *Levinge v. Director of Custodial Services*, 9 N.S.W.L.R. 546 (1987), the New South Wales court of appeals considered the *Eichmann* case and relevant Anglo-American precedents and stated "[w]here a person, however unlawfully, is brought into the jurisdiction and is before a court in this State, that court has undoubted jurisdiction to deal with him or her. But it also has discretion not to do so, where to exercise its discretion would involve an abuse of the court's process. . . . [S]uch conduct may exist, including wrongful and even unlawful involvement in bypassing the regular machinery for extradition and participation in unauthorized and unlawful removal of criminal suspects from one jurisdiction to another."

The South African Supreme Court adopted a different approach in *State v. Ebrahim*, 1991 (2) SALR 553. In *Ebrahim*, two men identifying themselves as South African police officers seized a South African member of the military wing of the anti-apartheid African National Congress in Swaziland in December 1986. Ebrahim was bound, gagged, blindfolded, and brought to Pretoria and charged with treason. Swaziland did not protest this abduction. Ebrahim argued that his abduction and rendition violated international law, and that the trial court was thus incompetent to try him because international law was a part of South African law.

Invoking Roman-Dutch common law, the Court concluded that it lacked jurisdiction to try a person brought before it from another state by means of state-sponsored abduction. These common law rules embodied fundamental legal principles, including "the preservation and promotion of human rights, friendly international relations, and the sound administration of justice." The Court continued:

> The individual must be protected from unlawful arrest and abduction, jurisdictional boundaries must not be exceeded, international legal sovereignty must be respected, the legal process must be fair towards those affected by it and the misuse thereof must be avoided in order to protect and promote the dignity and integrity of the judicial system. This applies equally to the State. When the State is itself party to a dispute, as for example in criminal cases, it must come to court "with clean hands" as it were. When the State is itself involved in an abduction across international borders as in the instant case, its hands cannot be said to be clean.

The Court also noted that "the abduction was a violation of the applicable rules of international law, that these rules are part of [South African] law, and that this violation of these rules deprived the trial court of competence to hear the matter." In a subsequent civil proceeding, Ebrahim was awarded compensation for the kidnapping.

Similar cases have come before European human rights bodies. Article 5 of the European Convention on Human Rights provides that "no one shall be deprived of his liberty" except in certain cases, including "lawful arrest or detention" for purposes of trial. *Ocalan v. Turkey*, App. No. 46221/99 (2005), involved the arrest of the leader of the Workers' Party of Kurdistan. In 1998, Ocalan was expelled from Syria, where he had lived for many years. After short stops in Greece, Russia, and Italy, Ocalan was taken to Kenya, where he stayed at the ambassador's residence. However, Kenya alleged that he entered the country improperly, and that his presence in the country constituted a security risk. After a meeting between the Greek Ambassador and Kenya's Foreign Minister, the Ambassador advised Ocalan that he was free to leave the country. Kenyan officials then picked up Ocalan to drive him to the airport. At the airport, Ocalan was taken to an aircraft where Turkish officials were waiting for him. He was then arrested and flown to Turkey, where he was convicted of terrorist acts by a national security court. The European Court of Human Rights rejected Ocalan's claim that his capture violated Article 5 of the European Convention on Human Rights:

> The Kenyan authorities did not perceive the applicant's arrest by the Turkish officials on board an aircraft at Nairobi Airport as being in any way a violation of Kenyan sovereignty. In sum, neither aspect of the applicant's detention—whether his interception by the Kenyan authorities before his transfer to the airport, or his arrest by the Turkish officials in the aircraft—led to an international dispute between Kenya and Turkey or to any deterioration in their diplomatic relations. The Kenyan authorities did not lodge any protest with the Turkish government on these points or claim any redress from Turkey, such as the applicant's return or compensation.

The Court concluded that Ocalan's arrest was not inconsistent with Kenyan sovereignty or international law, and did not violate the Convention.

What bearing, if any, do these cases have on the question before the court in *Dokmanovic?*

E. The ICTY Opines, Eventually

Dokmanovic argued that his arrest violated international law and divested the ICTY of jurisdiction to try him. After hearing testimony from Dokmanovic and UNTAES officials, the ICTY Trial Chamber concluded that Dokmanovic entered into Croatia "of his own free will" on the basis of his belief that he would be meeting with Transitional Administrator Klein to discuss his property in Croatia. As a result, the court determined that the prosecutor's "ruse" did not constitute a "forcible abduction or kidnaping." The court then determined that, absent an extradition treaty, "luring a suspect into another jurisdiction in order to effect his arrest is not an abuse of the suspect's rights or an abuse of process." Since the method used to arrest and detain Dokmanovic "was justified and *legal,*" the court did not have to decide "whether the International Tribunal has the authority to exercise jurisdiction over a defendant *illegally* obtained from abroad." *Prosecutor v. Mrskic, et al.,* Case No. IT-95-13a-PT (1997). Shortly after the close of evidence at his trial, but before a verdict was rendered, Dokmanovic committed suicide, and the ICTY Appeals Chamber had no occasion to consider the legality of Dokmanovic's arrest.

In the case of *Prosecutor v. Nikolic,* the Appeals Chamber did address the question of whether the ICTY could exercise personal jurisdiction over a defendant who had been kidnapped. The defendant in this action was abducted by the NATO-led stabilization force in Bosnia, acting in collusion with unknown individuals from Serbia and Montenegro.

Prosecutor v. Nikolic, Decision on Interlocutory Appeal Concerning Legality of Arrest

Case No. IT-94-2-AR73 (2003)

20. The impact of a breach of a State's sovereignty on the exercise of jurisdiction is a novel issue for this Tribunal. There is no case law directly on the point, and the [ICTY's] Statute and the Rules provide little guidance. . . . [As a result,] the Appeals Chamber will seek guidance from national case law, where the issue at hand has often arisen, in order to determine state practice on the matter.

21. In several national cases, courts have held that jurisdiction should not be set aside, even though there might have been irregularities in the manner in which the accused was

brought before them. [The court discussed a French case that upheld jurisdiction over a defendant kidnaped in Germany, a German court that upheld jurisdiction over a defendant improperly brought into Germany, and *Alvarez-Machain*.]

22. On the other hand, there have been cases in which the exercise of jurisdiction has been declined. [The court reviewed an incident in the 1930s when Germany released a suspect who it had kidnapped from Switzerland, and decisions by the Supreme Court of South Africa and the UK House of Lords where courts declined to exercise jurisdiction over defendants.]

23. With regard to cases concerning the same kinds of crimes as those falling within the jurisdiction of the [ICTY], reference may be made to *Eichmann* and *Barbie*. In *Eichmann*, the Supreme Court of Israel decided to exercise jurisdiction over the accused, notwithstanding the apparent breach of Argentina's sovereignty involved in his abduction. . . . In *Barbie*, the French Court of Cassation (Criminal Chamber) asserted its jurisdiction over the accused, despite [an irregular rendition], on the basis, *inter alia*, of the special nature of the crimes ascribed to the accused, namely, crimes against humanity.

24. Although it is difficult to identify a clear pattern in this case law . . . two principles seem to have support in State practice as evidenced by the practice of their courts. First, in cases of crimes such as genocide, crimes against humanity and war crimes . . . ("Universally Condemned Offenses"), courts seem to find in the special character of these offenses and, arguably, in their seriousness, a good reason for not setting aside jurisdiction. Second, absent a complaint by the State whose sovereignty has been breached or in the event of a diplomatic resolution of the breach, it is easier for courts to assert their jurisdiction. . . .

25. Universally Condemned Offenses are a matter of concern to the international community as a whole. There is a legitimate expectation that those accused of those crimes will be brought to justice swiftly. Accountability for these crimes is a necessary condition to the achievement of international justice, which plays a critical role in the reconciliation and rebuilding based on the rule of law of countries and societies torn apart by international and internecine conflicts.

26. . . . In the opinion of the Appeals Chamber, the damage caused to international justice by not apprehending fugitives accused of serious violations of international humanitarian law is comparatively higher than the injury, if any, caused to the sovereignty of a State by a limited intrusion in its territory. . . . Therefore, the Appeals Chamber does not consider that in cases of universally condemned offenses, jurisdiction should be set aside on the ground that there was a violation of the sovereignty of a State, when the violation is brought about by the apprehension of fugitives from international justice, whatever the consequences for the international responsibility of the State or organisation involved. . . .

[The tribunal then considered whether the violation of the accused's human rights divest the court of jurisdiction.]

30. . . . Although the assessment of the seriousness of the human rights violations depends on the circumstances of each case and cannot be made *in abstracto*, certain human rights violations are of such a serious nature that they require that the exercise of jurisdiction be declined. It would be inappropriate for a court of law to try the victims of these abuses. Apart from such exceptional cases, however, the remedy of setting aside jurisdiction will . . . usually be disproportionate. The correct balance must therefore be maintained between the fundamental rights of the accused and the essential interests of the international community in the prosecution of persons charged with serious violations of international humanitarian law.

[The Appeals Chamber concluded that the kidnapping of the accused did not divest the court of jurisdiction.]

Notes and Questions

1. How does the Appeals Chamber know that the "damage caused to international justice" by not apprehending individuals accused of serious violations of international humanitarian law is "comparatively higher" than the injury caused by violations of state sovereignty? Does *Eichmann* or state practice support this claim?

2. Is the Appeals Chamber suggesting that a suspect accused of universally condemned offenses somehow enjoys fewer rights than one accused of lesser crimes? What justification would there be for such a position?

3. Why did the Appeals Chamber rely upon the decisions of national tribunals? Is an irregular rendition to an international tribunal more justifiable than an irregular rendition to a national court?

F. Irregular Renditions by the United States of Suspected Terrorists

As *Alvarez-Machain* demonstrates, the U.S. government has historically engaged in a limited number of irregular renditions to bring suspects to trial in the United States. During the Clinton Administration, the United States participated in the rendition of suspects to third states for trial in those states. Following the September 11, 2001 attacks, President Bush broadened the CIA's authority to render terrorist suspects to other states, in particular authorizing the Agency to transfer individuals to third countries not simply to stand trial but also for purposes of intelligence gathering and detention. Thereafter, the United States transferred more than 100 individuals to Egypt, Jordan, Pakistan, Morocco, Saudi Arabia, Syria, Uzbekistan, and other states believed to employ harsh interrogation techniques, including torture and cruel, inhuman, or degrading treatment. Typically, these transferees were held incommunicado and neither formally charged with any crime nor permitted to challenge their detention before any authority; their detention remained secret, without notification to families or the International Committee of the Red Cross. Many former transferees allege that they were mistreated while in confinement.

The U.S. policy of irregular renditions sparked considerable outrage, particularly in Europe. In a series of reports, the Council of Europe strongly condemned U.S. rendition policy, and officials in Denmark, Ireland, Norway, Spain, and Sweden either undertook investigations into the use of European airspace by CIA-operated aircraft, protested the presence of CIA-operated planes in their territory, or asked the CIA to avoid use of their airspace for purposes incompatible with international law. Several states opened criminal investigations; in 2009, Italy's highest court affirmed the convictions, in absentia, of 22 CIA operatives who participated in the extraordinary rendition of Abu Omar, who was captured in Milan and flown to Egypt, where he was allegedly tortured.

Many of the legal criticisms leveled against the program center upon the prohibition of *refoulement*, i.e., the return of people to places where they will likely be subjected to persecution; the prohibition of enforced disappearances, which proscribes the concealment of the fate and whereabouts of individuals deprived of their liberty; and the prohibition against torture and cruel, inhuman, or degrading treatment. The prohibition on *refoulement* is found in a wide variety of human rights instruments. For example, Article 3 of the 1984 Convention Against Torture (CAT) provides that "[n]o State Party shall expel, return (*refouler*) or extradite a person to another State where there are substantial grounds for believing that he would be in danger of being subjected to torture."

The United States, which is a party to the CAT, claims that its policies and actions do not violate this obligation. For example, pursuant to a formal treaty understanding approved by the Senate and included in the U.S. instrument of ratification, the United States interprets CAT's "substantial grounds" provision to mean it is "more likely than not" that the transferee would be tortured. Critics claim that the U.S. position threatens to undermine the CAT's absolute prohibition on torture. The Committee Against Torture has indicated that "substantial grounds" means more than "mere theory or suspicion" but need not meet the test of being "highly probable."

Moreover, U.S. officials have emphasized that the United States obtains promises from the receiving state before transferring individuals to states where they face a risk of torture. For example, in December 2005 Secretary of State Condoleezza Rice stated that "the United States has not transported anyone, and will not transport anyone, to a country when we believe he will be tortured. Where appropriate, the United States seeks assurances that transferred persons will not be tortured."

The practice of relying upon diplomatic assurances has attracted substantial criticism from human rights advocates and international bodies; critics charge that the assurances are neither credible nor enforceable. In 2006, the Committee Against Torture issued a non-binding recommendation that the United States should only rely on "diplomatic assurances in regard to States which do not systematically violate the Convention's provisions, and after a thorough examination of the merits of each individual case. The [United States] should establish and implement clear procedures for obtaining such assurances, with adequate judicial mechanisms for review, and effective post-return monitoring arrangements."

Individuals subject to irregular renditions have found little relief in U.S. courts. Consider, for example, the case of Khaled El-Masri, a German citizen of Lebanese descent. On December 31, 2003, he was seized by Macedonian authorities while attempting to cross the border between Serbia and Macedonia. The Macedonian authorities held him incommunicado in a Skopje hotel room for 23 days, interrogating him continuously about purported associations with al Qaeda. El-Masri was then taken to an airport, transferred into CIA custody, and flown to Kabul, Afghanistan, where he was imprisoned for four months in a CIA-run facility, beaten, and interrogated about his alleged involvement with terrorists. Finally, in late May 2004, El-Masri was released in a remote area of northern Albania, after which he returned to his home to Germany. He was never charged with a crime. El-Masri contends that his captors told him that his detention resulted from a case of mistaken identity; his name is similar to that of Khalid al-Masri, a suspected al Qaeda operative. A Council of Europe investigation found that El-Masri's account of his rendition and detention was substantially accurate.

Following his release, El-Masri filed suit in the United States. The action was dismissed on the basis of the state secrets privilege, under which the government may prevent the disclosure of information in a judicial proceeding if there is a reasonable danger that such disclosure will expose military matters which, in the interest of national security, should not be divulged. *El-Masri v. United States*, 479 F.3d 296 (4th Cir.), *cert. denied*, 552 U.S. 947 (2007).

Detainees have enjoyed greater success at the European Court of Human Rights, and in July 2009, El-Masri filed an action there against Macedonia. On December 13, 2012, the Grand Chamber of the Court unanimously found multiple violations of the European Convention of Human Rights. The court found that Macedonia violated prohibitions against arbitrary detention and inhuman and degrading treatment when it held El-Masri in a hotel room. It also found that Macedonia was "directly responsible" for the torture at the Skopje airport by a CIA rendition team: "the acts complained of were carried out in the presence of officials of the respondent state and within its jurisdiction . . . [and] with the acquiescence or connivance of its authorities." In addition, the extrajudicial transfer of El-Masri to CIA agents "knowingly exposed him to real risks of ill-treatment" in violation of the Convention. Moreover, the Court found that the subsequent detention in Kabul was imputable to Macedonia, and thus that Macedonia was responsible for violating El-Masri's rights "during the entire period of his captivity." Given the "extreme seriousness of the violations of Convention," the court awarded him €60,000 (approximately $78,000).

In July 2014, the Court decided two cases involving "high value detainees" who had been in CIA custody and were transferred to a secret CIA detention facility in Poland. In both cases, the Court found that Poland had violated the European Convention on Human Rights through its complicity in the illegal treatment and detention of the detainees by U.S. officials on Polish territory. Both individuals were awarded non-pecuniary damages of €100,000. *Al-Nashiri v. Poland; Husayn (Abu Zubaydah) v. Poland.*

The Obama Administration has engaged in a limited number of irregular renditions. Notably, these renditions are for the purpose of bringing suspects to the United States for trial. For example, two Swedish citizens and a UK resident were arrested in Djibouti in August 2012 and, two months later, clandestinely taken into custody by the FBI and flown to the United States to stand trial for providing material support to al-Shabaab, an Islamist militia in Somalia that the United States considers a terrorist group. In June 2014, a joint Special Operations and FBI mission captured Ahmed Abu Khattala in a raid on his home near Benghazi, Libya. Abu Khattala is suspected of organizing the 2012 attack on the U.S. diplomatic compound in Benghazi that led to the deaths of four Americans. He was transferred to Washington, D.C., and has been indicted by a grand jury for murder, destruction of U.S. property, and providing material support and resources to terrorists resulting in death.

Notes and Questions

1. In *El-Masri*, the European Court of Human Rights held Macedonia responsible for its own conduct, such as transferring him to CIA agents knowing of the risk of mistreatment. What justifies the Court in finding Macedonia also responsible for unlawful acts by United States officials after El-Masri had been transferred to CIA agents in Kabul?

2. Under international law, does (or should) it matter whether the underlying purpose of an irregular rendition is to conduct an interrogation, as in the *El-Masri* case, or to put the suspect on trial?

IV. SOVEREIGN IMMUNITY: SUING ARGENTINA IN U.S. COURTS

Having examined the various ways that states assert authority, or jurisdiction, over people or activities, we now turn to certain situations where states have refrained from applying the general norms governing jurisdiction. Thus, states have excluded classes of entities—including foreign states; certain government officials, such as heads of state and diplomats; and international organizations—from the exercise of their jurisdiction in certain circumstances. Our focus will be on foreign state immunities, as this is the immunity most frequently raised in domestic court litigation.

The concept of state immunity from jurisdiction originated at a time when kings were considered to be the embodiment of a state's sovereignty, and when diplomatic envoys were considered to be rulers' personal representatives. The prevailing view was that, because they were of equal standing, one sovereign monarch could not be subject to the jurisdiction of another sovereign monarch: *par in parem non habet imperium.* Moreover, just as a king would not be subject to jurisdiction while visiting another state, so too the monarch's representatives were granted immunity.

Over time, the idea of an identity between state and ruler faded away, but states continued to extend to other states an absolute immunity from jurisdiction to adjudicate and jurisdiction to enforce. Governments justified these broad immunities by reference to the dignity, equality, and independence of states. However, pressures to limit various immunities grew as states and state instrumentalities became increasingly involved in international transactions. While recent developments have restricted traditional notions of sovereign immunity, the concept and policies underlying sovereign immunity remain important in much transnational litigation.

The materials that follow examine the historical development of the doctrine of sovereign immunity and its application in the United States. They will examine the role of domestic courts in determining foreign sovereign immunity; how well current doctrine serves the purposes underlying sovereign immunity; and whether current doctrine appropriately balances the interests of sovereigns and the non-state actors who deal with foreign state entities.

The goals for this Problem include:

- to understand the doctrinal and practical implications of the shift from the absolute theory to the restrictive theory of sovereign immunity;
- to understand the scope of the commercial activities exception to sovereign immunity; and
- to understand the controversies associated with litigation over sovereign debt.

A. *The Problem*

In 2001, the Republic of Argentina experienced a severe economic crisis. Inflation rose to over 40 percent, the stock market declined by roughly 60 percent, nearly half of the Argentine population was living below the poverty line, and looting and riots were common. In December of that year, Argentina's President declared a temporary moratorium on principal and interest payments on more than $100 billon of public external debt (i.e., money Argentina had borrowed from foreign creditors), triggering what at the time was the largest sovereign default ever. The size and complexity of Argentina's external debt problem—involving multiple bond issues held by hundreds of thousands of creditors all over the globe—gave rise to novel and difficult legal issues, some of which are explored below; Argentina's economic difficulties also led to dozens of disputes filed under various bilateral investment treaties, which are discussed in Chapter 11.

When a private company defaults, domestic bankruptcy procedures typically provide for an orderly resolution between creditors and the defaulting debtor. By contrast, no formal bankruptcy system exists for sovereign states. Thus, an informal system has developed, in which states attempt to restructure their debt with creditors, typically integrating debt relief with new funding and appropriate economic policy adjustment. In recent years, many states, including Russia, Mexico, and Greece have emerged from debt crises through these restructuring processes.

In the years following its default, Argentina successfully restructured much of its foreign debt. In particular, in 2005 and 2010, the government unilaterally offered to exchange the bonds on which it had defaulted in 2001 for new debt instruments, which were worth approximately 30 percent of the value of the original bonds. Given Argentina's refusal to make payments on the original bonds, most bondholders accepted the new terms, and these agreements covered 92.4 percent of the debt. By June 2014, Argentina had made timely payments of some $190 billion on this restructured debt.

A number of hedge funds, including Aurelius Capital, NML Capital, and EM Ltd., purchased on secondary markets hundreds of millions of dollars of original bonds issued by Argentina. These firms, which allegedly paid approximately 20 cents on the dollar, refused to tender their defaulted bonds for new securities. Rather, as the bonds were governed by New York law and provided for jurisdiction in New York, the firms filed lawsuits in New York City (and elsewhere) to collect the debt in full, plus interest. By 2014, these firms obtained final judgments in the United States District Court in New York City for nearly $2.4 billion. To collect on these unsatisfied judgments, the hedge funds attempted to attach various Argentine assets, including central bank funds on deposit at the Federal Reserve Bank in New York, the presidential airplane, and a navy vessel docked in Ghana.

In some actions, hedge funds relied on clauses in the original bonds providing that the payment obligations in the original bonds would rank equally with Argentina's other foreign debt obligations. The hedge funds argued that these clauses prohibited Argentina from paying the exchange bondholders unless it also made payments on the original bonds. In a 2012 opinion, a district court agreed, and ordered Argentina to specifically perform its contractual obligations by making "ratable payments" to the hedge funds whenever it makes payments to certain other bondholders. As the court later clarified, the order would effectively require Argentina to pay its debt to plaintiffs in full, an amount in excess of $1.4 billion, if it continued to pay the exchange bondholders. The injunction purported to enjoin Argentina from making payment outside the United States to bondholders outside the United States holding bonds governed by foreign law.

Argentina's President declared that the injunction amounted to "extortion," and its counsel stated in open court that the country would not comply with the injunction. Argentina claimed that if it paid plaintiffs in full, it would likewise have to pay other holders of the original bonds in full. In addition, it would also be obligated to pay the exchange bondholders in full, under a clause in the restructured bonds. Thus, Argentina claimed, the full cost of complying with the injunction would total over $120 billion, much more than Argentina could afford to pay. Argentina argues that the district court's injunction—pursued by interests owning just a small fraction of the original bonds—threatened to derail the complex restructuring plan that Argentina and the exchange bondholders had entered into.

Claiming that the injunction violated its sovereign immunity, Argentina sought review in the United States Supreme Court.

B. Development of Foreign Sovereign Immunity

In determining whether the doctrine of sovereign immunity limits the ability of plaintiffs to seek relief against Argentina in U.S. courts, it is important to understand how the doctrine has evolved over time.

1. The Classical View of Sovereign Immunity

The Schooner Exchange v. McFaddon, 11 U.S. 116 (1812), involved a vessel owned by two U.S. citizens that, while en route from the United States to Spain, was captured by the French Navy. The French Navy took the vessel to a French port, where it was converted into a French warship. Several months later, inclement weather forced the *Schooner Exchange* into port in Philadelphia, where the original owners filed an action in U.S. district court for the return of the vessel. The case eventually reached the Supreme Court, which upheld a claim of sovereign immunity.

The Schooner Exchange v. McFaddon
11 U.S. 116 (1812)

MARSHALL, C.J., delivered the opinion of the Court as follows:

This case involves the very delicate and important inquiry, whether an American citizen can assert, in an American court, a title to an armed national vessel, found within the waters of the United States. . . .

The jurisdiction of the nation within its own territory is necessarily exclusive and absolute. It is susceptible of no limitation not imposed by itself. Any restriction upon it, deriving validity from an external source, would imply a diminution of its sovereignty to the extent of the restriction, and an investment of that sovereignty to the same extent in that power which could impose such restriction.

All exceptions, therefore, to the full and complete power of a nation within its own territories, must be traced up to the consent of the nation itself. They can flow from no other legitimate source. . . .

This full and absolute territorial jurisdiction being alike the attribute of every sovereign, and being incapable of conferring extra-territorial power, would not seem to contemplate foreign sovereigns nor their sovereign rights as its objects. One sovereign being in no respect amenable to another; and being bound by obligations of the highest character not to degrade the dignity of his nation, by placing himself or its sovereign rights within the jurisdiction of another, can be supposed to enter a foreign territory only under an express license, or in the confidence that the immunities belonging to his independent sovereign station . . . are reserved by implication, and will be extended to him.

This perfect equality and absolute independence of sovereigns, and this common interest impelling them to mutual intercourse, have given rise to a class of cases in which every sovereign is understood to waive the exercise of a part of that complete exclusive territorial jurisdiction, which has been stated to be the attribute of every nation. . . .

When private individuals of one nation spread themselves through another as business or caprice may direct, mingling indiscriminately with the inhabitants of that other, or when merchant vessels enter for the purposes of trade, it would be obviously inconvenient and dangerous to society, and would subject the laws to continual infraction, and the government to degradation, if such individuals or merchants did not owe temporary and local allegiance, and were not amenable to the jurisdiction of the country. . . .

But in all respects different is the situation of a public armed ship. She constitutes a part of the military force of her nation; acts under the immediate and direct command of the sovereign; is employed by him in national objects. He has many and powerful motives for preventing those objects from being defeated by the interference of a foreign state. Such interference cannot take place without affecting his power and his dignity. The implied license therefore under which such vessel enters a friendly port, may reasonably be construed . . . as containing an exemption from the jurisdiction of the sovereign, within whose territory she claims the rites of hospitality. . . .

It seems then to the Court, to be a principle of public law, that national ships of war, entering the port of a friendly power open for their reception, are to be considered as exempted by the consent of that power from its jurisdiction. . . .

If the preceding reasoning be correct, the Exchange, being a public armed ship, in the service of a foreign sovereign, with whom the government of the United States is at peace, and having entered an American port open for her reception, on the terms on which ships of war are generally permitted to enter the ports of a friendly power, must be considered as having come into the American territory, under an implied promise, that while necessarily within it, and demeaning herself in a friendly manner, she should be exempt from the jurisdiction of the country.

Notes and Questions

1. Does *The Schooner Exchange* rest upon the application of international or domestic law?

2. Is the immunity granted in *The Schooner Exchange* a function of the juridical equality of all states? Or does the immunity granted here reflect an understanding that domestic courts can do little that is useful in such cases?

While *The Schooner Exchange* by its terms applies only to warships, subsequent English and American cases extended the rule of immunity to other vessels owned by foreign sovereigns and, eventually, to other kinds of property as well. For example, *Berizzi Bros. Co. v. S.S. Pesaro*, 271 U.S. 562 (1926), involved claims arising out of an Italian government-owned merchant vessel's delivery of damaged cargo in New York. The Supreme Court upheld dismissal of the action on immunity grounds. In *Ex parte Peru*, 318 U.S. 578 (1943), the Court held that vessels owned by foreign governments were immune from suit in courts in the United States, even if both the vessel and the claim were commercial. In this case, the State Department had formally "recognized and allowed" Peru's claim of immunity. The Court held that the State Department's determination "must be accepted by the courts as a conclusive determination by the political arm of the Government that the continued retention of the vessel interferes with the proper conduct of our foreign relations."

The principle of judicial deference to the political branches was reinforced in *Republic of Mexico v. Hoffman*, 324 U.S. 30 (1944), where the Court stated that:

> Every judicial action exercising or relinquishing jurisdiction over the vessel of a foreign government has its effect upon our relations with that government. Hence it is a guiding principle in determining whether a court should exercise or surrender its jurisdiction in such cases, that the courts should not so act as to embarrass the executive arm in its conduct of foreign affairs. . . .

Id. at 35. For this reason, the Court concluded that the judiciary should not "deny an immunity which our government has seen fit to allow, or to allow an immunity on new grounds which the government has not seen fit to recognize." *Id.*

2. The Tate Letter

Ex parte Peru and *Hoffman* granted the State Department broad authority to develop the doctrine of sovereign immunity and determine its application in particular cases. But scholars and practitioners argued that there was little justification for extending immunity to foreign governments when they engaged in commercial activity akin to that conducted by private parties, and the absolute theory of sovereign immunity articulated in *The Schooner Exchange* came under significant pressure. During the 1940s and 1950s, state practice moved away from the absolute theory. During this period, the State Department conducted a study of the relevant practices of other states and eventually reached the conclusion that immunity should not be granted in cases involving private, as contrasted with sovereign, acts. The Department set forth its position and reasoning in a May 1952 letter to the Department of Justice:

Letter from State Department Acting Legal Adviser Jack B. Tate

26 Dep't State Bull. 984 (1952)

MY DEAR MR. ATTORNEY GENERAL:

The Department of State has for some time had under consideration the question whether the practice of the Government in granting immunity from suit to foreign governments made parties defendant in the courts of the United States without their consent should not be changed. The Department has now reached the conclusion that such immunity should no longer be granted in certain types of cases. . . .

A study of the law of sovereign immunity reveals the existence of two conflicting concepts of sovereign immunity, each widely held and firmly established. According to the classical or absolute theory of sovereign immunity, a sovereign cannot, without his consent, be made a respondent in the courts of another sovereign. According to the newer or restrictive theory of sovereign immunity, the immunity of the sovereign is recognized with regard to sovereign or public acts (*jure imperii*) of a state, but not with respect to private acts (*jure gestionis*). . . .

The classical or virtually absolute theory of sovereign immunity has generally been followed by the courts of the United States, the British Commonwealth, Czechoslovakia, Estonia, and probably Poland. . . .

The decisions of the courts of Brazil, Chile, China, Hungary, Japan, Luxembourg, Norway, and Portugal may be deemed to support the classical theory of immunity if one or at most two old decisions anterior to the development of the restrictive theory may be considered sufficient on which to base a conclusion. . . .

The newer or restrictive theory of sovereign immunity has always been supported by the courts of Belgium and Italy. It was adopted in turn by the courts of Egypt and of Switzerland. In addition, the courts of France, Austria, and Greece, which were traditionally supporters of the classical theory, reversed their position in the 20's to embrace the restrictive theory. Rumania, Peru, and possibly Denmark also appear to follow this theory. . . .

Of related interest . . . is the fact that ten of the thirteen countries which have been classified above as supporters of the classical theory have ratified the Brussels Convention of 1926 under which immunity for government owned merchant vessels is waived. In addition the United States, which is not a party to the Convention, some years ago announced and has since followed, a policy of not claiming immunity for its public owned or operated merchant vessels. . . .

It is thus evident that with the possible exception of the United Kingdom little support has been found except on the part of the Soviet Union and its satellites for continued full acceptance of the absolute theory of sovereign immunity. . . . The reasons which obviously motivate state trading countries in adhering to the theory with perhaps increasing rigidity are most persuasive that the United States should change its policy. Furthermore, the granting of sovereign immunity to foreign governments in the courts of the United States is most inconsistent with the action of the Government of the United States in subjecting itself to suit in these same courts in both contract and tort and with its long established policy of not claiming immunity in foreign jurisdictions for its merchant vessels. Finally, the Department feels that the widespread and increasing practice on the part of governments of engaging in commercial activities makes necessary a practice which will enable persons doing business with them to have their rights determined in the courts. For these reasons it will hereafter be the Department's policy to follow the restrictive theory of sovereign immunity in the consideration of requests of foreign governments for a grant of sovereign immunity.

It is realized that a shift in policy by the executive cannot control the courts but it is felt that the courts are less likely to allow a plea of sovereign immunity where the executive has declined to do so. . . .

In order that your Department, which is charged with representing the interests of the Government before the courts, may be adequately informed it will be the Department's practice to advise you of all requests by foreign governments for the grant of immunity from suit and of the Department's action thereon.

———————————

The State Department's efforts to apply the principles set forth in the Tate Letter proved unsatisfactory. First, the Letter made no attempt to define the critical distinction between a state's "public" and "private" acts. Was the purchase of boots for a state's army a private or a public act? What about the purchase of bullets? In addition, the restrictive theory of immunity adopted in the Tate Letter turns on a legal analysis of the particular activity on which the claim is based. But in practice, the State Department faced political pressure from foreign governments to request immunity in cases where immunity was not warranted, placing the Department in difficult positions. Litigants quickly sensed that foreign policy considerations seemed to influence the Department's immunity determinations, and similar situations yielded different outcomes. Moreover, the courts still had to make immunity determinations in cases where the State Department chose not to intervene. As a result, different branches addressed immunity questions based on varying standards that were neither clearly articulated nor uniformly applied. Dissatisfaction with the perceived politicization of the process for deciding immunity and a desire for greater predictability led practitioners, scholars, and the State Department itself to urge reforms that would remove the Department from the process of determining immunity.

3. Codification of the Restrictive Theory: The Foreign Sovereign Immunities Act

Reform efforts bore fruit as Congress passed the Foreign Sovereign Immunities Act (FSIA) in 1976. This statute essentially codifies the U.S. view of the restrictive theory of sovereign immunity and is the exclusive means for obtaining jurisdiction over foreign states and their instrumentalities in courts in the United States. The statute provides that foreign states are immune from the jurisdiction of federal and state courts unless one or more statutory exceptions to immunity is applicable.

Foreign Sovereign Immunities Act of 1976

28 U.S.C. §§1602-1605

§1602. Findings and Declaration of Purpose

The Congress finds that the determination by the United States courts of the claims of foreign states to immunity from the jurisdiction of such courts would serve the interests of justice and would protect the rights of both foreign states and litigants in United States courts. Under international law, states are not immune from the jurisdiction of foreign courts insofar as their commercial activities are concerned, and their commercial property may be levied upon for the satisfaction of judgments rendered against them in connection with their commercial activities. Claims of foreign states to immunity should henceforth be decided by courts of the United States and of the States in conformity with the principles set forth in this Chapter.

§1603. Definitions

For purposes of this chapter—
(a) A "foreign state" . . . includes a political subdivision of a foreign state or an agency or instrumentality of a foreign state. . . .
(d) A "commercial activity" means either a regular course of commercial conduct or a particular commercial transaction or act. The commercial character of an activity shall be determined by reference to the nature of the course of conduct or particular transaction or act, rather than by reference to its purpose.
(e) A "commercial activity carried on in the United States by a foreign state" means commercial activity carried on by such state and having substantial contact with the United States.

§1604. Immunity of a Foreign State from Jurisdiction

Subject to existing international agreements to which the United States is a party at the time of enactment of this Act a foreign state shall be immune from the jurisdiction of the courts of the United States and of the States except as provided in sections 1605 to 1607 of this chapter.

§1605. General Exceptions to the Jurisdictional Immunity of a Foreign State

(a) A foreign state shall not be immune from the jurisdiction of courts of the United States or of the States in any case—
(1) in which the foreign state has waived its immunity either explicitly or by implication . . . ;
(2) in which the action is based upon a commercial activity carried on in the United States by the foreign state; or upon an act performed in the United States in connection with a commercial activity of the foreign state elsewhere; or upon an act outside the territory of the United States in connection with a commercial activity of the foreign state elsewhere and that act causes a direct effect in the United States;
(3) in which rights in property taken in violation of international law are at issue and that property or any property exchanged for such property is present in the United States in connection with a commercial activity carried on in the United States by the foreign state; . . .
(5) not otherwise encompassed in paragraph (2) above, in which money damages are sought against a foreign state for personal injury or death, or damage to or loss

of property, occurring in the United States and caused by the tortious act or omission of that foreign state or of any official or employee of that foreign state while acting within the scope of his office or employment; except this paragraph shall not apply to—

(A) any claim based upon the exercise or performance or the failure to exercise or perform a discretionary function regardless of whether the discretion be abused. . . .

Notes and Questions

1. Should the FSIA apply to conduct that took place prior to its enactment? In *Austria v. Altmann*, 541 U.S. 677 (2004), the heir of the original owner of paintings sued Austria for the return of paintings taken by the Nazis in violation of international law. Defendants argued that as of 1948, when much of their alleged wrongdoing took place, they would have enjoyed absolute immunity from suit in United States courts, and that the FSIA did not retroactively divest them of that immunity. The Supreme Court disagreed:

. . . [T]he preamble of the FSIA expresses Congress' understanding that the Act would apply to all postenactment claims of sovereign immunity. That section provides:

"*Claims* of foreign states to immunity should *henceforth* be decided by courts of the United States . . . in conformity with the principles set forth in this chapter." 28 U.S.C. §1602 (emphasis added).

. . . [T]his language is unambiguous: Immunity "claims"—not actions protected by immunity, but assertions of immunity to suits arising from those actions—are the relevant conduct regulated by the Act; those claims are "henceforth" to be decided by the courts. . . .

[A]pplying the FSIA to all pending cases regardless of when the underlying conduct occurred is most consistent with two of the Act's principal purposes: clarifying the rules that judges should apply in resolving sovereign immunity claims and eliminating political participation in the resolution of such claims. We have recognized that, to accomplish these purposes, Congress established a comprehensive framework for resolving any claim of sovereign immunity. . . . Quite obviously, Congress' purposes in enacting such a comprehensive jurisdictional scheme would be frustrated if, in postenactment cases concerning preenactment conduct, courts were to continue to follow the same ambiguous and politically charged "'standards'" that the FSIA replaced.

Is the *Altmann* holding fair to foreign states sued in U.S. courts?

2. By its terms, the FSIA applies to foreign states, which includes not only the foreign sovereign itself but also political subdivisions and agencies and instrumentalities of a foreign state. 28 U.S.C. §1603(a). The statute does not explicitly provide immunity to state officials. In *Samantar v. Yousuf*, 560 U.S. (2010), a unanimous Supreme Court held that the FSIA does not govern the immunity claims of foreign officials. Does refusing to apply the FSIA to government officials undermine the FSIA, by inviting plaintiffs to sue officials rather than the state itself?

C. What Is Commercial Activity?

Despite codification, sovereign immunity cases continue to raise difficult issues. One recurring issue is determining when an activity is commercial and when it causes a direct effect in the United States for purposes of the commercial activity exception set forth in §1605(a)(2).

The *Weltover* case, excerpted below, arises out of Argentina's foreign exchange crisis of the 1980s. To deal with this crisis, the Argentine Government entered into contracts with domestic borrowers to exchange local currency for U.S. dollars to enable these borrowers to pay their foreign debts. However, by 1982, Argentina's dollar reserves were insufficient to cover these contracts. As a result, Argentina refinanced these contracts by issuing government bonds, called Bonods, to the creditors. The Bonods provided that payment with specified interest would be made in dollars on scheduled dates in 1986 and 1987 into the holder's account in either New York, Frankfurt, Zurich, or London.

When the Bonods began to mature in May 1986, Argentina again lacked sufficient foreign currency reserves to retire the Bonods. The Argentine government then unilaterally rescheduled repayment of the Bonods. Two Panamanian corporations and a Swiss bank insisted on full payment into their New York accounts under the Bonods' terms. Argentina did not pay, and the three plaintiffs brought suit in federal court.

Republic of Argentina v. Weltover, Inc.

504 U.S. 607 (1992)

JUSTICE SCALIA delivered the opinion of the [unanimous] Court.

II

In the proceedings below, respondents relied only on the third clause of §1605(a)(2) [which removes immunity in actions based "upon an act outside the territory of the United States in connection with a commercial activity of the foreign state elsewhere and that act causes a direct effect in the United States"]. . . . The dispute pertains to whether the unilateral refinancing of the Bonods was taken "in connection with a commercial activity" of Argentina, and whether it had a "direct effect in the United States." We address these issues in turn.

A

The FSIA defines "commercial activity" to mean:

> "[E]ither a regular course of commercial conduct or a particular commercial transaction or act. The commercial character of an activity shall be determined by reference to the nature of the course of conduct or particular transaction or act, rather than by reference to its purpose."

This definition, however, leaves the critical term "commercial" largely undefined: The first sentence simply establishes that the commercial nature of an activity does *not* depend upon whether it is a single act or a regular course of conduct; and the second sentence merely specifies what element of the conduct determines commerciality (*i.e.*, nature rather than purpose), but still without saying what "commercial" means. Fortunately, however, the FSIA was not written on a clean slate. As we have noted, the Act (and the commercial exception in particular) largely codifies the so-called "restrictive" theory of foreign sovereign immunity first endorsed by the State Department in 1952. The meaning of "commercial" is the meaning generally attached to that term under the restrictive theory at the time the statute was enacted.

This Court did not have occasion to discuss the scope or validity of the restrictive theory of sovereign immunity until our 1976 decision in *Alfred Dunhill of London, Inc. v. Republic of Cuba*, 425 U.S. 682. . . . The plurality stated that . . . [a] foreign state engaging in "commercial" activities "do[es] not exercise powers peculiar to sovereigns"; rather, it "exercise[s] only those powers that can also be exercised by private citizens." *Id.* at 704. The dissenters did not disagree with this general description. . . .

In accord with that description, we conclude that when a foreign government acts, not as regulator of a market, but in the manner of a private player within it, the foreign sovereign's actions are "commercial" within the meaning of the FSIA. Moreover, because the Act provides that the commercial character of an act is to be determined by reference to its "nature" rather than its "purpose," the question is not whether the foreign government is acting with a profit motive or instead with the aim of fulfilling uniquely sovereign objectives. Rather, the issue is whether the particular actions that the foreign state performs (whatever the motive behind them) are the *type* of actions by which a private party engages in "trade and traffic or commerce." Thus, a foreign government's issuance of regulations limiting foreign currency exchange is a sovereign activity, because such authoritative control of commerce cannot be exercised by a private party; whereas a contract to buy army boots or even bullets is a "commercial" activity, because private companies can similarly use sales contracts to acquire goods.

The commercial character of the Bonods is confirmed by the fact that they are in almost all respects garden-variety debt instruments: They may be held by private parties; they are negotiable and may be traded on the international market (except in Argentina); and they promise a future stream of cash income. . . .

Argentina argues that the Bonods differ from ordinary debt instruments in that they "were created by the Argentine Government to fulfill its obligations under a foreign exchange program designed to address a domestic credit crisis, and as a component of a program designed to control that nation's critical shortage of foreign exchange." . . . Indeed, Argentina asserts that the line between "nature" and "purpose" rests upon a "formalistic distinction [that] simply is neither useful nor warranted." We think this line of argument is squarely foreclosed by the language of the FSIA. However difficult it may be in some cases to separate "purpose" (*i.e.,* the *reason* why the foreign state engages in the activity) from "nature" (*i.e.,* the outward form of the conduct that the foreign state performs or agrees to perform), the statute unmistakably commands that to be done. . . . [I]t is irrelevant *why* Argentina participated in the bond market in the manner of a private actor; it matters only that it did so. We conclude that Argentina's issuance of the Bonods was a "commercial activity" under the FSIA.

B

The remaining question is whether Argentina's unilateral rescheduling of the Bonods had a "direct effect" in the United States. . . . As the Court of Appeals recognized, an effect is "direct" if it follows "as an immediate consequence of the defendant's . . . activity." . . .

We . . . have little difficulty concluding that Argentina's unilateral rescheduling of the maturity dates on the Bonods had a "direct effect" in the United States. Respondents had designated their accounts in New York as the place of payment, and Argentina made some interest payments into those accounts before announcing that it was rescheduling the payments. Because New York was thus the place of performance for Argentina's ultimate contractual obligations, the rescheduling of those obligations necessarily had a "direct effect" in the United States: Money that was supposed to have been delivered to a New York bank for deposit was not forthcoming. We reject Argentina's suggestion that the "direct effect" requirement cannot be satisfied where the plaintiffs are all foreign corporations with no other connections to the United States. . . .

The Supreme Court also addressed the commercial activity exception in *Saudi Arabia v. Nelson*, 507 U.S. 349 (1993). Nelson, a U.S. citizen, was recruited in the United States to work in a government-owned hospital in Saudi Arabia. Nelson repeatedly advised hospital officials of certain defects in hospital equipment that endangered patients' lives. Hospital officials told Nelson to ignore these problems. In September 1984, hospital employees summoned Nelson to the hospital's security office, where Saudi government agents arrested him. The agents transported Nelson to a jail cell, where they allegedly tortured and beat him and kept him for four days without food. Nelson was then transferred to an overcrowded, rat-infested cell in another prison. For several days, the Saudi government failed to advise Nelson's family of his whereabouts, though a Saudi official eventually told Nelson's wife that he could arrange for her husband's release in exchange for sexual favors.

After Nelson was freed, he and his wife sued Saudi Arabia in federal court. The key legal issue was whether Nelson's claims fell within the commercial activity exception. Justice Souter delivered the opinion of the court:

Saudi Arabia v. Nelson

507 U.S. 349 (1993)

Unlike Argentina's activities that we considered in *Weltover*, the intentional conduct alleged here (the Saudi Government's wrongful arrest, imprisonment, and torture of Nelson) could not qualify as commercial under the restrictive theory. The conduct boils down to abuse of the power of its police by the Saudi Government, and however monstrous such abuse undoubtedly may be, a foreign state's exercise of the power of its police has long been understood for purposes of the restrictive theory as peculiarly sovereign in nature. Exercise of the powers of police and penal officers is not the sort of action by which private parties can engage in commerce. . . . The Nelsons and their *amici* urge us to give significance to their assertion that the Saudi Government subjected Nelson to the abuse alleged as retaliation for his persistence in reporting hospital safety violations, and argue that the character of the mistreatment was consequently commercial. One *amicus*, indeed, goes so far as to suggest that the Saudi Government "often uses detention and torture to resolve commercial disputes." But this argument does not alter the fact that the powers allegedly abused were those of police and penal officers. In any event, the argument is off the point, for it goes to purpose, the very fact the Act renders irrelevant to the question of an activity's commercial character. Whatever may have been the Saudi Government's motivation for its allegedly abusive treatment of Nelson, it remains the case that the Nelsons' action is based upon a sovereign activity immune from the subject-matter jurisdiction of United States courts under the Act.

[Justice White, joined by Justice Blackmun, wrote:]

To run and operate a hospital, even a public hospital, is to engage in a commercial enterprise. . . . By the same token, warning an employee when he blows the whistle and taking retaliatory action, such as harassment, involuntary transfer, discharge, or other tortious behavior, although not prototypical commercial acts, are certainly well within the bounds of commercial activity. . . .

Indeed, I am somewhat at a loss as to what exactly the majority believes petitioners have done that a private employer could not. As countless cases attest, retaliation for whistle-blowing is not a practice foreign to the marketplace. Congress passed a statute in response to such behavior, see Whistleblower Protection Act of 1989, as have numerous States. . . .

At the heart of the majority's conclusion . . . is the fact that the hospital in this case chose to call in government security forces. I find this fixation on the intervention of police officers, and the ensuing characterization of the conduct as "peculiarly sovereign in nature," to be misguided. To begin, it fails to capture respondents' complaint in full. Far from being directed solely at the activities of the Saudi police, it alleges that agents of the *hospital* summoned Nelson to its security office because he reported safety concerns and that the *hospital* played a part in the subsequent beating and imprisonment. Without more, that type of behavior hardly qualifies as sovereign. Thus, even assuming for the sake of argument that the role of the official police somehow affected the nature of petitioners' conduct, the claim cannot be said to "res[t] entirely upon activities sovereign in character." At the very least it "consists of both commercial and sovereign elements," thereby presenting the specific question the majority chooses to elude. The majority's single-minded focus on the exercise of police power, while certainly simplifying the case, thus hardly does it justice.

Reliance on the fact that Nelson's employer enlisted the help of public rather than private security personnel is also at odds with Congress' intent. The purpose of the commercial exception being to prevent foreign states from taking refuge behind their sovereignty when they act as market participants, it seems to me that this is precisely the type of distinction we should seek to avoid. Because both the hospital and the police are agents of the state, the case in my mind turns on whether the sovereign is acting in a commercial capacity, not on whether it resorts to thugs or government officers to carry on its business. That, when the hospital calls in security to get even with a whistle-blower, it comes clothed in police apparel says more about the state-owned nature of the commercial enterprise than about the noncommercial nature of its tortious conduct. . . .

Nevertheless, I reach the same conclusion as the majority because petitioners' commercial activity was not "carried on in the United States." . . . Neither the hospital's employment practices, nor its disciplinary procedures, has any apparent connection to this country. On that basis, I agree that the Act does not grant the Nelsons access to our courts.

Notes and Questions

1. A number of other states, including Australia, Canada, South Africa, and the United Kingdom, have codified the restrictive theory of sovereign immunity. That said, the shift from the absolute to the restrictive theory of immunity is hardly universal; China, India, Indonesia, and Russia, among others, still adhere to the absolute theory of immunity. What factors might prompt states to adopt the restrictive theory?

2. On December 2, 2004, the UN General Assembly adopted the UN Convention on Jurisdictional Immunities of States and Their Property. The treaty reflects more than two decades of negotiations and is the first modern multilateral instrument to address immunity issues comprehensively. The treaty provides, in general, that a state is immune from the jurisdiction of another state unless an enumerated exception to immunity applies. With respect to commercial transactions, the Convention states:

> If a State engages in a commercial transaction with a foreign . . . person and, by virtue of the applicable rules of private international law, differences relating to the commercial transaction fall within the jurisdiction of a court of another State, the State cannot invoke immunity from that jurisdiction in a proceeding arising out of that commercial transaction.

In determining whether a particular transaction is a "commercial transaction," the Convention provides that "reference should be made primarily to the nature of the contract or transaction, but its purpose should also be taken into account if the parties to the contract or transaction have so agreed, or if, in the practice of the State of the forum, that purpose is relevant to determining the non-commercial character of the contract or transaction." The Convention was opened for signature on January 17, 2005, and will enter into force when 30 states have deposited their instruments of ratification, acceptance, approval, or accession with the UN Secretary-General. As of early 2015, 16 states were party to the treaty.

The meaning of "commercial activities" for purposes of the FSIA was at issue in several proceedings in the litigation against Argentina. For example, in December 2005, Argentina's President directed Argentina's Central Bank to use certain funds on deposit at the Federal Reserve Bank in New York to repay Argentina's debt to the IMF and directed that, in exchange, the Republic would repay the Central Bank. Two of the hedge funds sought to attach over $100 million that the Central Bank had on deposit at the Federal Reserve Bank.* The Second Circuit addressed whether these funds were "used for a commercial activity" for purposes of the FSIA:

> According to the Supreme Court in *Weltover,* . . . Argentina engaged in "commercial activity" within the meaning of the FSIA when it issued commercially-available debt instruments, because the instruments were "in almost all respects garden-variety debt instruments: They may be held by private parties; they are negotiable and may be traded on the international market (except in Argentina); and they promise a future stream of cash income."
>
> The Republic's borrowing relationship with the IMF, and the repayment obligations assumed thereunder, are not similarly "commercial" for several reasons. First, when the Republic borrows from the IMF, it "exercise[s] powers peculiar to sovereigns." The IMF is a unique cooperative international institution established by treaty—the Bretton Woods Agreement—following the end of the Second World War. . . . Only sovereign nation states can become members of the IMF, and only members can avail themselves of IMF financing. . . .
>
> Second, the IMF's borrowing program is part of a larger regulatory enterprise intended to preserve stability in the international monetary system and foster orderly economic growth. See IMF Agreement art. IV §1 (describing requirement that each member "undertakes to collaborate with the Fund and other members to assure orderly exchange arrangements and to promote a stable system of exchange rates"); *id.* §3 (granting the IMF the power "to oversee the international monetary system in order to ensure its effective operation" by "exercis[ing] firm surveillance over the exchange rate policies of members"). The Republic's borrowing relationship with the IMF is regulatory in nature because the IMF's provision of foreign currency or IMF-specific assets in exchange for domestic currency generally requires regulatory action by the Republic. The Republic agreed to many economic policy and regulatory reform measures in exchange for the IMF loans that were ultimately repaid in 2005.
>
> Third, the terms and conditions of the Republic's borrowing relationship with the IMF are not governed by a "garden-variety debt instrument[ ]," but instead by the Republic's treaty obligations to the international organization, as supplemented by

---

* The FSIA provides for the immunity of central bank funds from attachment or execution. This immunity extends to funds which are held for the bank's "own account" as distinguished from funds used to finance the commercial transactions of other entities, including foreign states. The Second Circuit found that, notwithstanding the presidential decrees, the Central Bank was a separate legal entity and the funds on deposit were not the property of the Republic.

the terms and conditions contained in agreements associated with individual loans. If the Republic failed to comply with these obligations, it would be in breach of the IMF Agreement and as a result could lose its rights to use IMF borrowing facilities, participate in IMF governance, and ultimately, remain a member of the IMF. The vehicle for enforcing the Republic's obligations to the IMF is diplomatic and thus sovereign, not commercial.

Fourth, IMF loans are structured in a manner unique to the international organization, and are not available in the commercial market. Instead of obtaining currency in exchange for debt instruments, IMF debtors purchase "Special Drawing Rights" ("SDRs") or other currency from the IMF in exchange for their own currency. Because a nation state's borrowing relationship with the IMF takes place outside of the commercial marketplace, it cannot be considered "commercial" in nature.

EM Ltd. v. Republic of Argentina, 473 F.3d. 463, 482-484 (2d Cir. 2007).

Notes and Questions

1. Why did the court characterize the relevant activity as borrowing from and repaying funds *to the IMF* as opposed to borrowing and repaying funds in general? Are you persuaded by the court's efforts to distinguish *Weltover*?

2. The court emphasized that because the IMF often attaches conditions to its loans, IMF lending is "regulatory in nature." Is the IMF the only lender that attaches conditions to loans to debtors with poor credit histories?

3. What are the practical consequences of this decision? Why did the court permit Argentina to pursue a strategy that favors public creditors over private ones?

D. Efforts to Satisfy the Judgments Against Argentina

As the *EM* opinion suggests, obtaining a judgment against a foreign sovereign often triggers substantial legal efforts to collect on that judgment. The hedge funds in the Argentina litigation have spent over a decade seeking to discover, attach, and execute on Argentine property around the globe, spawning complex litigation in numerous jurisdictions.

1. Attachment and Execution

The FSIA provides that "the property in the United States of a foreign state shall be immune from attachment[,] arrest[,] and execution" except as provided elsewhere in the statute. 28 U.S.C. Sec. 1609. The property in the United States of a foreign state is subject to attachment, arrest, or execution if (1) it is "used for a commercial activity in the United States," *and* (2) another enumerated exception to immunity applies. The FSIA confers more robust immunities on designated property of international organizations, foreign central banks, and property used in connection with military activities.

Similar rules exist in other jurisdictions, and have frustrated the hedge funds' efforts to attach Argentine assets. For example, after obtaining judgments from U.S. courts, NML filed suit in French courts seeking the provisional garnishment of labor and corporate taxes and oil royalties owed to Argentina by the Argentine branches of three French companies. Argentina successfully argued in lower courts that the doctrine of sovereign immunity precluded garnishment. The cases were appealed to the Court of Cassation. As France has not enacted a statute addressing sovereign immunity, the Court applied the rules found in the UN Convention on Jurisdictional Immunities on the theory that they represented customary international law. The Court found that the particular asset classes that NML had attached were "necessarily connected to the exercise by the Argentine state of powers linked to its sovereignty," and immune from attachment.

In another effort to satisfy the New York judgments, in October 2012 NML obtained from the High Court (Commercial Division) in Accra, Ghana, an *ex parte* order of interlocutory injunction, effectively restraining the Argentine navy vessel ARA *Libertad* from leaving the port of Tema, Ghana, where it was docked. Argentina moved to set the order aside on grounds of sovereign immunity, but the High Court, relying upon a decision by the UK Supreme Court finding that Argentina had waived its sovereign immunity, found that Argentina was estopped from relitigating this issue.

In response, in November 2012, Argentina applied to the International Tribunal for the Law of the Sea (ITLOS) for provisional measures ordering the vessel's release. On December 15, ITLOS found that the ship enjoyed sovereign immunity and ordered that "Ghana should forthwith and unconditionally release the frigate ARA *Libertad*." *The "ARA Libertad" Case (Argentina v. Ghana)*, Case No. 20 (15 December 2012).

On December 19, 2012, Ghana's Attorney General filed a motion asking Ghana's Supreme Court to quash the interlocutory injunction. In June 2013, Ghana's Supreme Court issued its ruling. It noted that, in principle, Ghanaian courts could rely upon UK judgments for purposes of *res judicata*. However, it noted that under conflict of laws principles, the courts will not enforce a right arising under foreign law if doing so "would be inconsistent with the fundamental public policy of the law of the forum." The Court continued:

> Seizing military assets, particularly a warship, carries with it an inherent risk of generating military conflict, or at least diplomatic rows likely to undermine the security of the State. In principle, the law ought to allow the exclusion of foreign law, on public policy grounds, where the enforcement of a right under that foreign law contributes to such risk of military conflict or insecurity. . . . The fundamental public policy of the State should surely include the need to preserve its security.
>
> In sum . . . although [Argentina] waived its immunity . . . that waiver of immunity is not binding on the Ghanaian Courts, in so far as it relates to a military asset. Customary international law permits sovereign states to decide whether to accord a wider immunity in their municipal law than required under international law. . . .
>
> The Courts of Ghana ought not to promote conditions leading to possible military conflict, when they have the judicial discretion to follow an alternative path. This public policy consideration persuades us that waiver of sovereign State immunity over military assets should not be recognized under Ghanaian common law. . . .

The Republic v. High Court (Comm. Div.) Accra, Ex Parte; Attorney General, No. J5/10/2013 (20 June 2013).

2. The Injunction

Given the hedge funds' largely fruitless global efforts to attach and execute on Argentine assets, the injunction issued by the district court in New York represents a potentially powerful tool to induce payment by Argentina. It appears intended to give Argentina the unpalatable choice between paying holders of the original bonds in full, or defaulting on payments due to the exchange bondholders. Thus, Argentina sought review in the United States Supreme Court. Argentina argued that, under the FSIA, foreign state property is immune from attachment, arrest, and execution unless it is located in the United States and used in a commercial activity; hence property located outside the

United States lies beyond the reach of a U.S. court's enforcement authority. Argentina claimed that the injunctions "essentially invade the Treasury of a foreign sovereign, and commandeer its Legislative and Executive branches . . . to appropriate funds for a specific purpose while forbidding their appropriation for another purpose unless the first appropriation is made." The bondholders responded that the injunction is not an "attachment" because it did not entail the court's exercise of dominion over sovereign property, require Argentina to pay any bondholder any amount of money, or limit the other uses to which Argentina could put its fiscal reserves.

On June 16, 2014, the United States Supreme Court declined to hear the case, meaning that the injunction stayed in force. Payments to exchange bondholders were due June 30, 2014, with a 30-day grace period. In late June, Argentina deposited over $500 million, the amount of interest it owned to holders of the restructured bonds, with Bank of New York Mellon, the bondholder's trustee; however, Argentina refused to make payment to the hedge funds. As the bank was subject to the court's injunction, it did not distribute payments to the exchange bondholders. Despite a flurry of last-minute negotiations over payments to the hedge funds, no agreement was reached by the July 30 deadline. Thereafter, the bond rating firm Standard and Poor's declared Argentina to be in "selective default."

International reaction to the injunction was largely negative. For example, Christine Lagarde, Managing Director of the IMF, noted that "[o]ur concern is that the lower court's decision would undermine the ability of the debtors and creditors to reach agreement. In that respect it could be a threat to financial stability." The OAS issued a declaration stating that it is "essential for the stability and predictability of the international financial architecture to ensure that agreements reached between debtors and creditors in the context of sovereign debt-restructuring processes are respected by allowing that payment flows are distributed to cooperative creditors in accordance with the agreement reached with them in the process of consensual readjusting of the debt."

Notes and Questions

1. As this text goes to press, the dispute between Argentina and the hedge funds continues. In fall of 2014, Argentina enacted a law to replace the Bank of New York Mellon as the trustee for the restricted bonds with a state-owned bank in Argentina. The federal district court judge declared that this effort was "illegal and cannot be carried out," and found Argentina to be in contempt of court. Argentina's foreign minister denounced the contempt order as a "violation of international law."

2. In August 2014, Argentina filed suit against the United States in the ICJ, arguing that U.S. judicial decisions violated its sovereign immunity. The case will only proceed if the United States consents to ICJ jurisdiction over the action. Would the ICJ be an appropriate forum to resolve the issues raised by litigation in U.S. courts over Argentina's debt?

E. An Exception for Violation of Jus Cogens Norms?

In recent years, a vigorous debate has emerged over whether states should enjoy immunity for grave abuses of human rights. The International Court of Justice addressed these issues in *Jurisdictional Immunities of the State (Germany v. Italy)*, 2012 ICJ 99 (Feb. 3).

Near the end of World War II, German forces occupied much of Italy and committed many atrocities, including massacres of civilians and the deportation of civilians and

Italian troops for use in forced labor. In 1998, Luigi Ferrini, an Italian national who had been deported to Germany and forced to work in a munitions factory, filed suit against Germany in Italian courts. In 2004, the Italian Court of Cassation held that immunity does not apply where the underlying acts constitute an international crime. *Ferrini v. Federal Republic of Germany*, decision No. 5044/2004. Following the *Ferrini* opinion, other Italian claimants filed suit against Germany in Italian courts. In addition, Greek claimants who obtained default judgments against Germany in Greek courts for a 1944 massacre of civilians by German troops occupying Greece sought to enforce the judgment in Italy, and later registered a "legal charge" over property owned by Germany in Italy.

In 2008, Germany initiated proceedings at the ICJ, arguing that Italy violated Germany's sovereign immunity by permitting civil claims to be brought against it in Italian courts for conduct by German military forces during World War II. In 2012, the Court issued its judgment.

Jurisdictional Immunities of the State (Germany v. Italy: Greece intervening)

2012 I.C.J. 99 (Feb. 3)

[The Court noted that since there were no relevant treaties in force between Germany and Italy, the question of immunity was governed by customary international law.]

60. The Court is not called upon to address the question of how international law treats the issue of State immunity in respect of *acta jure gestionis* [private or commercial activity]. The acts of the German armed forces and other State organs which were the subject of the proceedings in the Italian courts clearly constituted *acta jure imperii* [i.e., sovereign activity]. . . .

61. Both Parties agree that States are generally entitled to immunity in respect of *acta jure imperii*. That is the approach taken in the United Nations, European and draft Inter-American Conventions, the national legislation in those States which have adopted statutes on the subject and the jurisprudence of national courts. It is against that background that the Court must approach the question raised by the present proceedings, namely whether that immunity is applicable to acts committed by the armed forces of a State . . . in the course of conducting an armed conflict. Germany maintains that immunity is applicable and that there is no relevant limitation on the immunity to which a State is entitled in respect of acta jure imperii. Italy . . . maintains that Germany is not entitled to immunity . . . because those acts involved the most serious violations of rules of international law of a peremptory character for which no alternative means of redress was available.

82. At the outset, however, the Court must observe that the proposition that the availability of immunity will be to some extent dependent upon the gravity of the unlawful act presents a logical problem. Immunity from jurisdiction is an immunity not merely from being subjected to an adverse judgment but from being subjected to the trial process. It is, therefore, necessarily preliminary in nature. Consequently, a national court is required to determine whether or not a foreign State is entitled to immunity as a matter of international law before it can hear the merits of the case brought before it and before the facts have been established. If immunity were to be dependent upon the State actually having committed a serious violation of international human rights law or the law of armed conflict, then it would become necessary for the national court to hold an enquiry into the merits in order to determine whether it had jurisdiction. If, on the other hand, the mere allegation that the State had committed such wrongful acts were to be sufficient

Notes and Questions

1. As a doctrinal matter, what justification does the ICJ give for privileging Germany's sovereign immunity over Italy's ability to exercise jurisdiction over acts on Italian soil? What normative principle supports the finding that Germany's sovereign immunity should take precedence over the right of Italian citizens to recover for widespread violations of core international legal norms? Note that, in analyzing the customary international law of sovereign immunity, the Court observed that

> the rule of State immunity occupies an important place in international law and international relations. It derives from the principle of sovereign equality of States, which, as Article 2, paragraph 1, of the Charter of the United Nations makes clear, is one of the fundamental principles of the international legal order. This principle has to be viewed together with the principle that each State possesses sovereignty over its own territory and that there flows from that sovereignty the jurisdiction of the State over events and persons within that territory. Exceptions to the immunity of the State represent a departure from the principle of sovereign equality. Immunity may represent a departure from the principle of territorial sovereignty and the jurisdiction which flows from it.

2. Are you persuaded by the ICJ's determination that "there is no conflict" between the rules of state immunity and *jus cogens* norms regarding war crimes and crimes against humanity?

3. Are you persuaded by the Court's statement that permitting an exception to sovereign immunity for serious violations of human rights law would require a court "to hold an enquiry into the merits in order to determine whether it had jurisdiction"? If so, does the same argument apply to permitting a commercial activity exception to sovereign immunity?

4. Can the judgments of the ICJ and the Italian Constitutional Court be harmonized? Can you justify judicial outcomes finding that international *jus cogens* norms cannot displace international legal immunities from jurisdiction, but fundamental constitutional rights can?

PART IV

The Protection of Human Dignity

Over the last several centuries, the formation and evolution of the modern, centralized, bureaucratic state has facilitated enormous economic growth, dramatic technological innovation, and lasting cultural and other forms of human achievement. But the unparalleled power of the modern state has also often been directed against individuals, and wars between states or struggles for power within states have cost at least 100 million lives in the last 70 years alone.

Modern international law emerged in tandem with the emergence of states as the preeminent form of political organization. In keeping with that history, international law until relatively recently focused almost exclusively on the rights and responsibilities of states. To the extent that individuals had rights in international law, they were derivative of the rights of the individual's state of nationality.

The status of the individual in international law has changed substantially in recent years, as states and other actors have increasingly sought to protect the basic human dignity of all individuals through law. In this regard, three rapidly developing, related, and to some extent overlapping bodies of law are relevant: international human rights, international humanitarian law, and international criminal law.

International humanitarian law is the oldest of the three bodies of law. As Professor Yoram Dinstein observes,

> Whereas the development of the international human rights of peacetime began in earnest only after Word War II, some fundamental freedoms of wartime had a seminal existence even before World War I. Insofar as many peacetime human rights are concerned, 1948—the year in which the U.N. General Assembly adopted the Universal Declaration of Human Rights—was the *die a quo* from which they first started to crystallize in international law. By contrast, as regards numerous wartime human rights, 1949—the year in which the Geneva Conventions were opened for ratification—was the *dies ad quem* which finalized their consolidation as binding legal norms. . . . [H]istorically the law of war is the most ancient part of international law.

Yoram Dinstein, *Human Rights in Armed Conflict: International Humanitarian Law, in* Human Rights in International Law 345, 347 (Theodor Meron ed., 1984).

ICRC = major role in Int'l Humanitarian Law

The International Committee of the Red Cross (ICRC), a non-governmental organization (NGO) that has played a major role in the development of international humanitarian law, offers the following description of the relationship between international human rights and international humanitarian law (IHL):

Both strive to protect the lives, health and dignity of individuals, albeit from a different angle.

Humanitarian law applies in situations of armed conflict, whereas human rights, or at least some of them, protect the individual at all times, in war and peace alike. However, some human rights treaties permit governments to derogate from certain rights in situations of public emergency. No derogations are permitted under IHL because it was conceived for emergency situations, namely armed conflict.

Humanitarian law aims to protect people who do not [take] or are no longer taking part in hostilities. The rules embodied in IHL impose duties on all parties to a conflict. Human rights, being tailored primarily for peacetime, apply to everyone. Their principal goal is to protect individuals from arbitrary behaviour by their own governments. Human rights law does not deal with the conduct of hostilities.

The duty to implement IHL and human rights lies first and foremost with States. Humanitarian law obliges States to take practical and legal measures, such as enacting penal legislation and disseminating IHL. Similarly, States are bound by human rights law to accord national law with international obligations. IHL provides for several specific mechanisms that help its implementation. Notably, States are required to ensure respect also by other States. Provision is also made for an enquiry procedure, [and] a Protecting Power mechanism. . . .

Human rights implementing mechanisms are complex and, contrary to IHL, include regional systems. Supervisory bodies, such as the UN Commission on Human Rights, are either based on the UN Charter or provided for in specific treaties. . . . The Human Rights [Council has] developed a mechanism of "special rapporteurs" and working groups, whose task is to monitor and report on human rights situations either by country or by topic. Six of the main human rights treaties also provide for the establishment of committees (e.g. the Human Rights Committee) of independent experts charged with monitoring their implementation. Certain regional treaties (European and American) also establish human rights courts. . . .

The international human rights instruments contain clauses that authorize States confronted with a serious public threat to suspend the rights enshrined in them. An exception is made for certain fundamental rights laid down in each treaty, which must be respected in all circumstances and may never be waived regardless of the treaty. In particular, these include the right to life, the prohibition of torture and inhuman punishment or treatment, slavery and servitude, and the principle of legality and non-retroactivity of the law. . . .

Since humanitarian law applies precisely to the exceptional situations which constitute armed conflicts, the content of human rights law that States must respect in all circumstances . . . tends to converge with the fundamental and legal guarantees provided by humanitarian law, e.g. the prohibition of torture and summary executions.

International Humanitarian Law: Answers to Your Questions, *www.icrc.org.*

There is also a close relationship between international humanitarian law and international criminal law. As the ICRC explains, states have an obligation to prosecute individuals who commit certain violations of the laws of war:

On becoming party to the Geneva Conventions, States undertake to enact any legislation necessary to punish persons guilty of grave breaches of the Conventions. States are also bound to prosecute in their own courts any person suspected of having committed a grave breach of the Conventions, or to hand that person over for judgment to another State. In other words, the perpetrators of grave breaches, i.e. war criminals, must be prosecuted at all times and in all places, and States are responsible for ensuring that this is done.

Generally speaking, a State's criminal laws apply only to crimes committed on its territory or by its own nationals. International humanitarian law goes further in that it requires States to seek out and punish any person who has committed a grave breach, irrespective of his nationality or the place where the offence was committed. This principle of universal jurisdiction is essential to guarantee that grave breaches are effectively repressed.

Such prosecutions may be brought either by the national courts of the different States or by an international authority. In this connection, the International Criminal Tribunals for the former Yugoslavia and Rwanda were set up by the UN Security Council in 1993 and 1994, respectively, to try those accused of war crimes committed during the conflicts in those countries.

Id.

But not all violations of international humanitarian law are subject to criminal prosecution. Moreover, international criminal law permits or requires prosecution of many offenses that are not part of the corpus of international humanitarian law—for example, drug trafficking, piracy, and aircraft hijacking. Accordingly, although there is a considerable overlap between these two bodies of law, they nonetheless differ in many ways.

Much has changed in international law since World War II. Perhaps most striking is the rapid development of legal norms and institutions intended to protect basic human dignity. As Nobel laureate Elie Wiesel notes:

> The defense of human rights has, in the last fifty years, become a kind of worldwide secular religion. . . . Statesmen, high officials, and diplomats serve as moral watchmen. . . . They make it their business to know and let other people know each time an opposition member is punished, a journalist stifled, a prisoner tortured. . . . Crimes against humanity are part of the public domain.

Elie Wiesel, *A Tribute to Human Rights, in* The Universal Declaration of Human Rights 2 (Yael Danieli, Elsa Stamatopoulou & Clarence Dias eds., 1999).

At the same time, efforts to render effective existing human rights, humanitarian law, and international criminal law are fraught with difficulty. Chapters 7, 8, and 9 examine the issues raised by each of these different but related areas.

7

The Claims of Individuals on States: International Human Rights

In the seventeenth and eighteenth centuries, there was no sharp distinction between international and national law. Individuals possessed legal personality—and with it the ability to assert legal rights—under both bodies of law. But the positivists who came to dominate legal theory in the nineteenth century viewed the law applicable to sovereign states in their interactions with each other as distinct from the law that applied to individuals. In this conception, only states could be viewed as subjects of international law, only states could participate in law making, and only states could possess and assert rights under international law. Thus, for example, the Statute of the Permanent Court of International Justice (PCIJ), and the statute of its successor, the International Court of Justice (ICJ), both provided that only states may be parties to cases before those courts. Individuals might be able to assert rights under municipal law in connection with international transactions, but they could not bring claims against states, at least not in international fora. Moreover, how a state treated its own nationals was viewed largely as an internal matter. Individuals could not assert rights against their own state on the international plane.

International law did take cognizance of the ways in which a state treated foreign nationals present in the state's territory, but in a strained and artificial way. Under the traditional law of state responsibility, all states have an obligation to treat foreign nationals within their jurisdiction in accordance with an ill-defined minimum standard of justice. Absent special agreements, states ordinarily have no obligations to admit foreign nationals to their territory, but if they do admit them, they must act toward them in ways consistent with those minimum international standards.

Foreign nationals, in turn, must ordinarily accept the legal regime of the state in which they find themselves. If a state injures a foreign national in a way that violates an international legal obligation—if, for example, a state unjustly expropriates a foreign national's property or deliberately or recklessly causes physical injury to a foreign national (whether the national is an individual or a corporation)—then the state may incur responsibility under international law. But under the traditional law of state responsibility, the responsibility of the state at issue does not extend directly to the injured foreign national. Instead, responsibility exists vis-à-vis the national's state, which may in its own discretion decide to assert a claim against the state responsible for the injury, provided the injured national has first exhausted local remedies. By espousing the claim of its national, the offended state exercises its own right of diplomatic protection. It is under no obligation to exercise that right, and if it succeeds in obtaining compensation from the offending state, it has no obligation to share that compensation with its injured national.

The traditional approach to state responsibility and diplomatic protection proceeded from the assumption that only states were subjects of international law and thus capable of exercising rights and accepting responsibilities under it. From this perspective, injuries to individuals could only be deemed violations of international law if viewed as injuries to their state. As the PCIJ put it,

> It is an elementary principle of international law that a State is entitled to protect its subjects, when injured by acts contrary to international law committed by another State, from whom they have been unable to obtain satisfaction through ordinary channels. By taking up the case of one of its subjects and by resorting to diplomatic action or international judicial proceedings on his behalf, a State is in reality asserting its own rights . . . to ensure, in the person of its subjects, respect for the rules of international law.

Mavrommatis Palestine Concessions (Greece v. United Kingdom), P.C.I.J. Ser. A, No. 2, at 12 (1924).

In some issue areas, states did manifest a concern for human welfare that extended beyond the treatment of their own nationals abroad. As early as the seventeenth century, states in Europe entered into treaties designed to confer limited protections on religious minorities in other states. In the nineteenth century, states in Europe (and eventually in the Americas) worked to outlaw slavery and the international trade in slaves through international conventions. And as we consider more fully in Chapter 8, modern international humanitarian law, the body of rules designed to render the conduct of warfare more humane, had its origins in the mid-nineteenth century.

The aftermath of World War I generated innovative experiments in the international legal treatment of minorities through the League of Nations minorities treaty system. Concerned about the possible destabilizing influence of national minorities, the victors in World War I imposed treaties on certain states in Eastern and Central Europe designed to guarantee fair treatment to members of ethnic, linguistic, or religious minorities. Moreover, international efforts to improve the lot of workers began around the same time, with the establishment of the International Labour Office (now the International Labour Organization (ILO)) in 1919. Since its formation, the ILO has promulgated numerous treaties, reports, and other instruments designed to improve the condition of workers and their families. But both the League treaties and the ILO's work were limited in their subject matter, and the former were also limited in their application to particular states. In general, most states continued to regard their treatment of their own nationals as largely their own affair.

The atrocities of World War II forced a reassessment of the position of individuals under international law. Reliance on the doctrine of state responsibility was clearly insufficient to deal with abuses committed by a state against its own nationals, since no state could be expected to bring an action against itself. Recognizing this, the Allied Powers during World War II—the United States, the United Kingdom, France, and the Soviet Union—pledged to prosecute individuals responsible for atrocities committed during the course of the war. This decision, and the Nuremberg and related trials that followed the war, marked a turning point in attitudes toward the individual's status in international law. Under the Nuremberg Charter, which is discussed in greater detail in Chapter 9, individuals could be prosecuted for crimes against peace, war crimes, and crimes against humanity. The last category was broad enough to encompass certain crimes committed by a state against its own nationals.

During and immediately after World War II, widespread revulsion at the Holocaust prompted civic and religious groups in many countries to call for inclusion of an international bill of rights in the UN Charter. Many organizations and individuals, including the American Law Institute, the ILO, the American Jewish Committee, and the American Bar Association, prepared draft bills of rights. At the Inter-American Conference on War and Peace, held in Mexico in early 1945, 21 Latin American states joined in the call for a bill of rights in the UN Charter, and three of those states later prepared a draft. Ultimately, other issues dominated the discussions in San Francisco during which the UN Charter was prepared, and no bill of rights was included in it. But the Charter contains multiple references to human rights. The Preamble to the Charter states the determination of the peoples of the United Nations "to reaffirm faith in international human rights," and Article 55 commits UN members to promote "universal respect for, and observance of, human rights and fundamental freedoms for all. . . ." Similarly, Article 56 of the UN Charter requires UN member states to cooperate in promoting human rights.

Moreover, Article 68 of the UN Charter contemplated the formation of a UN Commission on Human Rights to conduct research on human rights and to draft treaties and other instruments for the articulation and promotion of human rights. Indeed, as President Truman told the delegates to the San Francisco conference, the UN Charter provided "good reason to expect the framing of an international bill of rights, acceptable to all the nations involved," and one that "will be as much a part of international life as our own Bill of Rights is a part of our Constitution." The Human Rights Commission was formed in 1946.

In the years that followed, individual states, the United Nations, and various regional organizations, including the Council of Europe, the Organization of American States, and the Organization of African Unity, working with countless non-governmental human rights organizations, scholars, and lawyers, have developed an extensive body of human rights treaties, declarations, and related instruments in an effort to develop and clarify international human rights norms. These same actors have also developed a complex system of institutions designed to monitor and to some extent to implement existing norms. These institutions include regional human rights courts, treaty bodies, groups of experts, special rapporteurs, and more.

The following sections of this chapter illustrate the development and application of human rights law by looking at several illustrative problems. In Section I, we consider the application of universal instruments designed to protect fundamental liberty and personal security interests by examining the controversy surrounding recent U.S. interrogation policies. Section II examines disagreements over states' freedom to limit the scope of their obligations under human rights treaties through reservations. Section III examines economic, social, and cultural rights. As indicated in that section, the line between political and civil rights and economic, social, and cultural rights is often hard to draw, and the principal international human rights treaties often include both types of rights. Nonetheless, the theoretical and practical problems associated with each set of rights differ sufficiently to warrant separate consideration. Section IV of this chapter examines efforts to protect the rights of women and what happens when particular human rights conflict with each other or with important societal interests.

I. PROTECTING POLITICAL AND CIVIL RIGHTS: U.S. USE OF "ENHANCED INTERROGATION TECHNIQUES"

Contemporary articulations of political and civil rights, as claims of individuals on their society and government, find their principal historical roots in seventeenth and eighteenth century European political philosophy, though one can find related ideas in many cultures and periods. John Locke's insistence on rights to life, liberty, and property, and Jean Jacques Rousseau's proclamation that "man is born free," resonate in the 1776 American Declaration of Independence and its "self-evident" truth that "all men are created equal." Following the American Declaration, the newly proclaimed independent American states began drafting individual bills of rights, which influenced the 1789 French Declaration of the Rights of Man and the virtually contemporaneous Bill of Rights familiar to all American law students as the first ten amendments to the U.S. Constitution. The political philosophy animating these various instruments and the instruments themselves serve as the principal antecedents to contemporary international human rights treaties dealing with civil and political rights. In general, such instruments seek to guarantee everyone physical security and integrity through, for example, protections against torture and the arbitrary deprivation of life; equal treatment, through norms mandating nondiscrimination and the equal protection of the law; and basic liberties, such as the freedom to practice one's religion or express one's political views. In this section we seek to illustrate the development and application of political and civil rights through an examination of efforts to eliminate one of the most fundamental assaults on human dignity: torture.

The goals for this Problem include:

- to understand the philosophical and jurisprudential underpinnings of human rights;
- to understand the role human rights norms play—or should play—in shaping decisions by governments and private actors; and
- to understand the law on torture and its relationship to state interests in national security and individual interests in the rights to liberty and personal integrity.

A. *The Problem*

After the terrorist attacks of September 11, 2001, the Administration of President George W. Bush decided that the United States was in a "new kind of war." (For further discussion, see Chapter 14.) To prevail, the Bush Administration believed it vital to be able to obtain useful intelligence quickly from individuals suspected of possible terrorist activities directed against the United States.

During the course of the conflicts in Afghanistan and Iraq, and in connection with suspected al Qaeda activities elsewhere, the United States has detained thousands of individuals. The official interrogation policy in place when detentions began in 2001 was contained in U.S. Army Field Manual 34-52. The Manual permitted the use of psychological ploys, such as shouting at a detainee or banging on the table to invoke a sense of fear, but it expressly prohibited the use of "force, mental torture, threats, insults, or exposure to unpleasant and inhumane treatment of any kind."

In December 2001, the Defense Department's Office of the General Counsel sought information on "detainee exploitation" from the agency overseeing the U.S. military's Survival Evasion Resistance and Escape (SERE) training program. The SERE program exposes U.S. military personnel to techniques they might encounter if captured, in an effort to prepare them to resist interrogation. SERE techniques were modeled in part on methods used by China during the Korean War to elicit false confessions from captured U.S. military personnel. Such techniques include stress positions, enforced nudity, sleep deprivation, isolation, slapping, exposure to extreme temperatures, "walling," and waterboarding.

In March 2002, the Central Intelligence Agency (CIA) captured and began to interrogate a Saudi citizen named Abu Zubaydah. The CIA initially identified Zubaydah as a high-ranking al Qaeda member and a participant in the planning of the September 11 attacks, but later described him only as someone who "substantially supported" forces hostile to the United States. Senior Agency officials believed Zubaydah was withholding information that could not be obtained through then-authorized interrogation techniques. Accordingly, the CIA sought approval from the National Security Council for a new interrogation program aimed at high-value detainees. In particular, the CIA sought to use "enhanced interrogation techniques" (EITs) drawn from the SERE training program. At the same time, the CIA's Office of General Counsel sought legal advice from the Justice Department's Office of Legal Counsel (OLC). OLC concluded in several August 2002 memoranda that use of the proposed EITs would be lawful.

In September 2002, the commanding officer of the division in charge of interrogations at Guantánamo sought permission to use SERE-style techniques. His memorandum divided the proposed interrogation techniques into three categories, from the least aggressive to the most aggressive. Category I included yelling at detainees, deceiving detainees, and using multiple interrogators—techniques similar to those already permitted by Army Field Manual 34-52. Category II included the use of stress positions, such as forcing the detainee to stand for up to four hours, isolating the detainee for up to 30 days (with medical and psychological supervision), placing a hood over the detainee's head during transportation and questioning, depriving the detainee of light and auditory stimuli, and "[u]sing detainees' individual phobias (such as fear of dogs) to induce stress." Category III included "[u]se of a wet towel and dripping water to induce the misperception of suffocation," exposing the detainee to cold weather or water, and using "mild, non-injurious physical contact. . . ."

Asked for comment on the request, all four military branches raised significant concerns. For example, the Chief of the Army's International and Operational Law Division noted that some of the techniques would "likely constitute maltreatment" under the Uniform Code of Military Justice and "may violate the torture statute." On November 27, 2002, Department of Defense General Counsel William Haynes concluded that it was permissible to use techniques from categories I and II and one technique (mild physical contact) from Category III. Secretary Rumsfeld approved Haynes's recommendations.

As reports of detainee abuse at Guantánamo and elsewhere began to circulate, some Justice Department and military lawyers raised further concerns. As a result, Secretary Rumsfeld rescinded his approval of the additional interrogation techniques in January 2003, but simultaneously established a working group within the Department of Defense to review interrogation practices. On April 4, 2003, the Working Group issued a report recommending that Secretary Rumsfeld approve the 17 techniques already in use in accordance with Army Field Manual 34-52 and 18 new, more aggressive methods. Senior military lawyers in all branches immediately expressed serious legal and policy concerns and warned that the approved techniques might violate the Uniform Code of Military Justice, expose U.S. service members to prosecution abroad, invite reciprocal treatment of U.S. POWs, undermine morale, and undercut international support.

toward the preparation of a binding international human rights treaty, delays in the preparation of the two subsequent International Covenants left the Universal Declaration for many years as the primary and most heavily invoked international human rights instrument. Excerpts from the Universal Declaration pertinent to U.S. interrogation practices follow.

Universal Declaration of Human Rights

G.A. Res. 217A (1948)

Whereas recognition of the inherent dignity and of the equal and inalienable rights of all members of the human family is the foundation of freedom, justice and peace in the world,

Whereas disregard and contempt for human rights have resulted in barbarous acts which have outraged the conscience of mankind, and the advent of a world in which human beings shall enjoy freedom of speech and belief and freedom from fear and want has been proclaimed as the highest aspiration of the common people, . . .

ARTICLE 1

All human beings are born free and equal in dignity and rights. They are endowed with reason and conscience and should act towards one another in a spirit of brotherhood.

ARTICLE 2

Everyone is entitled to all the rights and freedoms set forth in this Declaration, without distinction of any kind, such as race, colour, sex, language, religion, political or other opinion, national or social origin, property, birth or other status. . . .

ARTICLE 4

Everyone has the right to life, liberty and security of person. . . .

ARTICLE 5

No one shall be subjected to torture or to cruel, inhuman or degrading treatment or punishment. . . .

ARTICLE 7

All are equal before the law and are entitled without any discrimination to equal protection of the law. All are entitled to equal protection against any discrimination in violation of this Declaration and against any incitement to such discrimination.

ARTICLE 8

Everyone has the right to an effective remedy by the competent national tribunals for acts violating the fundamental rights granted him by the constitution or by law.

ARTICLE 9

No one shall be subjected to arbitrary arrest, detention or exile. . . .

2. The International Covenant on Civil and Political Rights

In many respects, the International Covenant on Civil and Political Rights (ICCPR) closely resembles the first half of the Universal Declaration. Many of the political and civil rights in the Universal Declaration appear in almost identical form in the ICCPR; others are similar in substance though expressed in greater detail in the Covenant. In a few instances, political and civil rights found in one document are not included in the other. The Covenant, for example, does not include the right to own property, found in Article 17 of the UDHR, which became contentious due to the ideological conflict associated with the expropriation of foreign-owned assets, described in Chapter 2.

Despite the essential similarities between the ICCPR and the UDHR, there are also some significant differences. First, the Covenant is a formally binding treaty, not an aspirational declaration. Second, the Covenant establishes a formal international institution—the Human Rights Committee, a body of international human rights experts—to assist parties with the interpretation and implementation of the treaty's provisions. Among other things, the Human Rights Committee receives and reviews reports from parties concerning their compliance with the treaty's provisions. The Committee also issues periodic general comments articulating its interpretation of various treaty articles. Perhaps most significant, the Committee receives complaints from individuals concerning violations of the treaty with respect to states that have accepted the Committee's competence under the First Optional Protocol to the ICCPR, and transmits its views concerning those complaints to the affected state and the complainant. Third, the UDHR and the Covenant differ in their approach to articulating the circumstances under which specified rights and freedoms may be properly limited. The UDHR contains a single, general article on this issue.

Article 29

1. Everyone has duties to the community in which alone the free and full development of his personality is possible.

2. In the exercise of his rights and freedoms, everyone shall be subject only to such limitations as are determined by law solely for the purpose of securing due recognition and respect for the rights and freedoms of others and of meeting the just requirements of morality, public order and the general welfare in a democratic society.

3. These rights and freedoms may in no case be exercised contrary to the purposes and principles of the United Nations.

By contrast, the Covenant contains specific provisions applicable to specific rights. For example, Article 18 of the Covenant, which protects (among other things) the freedom to manifest one's religion or beliefs, provides that such freedom "may be subject only to such limitations as are prescribed by law and are necessary to protect public safety, order, health, or morals or the fundamental rights and freedoms of others." In addition, and more broadly, the Covenant permits the limitation—or derogation—of most rights during times of public emergency:

Article 4

1. In time of public emergency which threatens the life of the nation and the existence of which is officially proclaimed, the States Parties to the present Covenant may take measures derogating from their obligations under the present Covenant to the extent strictly required by the exigencies of the situation, provided that such measures are not

inconsistent with their other obligations under international law and do not involve discrimination solely on the ground of race, colour, sex, language, religion or social origin.

2. No derogation from articles 6 [right to life], 7 [ban on torture], 8 (paragraphs 1 and 2) [ban on slavery], 11 [ban on imprisonment for debt], 15 [ban on ex post facto crimes], 16 [recognition as a person before the law] and 18 [freedom of thought, conscience, and religion] may be made under this provision.

3. Any State Party to the present Covenant availing itself of the right of derogation shall immediately inform the other States Parties to the present Covenant, through the intermediary of the Secretary-General of the United Nations, of the provisions from which it has derogated and of the reasons by which it was actuated. A further communication shall be made, through the same intermediary, on the date on which it terminates such derogation.

3. The Convention Against Torture

In 1975, the UN General Assembly adopted a declaration calling for an end to torture and other cruel, inhuman, and degrading treatment. Thereafter, human rights NGOs pressed for the preparation of a binding convention that would expand on the obligation not to torture contained in Article 7 of the ICCPR. In 1984, the UN General Assembly adopted the Convention Against Torture and Other Cruel, Inhuman or Degrading Treatment or Punishment. The Convention strengthens existing norms against torture in a number of ways. Among other things, the Convention requires state parties to present reports focused explicitly on torture, and creates an expert committee to review those reports and make recommendations. The Convention also includes an optional individual complaints procedure. Perhaps most important, the Convention requires states either to prosecute anyone who has committed torture and is found within their jurisdiction or to extradite such persons to another state for prosecution. As of early 2015, 155 states were party to the Convention. The U.S. became a party in 1994. Particularly relevant are the following provisions:

Convention Against Torture and Other Cruel, Inhuman or Degrading Treatment or Punishment
1465 U.N.T.S. 85 (1984)

Article 1

1. For the purposes of this Convention, the term "torture" means any act by which severe pain or suffering, whether physical or mental, is intentionally inflicted on a person for such purposes as obtaining from him or a third person information or a confession, punishing him for an act he or a third person has committed or is suspected of having committed, or intimidating or coercing him or a third person, or for any reason based on discrimination of any kind, when such pain or suffering is inflicted by or at the instigation of or with the consent or acquiescence of a public official or other person acting in an official capacity. It does not include pain or suffering arising only from, inherent in or incidental to lawful sanctions. . . .

Article 2

1. Each State Party shall take effective legislative, administrative, judicial or other measures to prevent acts of torture in any territory under its jurisdiction.

2. No exceptional circumstances whatsoever, whether a state of war or a threat of war, internal political instability or any other public emergency, may be invoked as a justification of torture.

3. An order from a superior officer or a public authority may not be invoked as a justification of torture. . . .

Article 4

1. Each State Party shall ensure that all acts of torture are offences under its criminal law. The same shall apply to an attempt to commit torture and to an act by any person which constitutes complicity or participation in torture.

2. Each State Party shall make these offences punishable by appropriate penalties which take into account their grave nature. . . .

Article 10

1. Each State Party shall ensure that education and information regarding the prohibition against torture are fully included in the training of law enforcement personnel, civil or military, medical personnel, public officials and other persons who may be involved in the custody, interrogation or treatment of any individual subjected to any form of arrest, detention or imprisonment.

Article 11

Each State Party shall keep under systematic review interrogation rules, instructions, methods and practices as well as arrangements for the custody and treatment of persons subjected to any form of arrest, detention or imprisonment in any territory under its jurisdiction, with a view to preventing any cases of torture. . . .

Article 14

1. Each State Party shall ensure in its legal system that the victim of an act of torture obtains redress and has an enforceable right to fair and adequate compensation, including the means for as full rehabilitation as possible. In the event of the death of the victim as a result of an act of torture, his dependants shall be entitled to compensation.

Article 16

1. Each State Party shall undertake to prevent in any territory under its jurisdiction other acts of cruel, inhuman or degrading treatment or punishment which do not amount to torture as defined in article 1, when such acts are committed by or at the instigation of or with the consent or acquiescence of a public official or other person acting in an official capacity. . . .

4. The Extraterritorial Reach of Human Rights Treaties

Most human rights treaties contain general language governing the scope of their application. Thus, Article 2 of the ICCPR, for example, requires a state to ensure the rights of all individuals "within its territory and subject to its jurisdiction." Such provisions have given rise to vigorous debate about whether and under what circumstances human rights treaties apply extraterritorially.

The Human Rights Committee stated in its General Comment No. 31 that "a State Party must respect and ensure the rights laid down in the Covenant to anyone within the power or effective control of that State Party, even if not situated within the territory of that State party." Similarly, the International Court of Justice in its 2004 Advisory Opinion on *Legal Consequences of the Construction of a Wall in the Occupied Palestinian Territory* (excerpted in Chapter 8) stated that the ICCPR "is applicable in respect of acts done by a State in the exercise of its jurisdiction outside its own territory."

The European Court of Human Rights, however, decided in 2001 that the European Convention on Human Rights applies extraterritorially only in exceptional circumstances, such as when a state exercises "effective control of the relevant territory and its inhabitants as a consequence of military occupation" or "exercises all or some of the public powers normally to be exercised by" the government of the territory. *Bankovic and Others v. Belgium and 16 Other Contracting States*, 2001-XII Eur. Ct. H.R. 33. Accordingly, the Court declared inadmissible a claim that NATO members violated the right to life in a bombing attack on a Federal Republic of Yugoslavia radio and television station during the Kosovo conflict.

In 2011, the European Court of Human Rights revisited the issue in *Al Skeini v. United Kingdom*, a case involving the killing of civilians in Iraq by British soldiers. The Court outlined two principal bases for "exceptional circumstances" justifying the extraterritorial exercise of jurisdiction, one based on control of persons and one based on control over foreign territory. In the former category, involving "state agent authority and control" over individuals, the Court included (1) "acts of diplomatic and consular agents, who are present on foreign territory in accordance with international law"; (2) situations "when, through the consent, invitation or acquiescence of the Government [of another state, a Contracting State] exercises all or some of the public powers normally to be exercised by that Government"; and (3) situations in which "the use of force by a State's agents operating outside its territory may bring the individual . . . into custody of State agents abroad." The Court provided a number of examples, including irregular rendition and mistreatment of prisoners. The Court added that "[w]hat is decisive in such cases is the exercise of physical power and control over the person in question."

The United States, on the other hand, has long maintained that neither the ICCPR nor the Convention Against Torture applies extraterritorially. In 2006, for example, during the U.S. presentation to the Human Rights Committee, the U.S. delegation stated that under Article 2 of the ICCPR, the Covenant on its face applies "only to individuals who are BOTH *within* the territory of a State Party *and* subject to its jurisdiction." The United States also relied on the ICCPR's negotiating record, noting that "the reference to 'within its territory' in Article 2(1) was adopted as a result of a proposal made over fifty years ago by U.S. delegate Eleanor Roosevelt," in keeping with the U.S. concern that it might otherwise be held to have assumed "an obligation to ensure the rights recognized in [the ICCPR] to the citizens of countries under United States occupation" in Germany, Austria, and Japan.

In 2010, then State Department Legal Adviser Harold Koh wrote a lengthy classified memorandum arguing that the "best reading" of the ICCPR is that it does "impose certain obligations on a State Party's extraterritorial conduct." Koh wrote another lengthy memorandum in 2013, just before leaving his State Department post, arguing that "it is not legally available to policy makers to claim" that the Torture Convention does not apply extraterritorially. In late 2013, the U.S. submitted a report to the Committee Against Torture that declined to "address the geographic scope of the Convention as a legal matter," but stated that under U.S. constitutional and statutory law, it "is unlawful for U.S. actors to commit an act of torture, under any circumstances, anywhere in the world."

Notes and Questions

1. Why do you think the United States and the Soviet Union initially preferred a non-binding declaration of human rights to a treaty?

2. What is the current legal status of the rights contained in the Universal Declaration? The Declaration is not itself legally binding, but many of its provisions are now part of customary international law. After the UN Charter, the Universal Declaration is often considered to be the most influential international law instrument of the twentieth century.

3. Why do the UDHR and the ICCPR take different approaches to the circumstances under which particular rights and freedoms may be limited? What might explain the selection of the particular articles listed as non-derogable in Article 4 of the ICCPR?

4. Should the ICCPR and other human rights treaties apply extraterritorially? Should the answer turn on the state's degree of control over territory or over an individual abroad?

5. Implementation Mechanisms

Unlike the UDHR, the ICCPR includes implementation mechanisms that consist of state reporting requirements, Human Rights Committee comments and recommendations, and an optional protocol permitting the Committee to consider individual complaints. As of early 2015, 115 states were parties to that optional protocol. This implementation machinery has often been contrasted unfavorably with the adjudicatory procedures available in the European and, to a lesser extent, the Inter-American regional human rights systems. Under the ICCPR procedures, states are often late, sometimes many years late, in submitting reports, and they often pay relatively little attention to the recommendations of the Human Rights Committee. Moreover, decisions of the Committee under the optional protocol are not officially binding, though they have considerable persuasive value to many governments. To date there has been little enthusiasm among governments for a global international human rights court of the sort suggested in 1947. The UN Human Rights Commission, formed in 1946, often came under sharp criticism for being political and ineffective. States often sought membership to shield themselves and allies from criticism rather than to promote human rights, and the UN General Assembly periodically elected to the Commission states with poor human rights records, such as Sudan, Zimbabwe, Pakistan, Libya, and Saudi Arabia. In 2006, the General Assembly created a new Human Rights Council to replace the Commission. The Council meets year-round. The General Assembly now approves new members individually (rather than as members of a regional group), and members are subject to a mandatory review of their human rights record.

In June 2007, one year after it was formed, the Council established a Universal Periodic Review to assess the human rights situation in all UN member states. With some changes, the Council also renewed the mandate of most of the Commission's thematic and country rapporteurs, and established a new complaints procedure "to address consistent patterns of gross and reliably attested violations of human rights." Like its predecessor, however, the Council has focused disproportionately on Israel, included as members states with poor human rights records, and ignored serious human rights violations in countries with allies on the Council. Bloc voting by regional groups has generated particular concern. In an especially controversial action, the Council in March 2009 adopted a resolution proposed by Pakistan on behalf of the Organization of the Islamic Conference declaring "defamation of religion" to be a human rights violation. The vote was 21-10, with 14 abstentions; most of the Western states on the Council voted against the resolution.

Under the Bush Administration, the United States declined to seek a seat on the Council. The Obama Administration sought and received a seat on the Council in May 2009.

6. Court Decisions on Torture

Both international and national courts have had occasion to consider the legality of interrogation practices alleged to violate international human rights law. Among the most prominent of these decisions is the ruling of the European Court of Human Rights in *Ireland v. United Kingdom.* The European Court adjudicates cases brought under the European Convention on Human Rights, the world's first general human rights treaty. As you read the excerpt below, consider whether and to what extent its reasoning and analysis might be deemed applicable to U.S. interrogation practices.

Republic of Ireland v. United Kingdom
2 ECHR (Ser. A) at 25 (1978)

[The United Kingdom acknowledged that in combating terrorism in Northern Ireland in the early 1970s, British security forces employed a number of methods that violated international human rights law. By the time of the decision, the UK had already taken steps to eliminate the use of those methods. Nonetheless, the Court felt obliged to consider their legality under Article 3 of the European Convention on Human Rights, which prohibits torture and inhuman or degrading treatment or punishment. The interrogation techniques at issue included: "forcing the detainees to remain for periods of some hours in a 'stress position'"; "putting a black or navy coloured bag over the detainees' heads and, at least initially, keeping it there all the time except during interrogation"; "holding the detainees in a room where there was a continuous loud and hissing noise"; sleep deprivation; and deprivation of food and drink.]

QUESTIONS CONCERNING THE MERITS

162. As was emphasised by the Commission, ill-treatment must attain a minimum level of severity if it is to fall within the scope of Article 3. The assessment of this minimum is, in the nature of things, relative; it depends on all the circumstances of the case, such as the duration of the treatment, its physical or mental effects and, in some cases, the sex, age and state of health of the victim, etc.

163. The Convention prohibits in absolute terms torture and inhuman or degrading treatment or punishment, irrespective of the victim's conduct. Unlike most of the substantive clauses of the Convention and of Protocols 1 and 4, Article 3 makes no provision for exceptions and, under Article 15 (2), there can be no derogation therefrom even in the event of a public emergency threatening the life of the nation. . . .

167. The five techniques were applied in combination, with premeditation and for hours at a stretch; they caused, if not actual bodily injury, at least intense physical and mental suffering to the persons subjected thereto and also led to acute psychiatric disturbances during interrogation. They accordingly fell into the category of inhuman treatment within the meaning of Article 3. The techniques were also degrading since they were such as to arouse in their victims feelings of fear, anguish and inferiority capable of humiliating and debasing them and possibly breaking their physical or moral resistance. . . .

In the Court's view, [the] distinction [between torture and cruel, inhuman and degrading treatment] derives principally from a difference in the intensity of the suffering inflicted.

The Court considers . . . that it was the intention that the Convention, with its distinction between 'torture' and 'inhuman or degrading treatment', should by the first of these terms attach a special stigma to deliberate inhuman treatment causing very serious and cruel suffering. . . .

Although the five techniques, as applied in combination, undoubtedly amounted to inhuman and degrading treatment, although their object was the extraction of confessions, the naming of others and/or information and although they were used systematically, they did not occasion suffering of the particular intensity and cruelty implied by the word torture as so understood.

———————

Although *Republic of Ireland v. United Kingdom* remains a widely cited case, recently discovered documents relating to the impact of the five techniques on internees and the role of the UK government in authorizing use of the techniques led the Irish government in late 2014 to petition the Court to reopen the case.

In 1999, the Israeli Supreme Court ruled on the legality of interrogation practices conducted by Israel's General Security Serivce (GSS), in a case brought by several Israeli human rights groups, including the Public Committee Against Torture, on behalf of Palestinian interrogees.

Public Committee Against Torture in Israel v. State of Israel

38 I.L.M. 1471 (1999)

Background:

1. The State of Israel has been engaged in an unceasing struggle for both its very existence and security, from the day of its founding. Terrorist organizations have established as their goal Israel's annihilation. Terrorist acts and the general disruption of order are their means of choice. In employing such methods, these groups do not distinguish between civilian and military targets. They carry out terrorist attacks in which scores are murdered in public areas, public transportation, city squares and centers, theaters and coffee shops. . . .

The purpose of [the GSS] interrogations is, among others, to gather information regarding terrorists and their organizing methods for the purpose of thwarting and preventing them from carrying out these terrorist attacks.

[The Court's opinion describes in considerable detail the challenged interrogation practices, which include "the forceful shaking of the suspect's upper torso," prolonged sitting on a low, tilted chair, with hands tied behind the back and head covered by an opaque sack, excessive tightening of handcuffs, and sleep deprivation.]

15. . . . With respect to the physical means employed by the GSS, the State argues that these do not violate International Law. . . .

[T]he State notes that the use of physical means by GSS investigators is most unusual and is only employed as a last resort in very extreme cases. Moreover, even in these rare cases, the application of such methods is subject to the strictest of scrutiny and supervision. . . . This having been said, when the exceptional conditions requiring the use of these means are in fact present, the above described interrogation methods are funda-mental to saving human lives and safeguarding Israel's security. . . .

22. . . . In crystallizing the interrogation rules, two values or interests clash. *On the one hand,* lies the desire to uncover the truth, thereby fulfilling the public interest in exposing crime and preventing it. *On the other hand,* is the wish to protect the dignity and liberty of the individual being interrogated. This having been said, these interests and values are not absolute. A democratic, freedom-loving society does not accept that investigators use any means for the purpose of uncovering the truth. . . . At times, the price of truth is so high that a democratic society is not prepared to pay it. To the same extent, however, a democratic society, desirous of liberty, seeks to fight crime and to that end is prepared to accept that an interrogation may infringe upon the human dignity and liberty of a sus-pect provided it is done for a proper purpose and that the harm does not exceed that which is necessary. . . . Our concern, therefore, lies in the clash of values and the bal-ancing of conflicting values. The balancing process results in the rules for a "reasonable interrogation". . . .

23. . . . [A] number of general principles are . . . worth noting:

> *First,* a reasonable investigation is necessarily one free of torture, free of cruel, inhu-man treatment of the subject and free of any degrading handling whatsoever. . . . This conclusion is in perfect accord with (various) International Law treaties—to which Israel is a signatory—which prohibit the use of torture, "cruel, inhuman treatment" and "degrading treatment". These prohibitions are "absolute". There are no exceptions to them and there is no room for balancing. Indeed, violence directed at a suspect's body or spirit does not constitute a reasonable investigation practice. . . .
>
> *Second,* a reasonable investigation is likely to cause discomfort; It may result in insuf-ficient sleep; The conditions under which it is conducted risk being unpleasant. . . . In the end result, the legality of an investigation is deduced from the propriety of its purpose and from its methods. Thus, for instance, sleep deprivation for a prolonged period, or sleep deprivation at night when this is not necessary to the investigation time wise may be deemed a use of an investigation method which surpasses the least restric-tive means.

From the General to the Particular

24. . . . Plainly put, shaking is a prohibited investigation method. It harms the sus-pect's body. It violates his dignity. It is a violent method which does not form part of a legal investigation. It surpasses that which is necessary. . . .

[Reviewing the other interrogation methods at issue, the Court found that each has elements that may be permissible when carried out humanely (e.g., handcuffing) but that when carried out unreasonably "impinge upon the suspect's dignity, his bodily integrity, and his basic rights" and cannot then "be deemed as included within the general power to conduct interrogations."]

Physical Means and the "Necessity" Defence

33. [A]n explicit authorization permitting GSS to employ physical means is not to be found in our law. An authorization of this nature can, in the State's opinion, be obtained in specific cases by virtue of the criminal law defense of "necessity", prescribed in the Penal Law. . . . The State maintains that an act committed under conditions of "neces-sity" does not constitute a crime. Instead, it is deemed an act worth committing in such circumstances in order to prevent serious harm to a human life or body. . . . In the course of their argument, the State's attorneys submitted the "ticking time bomb" argument. A

given suspect is arrested by the GSS. He holds information respecting the location of a bomb that was set and will imminently explode. There is no way to defuse the bomb without this information. If the information is obtained, however, the bomb may be defused. If the bomb is not defused, scores will be killed and maimed. Is a GSS investigator authorized to employ physical means in order to elicit information regarding the location of the bomb in such instances? . . .

36. In the Court's opinion, a general authority to establish directives respecting the use of physical means during the course of a GSS interrogation cannot be implied from the "necessity" defence. . . . This defence deals with deciding those cases involving an individual reacting to a given set of facts; It is an ad hoc endeavour, in reaction to an event. . . . Thus, the very nature of the defence does not allow it to serve as the source of a general administrative power. The administrative power is based on establishing general, forward looking criteria. . . .

Moreover, the "necessity" defence has the effect of allowing one who acts under the circumstances of "necessity" to escape criminal liability. The "necessity" defence does not . . . authorize the use of physical means for the purposes of allowing investigators to execute their duties in circumstances of necessity. The very fact that a particular act does not constitute a criminal act (due to the "necessity" defence) does not in itself authorize the administration to carry out this deed, and in doing so infringe upon human rights. The Rule of Law (both as a formal and substantive principle) requires that an infringement on a human right be prescribed by statute, authorizing the administration to this effect. . . .

37. If the State wishes to enable GSS investigators to utilize physical means in interrogations, they must seek the enactment of legislation for this purpose. . . .

A Final Word

39. This decision opens with a description of the difficult reality in which Israel finds herself security wise. . . . We are aware that this decision does not ease dealing with that reality. This is the destiny of democracy, as not all means are acceptable to it, and not all practices employed by its enemies are open before it . . . . If it will nonetheless be decided that it is appropriate for Israel, in light of its security difficulties to sanction physical means in interrogations (and the scope of these means which deviate from the ordinary investigation rules), this is an issue that must be decided by the legislative branch which represents the people. . . .

40. Deciding these applications weighed heavy on this Court. True, from the legal perspective, the road before us is smooth. We are, however, part of Israeli society. Its problems are known to us and we live its history. We are not isolated in an ivory tower. We live the life of this country. We are aware of the harsh reality of terrorism in which we are, at times, immersed. Our apprehension is that this decision will hamper the ability to properly deal with terrorists and terrorism disturbs us. We are, however, judges. Our brethren require us to act according to the law. This is equally the standard that we set for ourselves. When we sit to judge, we are being judged. . . .

Notes and Questions

1. Did either the European Court of Human Rights or the Israeli Supreme Court conclude that the interrogation practices at issue in each case amounted to torture? Does the relevant international law compel that conclusion in either case?

included dietary manipulation, nudity, slapping, wall standing, stress positions, sleep deprivation, and waterboarding. The first memorandum spelled out the precautions in place to minimize harm to detainees, and concluded that none of the techniques were likely to cause the severe pain and suffering actionable under the torture statute. With regard to waterboarding, the memorandum acknowledged that a detainee "will experience the physical sensation of drowning," even if he "knows he is not going to drown." Nonetheless, noting that the waterboard had been used on prior detainees and that medical doctors concluded they "did not experience physical pain," the memorandum concluded that "the authorized use of the waterboard by adequately trained interrogators could not reasonably be considered specifically intended to cause 'severe physical pain.'" The memorandum added that waterboarding does not cause "severe mental pain or suffering" because it does not produce "prolonged mental harm" beyond "the distress that directly accompanies its use and the prospect that it will be used again." An accompanying memorandum concluded that "the combination of techniques in question here would not be 'extreme and outrageous' and thus would not reach the high bar established by Congress in sections 2340-2340A. . . ."

On May 30, 2005, OLC provided another memorandum to the CIA, analyzing the legality of EITs under Article 16 of the Torture Convention. Applying a "shocks the conscience" test derived from U.S. Fifth Amendment jurisprudence, OLC concluded that the CIA interrogation program was neither "'constitutionally arbitrary' nor so egregious or outrageous 'that it may fairly be said to shock the contemporary conscience.'"

Notes and Questions

1. Did U.S. interrogation policy change as a result of the December 30, 2004 OLC memorandum disavowing portions of the August 2002 OLC memoranda?

2. Defense Department investigations of abuses at Abu Ghraib focused on the acts of a few individuals, and Bush Administration officials strongly denied that official interrogation policies contributed to those abuses. However, the 2008 Senate Armed Services Committee Report on Inquiry into the Treatment of Detainees in U.S. Custody concludes that official policies "conveyed the message that physical pressures and degradation were appropriate treatment for detainees in U.S. military custody." For discussion of the various Abu Ghraib investigations and prosecutions of individuals involved in abuses there, see Chapter 9.

b. Congress Responds: The Detainee Treatment Act

In late 2005, Senator John McCain, who was tortured as a prisoner of war in Vietnam, introduced an amendment to a 2006 Department of Defense Appropriations bill providing that "no person in the custody or under the effective control of the Department of Defense . . . shall be subject to any treatment or technique of interrogation not authorized by and listed in the United States Army Field Manual on Intelligence Interrogation." The amendment provided further:

(a) In General—No individual in the custody or under the physical control of the United States Government, regardless of nationality or physical location, shall be subject to cruel, inhuman, or degrading treatment or punishment.

(b) Construction—Nothing in this section shall be construed to impose any geographical limitation on the applicability of the prohibition against cruel, inhuman, or degrading treatment or punishment under this section.

The Bush Administration initially opposed the legislation, and later sought an exception for CIA personnel; however, after both houses of Congress voted overwhelmingly to support the legislation, the Bush Administration dropped its opposition.

President Bush signed the legislation, known as the Detainee Treatment Act, on December 30, 2005. But in a signing statement, Bush declared that the Executive Branch would interpret the Act "in a manner consistent with the constitutional authority of the President," and added that, in the Administration's view, the legislation did not create a private right of action. In addition to the McCain amendment, the Detainee Treatment Act contained new protections for U.S. personnel engaged in interrogations. Among other things, the Act provided that "in any civil action or criminal prosecution" against such personnel in connection with

> specific operational practices, that involve detention and interrogation of aliens who the President or his designees have determined are believed to be engaged in or associated with international terrorist activity that poses a serious, continuing threat to the United States, its interests, or its allies, and that were officially authorized and determined to be lawful at the time that they were conducted, it shall be a defense that such [personnel] did not know that the practices were unlawful and a person of ordinary sense and understanding would not know the practices were unlawful. Good faith reliance on advice of counsel should be an important factor, among others, to consider in assessing whether a person of ordinary sense and understanding would have known the practices to be unlawful.

Finally, the Detainee Treatment Act also contains provisions limiting habeas corpus for detainees at Guantánamo, a topic discussed in detail in Chapter 14.

Notes and Questions

1. Does the President's signing statement effectively take away the legal protections the McCain amendment sought to provide detainees? Is the Detainee Treatment Act consistent with international law?

2. Should evidence obtained through torture be admissible in court? In December 2005, the United Kingdom's highest court, the House of Lords, considered this issue in depth. The British government argued that although evidence procured by torture carried out by or with the complicity of British authorities should not be admissible, evidence procured without any taint of complicity should not be excluded. The Law Lords, however, ruled unanimously that evidence procured by torture may not be admitted into evidence in British courts, regardless of its source. Consider the remarks of Lord Hope of Craighead:

> The use of such evidence is excluded not on grounds of its unreliability—if that was the only objection to it, it would go to its weight, not to its admissibility—but on grounds of its barbarism, its illegality and its inhumanity. The law will not lend its support to the use of torture for any purpose whatever. It has no place in the defence of freedom and democracy, whose very existence depends on the denial of the use of such methods to the executive.

A and Others v. Secretary of State for the Home Department, [2005] UKHL 71. The Law Lords agreed, however, that the executive could utilize evidence procured by torture to avert an attack or make an arrest. The European Court of Human Rights has also held, in a series of cases, that evidence procured by torture is inadmissible.

c. The Committee Against Torture Reacts

As international criticism of U.S. detention and interrogation policies intensified, the Committee Against Torture (CAT) in July 2006 offered the following comments on the U.S. report to the Committee:

- Expressed regret at the U.S. view that the Convention did not apply in the context of armed conflict. . . .
- Regretted the U.S. view that key Convention provisions do not apply extraterritorially.
- Noted "that detaining persons indefinitely without charge constitutes per se a violation of the Convention," expressed concern "that detainees are held for protracted periods at Guantánamo Bay, without sufficient legal safeguards and without judicial assessment of the justification for their detention (arts. 2, 3 and 16)," and urged the U.S. to close the Guantánamo Bay facility.
- Urged the United States to "rescind any interrogation technique, including methods involving sexual humiliation, 'waterboarding,' 'short shackling,' and using dogs to induce fear, that constitutes torture or cruel, inhuman or degrading treatment or punishment."
- Expressed concern at "reliable reports of acts of torture or cruel, inhuman and degrading treatment or punishment committed by certain members of the State party's military or civilian personnel in Afghanistan and Iraq," and at "lenient sentences" given in such cases, "including of an administrative nature or less than one year's imprisonment."

In 2013, the United States submitted a new report to the Committee Against Torture, addressing the criticisms raised by the committee. The report stated that under a 2009 Executive Order, all interrogations of individuals detained in armed conflict, whether conducted by the military, the CIA, or any other agency, must comply with the Army Field Manual. The report added that:

108. Actions prohibited by the Army Field Manual with respect to intelligence interrogations include, but are not limited to: forcing the detainee to be naked, perform sexual acts, or pose in a sexual manner; placing hoods or sacks over the head of a detainee or using duct tape over the eyes; applying beatings, electronic shock, burns, or other forms of physical pain; "waterboarding"; using military working dogs; inducing hypothermia or heat injury; conducting mock executions; and depriving the detainee of necessary food, water, or medical care. The Army Field Manual also provides guidance to be used while formulating interrogation plans for approval. It states: "In attempting to determine if a contemplated approach or technique should be considered prohibited . . . consider these two tests before submitting the plan for approval:

- If the proposed approach technique [sic] were used by the enemy against one of your fellow soldiers, would you believe the soldier had been abused?
- Could your conduct in carrying out the proposed technique violate a law or regulation? Keep in mind that even if you personally would not consider your actions to constitute abuse, the law may be more restrictive.

If you answer yes to either of these tests, the contemplated action should not be conducted."

3. Beyond the Torture Convention: The Supreme Court, Congress, and the President Reinterpret the Geneva Conventions

In June 2006, the U.S. Supreme Court decided *Hamdan v. Rumsfeld*, 548 U.S. 557 (2006). The decision, excerpted in Chapter 14, rejected the U.S. position that the 1949 Geneva Conventions do not apply to the conflict with al Qaeda. Without deciding the extent to which the Conventions might apply, the Court determined that, at a minimum, Common Article 3 of the Conventions does apply.

Common Article 3 establishes minimum standards for non-international armed conflicts. It requires that "[p]ersons taking no active part in the hostilities . . . shall in all circumstances be treated humanely," and prohibits "cruel treatment and torture" as well as "outrages upon personal dignity." Under the U.S. War Crimes Act, a violation of Common Article 3 constitutes a federal offense.

The Supreme Court's decision in *Hamdan* forced the Bush Administration to reconsider its interrogation policies and negotiate with Congress over procedures for military commissions and related issues, including interrogations and criminal liability of U.S. personnel for war crimes. These negotiations produced the Military Commissions Act of 2006 (MCA). Section 6 of the MCA amended the War Crimes Act to specify nine separate offenses that would constitute grave breaches of Common Article 3, including torture and cruel and inhuman treatment. Section 6 defines torture to require a specific intent "to inflict severe physical or mental pain or suffering," which is in turn defined as "bodily injury" that involves "a substantial risk of death," "extreme physical pain," a serious burn or physical disfigurement, or "significant loss or impairment of the function of a bodily member, organ, or mental faculty."

Following passage of the MCA, the CIA sought approval for the use of six EITs, including the "facial hold," the "attention grasp," the "abdominal slap," the "insult (or facial) slap," dietary manipulation, and extended sleep deprivation. In a lengthy 2007 memorandum, OLC opined that all six techniques would be consistent with the DTA, the MCA, and Common Article 3. OLC noted that prior to the enactment of the MCA, CIA Director Michael Hayden briefed the full membership of the House and Senate Intelligence Committees on CIA interrogation techniques, and none of them favored stopping the program.

Notes and Questions

1. Did either *Hamdan* or the MCA force changes to U.S. interrogation policies? Why does the MCA specify that torture and cruel, inhuman, and degrading treatment constitute grave breaches of Common Article 3 but simultaneously bar invocation of the Geneva Conventions in habeas or civil actions in U.S. courts?

2. Is OLC's analysis of Common Article 3 convincing?

3. Should the United States apply human rights law or humanitarian law to detainee interrogations? Does it matter which body of law is applied?

On his third day in office, President Obama signed three executive orders departing from his predecessor's approach to detention and interrogation policies. Obama's

Executive Order on "Ensuring Lawful Interrogation" required the CIA to close any detention facilities it might have and established a special interagency task force to review detention and interrogation policies. Section 2 of the order stipulated that terms such as "treated humanely" shall have the same meaning as the same terms in Common Article 3 of the Geneva Conventions. Section 3 established Common Article 3 as a minimum baseline for treatment of "individuals detained in any armed conflict" whenever "such individuals are in the custody or under the effective control of an officer, employee, or other agent of the United States Government. . . ." Section 3 also barred U.S. officials or agents from relying "upon any interpretation of the law governing interrogation . . . issued by the Department of Justice between September 11, 2001, and January 20, 2009." Later that year, Congress passed the Military Commissions Act of 2009, which mitigated some of the harsher provisions of the 2006 MCA. For example, under the 2009 Act, testimony procured through coercion may not be introduced as evidence.

As discussed in Chapter 9, in April 2009, President Obama and Attorney General Eric Holder ordered "a preliminary review into whether federal laws were violated in connection with the interrogation of specific detainees at overseas locations." However, the Attorney General reiterated an earlier pledge by the President "that the Department of Justice will not prosecute anyone who acted in good faith and within the scope of the legal guidance given by the Office of Legal Counsel regarding the interrogation of detainees." As the Human Rights Committee noted in its March 2014 concluding observations on the fourth report of the United States under the ICCPR, "all reported investigations into enforced disappearances, torture and other cruel, inhuman or degrading treatment committed in the context of the CIA secret rendition, interrogation and detention programmes were closed in 2012, resulting in only a meagre number of criminal charges being brought against low-level operatives."

In December 2012, the Senate Select Committee on Intelligence adopted a comprehensive 6,700-page report on the CIA's role in interrogations. In April 2014, the committee voted to release the 500-page executive summary to the public, and after an eight-month delay, the summary was released to the public in December 2014. The summary concludes that the CIA misled the Justice Department, the President, and Congress on the scope and effectiveness of CIA interrogations and that no significant intelligence was obtained through torture that could not have been acquired through other methods.

II. NARROWING HUMAN RIGHTS TREATIES: THE UNITED STATES AND THE INTERNATIONAL COVENANT ON CIVIL AND POLITICAL RIGHTS

As discussed in Chapter 2, states may make reservations to treaties in order to modify or exclude the application to the reserving state of a particular provision or provisions of the treaty, provided that the reservation is not prohibited by the treaty and is compatible with its object and purpose. In its Advisory Opinion concerning reservations to the Genocide Convention, the ICJ suggested that it was particularly important to permit reservations to human rights and humanitarian law treaties — that is, to treaties "adopted for a purely humanitarian and civilizing purpose," for which the contracting parties desired that "as many States as possible should participate." Reservations to the Convention on the Prevention and Punishment of the Crime of Genocide, 1951 I.C.J. 15, 24.

Most multilateral treaties are ratified with few or no reservations. When states do make reservations to multilateral treaties, the reservations usually relate to the dispute settlement provisions of the treaty or other matters that do not go to the substantive heart of the treaty. By contrast, reservations to multilateral human rights treaties are frequent, and often apply to important substantive provisions of the treaties. As a result, human rights NGOs and treaty bodies frequently argue that the reservations significantly impair the protective purposes of the treaties. Yet only rarely do states object to reservations to human rights treaties. Even less often do states insist that a reservation is incompatible with the object and purpose of a treaty. The U.S. reservations to the ICCPR illustrate some of the issues associated with reservations to human rights treaties.

A. *The Problem*

The United States played a leading role in the drafting of the ICCPR, and the provisions of that treaty fit comfortably within the liberal political tradition of the U.S. Bill of Rights. Yet the United States did not ratify the ICCPR until 1992, more than 25 years after the Covenant was first opened for signature. Reluctance by the United States to ratify the ICCPR is part of a larger pattern. Although the United States has long supported the development of human rights treaties and routinely presses other countries to ratify and abide by them, the United States has long been reluctant to accept international scrutiny of its own human rights practices.

Several reasons help explain the U.S. attitude to human rights treaties. As discussed in Section I of Chapter 5, conservatives in the United States in the 1950s feared that rapidly developing international human rights norms would threaten segregation and other racially discriminatory practices then prevalent in the United States, expand the power of the federal government at the expense of the states, and undermine the latter's constitutional authority to regulate matters previously considered "local." These concerns drove support for a proposed constitutional amendment, the Bricker Amendment, that would sharply limit the reach of the federal government's treaty power. To defeat this proposed amendment, the Eisenhower Administration announced in 1953 that it did not view human rights treaties "as the proper and most effective way to spread throughout the world the goals of human liberty," and that it would not in the future support ratification of any human rights treaty.

Although subsequent administrations disavowed the Eisenhower Administration's blanket opposition to all human rights treaties, critics continue to argue that such treaties inappropriately transfer decisionmaking authority from Congress and the states to international bodies. Accordingly, the United States to date has ratified only a handful of major human rights treaties, usually long after most other developed states. President Truman submitted the Genocide Convention to the Senate for its advice and consent in 1949, but the United States did not ratify it until 1988. The United States did not ratify the Convention Against Torture or the International Convention on the Elimination of All Forms of Racial Discrimination until 1994. The United States has not ratified the International Covenant on Economic, Social and Cultural Rights or the Convention on the Elimination of Discrimination Against Women. Only the United States, Somalia, and South Sudan have failed to ratify the Convention on the Rights of the Child, and the latter two have both committed to ratification.

When the United States does ratify an international human rights treaty, it typically attaches to its instrument of ratification a detailed list of reservations, understandings, and declarations (RUDs) designed to limit the extent of U.S. obligations under the treaty. These RUDs have generated considerable controversy. Critics generally view the RUDs as a means to undercut the utility of treaties as a vehicle for encouraging states to improve their domestic human rights practices. The U.S. RUDs to the ICCPR are a case in point.

B. *The Effects of U.S. Reservations*

As you review the excerpts of the ICCPR set out below, consider which, if any, of the ICCPR's articles might be viewed as problematic by the U.S. government.

International Covenant on Civil and Political Rights

999 U.N.T.S. 171 (1966)

Article 2

1. Each State Party to the present Covenant undertakes to respect and to ensure to all individuals within its territory and subject to its jurisdiction the rights recognized in the present Covenant, without distinction of any kind, such as race, colour, sex, language, religion, political or other opinion, national or social origin, property, birth or other status. . . .

3. Each State Party to the present Covenant undertakes:

(a) To ensure that any person whose rights or freedoms as herein recognized are violated shall have an effective remedy, notwithstanding that the violation has been committed by persons acting in an official capacity. . . .

Article 6

1. Every human being has the inherent right to life. This right shall be protected by law. No one shall be arbitrarily deprived of his life.

2. In countries which have not abolished the death penalty, sentence of death may be imposed only for the most serious crimes in accordance with the law in force at the time of the commission of the crime. . . .

5. Sentence of death shall not be imposed for crimes committed by persons below eighteen years of age and shall not be carried out on pregnant women.

Article 9

1. Everyone has the right to liberty and security of person. No one shall be subjected to arbitrary arrest or detention. No one shall be deprived of his liberty except on such grounds and in accordance with such procedure as are established by law. . . .

Article 14

1. All persons shall be equal before the courts and tribunals. In the determination of any criminal charge against him, or of his rights and obligations in a suit at law, everyone shall be entitled to a fair and public hearing by a competent, independent and impartial tribunal established by law. . . .

3. In the determination of any criminal charge against him, everyone shall be entitled to the following minimum guarantees, in full equality:

(a) To be informed promptly and in detail in a language which he understands of the nature and cause of the charge against him;

(b) To have adequate time and facilities for the preparation of his defence and to communicate with counsel of his own choosing;

(c) To be tried without undue delay;

(d) To be tried in his presence, and to defend himself in person or through legal assistance of his own choosing; to be informed, if he does not have legal assistance, of this right; and to have legal assistance assigned to him, in any case where the interests of justice so require, and without payment by him in any such case if he does not have sufficient means to pay for it;

(e) To examine, or have examined, the witnesses against him and to obtain the attendance and examination of witnesses on his behalf under the same conditions as witnesses against him;

(f) To have the free assistance of an interpreter if he cannot understand or speak the language used in court;

(g) Not to be compelled to testify against himself or to confess guilt.

4. In the case of juvenile persons, the procedure shall be such as will take account of their age and the desirability of promoting their rehabilitation.

5. Everyone convicted of a crime shall have the right to his conviction and sentence being reviewed by a higher tribunal according to law. . . .

7. No one shall be liable to be tried or punished again for an offence for which he has already been finally convicted or acquitted in accordance with the law and penal procedure of each country. . . .

Article 17

1. No one shall be subjected to arbitrary or unlawful interference with his privacy, family, home or correspondence, nor to unlawful attacks on his honour and reputation.

Article 18

1. Everyone shall have the right to freedom of thought, conscience and religion. . . .

3. Freedom to manifest one's religion or beliefs may be subject only to such limitations as are prescribed by law and are necessary to protect public safety, order, health, or morals or the fundamental rights and freedoms of others.

Article 19

1. Everyone shall have the right to hold opinions without interference.

2. Everyone shall have the right to freedom of expression; this right shall include freedom to seek, receive and impart information and ideas of all kinds, regardless of frontiers, either orally, in writing or in print, in the form of art, or through any other media of his choice.

3. The exercise of the rights provided for in paragraph 2 of this article carries with it special duties and responsibilities. It may therefore be subject to certain restrictions, but these shall only be such as are provided by law and are necessary:

(a) For respect of the rights or reputations of others;

(b) For the protection of national security or of public order (*ordre public*), or of public health or morals.

Article 20

1. Any propaganda for war shall be prohibited by law.
2. Any advocacy of national, racial or religious hatred that constitutes incitement to discrimination, hostility or violence shall be prohibited by law.

Article 23

1. The family is the natural and fundamental group unit of society and is entitled to protection by society and the State.
2. The right of men and women of marriageable age to marry and to found a family shall be recognized.
3. No marriage shall be entered into without the free and full consent of the intending spouses.
4. States Parties to the present Covenant shall take appropriate steps to ensure equality of rights and responsibilities of spouses as to marriage, during marriage and at its dissolution . . . .

Article 25

Every citizen shall have the right and the opportunity, without any of the distinctions mentioned in article 2 and without unreasonable restrictions:
(a) To take part in the conduct of public affairs, directly or through freely chosen representatives;
(b) To vote and to be elected at genuine periodic elections which shall be by universal and equal suffrage and shall be held by secret ballot, guaranteeing the free expression of the will of the electors;
(c) To have access, on general terms of equality, to public service in his country.

The Carter Administration announced in 1977 that it would make the promotion of respect for human rights an important component of U.S. foreign policy. In keeping with that pledge, President Carter submitted both the ICCPR and the International Covenant on Economic, Social and Cultural Rights (ICESCR) to the Senate for its advice and consent in 1978. The Carter Administration prepared a package of RUDs to accompany each treaty. As President Carter told the Senate in his ICCPR transmittal message, "whenever a provision is in conflict with United States law, a reservation, understanding or declaration has been submitted." But the Senate took no action on the treaties, and the Reagan Administration, which was critical of Carter's human rights policy for allegedly undermining friendly authoritarian regimes in Latin America and elsewhere, did not pursue ratification. In August 1991, the first Bush Administration reformulated the package of RUDs originally prepared by the Carter Administration and asked the Senate Foreign Relations Committee to renew its consideration of the ICCPR. Following Senate approval, the United States ratified the ICCPR in June 1992.

The U.S. acceptance of the ICCPR is qualified by five reservations, four understandings, and four declarations. The reservations limit the effect of ICCPR provisions dealing with war propaganda and hate speech (Article 20), capital punishment (Article 6), the definition of "cruel, inhuman or degrading treatment" (Article 7), reduction of penalties for criminal offenses (Article 15(1)), and segregation of juvenile and adult offenders (Articles 10(2) and 14(4)). The understandings state U.S. interpretations of ICCPR provisions dealing with nondiscrimination (Articles 2 and 26), compensation for unlawful arrest (Articles 9(5) and 14(6)), segregation of accused and convicted persons (Article 10(2)), the purposes of incarceration (Article 10(3)), the rights to counsel, compelled attendance of witnesses, the prohibition of double jeopardy (Article 14(3)), and federal-state relations (Article 50). The U.S. declarations deal primarily with the means by which states implement their obligations under the ICCPR. Most important are the first declaration, which declares provisions 1-27 of the Covenant to be non-self-executing, and the third declaration, which "accepts the competence of the Human Rights Committee to receive and consider communications under Article 41 in which a State Party claims that another State Party is not fulfilling its obligations under the Covenant."

The Senate Foreign Relations Committee Report explains the U.S. approach to the ICCPR and includes the Bush Administration's explanation for its proposed reservations, understandings, and declarations.

Senate Committee on Foreign Relations, Report on the International Covenant on Civil and Political Rights

Senate Executive Rep. 102-123 (102d Cong. 2d Sess. 1992)

... The overwhelming majority of the provisions in the Covenant are compatible with existing U.S. domestic law. In those few areas where the two diverge, the Administration has proposed a reservation or other form of condition to clarify the nature of the obligation being undertaken by the United States. This approach has caused concern among some private groups and individuals in the human rights field who argue that U.S. law should be brought into conformance with international human rights standards in those areas where the international standards are superior.

The Committee recognizes the importance of adhering to internationally recognized standards of human rights. Although the U.S. record of adherence has been good, there are some areas in which U.S. law differs from the international standard. For example, the Covenant prohibits the imposition of the death penalty for crimes committed by persons below the age of eighteen but U.S. law allows it for juveniles between the ages of 16 and 18. In areas such as these, it may be appropriate and necessary to question whether changes in U.S. law should be made to bring the United States in to full compliance at the international level. However, the Committee anticipates that changes in U.S. law in these areas will occur through the normal legislative process.

The approach taken by the Administration and the Committee in its resolution of ratification will enable the United States to ratify the Covenant promptly and to participate with greater effectiveness in the process of shaping international norms and behavior in the area of human rights. It does not preclude the United States from modifying its obligations under the Covenant in the future if changes in U.S. law allow the United States to come into full compliance. In view of this situation, ratification with the Administration's proposed reservations, understandings, and declarations is supported by a broad coalition of human rights and legal groups and scholars in the United States, notwithstanding concerns any of them may have with respect to particular conditions. . . .

VII. EXPLANATION OF BUSH ADMINISTRATION CONDITIONS

The Bush Administration . . . submitted the following explanation of its proposals. . . .

expresses" its intention not to be bound, the treaty does not enter into force between the objecting and the reserving state. Of course, a particular treaty may contain its own treaty-specific rules regarding the acceptability of reservations.

Although the ICCPR itself contains no provisions dealing with reservations, the Human Rights Committee issued the following general comment on reservations.

Human Rights Committee, General Comment 24

U.N. Doc. A/50/40, Vol. 1, at 119 (1995)

1. As of 1 November 1994, 46 of the 127 States parties to the International Covenant on Civil and Political Rights had, between them, entered 150 reservations of varying significance to their acceptance of the obligations of the Covenant. Some of these reservations exclude the duty to provide and guarantee particular rights in the Covenant. Others are couched in more general terms, often directed to ensuring the continued paramountcy of certain domestic legal provisions. Still others are directed at the competence of the Committee. The number of reservations, their content and their scope may undermine the effective implementation of the Covenant and tend to weaken respect for the obligations of States Parties. . . .

8. Reservations that offend peremptory norms would not be compatible with the object and purpose of the Covenant. Although treaties that are mere exchanges of obligations between States allow them to reserve *inter se* application of rules of general international law, it is otherwise in human rights treaties, which are for the benefit of persons within their jurisdiction. Accordingly, provisions in the Covenant that represent customary international law (and *a fortiori* when they have the character of peremptory norms) may not be the subject of reservations. Accordingly, a State may not reserve the right to engage in slavery, to torture, to subject persons to cruel, inhuman or degrading treatment or punishment, to arbitrarily deprive persons of their lives, to arbitrarily arrest and detain persons, to deny freedom of thought, conscience and religion, to presume a person guilty unless he proves his innocence, to execute pregnant women or children, to permit the advocacy of national, racial or religious hatred, to deny to persons of marriageable age the right to marry, or to deny to minorities the right to enjoy their own culture, profess their own religion, or use their own language. And while reservations to particular clauses of Article 14 may be acceptable, a general reservation to the right to a fair trial would not be. . . .

10. The Committee has further examined whether categories of reservations may offend the "object and purpose" test . . . . While there is no hierarchy of importance of rights under the Covenant, the operation of certain rights may not be suspended, even in times of national emergency. This underlines the great importance of non-derogable rights. But not all rights of profound importance, such as articles 9 and 27 of the Covenant, have in fact been made non-derogable. One reason for certain rights being made non-derogable is because their suspension is irrelevant to the legitimate control of the state of national emergency (for example, no imprisonment for debt, in article 11). Another reason is that derogation may indeed be impossible (as, for example, freedom of conscience). At the same time, some provisions are non-derogable exactly because without them there would be no rule of law. A reservation to the provisions of article 4 itself, which precisely stipulates the balance to be struck between the interests of the State and the rights of the individual in times of emergency, would fall in this category. And some non-derogable rights, which in any event cannot be reserved because of their status as peremptory norms, are also of this character—the

prohibition of torture and arbitrary deprivation of life are examples. While there is no automatic correlation between reservations to non-derogable provisions, and reservations which offend against the object and purpose of the Covenant, a State has a heavy onus to justify such a reservation.

11. The Covenant consists not just of the specified rights, but of important supportive guarantees. These guarantees provide the necessary framework for securing the rights in the Covenant and are thus essential to its object and purpose . . . . Reservations designed to remove these guarantees are thus not acceptable. Thus, a State could not make a reservation to article 2, paragraph 3, of the Covenant, indicating that it intends to provide no remedies for human rights violations . . . .

12. . . . Of particular concern are widely formulated reservations which essentially render ineffective all Covenant rights which would require any change in national law to ensure compliance with Covenant obligations. No real international rights or obligations have thus been accepted. And when there is an absence of provisions to ensure that Covenant rights may be sued on in domestic courts, and, further, a failure to allow individual complaints to be brought to the Committee under the first Optional Protocol, all the essential elements of the Covenant guarantees have been removed. . . .

17. As indicated above, it is the Vienna Convention on the Law of Treaties that provides the definition of reservations and also the application of the object and purpose test in the absence of other specific provisions. But the Committee believes that its provisions on the role of State objections in relation to reservations are inappropriate to address the problem of reservations to human rights treaties. Such treaties, and the Covenant specifically, are not a web of inter-State exchanges of mutual obligations. They concern the endowment of individuals with rights. The principle of inter-State reciprocity has no place, save perhaps in the limited context of reservations to declarations on the Committee's competence under article 41. And because the operation of the classic rules on reservations is so inadequate for the Covenant, States have often not seen any legal interest in or need to object to reservations. The absence of protest by States cannot imply that a reservation is either compatible or incompatible with the object and purpose of the Covenant. Objections have been occasional, made by some States but not others, and on grounds not always specified; when an objection is made, it often does not specify a legal consequence, or sometimes even indicates that the objecting party nonetheless does not regard the Covenant as not in effect as between the parties concerned. In short, the pattern is so unclear that it is not safe to assume that a non-objecting State thinks that a particular reservation is acceptable. . . .

18. It necessarily falls to the Committee to determine whether a specific reservation is compatible with the object and purpose of the Covenant. This . . . is a task that the Committee cannot avoid in the performance of its functions. In order to know the scope of its duty to examine a State's compliance under article 40 or a communication under the first Optional Protocol, the Committee has necessarily to take a view on the compatibility of a reservation with the object and purpose of the Covenant and with general international law. Because of the special character of a human rights treaty, the compatibility of a reservation with the object and purpose of the Covenant must be established objectively, by reference to legal principles, and the Committee is particularly well placed to perform this task. The normal consequence of an unacceptable reservation is not that the Covenant will not be in effect at all for a reserving party. Rather, such a reservation will generally be severable, in the sense that the Covenant will be operative for the reserving party without benefit of the reservation.

3.1.5.3 Reservations to a provision reflecting a customary rule

The fact that a treaty provision reflects a rule of customary international law does not in itself constitute an obstacle to the formulation of a reservation to that provision.

3.1.5.4 Reservations to provisions concerning rights from which no derogation is permissible under any circumstances

A State or an international organization may not formulate a reservation to a treaty provision concerning rights from which no derogation is permissible under any circumstances, unless the reservation in question is compatible with the essential rights and obligations arising out of that treaty. In assessing that compatibility, account shall be taken of the importance which the parties have conferred upon the rights at issue by making them non-derogable.

4.4.2 Absence of effect on rights and obligations under customary international law

A reservation to a treaty provision which reflects a rule of customary international law does not of itself affect the rights and obligations under that rule, which shall continue to apply as such between the reserving State or organization and other States or international organizations which are bound by that rule.

4.4.3 Absence of effect on a peremptory norm of general international law (*jus cogens*)

1. A reservation to a treaty provision which reflects a peremptory norm of general international law (*jus cogens*) does not affect the binding nature of that norm, which shall continue to apply as such between the reserving State or organization and other States or international organizations.

2. A reservation cannot exclude or modify the legal effect of a treaty in a manner contrary to a peremptory norm of general international law.

3.2.1 Competence of the treaty monitoring bodies to assess the permissibility of reservations

1. A treaty monitoring body may, for the purpose of discharging the functions entrusted to it, assess the permissibility of reservations formulated by a State or an international organization.

2. The assessment made by such a body in the exercise of this competence has no greater legal effect than that of the act which contains it.

3.2.4 Bodies competent to assess the permissibility of reservations in the event of the establishment of a treaty monitoring body

When a treaty establishes a treaty monitoring body, the competence of that body is without prejudice to the competence of the contracting States or contracting organizations to assess the permissibility of reservations to that treaty, or to that of dispute settlement bodies competent to interpret or apply the treaty.

4.5.3 Status of the author of an invalid reservation in relation to the treaty

1. The status of the author of an invalid reservation in relation to a treaty depends on the intention expressed by the reserving State or international organization on whether it intends to be bound by the treaty without the benefit of the reservation or whether it considers that it is not bound by the treaty.

2. Unless the author of the invalid reservation has expressed a contrary intention or such an intention is otherwise established, it is considered a contracting State or a contracting organization without the benefit of the reservation.

3. Notwithstanding paragraphs 1 and 2, the author of the invalid reservation may express at any time its intention not to be bound by the treaty without the benefit of the reservation.

4. If a treaty monitoring body expresses the view that a reservation is invalid and the reserving State or international organization intends not to be bound by the treaty without the benefit of the reservation, it should express its intention to that effect within a period of twelve months from the date at which the treaty monitoring body made its assessment.

Notes and Questions

1. Which, if any, of the U.S. reservations to the ICCPR are incompatible with the object and purpose of that treaty? Is the package of RUDs, taken as a whole, incompatible with the object and purpose of the treaty?

2. What is the basis for the Human Rights Committee's claim that it is particularly well placed to assess the validity of reservations to the ICCPR? Should the Committee's assessment of reservations be treated as authoritative?

3. Which is the better view of the consequences of an unacceptable reservation, that of the Committee or the ILC Guide? If the Committee's approach to unacceptable reservations became generally accepted, what changes might states make in their approach to ratification of human rights treaties?

4. Why would the United States ratify the Covenant if it was unwilling to change its laws? Critics charge that with its package of RUDs, the United States "is pretending to assume international obligations, but is in fact undertaking nothing," and seeks the benefits of participating in human rights treaties "without assuming any obligations or burdens." One critic suggests that "Senator Bricker lost his battle, but his ghost is now enjoying victory." Do you agree?

III. GUARANTEEING ECONOMIC, SOCIAL, AND CULTURAL RIGHTS: A RIGHT TO FOOD?

The Universal Declaration of Human Rights sets out both civil and political rights and economic, social, and cultural rights. But the relationship and relative status of the two sets of rights has long been controversial. Some states, particularly socialist and developing countries, have taken the position that the achievement of a minimum standard of economic and social welfare is an essential precondition to the realization of political and civil rights. Other states have emphasized the importance of political and civil rights to economic progress; some have questioned whether economic and social rights can properly be considered rights at all.

These political and philosophical differences, exacerbated by Cold War politics, played out in the debates over a successor covenant to the Universal Declaration of Human Rights. In 1948, the UN General Assembly proposed the promulgation of a single covenant to give binding legal effect to the principles enunciated in the Universal Declaration. But when the time came to begin drafting such a covenant, some Western states questioned the desirability and feasibility of including economic and social rights. To those states, and to the United States in particular, the ICCPR appeared to fall far more comfortably within the Western tradition of respect for liberal democratic rights than did the companion International Covenant on Economic, Social and Cultural Rights. The former was seen as a natural descendant of Western theories of political liberty and civil rights, as reflected in antecedents such as the French Declaration of the Rights of Man and the Citizen and the Bill of Rights to the U.S. Constitution; the latter was seen as a more recent successor to the early twentieth-century constitutions of states such as the Soviet Union and Mexico. As a result, the first draft covenant prepared by the United Nations Human Rights Commission contained only political and civil rights.

But in 1950, developing and socialist states managed to push through the General Assembly a resolution urging the Human Rights Commission "to include in the draft covenant a clear expression of economic, social and cultural rights in a manner which relates them to the civil and political freedoms proclaimed by the draft covenant." Western states then insisted that the single Covenant contemplated by the Commission be split into two separate Covenants. After a long debate, the General Assembly reaffirmed that the two sets of rights are "interconnected and interdependent," and emphasized that "when deprived of economic, social and cultural rights, man does not represent the human person whom the Universal Declaration regards as the ideal of the free man." G.A. Res. 421 (1950).

In 1952, the General Assembly accepted the Western demand for two covenants, but stipulated that the two should be promulgated simultaneously to reaffirm their interdependence. The different views concerning the demand for two covenants are described in the following analysis prepared by the UN Secretariat in 1955:

> 8. Those who were in favour of drafting a single covenant maintained that human rights could not be clearly divided into different categories, nor could they be so classified as to represent a hierarchy of values. All rights should be promoted and protected at the same time. Without economic, social and cultural rights, civil and political rights might be purely nominal in character; without civil and political rights, economic, social and cultural rights could not be long ensured. . . .

> 9. Those in favour of drafting two separate covenants argued that civil and political rights were enforceable, or justiciable, or of an "absolute" character, while economic, social and cultural rights were not or might not be; that the former were immediately applicable, while the latter were to be progressively implemented; and that, generally speaking, the former were rights of the individual "against" the State, that is, against unlawful and unjust action of the State, while the latter were rights which the State would have to take positive action to promote. Since the nature of civil and political rights and that of economic, social and cultural rights, and the obligations of the State in respect thereof, were different, it was desirable that two separate instruments should be prepared.

> 10. The question of drafting one or two covenants was intimately related to the question of implementation. If no measures of implementation were to be formulated, it would make little difference whether one or two covenants were to be drafted. Generally speaking, civil and political rights were thought to be "legal" rights and could best be implemented by the creation of a good offices committee, while economic, social and cultural rights were thought to be "programme" rights and could best be implemented by the establishment of a system of periodic reports. Since the rights could be divided into two broad categories, which should be subject to different procedures of implementation, it would be both logical and convenient to formulate two separate covenants.

> 11. However, it was argued that not in all countries and territories were all civil and political rights "legal" rights, nor all economic, social and cultural rights "programme" rights. A civil or political right might well be a "programme" right under one regime, an economic, social or cultural right a "legal" right under another. A covenant could be drafted in such a manner as would enable States, upon ratification or accession, to

announce, each in so far as it was concerned, which civil, political, economic, social and cultural rights were "legal" rights, and which "programme" rights, and by which procedures the rights would be implemented.

Annotations on the Text of the Draft International Covenants on Human Rights, U.N. Doc. A/2929 at 7 (1955).

The goals for this Problem include:

- to consider whether there are meaningful differences between political and civil rights and economic, social, and cultural rights;
- to understand the reasons behind the U.S. reluctance to ratify the Covenant on Economic, Social and Cultural Rights; and
- to examine the nature and extent of any international legal obligations imposed on states in connection with the effort to combat hunger.

A. *The Problem*

Although considerable progress has been made over the last 30 years toward meeting the world's basic food needs, the UN Food and Agriculture Organization estimates that as of 2014 roughly 805 million people—about 1 in 9—are "chronically undernourished." This number has declined by over 100 million in the last ten years and by over 200 million since 1990. Nonetheless, millions die of hunger every year. Although many lack food as the result of drought or war, most hunger-related deaths occur as the result of chronic malnutrition. The problem stems principally from the grinding poverty that affects large portions of the developing world, where a fifth of the population subsists on less than $1.25 a day. Food distribution is also a serious challenge. As Olivier de Schutter, U.N. Special Rapporteur on the Right to Food, 2008–2014, explains:

> [T]he food systems we have inherited from the twentieth century have failed. Of course, significant progress has been achieved in boosting agricultural production over the past fifty years. But this has hardly reduced the number of hungry people, and the nutritional outcomes remain poor . . . .
>
> [B]ecause global food systems have been shaped to maximize efficiency gains and produce large volumes of commodities, they have failed to take distributional concerns into account. The increases in production far outstripped population growth during the period from 1960 to 2000. But these increases went hand in hand with regional specialization in a relatively narrow range of products, a process encouraged by the growth of international trade in agricultural products. The associated technological and policy choices concentrated benefits in the hands of large production units and landholders at the expense of smaller-scale producers and landless workers, resulting in the growth of inequality in rural areas and a failure to address the root causes of poverty.

http://www.srfood.org/images/stories/pdf/officialreports/20140310_finalreport_en.pdf.

Although the problem of hunger is greatest in the developing world, particularly in sub-Saharan Africa, many people in developed countries also go hungry. A September 2014 report from the U.S. Department of Agriculture found that in 2013 roughly 14 percent of U.S. households "were food insecure at least some time during the year, including 5.6 percent with very low food security—meaning that the food intake of some household members was reduced and normal eating patterns were disrupted at times during the year due to limited resources." The problem was particularly acute among black and Hispanic households.

At a 2008 world food summit, UN officials estimated it would cost $30 billion annually to end world hunger. Despite some progress, the World Bank recently concluded that we now live in a " 'new normal' of high and volatile food prices." According to the Bank,

> Managing this volatility will require sustained commitment, co-ordination, and vigilance from the international community to help governments put policies in place to help people better cope.
>
> Some countries with high poverty and weak safety nets tend to respond to chronic price volatility by scaling up consumer food subsidies, which are often counter-productive. When faced with high food prices, many of the poorest families cope by pulling their children out of school and eating cheaper, less nutritious food, which can have catastrophic life-long effects on the social, physical, and mental well-being of millions of young people. Malnutrition contributes to infant, child, and maternal illness; decreased learning capacity; lower productivity, and higher mortality. One-third of all child deaths globally are attributed to under-nutrition . . . .

World Bank, Food Security Overview, http://www.worldbank.org/en/topic/foodsecurity/overview#1.

B. Background on Economic, Social, and Cultural Rights

In some respects, the ICCPR and the ICESCR are obviously similar. The Preambles and Articles 1 (self-determination), 3 (equal rights of men and women to enjoy Covenant rights), and 5 (prohibiting reliance on the Covenant as a ground for limiting rights) of the two covenants are essentially identical. In other respects the two covenants differ significantly, as will be evident when you review the following excerpts.

International Covenant on Economic, Social and Cultural Rights

993 U.N.T.S. 3 (1966)

The States Parties to the present Covenant, . . .

Recognizing that, in accordance with the Universal Declaration of Human Rights, the ideal of free human beings enjoying freedom from fear and want can only be achieved if conditions are created whereby everyone may enjoy his economic, social and cultural rights, as well as his civil and political rights, . . .

Agree upon the following articles:

Article 2

1. Each State Party to the present Covenant undertakes to take steps, individually and through international assistance and co-operation, especially economic and technical, to the maximum of its available resources, with a view to achieving progressively the full realization of the rights recognized in the present Covenant by all appropriate means, including particularly the adoption of legislative measures.

2. The States Parties to the present Covenant undertake to guarantee that the rights enunciated in the present Covenant will be exercised without discrimination of any kind as to race, colour, sex, language, religion, political or other opinion, national or social origin, property, birth or other status.

3. Developing countries, with due regard to human rights and their national economy, may determine to what extent they would guarantee the economic rights recognized in the present Covenant to non-nationals.

Article 4

The States Parties to the present Covenant recognize that, in the enjoyment of those rights provided by the State in conformity with the present Covenant, the State may subject such rights only to such limitations as are determined by law only in so far as this may be compatible with the nature of these rights and solely for the purpose of promoting the general welfare in a democratic society.

Article 6

1. The States Parties to the present Covenant recognize the right to work, which includes the right of everyone to the opportunity to gain his living by work which he freely chooses or accepts, and will take appropriate steps to safeguard this right.
2. The steps to be taken by a State Party to the present Covenant to achieve the full realization of this right shall include technical and vocational guidance and training programmes, policies and techniques to achieve steady economic, social and cultural development and full and productive employment under conditions safeguarding fundamental political and economic freedoms to the individual.

Article 7

The States Parties to the present Covenant recognize the right of everyone to the enjoyment of just and favourable conditions of work, which ensure, in particular:
(a) remuneration which provides all workers, as a minimum, with:
(i) fair wages and equal remuneration for work of equal value without distinction of any kind, in particular women being guaranteed conditions of work not inferior to those enjoyed by men, with equal pay for equal work;
(ii) a decent living for themselves and their families in accordance with the provisions of the present Covenant;
(b) safe and healthy working conditions;
(c) equal opportunity for everyone to be promoted in his employment to an appropriate higher level, subject to no considerations other than those of seniority and competence;
(d) rest, leisure and reasonable limitation of working hours and periodic holidays with pay, as well as remuneration for public holidays.

Article 9

The States Parties to the present Covenant recognize the right of everyone to social security, including social insurance.

Article 11

1. The States Parties to the present Covenant recognize the right of everyone to an adequate standard of living for himself and his family, including adequate food, clothing and housing, and to the continuous improvement of living conditions. The States Parties will take appropriate steps to ensure the realization of this right, recognizing to this effect the essential importance of international co-operation based on free consent.

2. The States Parties to the present Covenant, recognizing the fundamental right of everyone to be free from hunger, shall take, individually and through international co-operation, the measures, including specific programmes, which are needed:

(a) to improve methods of production, conservation and distribution of food by making full use of technical and scientific knowledge, by disseminating knowledge of the principles of nutrition and by developing or reforming agrarian systems in such a way as to achieve the most efficient development and utilization of natural resources;

(b) taking into account the problems of both food-importing and food-exporting countries, to ensure an equitable distribution of world food supplies in relation to need.

Article 12

1. The States Parties to the present Covenant recognize the right of everyone to the enjoyment of the highest attainable standard of physical and mental health. . . .

Notes and Questions

1. What steps are parties to the ICESCR required to take to combat hunger?

2. To what extent and in what ways are the rights enumerated different in kind from political and civil rights? Do you agree with the General Assembly that economic, social, and cultural rights and political and civil rights are "interconnected and interdependent," or do you agree with Western states who argued in favor of two separate covenants?

3. The decision to promulgate two separate covenants turned in part on the question of implementation. How would states go about implementing, for example, the right to an "adequate standard of living"? Would implementation of economic, social, and cultural rights generally require an approach different from implementation of political and civil rights?

4. Compare Article 2 of the ICESCR with Article 2 of the ICCPR. What obligations does each article impose? Under Article 16 of the ICESCR, states are required to submit reports "on the measures they have adopted and the progress made in achieving observance of" ICESCR rights. In 1985, the UN Economic and Social Council set up a Committee on Economic, Social and Cultural Rights modeled on the Human Rights Committee established under Article 28 of the ICCPR. The Committee is to monitor state reports and issue comments and recommendations on state compliance with the ICESCR. How should the Committee ascertain whether a party to the ICESCR is taking steps to realize Covenant rights "to the maximum of its available resources"? In 2003, in its General Comment 3, the Committee stated:

> 10. On the basis of . . . more than a decade of examining States parties' reports the Committee is of the view that a minimum core obligation to ensure the satisfaction of, at the very least, minimum essential levels of each of the rights is incumbent upon every State party. Thus, for example, a State party in which any significant number of individuals is deprived of essential foodstuffs, of essential primary health care, of basic shelter and housing, or of the most basic forms of education is, prima facie, failing to discharge its obligations under the Covenant. . . . By the same token, it must be noted that any assessment as to whether a State has discharged its minimum core obligation must also take account of resource constraints applying within the country concerned. Article 2(1) obligates each State party to take the necessary steps "to the maximum of its available resources". In order for a State party to be able to attribute its failure to meet at least its minimum core obligations to a lack of available resources it must demonstrate

that every effort has been made to use all resources that are at its disposition in an effort to satisfy, as a matter of priority, those minimum obligations.

11. The Committee wishes to emphasize, however, that even where the available resources are demonstrably inadequate, the obligation remains for a State party to strive to ensure the widest possible enjoyment of the relevant rights under the prevailing circumstances.

In a 2007 statement, the Committee added that:

8. In considering a communication concerning an alleged failure of a State party to take steps to the maximum of available resources, . . . the Committee may take into account, *inter alia*, the following considerations:

(a) the extent to which the measures taken were deliberate, concrete and targeted towards the fulfilment of economic, social and cultural rights;

(b) whether the State party exercised its discretion in a non-discriminatory and nonarbitrary manner; . . .

(d) where several policy options are available, whether the State party adopts the option that least restricts Covenant rights;

(e) the time frame in which the steps were taken;

(f) whether the steps had taken into account the precarious situation of disadvantaged and marginalized individuals or groups and . . . whether they prioritized grave situations or situations of risk.

[The Committee noted, however, that it "always respects the margin of appreciation of States to take steps and adopt measures most suited to their specific circumstances."]

Committee on Economic, Social, and Cultural Rights, An Evaluation of the Obligation to Take Steps to the "Maximum of Available Resources" Under an Optional Protocol to the Covenant, E/C.12/2007/1 (2007).

5. Many states routinely fail to comply with their reporting obligations under the ICESCR. They either fail to present their reports at all or present their reports years after they were due. As of early 2015, 71 reports were overdue under the ICESCR, 86 under the ICCPR, and 100 under CERD. Thirty of the ICESCR reports were more than 10 years overdue; 31 of the ICCPR and 25 of the CERD reports were also more than 10 years overdue. According to a 2012 report by the UN High Commissioner on Human Rights, only 16 percent of the reports due to UN human rights treaty bodies in 2010 and 2011 were submitted when due. The report adds that,

"As a consequence **a State that complies with its reporting obligations faithfully will be reviewed more frequently by the concerned treaty body compared to a State that adheres to its obligations less faithfully . . . .**

Under some treaties such as ICESCR, CAT and the ICCPR, around 20% of States parties have never submitted an initial report . . . . In other words, a significant proportion of ratifications has never resulted in a report or a review.

Navanathem Pillay, Strengthening the United Nations Human Rights Treaty Body System, June 2012, at 22 (emphasis in the original). Why do states often ignore their reporting obligations? How effective is reporting likely to be as an implementation mechanism?

6. Human rights advocates for many years urged adoption of an optional protocol to the ICESCR to provide for an individual complaints procedure. The General Assembly finally approved an optional protocol in 2008; the protocol entered into force in 2013. As of early 2015, 18 states had ratified it.

C. *The U.S. Position on Economic, Social, and Cultural Rights*

The United States played a lead role in pressing for separate covenants and has expressed considerable skepticism regarding the status of economic, social, and cultural rights. But the U.S. position has varied considerably from administration to administration. In January 1941, President Franklin Roosevelt delivered his famous "Four Freedoms" speech, warning the country of the need to strengthen democracy and combat totalitarianism, in part by protecting "four essential human freedoms," among them "freedom from want—which, translated into world terms, means economic understandings which will secure to every nation a healthy peacetime life for its inhabitants—everywhere in the world." 87 Cong. Rec. 44, 46-47 (1941).

Roosevelt elaborated on the four freedoms theme in his 1944 State of the Union message:

> We cannot be content . . . if some fraction of our people—whether it be one-third or one-fifth or one-tenth—is ill-fed, ill-clothed, ill-housed, and insecure. . . .
>
> We have come to a clear realization of the fact that true individual freedom cannot exist without economic security and independence. "Necessitous men are not free men." People who are hungry and out of a job are the stuff of which dictatorships are made.
>
> In our day these economic truths have become accepted as self-evident. We have accepted, so to speak, a second Bill of Rights under which a new basis of security and prosperity can be established for all—regardless of station, race, or creed.
>
> Among these are:
>
> The right to a useful and remunerative job in the industries or shops or farms or mines of the Nation;
>
> The right to earn enough to provide adequate food and clothing and recreation;
>
> . . . The right of every family to a decent home;
>
> The right to adequate medical care and the opportunity to achieve and enjoy good health;
>
> The right to adequate protection from the economic fears of old age, sickness, accident, and unemployment;
>
> The right to a good education.

90 Cong. Rec. 55, 57 (1944)

President Carter signed the ICESCR in 1978 and sent it to the Senate for its advice and consent. The Covenant languished there, and the Reagan and first Bush Administrations both opposed its ratification. Indeed, the Reagan and Bush Administrations rejected the idea that economic and social rights could properly be considered rights at all. Elliott Abrams, Assistant Secretary of State for Human Rights and Humanitarian Affairs in the Reagan Administration, explained why:

> The great men who founded the modern concern for human rights . . . wanted to focus the idealism of mankind by defining very precisely the rights that are truly inalienable. They sought to do this by separating those goods the government ought to encourage over the long term from the rights the government *has an absolute duty to respect* at any time . . . . [W]e must not blur the distinction between two categories. The rights that no government *can violate* should not be watered down to the status of rights that governments should *do their best* to secure. The right to be free from torture or to freedom of speech can and should be easily respected by every Government. No government has to torture or censor its people. But the rights to an adequate standard of living or to holidays with pay or to technical and professional education pose enormous challenges to desperately poor nations. The policies likely to produce conditions where